RCAHMS

Tolbooths and Town-houses
Civic Architecture in Scotland to 1833

Tolbooths and Town-houses

Civic Architecture in Scotland to 1833

THIS HOUSE LOVES PEACE HATES KNAVES CRIMES PUNISHETH
PRESERVES THE LAWS AND GOOD MEN HONOURETH

ROYAL COMMISSION
ON THE ANCIENT
AND HISTORICAL
MONUMENTS
OF SCOTLAND
1996

Applications for reproduction should be made to The Stationery Office.

British Library Cataloguing in Publication Data

A catalogue record for this book is available from the British Library

Royal Commission on the Ancient and Historical Monuments of Scotland
John Sinclair House, 16 Bernard Terrace, Edinburgh EH8 9NX
0131-662 1456

The Royal Commission, which was established in 1908, is responsible for compiling a national record of archaeological sites and historic buildings of all types and periods. The Royal Commission makes this record available both through its publications (details of which can be obtained from the above address) and through the maintenance of a central archive of information, known as the National Monuments Record of Scotland. This contains the national collection of pictorial and documentary material relating to Scotland's ancient monuments and historic buildings and is open Monday to Friday for public reference at the above address.

ISBN 0 11 495799 1

CONTENTS

The Royal Commission on the Ancient and Historical Monuments of Scotland

PREFACE

This volume represents a new development by RCAHMS in its approach to architectural survey and publication. For more than eighty years topographical survey was concerned with the identification and recording of both archaeological and architectural material, the ultimate objective being to complete an assessment of the entire national heritage at the same level of detailed appraisal. As originally conceived, the completed record was to consist of a series of published *Inventories*, the contents of which would chart a gradual county-by-county progress towards a finite goal.

It is now widely realised that to cover the entire country in similar detail would have taken far too long, and countless monuments and buildings would have succumbed to the pressures of development or decay before their significance, or perhaps even their existence, could be recognised. It is also plain that any concept of a 'finite' record is outmoded and impractical, as advances in recording technology, the deepening of archaeological and historical insights, and changing social values will constantly combine to widen the field of reference for those assessing the built environment of Scotland's past.

Accordingly, the 'Inventory of Ancient and Historical Monuments', which Commissioners are charged by Royal Warrant to compile, is now construed as the total archive of the National Monuments Record of Scotland, where full details of all Royal Commission survey programmes are publicly accessible. Survey publications, such as *Tolbooths and Town-Houses*, will thus present a distillation of the information available in the national archive, as a means both of heightening public awareness of a particular group or class of buildings and of highlighting the quality of information available in the NMRS. Whether in book form, or as a series of Record entries, however, the overall concern will remain the same as in the past: to help contemporary society learn more about the culture, civilisation and conditions of life experienced by the people of Scotland in earlier times.

In respect of architectural survey, Commissioners decided that following the conclusion of the architectural inventory programme in 1992 when the final volume in the *Inventory of Argyll* series was published, a thematic approach to survey and publication was to be adopted. Building- and monument-types that are redundant in terms of their original functions and are particularly representative of Scottish architecture and society would be selected for thematic survey and publication, drawing, where necessary, upon the work and experience of the accompanying threatened building and industrial survey programmes. The first subject to be selected for this treatment, *Tolbooths and Town-Houses*, will be followed by publications on Early Medieval Sculpture in the West Highlands and Historic Burgh Schools.

This volume takes as its principal theme those buildings that were designed, or adapted, to serve as centres of local burgh administration, justice and ceremonial prior to the Municipal Reform Act of 1833. This legislation was a watershed in the history of local government in Scotland, marking the beginnings of democratically-elected councils and the emergence of modern town-halls. Tolbooths and town-houses continued in use, however, and it was not until 1975 that centuries-old traditions of burgh and county government in Scotland finally came to an end, a situation which was confirmed by further local government reorganisation in 1996.

Tolbooths are known to have existed in medieval times, but the earliest surviving examples of civic architecture represented in this volume date from a period of about 250 years before the 1833 Act. An introduction provides the historical and architectural background to the 87 entries contained in the descriptive gazetteer. In cases where more than one pre-1833 municipal building survives, the article-heading in the gazetteer refers to the name of the burgh rather than to a specific building, each building being given a sub-heading in the text. The same treatment has been adopted for the demolished tolbooths in Edinburgh and Leith, whilst an appendix provides brief summary notes of another 106 demolished or much-altered buildings of which there is some surviving record. The bulk of survey work has been undertaken between 1991 and 1995.

RCAHMS wishes to acknowledge the assistance given by all the owners and occupants of the buildings who have allowed access for study and survey. For assistance and information, thanks are due to the staff of local libraries, archives and museums throughout Scotland, of the National Library of Scotland, the Royal Museum of Scotland, the Scottish Record Office, the National Register of Archives (Scotland), the National Trust for Scotland, and particularly to the following individuals: David Alston, Sheena Andrew, Norman Atkinson, Geoffrey Bailey, Dorothy Bennett, Rachel Benvie, Hildegarde Berwick, Ian Brown, Charles Burnett, Helen Clark, Dr Tristram Clarke, Brenda Cluer, Lesley Couparwhite, Judith Cripps, George Dixon, Dr David Devereux, John Gifford, Derek Hall, James Hunter, Michael King, Margaret McCance, Murdo Macdonald, Aonghus McKechnie, Janet Meikle, Estelle Quick, Siobhan Ratchford, Alison Reid, Margaret Robertson, Fiona Scharlau, Dr Allen Simpson, Marion Stavert, Daniel Stewart, Marion Stewart, Robert Stewart and Marion Wood.

The text of this volume has been written by Neil Cameron and Ian Fisher, with contributions by Simon Green and Geoffrey Stell; historical research has been undertaken by Caroline MacGregor and the volume has been edited by Ian Fisher. Measured survey work and preparation of finished drawings have been undertaken principally by John Borland, and by Douglas Boyd, Angela Gannon, Jane Green, Alan Leith, Kevin Macleod, Ian Parker, Sam Scott and Heather Stoddart. The photographs were taken by John Keggie, Angus Lamb and Stephen Wallace. The layout has been designed by John Stevenson and Kate George.

The suggestion that tolbooths would form a particularly appropriate subject for thematic architectural survey was initially made by Sir Howard Colvin, a former Commissioner, and was agreed by the Royal Commission's Buildings Programme Committee under the chairmanship of Professor Sir James Dunbar-Nasmith. Throughout, the project has greatly benefited from the advice and support of that committee.

EDITORIAL NOTES

Gazetteer entries

Entry headings normally give the name of the building, with its Council Area (as introduced in 1996) and the National Grid Reference. In burghs where more than one pre-1833 building survives, or where a demolished tolbooth was of exceptional importance, individual building-names and grid-references are included in sub-headings. Former burghal status and local government areas are indicated in the table accompanying the location-map (p.xi). The appendix (pp.202-14) lists demolished or much-altered buildings for which information is available, and some of doubtful status, and is arranged by royal burghs, those of regality and barony, and other places.

Square brackets in the text of an inscription indicate that illegible letters have been restored. Letters in round brackets indicate that contractions have been expanded for the sake of clarity.

Illustrations

All illustrations are classed as figures and are cited in the margins by the number of the page on which they appear, with an appropriate letter suffix. Plans and elevations, including those from archival sources, are normally reproduced at a standard scale of 1:200 (1:400 in the appendix), and where an elevation is separated from the accompanying plan the same scale-line applies to both. The labels attached to individual rooms refer to their historical use, as described in the text, rather than to modern functions.

Copyright

Unless otherwise specified, the contents of this volume are Crown Copyright. Copies of Commission photographs and drawings (identified respectively by the negative numbers in the captions and by their figure-numbers) can be purchased on application to:

> The Secretary
> The Royal Commission on the Ancient
> and Historical Monuments of Scotland
> John Sinclair House
> 16 Bernard Terrace
> Edinburgh EH8 9NX

The records of the Commission, which may be consulted in the National Monuments Record of Scotland at the same address, include a large collection of unpublished photographs of the buildings described in this volume. Historical research-files on individual buildings, including transcripts and copies from primary sources, are housed in the manuscripts collection.

Acknowledgements for illustrations

We are indebted to the following individuals and institutions for supplying photographs and for permission to reproduce copyright material:

Aberdeen City Archives: Figs.2A, 17B, 31C.
Angus Council, Cultural Services (Montrose Museum): Fig.146B.
Ayr, Carnegie Library: Figs.14B, 38B,D,E, 40B.
Mr R M Bremner, Dingwall: Fig.70B.
Bute Museum: Fig.16.
Dumfries and Galloway Council (Wigtownshire Museums Service): Fig.6B.
Dumfries Museum: Figs.74A, 140A.
East Fife Museums Service: Fig.6A.
Falkirk Council, History Research Centre: Figs.88, 89A.
Fife Council Libraries (Cupar Library, George Normand Collection): Fig.4D.
Highland Council, Nairn office: Fig.152B.
Historic Scotland: Fig.95B.
Inverclyde Council (Watt Library, Greenock): Figs.11A, 175A.
Mr A Mackechnie: Fig.209B.
Trustees of the National Library of Scotland: Fig.206C.
Trustees of the National Museums of Scotland: Figs.5A,B, 84B.
The Peoples' Story Museum, Canongate Tolbooth: Fig.17A.
Public Record Office: Fig.122B (MPHH 37).
Selkirkshire Antiquarian Society: Fig.183B,C.
Sheriff D B Smith: Fig.206B.
The Trustees of Sir John Soane's Museum: Figs.64C,D.
Ms E Strong: Fig.203B.

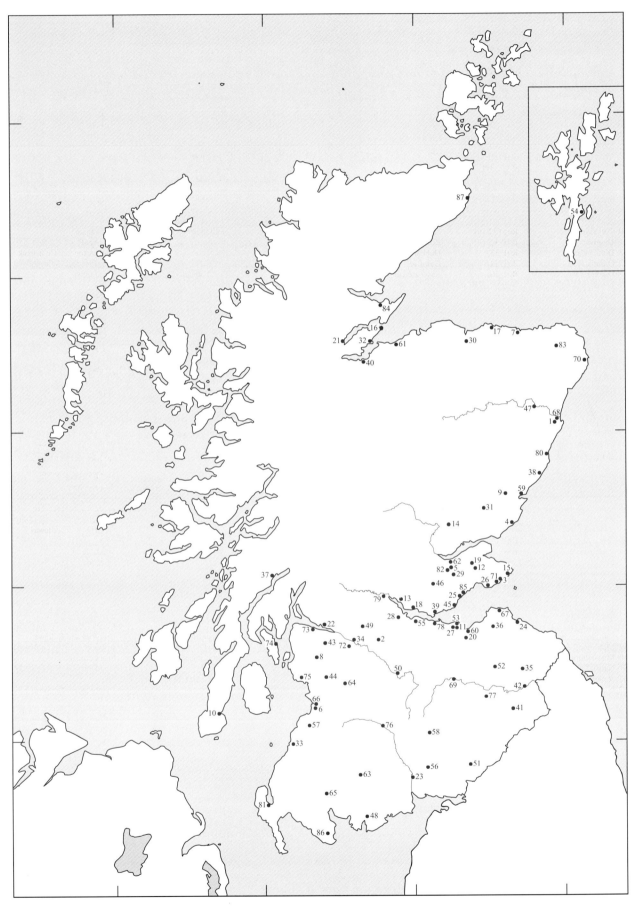

Location of gazetteer entries (based upon the Ordnance Survey map, Crown Copyright)

TOLBOOTHS AND TOWN-HOUSES

The following abbreviations are used: B, burgh of barony; R, royal burgh; Reg, burgh of regality; P, reference in Pryde, GS, *The Burghs of Scotland* (1965).

		Status	County	Region	District	Council
1	Aberdeen	R (P 7)	Aberdeen	Grampian	City of Aberdeen	City of Aberdeen
2	Airdrie	B (P 480)	Lanark	Strathclyde	Monklands	North Lanarkshire
3	Anstruther Wester	R (P 61)	Fife	Fife	North-east Fife	Fife
4	Arbroath	R (P 69)	Angus	Tayside	Angus	Angus
5	Auchtermuchty	R (P 54)	Fife	Fife	North-east Fife	Fife
6	Ayr	R (P 31)	Ayr	Strathclyde	Kyle and Carrick	South Ayrshire
7	Banff	R (P 27)	Banff	Grampian	Banff and Buchan	Aberdeenshire
8	Beith	none	Ayr	Strathclyde	Cunninghame	North Ayrshire
9	Brechin	R (P 77)	Angus	Tayside	Angus	Angus
10	Campbeltown	R (P 80)	Argyll	Strathclyde	Argyll and Bute	Argyll and Bute
11	Canongate	Reg (P 239)	Midlothian	Lothian	City of Edinburgh	City of Edinburgh
12	Ceres	B (P 306)	Fife	Fife	North-east Fife	Fife
13	Clackmannan	B (P 230)	Clackmannan	Central	Clackmannan	Clackmannan
14	Coupar Angus	B (P 281)	Perth	Tayside	Perth and Kinross	Perthshire and Kinross
15	Crail	R (P 16)	Fife	Fife	North-east Fife	Fife
16	Cromarty	R/B (P 36, 423)	Ross and Cromarty	Highland	Ross and Cromarty	Highland
17	Cullen	R (P 28)	Banff	Grampian	Banff and Buchan	Aberdeenshire
18	Culross	R (P 65)	Fife	Fife	Dunfermline	Fife
19	Cupar	R (P40)	Fife	Fife	North-east Fife	Fife
20	Dalkeith	Reg (P 216)	Midlothian	Lothian	Midlothian	Midlothian
21	Dingwall	R (P 34)	Ross and Cromarty	Highland	Ross and Cromarty	Highland
22	Dumbarton	R (P 33)	Dunbarton	Strathclyde	Dumbarton	Dumbarton and Clydebank
23	Dumfries	R (P 24)	Dumfries	Dumfries and Galloway	Nithsdale	Dumfries and Galloway
24	Dunbar	R (P 50)	East Lothian	Lothian	East Lothian	East Lothian
25	Dysart	R (P 67)	Fife	Kirkcaldy	Fife	Fife
26	Earlsferry	R (P 62)	Fife	Fife	North-east Fife	Fife
27	Edinburgh	R (P 4)	Midlothian	Lothian	City of Edinburgh	City of Edinburgh
28	Falkirk	Reg (P 266)	Stirling	Central	Falkirk	Falkirk
29	Falkland	R (P 51)	Fife	Fife	North-east Fife	Fife
30	Fochabers	B (P 261)	Moray	Grampian	Moray	Moray
31	Forfar	R (P 23)	Angus	Tayside	Angus	Angus
32	Fortrose	R (P 64)	Ross and Cromarty	Highland	Ross and Cromarty	Highland
33	Girvan	B (P 382)	Ayr	Strathclyde	Kyle and Carrick	South Ayrshire
34	Glasgow	R (P 70)	Lanark	Strathclyde	City of Glasgow	City of Glasgow
35	Greenlaw	B (P 256)	Berwick	Borders	Berwickshire	Scottish Borders
36	Haddington	R (P 9)	East Lothian	Lothian	East Lothian	East Lothian
37	Inveraray	R (P 79)	Argyll	Strathclyde	Argyll and Bute	Argyll and Bute
38	Inverbervie	R (P 44)	Kincardine	Grampian	Kincardine and Deeside	Aberdeenshire
39	Inverkeithing	R (P 19)	Fife	Fife	Kirkcaldy	Fife
40	Inverness	R (P 20)	Inverness	Highland	Inverness	Highland
41	Jedburgh	R (P 17)	Roxburgh	Borders	Roxburgh	Scottish Borders
42	Kelso	R (P 293)	Roxburgh	Borders	Roxburgh	Scottish Borders
43	Kilbarchan	B (P 448)	Renfrew	Strathclyde	Renfrew	Renfrewshire
44	Kilmaurs	B (P 210)	Ayrshire	Strathclyde	Kilmarnock and Loudoun	East Ayrshire
45	Kinghorn	R (P 21)	Fife	Fife	Kirkcaldy	Fife
46	Kinross	Reg (P 218)	Kinross	Tayside	Perth and Kinross	Perthshire and Kinross
47	Kintore	R (P 26)	Aberdeen	Grampian	Gordon	Aberdeenshire
48	Kirkcudbright	R (P 43)	Kirkcudbright	Dumfries and Galloway	Stewartry	Dumfries and Galloway
49	Kirkintilloch	B (P 207)	Dunbarton	Strathclyde	Strathkelvin	East Dunbartonshire
50	Lanark	R (P 18)	Lanark	Strathclyde	Clydesdale	South Lanarkshire
51	Langholm	Reg (P 310)	Dumfries	Dumfries and Galloway	Annandale and Eskdale	Dumfries and Galloway
52	Lauder	R (P 39)	Berwick	Borders	Ettrick and Lauderdale	Scottish Borders
53	Leith	B (P 337)	Midlothian	Lothian	City of Edinburgh	City of Edinburgh
54	Lerwick	B (P 478)	Shetland	Shetland Islands	Mainland	Shetland Islands
55	Linlithgow	R (P 14)	West Lothian	Lothian	West Lothian	West Lothian
56	Lochmaben	R (P 49)	Dumfries	Dumfries and Galloway	Annandale and Eskdale	Dumfries and Galloway
57	Maybole	B (P 205)	Ayr	Strathclyde	Kyle and Carrick	South Ayrshire
58	Moffat	Reg (P 347)	Dumfries	Dumfries and Galloway	Annandale and Eskdale	Dumfries and Galloway
59	Montrose	R (P 15)	Angus	Tayside	Angus	Angus
60	Musselburgh	Reg (P 234)	Midlothian	Lothian	East Lothian	East Lothian
61	Nairn	R (P 25)	Nairn	Highland	Nairn	Highland
62	Newburgh	R (P 75)	Fife	Fife	North-east Fife	Fife
63	New Galloway	R (P 74)	Kirkcudbright	Dumfries and Galloway	Stewartry	Dumfries and Galloway
64	Newmilns	Reg (P 166)	Ayr	Strathclyde	Kilmarnock and Loudoun	East Ayrshire
65	Newton on Ayr	B (P 252)	Ayr	Strathclyde	Kyle and Carrick	South Ayrshire
66	Newton Stewart	B (P 406)	Wigtown	Dumfries and Galloway	Wigtown	Dumfries and Galloway
67	North Berwick	R (P 47)	East Lothian	Lothian	East Lothian	East Lothian
68	Old Aberdeen	B (P 162)	Aberdeen	Grampian	City of Aberdeen	City of Aberdeen
69	Peebles	R (P 10)	Peebles	Borders	Tweeddale	Scottish Borders
70	Peterhead	B (P 240)	Aberdeen	Grampian	Banff and Buchan	Aberdeenshire
71	Pittenweem	R (P 56)	Fife	Fife	North-east Fife	Fife
72	Pollokshaws	B (P 474)	Renfrew	Strathclyde	City of Glasgow	City of Glasgow
73	Port Glasgow	free port	Renfrew	Strathclyde	Inverclyde	Inverclyde
74	Rothesay	R (P 46)	Bute	Strathclyde	Argyll and Bute	Argyll and Bute
75	Saltcoats	B (P 212)	Ayr	Strathclyde	Cunninghame	North Ayrshire
76	Sanquhar	R (P 68)	Dumfries	Dumfries and Galloway	Nithsdale	Dumfries and Galloway
77	Selkirk	R (P 41)	Selkirk	Borders	Ettrick and Lauderdale	Scottish Borders
78	South Queensferry	R (P 76)	West Lothian	Lothian	City of Edinburgh	City of Edinburgh
79	Stirling	R (P 6)	Stirling	Central	Stirling	Stirling
80	Stonehaven	B (P 241)	Kincardine	Grampian	Kincardine and Deeside	Aberdeenshire
81	Stranraer	R (P 71)	Wigtown	Dumfries and Galloway	Wigtown	Dumfries and Galloway
82	Strathmiglo	B (P 188)	Fife	Fife	North-east Fife	Fife
83	Strichen	none	Aberdeen	Grampian	Banff and Buchan	Aberdeenshire
84	Tain	R (P 48)	Ross and Cromarty	Highland	Ross and Cromarty	Highland
85	West Wemyss	B (P 196)	Fife	Fife	North-east Fife	Fife
86	Whithorn	R (P 53)	Wigtown	Dumfries and Galloway	Wigtown	Dumfries and Galloway
87	Wick	R (P 63)	Sutherland	Highland	Sutherland	Highland

A. Linlithgow (No.55) from W, view by Slezer c.1690   (WLD/37/2)

B. Glasgow Tolbooth (No.34) from SE, view by Knox c.1826   (GWD/19/3)

C. Falkirk Town Steeple (No.28) from W, c.1820   (Falkirk Museum)

D. Stirling Town-house (No.79), steeple from SW   (ST/430)

E. Dundee Town-house (appendix, no.6) from NW, c.1930   (AN/22)

HISTORICAL INTRODUCTION

TOLBOOTHS AND TOWN-HOUSES

The tolbooth or town-house was the centre of local administration, justice and ceremonial in Scottish burghs from the medieval period until the 19th century. The royal burghs founded in Scotland from the 12th century onwards were empowered to hold markets and to levy tolls and customs which formed a substantial part of their income. The Latin word *tolloneum* and its vernacular equivalent *tolbuith* were applied to the buildings erected for the collection of such tolls, but these also served for meetings of the burgh councils and courts, and for the imprisonment both of suspected criminals and of debtors.

A. **Maybole** *(No.57), burgh arms on gable of town hall*   *(B 58111)*

B. **Saltcoats** *(No.75), pediment of town hall*   *(B 47659)*

The earliest reference to a tolbooth in a Scottish burgh, at Berwick in the second half of the 13th century, already shows the *tolbotha* being used for the regular 'head courts' or general assemblies of the burgesses.[1] The status of the tolbooth as the recognised place for doing justice was acknowledged at Dunbar (No.24) in 1545-6, when it was stated that 'quhair ever the Bailies holdis the Court, that is ther Towbuth'. The same application of the term is seen in a royal charter of 1593,

confirming the use of part of the priory at Pittenweem (No.71) for building '*pretorium, carcerem domumque ponderum et telonium*', translated as 'the tolbuith, prissoun, weyhous and customehous'.[2] From the 17th century the word *tolbuith* was often synonymous with 'prison' (although the more specific 'wardhouse' was also used, as at Aberdeen). 'The Tolbooth' was even applied as the name of a crannog in Loch Kinord (Aberdeenshire) which had traditionally been used for that purpose.[3]

As the name 'tolbooth' acquired this unpleasant significance, the descriptions 'Council-house', 'Town's house' or 'Town-house' became increasingly common, although many tolbooths continued to be known as such until the 20th century.[4] Increasing co-operation with county authorities from the late 18th century onwards led to the erection in several burghs of shared 'Town and County Buildings'. During the following century many new 'Municipal Buildings' and 'Town Halls'[5] were built, but in other burghs the original town-houses remained the meeting-places of the town councils until local government reform in 1975.

SOURCES

There is an extensive literature on the origins, development and social structure of Scottish burghs.[6] There is also a wide range of documentary sources for the history of individual tolbooths and town-houses, recording their construction, use, dilapidation and demolition. These include royal charters and Acts of Parliament permitting or enjoining their erection; instructions from the Privy Council regarding their maintenance and the reception or escape of prisoners; and official reports such as those of the Royal Commission on Municipal Corporations (1835-6)[7] and the prison inspectors of the same period. The published records of the Convention of Royal Burghs include many grants of financial assistance for the construction and repair of tolbooths, and reports on their condition. Burghs had a close relationship with county administration and much relevant material is found in the records of commissioners of supply[8] and sheriff courts.

C. **Tain** *(No.84), model of tolbooth steeple and court-house, c.1848*   *(C 48421)*

A. Aberdeen Tolbooth (No.1) from SW, view on letter-head, c.1801   (C 17903)

The most important sources are the records of the burghs
themselves, notably their council minute-books and accounts.
Selections from some of these have been published by the
Scottish Burgh Records Society or individual burgh councils.[9]
However, most remain in manuscript in the care of local
authorities or the Scottish Record Office. The control of
building-operations was often devolved to a committee, and in
rare cases their minute-books survive, as for Dumfries
Midsteeple (No.23) in 1703-8. Building-contracts and
correspondence may survive as separate documents, as at
Forfar and Linlithgow (Nos.31, 55), or copied into council
minutes as at Edinburgh (No.27) in 1502 and Aberdeen (No.1)
in 1616.

Documents relating to burghs of barony and regality often
remain in private archives, many of which are deposited in the
Scottish Record Office. Examples include the account for the
purchase of a bell at Moffat (No.58) in 1660 and documents
and plans for the construction of Fochabers Town-house
(No.30) in 1790-2. In some cases even a royal burgh relied for
the financing of a new town-house on the munificence of the
local magnate, and abundant documentation survives in estate
archives for rebuilding at Sanquhar (No.76) in 1735-9 and in
the new town of Cullen (No.17) in 1822-3.

Early travellers' accounts and local histories give most
attention to Aberdeen (No.1), Edinburgh (No.27) and Glasgow
(No.34), but conditions in many Scottish tolbooths were
described by the prison-reformers, John Howard (1779-83),
James Neild (1812) and Joseph Gurney (1819).[10] Similar
descriptions are found in many of the parish entries, of the
1790s and 1840s respectively, in the Old and New *Statistical
Accounts*. From the late 18th century, newspapers provide a
constant commentary on civic affairs and give detailed
accounts of ceremonies such as the laying of foundation-
stones, and more recently they have afforded a valuable
medium for the publication of local historical research.

Numerous biographies and memoirs portray civic life in the
19th century.[11] Vivid and critical glimpses of the old town
councils were given by Henry, Lord Cockburn, himself a
leading reformer, in *Memorials of his Time* and in his
Journals, while in *Circuit Journeys* he recorded the
professional and leisure activities of judges on circuit at such
towns as Inveraray, Inverness and Kirkcudbright. The greatest
of Scottish novelists, Sir Walter Scott, immortalised the Old
Tolbooth of Edinburgh (No.27) in *The Heart of Midlothian*
(1818); in *Rob Roy* (1817) he represented the detention of a
debtor in Glasgow Tolbooth (No.34), 'one of the legal
fortresses of Scotland'; and in *Guy Mannering* (1815), he
narrated the violent death of the smuggler Dirk Hatteraick in
the tolbooth of 'Freeport', which was modelled on
Kirkcudbright. John Galt, in *The Provost* (1822), portrayed
the civic ceremonial and intrigues, riots and executions, in the
burgh of 'Gudetoun', inspired by his native town of Irvine.

Visual sources include architects' drawings from the 17th

century onwards; topographical views beginning with a late-
16th century perspective plan of St Andrews, continuing in the
following century with the urban landscapes of Gordon of
Rothiemay and Slezer, and including important paintings of
Aberdeen (No.1), Edinburgh (No.27), Glasgow (No.34) and
Montrose (No.59); engraved medals and architects' models;
early photographs; and town plans, of which the largest
collection was surveyed by John Wood in the 1820s.[12]

CHRONOLOGICAL SUMMARY

The use of a tolbooth at Berwick for burgh courts in the
second half of the 13th century has been referred to (*supra*,
p.1). Further evidence of substantial municipal buildings in
Scottish burghs is provided by a series of 14th-century royal
grants of plots of ground of specified size for building or
enlarging a *tolloneum* or a *pretorium* (court-house). The
earliest such grant, at Dundee in 1325, was for the
construction of 'a tolbooth and a prison', which was enlarged
in 1363.[13] Similar grants were made to Edinburgh (No.27) in

B. Irvine Tolbooth (appendix, no.12) from SW, c.1840   (C 47327)

1365 and, on a new site, in 1386; to Montrose (No.59) in
1375; and to Irvine in 1386. The grant of 1393 to Aberdeen
(No.1) is unique in specifying that the *pretorium* was not to be
built 'in the middle of the market-place', but the site chosen,
still occupied by the municipal buildings, was immediately N
of the medieval market. At this period, however, it was not
uncommon for burgh and sheriff courts, and council meetings,
to be held in the open air or in a private house.[14]

With the exception of the excavated footings of a tolbooth in
Peebles (No.69) and some portions of churches which were
later used for burgh purposes (e.g. Fortrose, No.32; Greenlaw,
No.35), there are no surviving tolbooths of medieval date. The
only building of this period which is known from graphic as
well as documentary sources is the Old Tolbooth of Edinburgh
(No.27), Scott's 'Heart of Midlothian', which was demolished
in 1817. Several tolbooths survive from the last quarter or end
of the 16th century, including the steeples of Crail and Dysart
(Nos.15, 25), and complete structures at Canongate and
Musselburgh (Nos.11, 60).[15]

At Aberdeen (No.1) the E end of the town-house was rebuilt
in 1616-30 as the massive 'wardhouse' tower, still extant,
which provided a first-floor vestibule to the court-house and
prison cells on the upper floors. This work was carried out in
compliance with an Act of 1597 that obliged royal burghs to
house prisoners from the surrounding counties as well as their
own inhabitants (*infra*, pp.8-9). This duty, as well as the
responsibility of head (county) burghs to accommodate the
sheriff courts, was a powerful incentive to rebuild or repair
tolbooths. The most remarkable civic building of the 17th
century was the five-storeyed tolbooth in Scots Renaissance
style at Glasgow (1626-7; No.34), which was rebuilt, except
for its crown steeple, in 1814. Other notable buildings of this
century are at Kirkcudbright (1627-9 and later; No.48) and

Linlithgow (1668-70; No.55).

The first decade of the 18th century saw the construction of two well-documented town-houses, in Renaissance style but with belfries of a traditional Scottish type, at Dumfries and Stirling (Nos.23, 79). At Aberdeen, however, the extension of the wardhouse to the rear in 1704-6, to designs by James Smith, matched the rough masonry and corbelled wall-head of the original tower. Later examples of the classical style survive at Sanquhar (William Adam, 1735-9; No.76) and in the Palladian wing added in 1731 to Musselburgh (No.60). The major building of this period, designed by William Adam in 1731 and demolished in 1932, was the town-house of Dundee (appendix,no.6).

In 1749 the town council of Peebles (No.69) stated that other royal burghs 'have of late built new Houses, commonly called Town Houses', and many such buildings were erected in the second half of the 18th century. One incentive to replace inconvenient and dilapidated tolbooths was the financial support of burgesses and the neighbouring gentry, who took an increasing interest in balls and assemblies and required suitable rooms for these and other social events. A fine example of an assembly-room, which is still used for the purpose, is that in the wing added to Haddington Town-house (No.36) in 1788. At Aberdeen (No.1) the second floor of the town-house was sumptuously refurbished in the 1750s to form the 'Great Room' for banquets and other civic functions (infra, p.18).

About one-third of the surviving town-houses were built or rebuilt in the first third of the 19th century. In some cases this resulted from increasing separation of functions. At Selkirk (No.77) a new court-house was built in 1803-5 close to the site of the tolbooth, which had been condemned as unfit by Sir Walter Scott, the sheriff-depute of the county, and a purpose-built prison was placed on the outskirts of the burgh. Even before an Act of Parliament in 1819 authorised counties to contribute to the building and maintenance of prisons, a number were jointly rebuilt. Several joint 'Town and County Buildings' were erected, following the precedent of Forfar (1786-8; No.31). The financial contributions made by burghs varied from the gift of a free site to the equal sharing of costs, and the provision made for burgh functions varied accordingly (see Ayr, Dumbarton, Glasgow, Nairn, Rothesay; Nos.6, 22, 34, 61, 74). At Linlithgow (No.55) a wing to house the County Buildings was added in 1819-21 adjoining the town-house, which still contained the prison, whereas at Cupar, Edinburgh, Kinross and Perth the new County Buildings were independent of the burgh ones. This period saw the construction of some of the most impressive of Scotland's civic buildings, including the town steeples that dominate Ayr and Port Glasgow (Nos.6, 73), and elegant Georgian town-houses in small burghs such as Falkland (No.29).

The period following the Municipal Reform Act of 1833[16] saw stricter financial control of Scottish burghs, and little new building or major alteration to town-houses was carried out before the middle of the century. The main exception was in the remodelling of prisons, which from 1835 were subject to annual inspection and from 1839 came under the authority of General and County Prison Boards.[17] Self-contained prisons on new sites were often built, but existing cell-blocks were remodelled or new ones added to town-houses in the 1840s, as at Cromarty and Nairn (Nos.16, 61). In the second half of the 19th century many town halls were built in response to the public demand for suitable venues for evangelical and other meetings and concerts, as well as civic events.[18] In many cases these were on new sites, but at Ayr (No.6) the town-house was extended in 1878-81 to contain a large hall. During this period Aberdeen Town-house (No.1) was rebuilt, to a baronial design by Peddie and Kinnear, as the County and Municipal Buildings, and Glasgow's new Municipal Buildings were built to a spectacular Renaissance design by William Young. In Edinburgh, however, the city council preferred to extend the 18th-century City Chambers (No.27).

*A. **Aberdeen** (No.1), County and Municipal Buildings from SE, c.1890 (A 33181)*

*B. **Glasgow** (No.34), Municipal Buildings from NW, c.1890   (GW/2113)*

*C. **Ayr** (No.6), interior of town hall of 1878-81   (C 4354)*

Many town-houses remained in use for burgh administration until the local government re-organisation of 1975. While some are now in private ownership, many still serve a wide range of public functions — sheriff courts, police stations, halls for meetings and social events, libraries and museums, art centres and studios, registrar's offices — as well as continuing administrative use by the new organs of local government.

BURGHAL STATUS

Throughout Europe in the medieval period new urban communities were established by kings and princes, and existing ones taken under their protection.[19] As well as these royal burghs, many other towns were established by ecclesiastical or secular landlords. In Scotland these came to be known as burghs of barony or regality, the distinction depending on the legal jurisdiction of their founders. Lords of regalities, many of which originated as ecclesiastical or noble estates, had wider judicial powers than lords of baronies.[20]

A. *Edinburgh (No.27), Lord Provost*   (Whitson)
George Drummond, engraving after Alexander, 1752

B. *Cupar (No.19), one of three Chinese*   (C 65084)
porcelain punch-bowls presented in 1784

C. *Montrose (No.59)*   (B 58152)
   thumbscrews from
   old tolbooth

D. *Cupar (No.19), meeting of town council, c.1830*   (C 62921)

Of the seventy-one burghs that were recognised as royal burghs in the 18th century,[21] fifty-two preserve substantial remains of tolbooths or town-houses, and there are varying degrees of information about the demolished buildings in the others (appendix, pp. 202-7). These royal burghs held crown charters or prescriptive rights which conferred extensive monopolies in foreign and local trade and the practice of crafts. They were authorised to govern themselves by elected councils, usually led by a provost and two or more bailies who acted as magistrates. In most cases, however, following an Act of 1469, the outgoing council took the predominant rôle in appointing its successor. The 'setts' or constitutions of the various councils specified the balance between merchants and craftsmen,[22] and places were often reserved for the 'deacons' or heads of individual craft-incorporations. From the 14th century to 1707 the royal burghs sent Commissioners to the Scottish Parliament or 'Estates'. After the Union of the Parliaments, in small groups (except for Edinburgh which had its own representative), their councils elected members to fifteen seats at Westminster.[23]

The celebrated lawyer Sir George Mackenzie noted in 1686 that the royal burghs 'having great freedoms and privileges from the king', were subject to correspondingly heavy burdens.[24] He was referring particularly to their responsibility for maintaining burgh and, in some cases, county prisons (*infra*). Their burgesses were liable for an important share of national taxation, where a block sum voted by the Estates would (from the mid 16th century) be apportioned between the individual burghs by the Convention of Royal Burghs.

Of the remaining thirty-five communities represented in the gazetteer, twenty-five were burghs of barony and eight were burghs of regality. The degree of self-government allowed to these burghs depended on the wishes of the superior and in some cases courts were held and regulations enacted by his baron-bailie while in others (e.g. Old Aberdeen, No.68) there was an elected council. Despite the much greater numbers of these dependent burghs, only a small proportion preserve their buildings, but some of these are of high architectural merit, including Old Aberdeen Town-house (No.68), Falkirk Town Steeple (No.28) and Port Glasgow Town Buildings (No.73). Two of the earliest surviving complete tolbooths, Canongate and Musselburgh (Nos.11, 60), belonged to burghs of regality. In the two communities that never had burgh status, the town-house at Beith (No.8) was built by subscription, while that at

Strichen (No.83) was initiated by an improving landlord.

When increased reponsibilities for holding sheriff courts and detaining prisoners were placed on head burghs in the late 16th century it was found that some counties contained no active royal burghs. The burghs of barony at Clackmannan (No.13) and Stonehaven (No.80) were therefore designated as head burghs, and in 1592 Parliament ordered a tolbooth to be built at the former. In several cases the status of a burgh of barony was not relevant to the erection of the existing building, since the superior was not involved. This was the case at Kilbarchan (No.43), where a steeple of characteristic tolbooth style was built by the parish heritors in 1755 along with a parish school and meal-market. At Lerwick (No.54) the tolbooth was rebuilt by the Commissioners of Supply in 1767, although the burgh of barony was not created until 1818. Pollokshaws Town-house (No.72) was built by a self-styled 'Community or Common Council of the Town of Pollokshaws' in 1803, some ten years before it secured the status of a burgh of barony. Similar local community spirit led to the building of the town-house at Saltcoats (No.75) in 1825-6 by a group of subscribers, 'considering that few towns of its size are destitute of some ornamental spire'. At Leith (No.53), which was a burgh of barony dependent on the City of Edinburgh, the historic tolbooth was rebuilt in 1824, but the existing town hall was built a few years later by 'the Magistrates and Masters', a body with local representation established by a Police Act of 1827.

Following the Parliamentary and Municipal Reform Acts of 1832 and 1833, new categories of burghs were created. Existing burghs of barony such as Leith (No.53), and towns of recent growth such as Portobello, were added to the groups of parliamentary burghs. These and numerous other burghs also received the status of police burghs, under successive general and local Police Acts, and in 1896 the number of royal, parliamentary and police burghs in Scotland had risen to two hundred and three.[25]

courts.[29] Some tolbooths in major burghs, notably Edinburgh (No.27), were also used by Parliament, royal councils and courts and the Convention of Royal Burghs. The expense of such obligations was balanced by the status and lucrative trade that they conferred, and at Edinburgh in 1562 new accommodation was provided for the royal courts after their threatened withdrawal to St Andrews because of the dangerous condition of the tolbooth. This threat had been anticipated at the beginning of the century in William Dunbar's poem 'To the Merchantis of Edinburgh':[30]

Sen (since) for the Court and the Sessioun,
The great repair of this regioun
Is in your burgh, thairfoir be boun
To mend all faultis that ar to blame,
    And eschew schame;
Gif thai pas to ane uther toun,
Ye will decay, and your great name.

Similar motives induced the citizens of the capital in the 1630s to accept the burden of erecting the Parliament House, and Charles I, in a letter of 1634, styled the unfinished structure 'the New Tolbooth', since it would replace the use of various civic buildings for royal purposes.[31]

82A

The use of a burgh bell was one of the first civic functions to be recorded, in the guildhall at Berwick in 1284,[32] and Edinburgh Tolbooth (No.27) was described as 'the belhous' in the endorsement of a royal charter of 1386. Steeples or bellcots were a normal feature of the buildings recorded here, and most of them had bells and clocks, many of which survive (*infra*,pp.15-16, 22-3).

Executions, which were supervised by the magistrates, were often held in front of tolbooths, as at Dalkeith and Glasgow (Nos.20, 34). At Edinburgh after 1785 they took place on 'the west end', the flat roof of an annexe to the tolbooth (No.27), with the gallows beam fitted into a socket in the adjacent gable-wall. A spike fixed on the same gable was used to display the heads of notable victims, including those of the

A. **Edinburgh** (No.27), hall of Old Tolbooth, drawing by Archer, 1817   (National Museums of Scotland)

B. **Edinburgh** (No.27), guard-house in Old Tolbooth, drawing by Archer, 1817   (National Museums of Scotland)

FUNCTIONS

Tolbooths and town-houses made tangible the civic pride and sense of community of the Scottish burgh, or the generosity of its patrons. Their most important practical uses were as meeting-places for councils and courts, and as prisons (*infra*). Burgh councils met regularly, on pain of fines for non-attendance,[26] and meetings of both councils and courts were held with strict formality, the magistrates often being attended by macers or officers bearing halberds.[27] Other formal occasions included burgh or county elections, the admission of new burgesses, and assembling to drink the king's health or for processions to church.[28]

In addition to the burgh courts conducted by the bailies and other officials such as the dean of guild, head burghs were required to house a wide range of county and sometimes royal

Marquis of Montrose from 1650 to 1661 and of his great opponent the Marquis of Argyll from 1661 to 1664.[33] Less severe but humiliating public punishments were also administered at the tolbooth or the mercat cross, and jougs (iron neck-collars) remain attached to the outer walls of several tolbooths. A whipping-post and stocks were fixed to the platform of the forestair at Paisley,[34] although at Canongate and Edinburgh the stocks were inside the tolbooth (Nos.11, 27). The town guard, who in many burghs performed the rôle of police until the early 19th century, often had their guard-house on the ground floor of the tolbooth.

115A, 124C, 157A

Despite the origin of the name 'tolbooth', rooms used for the collection of tolls and customs are rarely identifiable, although chambers for town clerks and their assistants were

A. **St Andrews** *(East Fife Museums Service)*
(appendix, no.20)
Scots pint measure, 1574

often provided. At Glasgow in the 17th century, however, a room was provided on the ground storey of the tolbooth (No.34) for the collector of excise. Weigh-houses for storing the standard weights and measures that each burgh kept for local or, in some cases, national use were often housed in tolbooths.[35] The weigh-house of the small rural burgh of Ceres (No.12), which was also used as a prison, has a balance carved above its entrance. Linear measures were commonly attached to the walls of tolbooths by chains, or built into them as at Dumfries (No.23).[36] In addition to their own records, head burghs were required to provide safe storage-space for county and court records, and this obligation was strictly enforced from the early 19th century.[37] Tolbooths and town-houses were also used for the storage of many kinds of burgh property, including armour and weapons, as at Aberdeen (No.1), fire-engines at Kilbarchan and Linlithgow (Nos.43, 55), and the equipment of such officials as town criers, drummers and pipers, or the town guard.

As well as their official functions, tolbooths and town-houses served a variety of other public and private uses, many of which brought revenue to the burgh, or avoided expenditure on separate buildings. The provision of a school was an obligation on all royal burghs, often met by the use of a room in the town-house (e.g. Anstruther Wester, Falkland, Inveraray; Nos.3, 29, 37). At Kilbarchan, it was the requirement for a new parish school that led to the erection of the steeple (No.43). The popularity of assemblies in the second half of the 18th century led to a demand for regular or seasonal dancing-classes. At Montrose (No.59), one of the first town-

54B

148D

B. **Wigtown** *(appendix, no.21)* *(Stranraer Museum)*
wine gallon, 1707

D. **Ceres Weigh-house** *(No.12), carved panel above door-lintel*

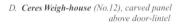

E. **Culross Town-house** *(No.18), imperial measures, 1824* *(C 23783)*

C. **Culross** *(C 23786)*
Town-house *(No.18)*
stone weight, 1618

F. **Culross Town-house** *(No.18)* *(C 23781)*
burgh drum

houses to have an assembly-room, it was also used by the local Musical Society in the 1760s for regular concerts. At North Berwick (No.67) entertainment was provided in the 1770s by 'strolling companys of show and playactors', and at Old Aberdeen (No.68) in 1796 by 'gentlemen of the theatre'. In 1824 the records of the same burgh have the intriguing entry, 'use of town hall, combustible lady, 15s', while in the 1750s Hawick town council received payment from 'a man with wild beasts in the tolbooth'.[38] In the early 19th century public reading-rooms and libraries became popular, and were sometimes housed in town-houses (e.g. Ayr, Beith, Cupar, Montrose, Newburgh; Nos.6, 8, 19, 59, 62).

In the 18th and early 19th centuries some burghs received financial support from two bodies whose membership often overlapped with that of the town council, the guildry (e.g. Brechin, Montrose; Nos.9, 59) and the local masonic lodge (e.g. Campbeltown, Old Aberdeen; Nos.10, 68). In such cases these bodies were often granted exclusive or preferential use of a room in the town-house for their meetings and social functions, as were the county gentlemen who contributed for the building of assembly-rooms (e.g. Haddington, Lanark; Nos.36, 50).

From the medieval period onwards it was common in Scotland, as elsewhere in Western Europe,[39] for the ground storeys of tolbooths to include covered space for market traders, or an exchange where merchants could transact business. During the 18th century an enclosed meal-market with a store or girnel was sometimes also provided, as at Kilbarchan (No.43).[40] A more permanent arrangement by which booths or shops were rented to merchants or craftsmen brought a steady revenue to many burghs, and their prominent locations were often highly valued. One of the rented properties below Dundee Town-house was a bank, which in 1788 was broken into through the floor of the guildry-room above.[41] When Johnson and Boswell visited Montrose (No.59) in 1773, they saw 'rooms for tea-drinking', and coffee-rooms were included in the Ayr Town Buildings of 1828-30 (No.6) and several other town-houses. However, Scotland appears to have had no equivalent of the municipal cellars and taverns that were a feature of many continental town-houses. The tap-rooms at Edinburgh and Glasgow Tolbooths (Nos.27, 34) were intended for prisoners and their visitors, and the wine-store at Aberdeen (No.1) was for councillors and their guests.

84B

Individual buildings were put to a variety of other uses. At Kilbarchan (No.43), the room above the meal-market was reserved exclusively for the local ladies, particularly when attending hunts and in the intervals between church services. Perhaps the most remarkable use was at Montrose (No.59) where, in 1819, the town-house was extended to cover part of the parish churchyard, which was retained as an enclosed

145E burial-vault. This includes the monuments of successive town clerks, and remained in use until the middle of the 19th century.

COSTS AND FUNDING

The obligation on royal burghs to maintain prisons and court-houses was an onerous one, as well as a source of civic pride, and the cost of building-works often led to prolonged debate in councils or criticism from reluctant contributors (e.g. Rothesay, No.74). Comparisons of cost are difficult because of the changing value of money, the frequent division of work between several contractors, the universal tendency for estimated or contract prices to be exceeded, and the hidden benefits sometimes received from the re-use or gift of materials and fittings. However, some examples illustrate variations in cost, and the heavy burden imposed on major burghs as standards of accommodation rose in the early 19th century.

At Aberdeen (No.1), the contract-price for the wardhouse in 1616 was £280,[42] while the addition made to that structure in 1704 cost £674. Tobias Bachup's contract of 1705 for

Dumfries Midsteeple (No.23) was for £1,045, but this does not include sums paid to the designer, John Moffat, and the value of materials already obtained by the burgh. William Adam's estimate of 1732 for Dundee Town-house was £2,852, but by 1737 expenditure had reached £4,000 and the building was not completely furnished for many years. In the 1770s the contract-price for Lanark Town-house (No.50) was £215, for Stranraer Town-house (No.81) it was £270, and Cromarty Court-house (No.16) cost between £400 and £500, but in 1789 Inverness Steeple (No.40), exclusive of the adjacent court-house, cost £1,598.

In the early 19th century, the contract-price for Airdrie Town-house (No.2) was £1,075, and the total outlay on Nairn Town and County Buildings was £1,392. Of the major civic buildings of that period, Ayr Assembly Rooms and Steeple (No.6) cost £9,965 and Port Glasgow Town Buildings (No.73) as much as £12,000. The £30,000 required for Ayr Town and County Buildings and prison (No.6) was mainly covered by an assessment on the burgh and county, but the entire cost of £34,811 for Glasgow Green Court-house (No.34) and the adjacent prison was borne by the Corporation of Glasgow.

The normal source of income available to royal burghs was the 'Common Good', which might be derived from tolls and customs on goods brought to market; rents from urban property including 'booths' and permanent market-stalls,

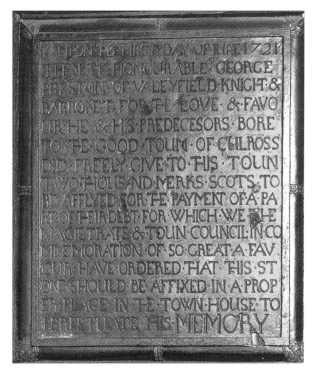

Culross Town-house (No.18), stone panel recording donation   (C 23767)

mills, and the 'common muir' or other rural lands; trading ventures, which at Edinburgh were known as the 'wild adventures'; and court fines. In many burghs, income from these sources declined with the concentration of trade in the larger burghs and ports, while it was further diminished by the alienation of common lands, often to members of the ruling oligarchy.[43] Burghs, like other institutions, received or administered 'mortifications' or charitable funds from individuals, and such gifts are recorded on painted boards at Aberdeen (No.1) and on a stone panel of 1721 at Culross (No.18), but these were commonly attached to specific purposes. Deans of Guild might have their own income, and in some cases, as at Aberdeen (No.1) in 1704, these funds were used for building-operations. Aberdeen also had a permanent 'Guild Wine fund', levied on new burgesses and devoted mainly to civic entertainments, and an 'arms-money'

7

fund for the maintenance of the burgh armoury, and both of these were sometimes used for work on the town-house.[44] Burghs sometimes received considerable sums for the sites and materials of earlier buildings, although the £3,300 thus raised at Ayr (No.6) in 1826 was exceptional.

There were many demands on the Common Good and other civic revenue, including the salaries of jailers, bell-ringers, clock-winders and other officials, and substantial building-operations could seldom be financed from these sources alone. Councils had the power to impose a local 'stent' or tax on inhabitants for specific ends, as well as demanding labour in kind, usually in the form of carting services.[45] Royal authority to levy other local taxes was sometimes granted, as with the duty on ale and malt at Linlithgow (No.55) in 1666 and on ale at Dunbar (No.24) in 1714. Grants in aid of tolbooths and other public works were often made by the Convention of Royal Burghs, although these normally took the form of exemptions from attendance at forthcoming meetings of the convention, rather than cash advances. However, a grant of revenue from the Scottish customs, which was obtained by the convention in 1696 and divided among the burghs, was used at Dumfries to build the Midsteeple (No.23). Direct grants from central government were rarely obtained, and in the 1630s the citizens of Edinburgh were required to provide the new Parliament House and Supreme Courts at their own expense.[46]

It is thus not surprising that councils had to resort to a combination of sources of funding, and were particularly reliant upon loans and private donations. Since the councils normally included some of the wealthiest burgesses, they were often able to obtain substantial loans from among their own members or other local worthies, such as the Bailie John Adamson who lent £700 for the new town-house at Newburgh (No.62) in 1808, or the four merchants of Port Glasgow (No.73), whose combined loans in 1815 amounted to £5,500. Local institutions such as churches, hospitals, and schools also appear among the lenders. After the town council of Dundee decided in 1731 to execute William Adam's design for the new town-house, their provost was sent to Edinburgh 'to ascertain on what terms the Banks would advance the necessary funds for this building',[47] and this was to become an increasingly important source of finance. The result was that many burghs carried a heavy burden of debt, with complex financial schemes to avoid insolvency, and by the early 1830s the City of Edinburgh was spectacularly bankrupt.[48]

Outright donations were particularly valued, and those from guildries and masonic lodges have been mentioned, while 'trades' or craft-incorporations also contributed (p.163). Furniture was sometimes donated, for example the chairs, tables and forms for Campbeltown Town-house (No.10) were gifted by the local masonic lodge in 1769.[49] More general support from the burgh and its hinterland was often obtained by the circulation of subscription-papers, a method whose public nature stimulated the generosity of donors. Local noblemen and members of parliament were generous contributors to these subscriptions, or made direct donations such as the £150 gifted by the 3rd Marquis of Annandale to Lochmaben (No.56) in 1741. They also appear frequently as donors of bells, clocks and other artefacts, and a panel on the S front of Kinross Town-house (No.46) records that Robert Adam, while member for Kinross-shire, 'decorated this front at his own expense'. The element of electioneering in these donations is explicit in Sir Hew Dalrymple's subscription to Haddington (No.36) in 1741 for £50, 'or if I sit in the present parliament, for £100 sterling'.[50] Sir Hew was again successful in the 1761 election for the Haddington group of burghs, which included Jedburgh, after paying for the completion of the Newgate there (No.41).

In those head burghs that were not royal ones, a tolbooth for use by the sheriff might be financed by a general levy on the county, as at Clackmannan (No.13) in 1592. At Aberdeen (No.1) in 1616 an approach was made to the Marquis of Huntly, then sheriff, for assistance in building the wardhouse,

Kinross Town and County House (No.46), inscription on S front   (C 48024)

'for the gude and benefitt of the whole shyre ... albeit for the use of our awin inhabitantis, the tolbuith itselff wes alreddie a sufficient wardhous'.[51] This application was ignored, and in general royal burghs were held to the Act of 1597 (*infra*) which placed upon them the sole reponsibility for providing and maintaining prisons. By the middle of the 18th century their inability to do this adequately, and the increasing demand for better court facilities, as well as rooms for general meetings and social events, led some counties to make voluntary contributions. An early example was at Inveraray (No.37), where the town-house of 1751-5 was paid for by the county, largely through a 'donation' by a former sheriff-depute who had collected excess taxes many years earlier. The 'Town and County Buildings' of 1786-8 at Forfar (No.31) were followed by several other joint ventures, even before the legal right of counties to contribute to the cost of new prisons was recognised by an Act of 1819.[52] The contributions made from burgh resources varied from the site alone (in itself a valuable asset), at Jedburgh (No.41), or the site and a £500 subscription at Ayr (No.6), to an equal division of all costs at Nairn (No.61) or one in which the burgh paid the greater amount as at Wick (No.87). Where a general assessment was levied (e.g. Ayr), the inhabitants of the burgh as well as the county were liable for payment.

In the exceptional cases of the royal burghs of Sanquhar (No.76) in the 1730s and Cullen (No.17), which was part of a new planned town, in the 1820s, the new town-houses were financed entirely by the local magnates. Such patronage was more common in burghs of barony and regality, such as the new village of Fochabers (No.30), and inscriptions testify to similar generosity in the early 18th century at Greenlaw and West Wemyss (Nos.35, 85). Kelso Town Hall (No.42) was rebuilt in 1816 by the 5th Duke of Roxburghe, with assistance from local subscribers. In other burghs where the initiative for building came from the local community, such as Newton on Ayr and Saltcoats (Nos.65, 75), it was solely responsible for financing the work. Many of the expedients familiar in royal burghs were employed, with subscription being especially popular.

PRISONS AND PRISONERS[53]

The construction of a tolbooth and prison was authorised at Dundee in 1325 (*supra*), and 'the prison of the court-house' (*carcer pretorii*) was used for the detention of inhabitants of Aberdeen (No.1) in 1398.[54] The sheriff of Aberdeenshire had already been reimbursed by the Crown for building a prison there in 1358, and during the later middle ages the division between county and burgh prisons was maintained, with sheriffs often making use of royal castles. From the late 16th century, state prisoners continued to be held in castles, but in 1597 burghs were made responsible for receiving all county prisoners whose offences fell outside the jurisdiction of barony and regality courts. This Act, 'that prison-houses suld be biggit in all burrows', recited that 'sindry rebelles and transgressoures of the lawes' had escaped unpunished, and ordained that, 'within the space of three zeires [years], in all burghs within this realme there be sufficient and sure jailles and warde-houses, bigged, uphalden, and maintained be the provost, baillies, councell, and communities of the said burrowes, upon their awin [own] common gude, or utherways upon the charges of the burgh'.[55] This burden became increasingly onerous until the responsibility was transferred in 1839 to County Boards, some of whom thus assumed ownership of parts of town-houses (e.g. Haddington, Linlithgow; Nos.36, 55).

Until the latter part of the period covered by this survey, those detained were mainly suspected criminals awaiting trial, when a fine or physical punishment might be imposed, or debtors committed by their creditors. Imprisonment as a punishment became common only in the late 18th century, with the introduction of 'Bridewells' where corrective labour was imposed.[56] However, suspects might be held for long periods before trial, at the expense of the burgh. The period of detention for debtors was sometimes moderated by the requirement on creditors, by the 'Act of Grace' of 1696,[57] to pay aliment for those who could not maintain themselves, but in practice the burghs frequently bore this expense also. A particularly obnoxious burden was the heavy fine payable to the Crown if a prisoner escaped, or in the case of an absconding debtor the liability for payment of his debts. Wick town council was fined £260 in 1820 for the escape of a prisoner from their tolbooth, and they faced a writ for a further £700 for the escape of five smugglers.[58]

Political prisoners were commonly held in state prisons such as Edinburgh Castle or the Bass Rock, but the Marquises of Montrose in 1650 and Argyll in 1661 both suffered the ignominy of imprisonment in Edinburgh Tolbooth (No.27) in the final days before their executions at the nearby mercat cross. An ingenious deception by a Royalist prisoner in Sanquhar Tolbooth (No.76) in 1653 led to panic and fighting between two detachments of Cromwellian forces.[59] Many Jacobite prisoners were held in tolbooths in 1715 and 1746, and a group of Jacobite soldiers were liberated from Leith Tolbooth (No.53) in 1715 after their comrades had seized control of the port.

Religious dissenters were also detained in tolbooths from the early days of the Reformation, and at Edinburgh in 1569 the dean of guild was ordered to 'caus mak ane poupat, portative (portable pulpit), to be set up in the Over Tolbuth for preiching to the papistis'.[60] During the 17th century 'Popish priests' continued to be subject to immediate arrest and many Covenanters were held at Edinburgh and Canongate awaiting trial or transportation.[61] Among those detained in Edinburgh Tolbooth in 1684 was Lady Colvill, 'for breiding up hir sone the Lord Colvill in phanaticisme'.[62] At Dumfries, which lay close to the main area of Covenanter activity, Graham of Claverhouse complained in 1679 that 'there is here in prison a minister ... has had the liberty of an open prison; and more conventicles have been kept by him there, than has been in any one house in the kingdom. That prison is more frequented than the kirk'.[63] During the 18th century non-juring Episcopalians were also subject to penal laws because of their Jacobite sympathies. In a celebrated incident at Stonehaven in 1748-9, three clergymen conducted daily worship and administered baptism through the window of their cell in the tolbooth (No.80).

Quakerism made many converts during the reign of Charles II, and its adherents both in England and Scotland were subject to persecution. Those imprisoned in Aberdeen Tolbooth (No.1) included two notable local landowners, Alexander Jaffray of Kingswells and Robert Barclay of Urie. Barclay was an eminent theologian who employed his five-month imprisonment in 1677 in writing a treatise on 'Universal Love'.[64] His father, David Barclay, who was also imprisoned at Aberdeen, had himself been converted to Quakerism in Edinburgh Castle in 1665 by a fellow-prisoner, John Swinton of Swinton,[65] who was an ancestor of Sir Walter Scott's mother. Scott also related with pride that his paternal

great-great-grandfather, Walter Scott of Raeburn, was imprisoned in 1666 in Edinburgh Tolbooth where, by contact with other Quakers, 'he [was] hardened in his pernitious opinions and principles'.[66]

Suspected witches were frequent inmates of Scottish tolbooths from 1563, when witchcraft was made a capital offence, until the repeal of this legislation in 1735. They were normally subjected to torture or to violent 'pricking', under the supervision of the local kirk-session, to extract confessions.[67] Another group of female prisoners, who inspired greater public sympathy, were those accused of murdering their new-born infants or concealing their pregnancy. There were many real-life examples to set alongside the famous fictional characters, Effie Deans in Scott's *Heart of Midlothian* and the less fortunate Jean Gaisling in Galt's *The Provost*.[68]

Despite the onerous penalties imposed on burghs for the escape of prisoners, Scottish tolbooths were notoriously insecure. The inadequate design and poor maintenance of many of the buildings were compounded by the meagre pay of the jailers, few of whom were resident overnight. It was noted that Edinburgh Tolbooth (No.27) 'had no power of retention over people of quality', and even where bribery or connivance were not suspected prisoners might escape by deception, disguised or concealed in a container.[69] Escapes might also be contrived by cutting through or under walls which were often held to be inadequate (e.g Tain; No.84); by the complete removal of window-grilles (Inveraray), or by cutting them with saws or acid[70]; by breaking upwards onto a roof (Leith) or down through a vault as at Aberdeen (No.1) in 1673; or by main force from outside. It was often perilous for burghs to imprison those with powerful friends or enemies. In 1561 the magistrates of Edinburgh had themselves to take refuge in the tolbooth (No.27) from an armed mob who had already liberated the prisoners from there.[71] In 1715 a Jacobite force broke into Leith Tolbooth (No.53) to release their imprisoned comrades, and in 1832 supporters of Parliamentary Reform stormed Dundee Town-house to rescue those held during a previous riot.[72] At Lauder (No.52) in 1598 the Earl of Home burnt the tolbooth after removing and killing one of the bailies, who had been involved in a family feud with one of the Earl's supporters. In the most celebrated of all tolbooth 'breakings', in 1736, Captain John Porteous vainly attempted to evade removal from Edinburgh Tolbooth by a mob bent on his execution which burnt down the entrance-door.[73] However, in at least two cases fugitives in the capital eluded pursuit by concealing themselves in that building.[74]

The conditions in which prisoners were kept varied widely, from place to place and within a single prison. The medieval tradition was that accused burgesses should voluntarily 'enter into ward' in their tolbooth, and at Paisley this was preserved until the 18th century in the custom of presenting the tolbooth key to a burgess so that he could admit himself.[75] In many cases, and most commonly at Edinburgh and Glasgow, where the jailers kept tap-rooms, friends were allowed to visit and drink with inmates. There were frequent complaints that prisoners could converse with those outside through ground-floor windows, or let down baskets or bottles from upper windows to receive gifts of food or drink.

In contrast, difficult or 'refractory' prisoners, and those convicted of serious crimes, were kept in seclusion and often heavily manacled. Until 1839 it was almost universal for those *28C, 148C* condemned to execution to be manacled to a 'gad' or iron floor-bar, of the type that survives at Aberdeen (No.1).[76] This *29B* use of the gad in the tolbooth of 'Freeport' (modelled on Kirkcudbright) is graphically described in Scott's account of the death of Dirk Hatteraick.[77] At Edinburgh an iron 'cage' for solitary confinement stood in the 'iron house', and several timber-built cages were built in the criminals' rooms in Perth Tolbooth in the late 18th century. Many tolbooths had an unlit 'black hole' or 'thieves' hole', which might be used for vagrants or drunkards as well as for high-security prisoners,

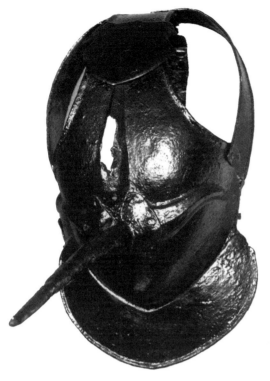

Culross, No.18) for burgess or gentleman debtors, whose status and means of livelihood would be forfeited if they absconded. Conditions for non-burgess debtors often remained very bad, partly on the grounds that creditors expected the *squalor carceris* ('filth of the prison') to induce them to make rapid repayment, and some burghs were even fined for allowing debtors to take exercise. An inscription[78] seen in Perth Tolbooth before 1812 gave a stern warning to debtors:

THINK WITH THYSELF WHILST THOU ART ON THE VAY,
AND TAKE SOME COURSE THY CREDITOR TO PAY
LEST THOU BY HIM BEFORE A JUDGE BE CALLD
AND BY ANE OFFICER BE HERE INTHRALLD
TILL UTMOST FARTHING SHALL BY THEE BE PAID
THOU SHALT BE CLOSE WITHIN THIS PRISON
STAID.

From the last quarter of the 18th century, many Scottish tolbooths were visited by John Howard and his successors who were active as penal reformers in England. Apart from lack of hygiene and exercise-space, one of their most common criticisms was that overcrowding prevented 'classification', or the separation of those awaiting trial from convicts, juveniles from adults, criminals from civil detainees, and even males from females. Their publications helped to stimulate a demand for reform which strengthened the involvement of counties in the construction of new prisons, and many were built in this period. Because of changing standards, however, and increasing emphasis on the need for classification, buildings of this type such as the County Jail of 1810-13 at Cupar (No.19) were themselves to be condemned by the official inspector of the 1830s as extravagant and unsuitable. The inspectors placed great importance on the system of solitary confinement, and prison designs of the 1840s and later were characterised by the construction of numerous small individual cells.

A. **Montrose** *(No.59), branks' bridles from tolbooth (B 58143)*

and 'lock-ups' for this purpose were common until the 19th century. A frequent source of public dissatisfaction was the committal to prison of innocent lunatics, and revulsion at the conditions in which they were kept at Montrose (No.59) led to the foundation of the asylum there in 1781.

Special provision was often made for those of superior class and wealth, who could afford to pay for better facilities. Thus, Edinburgh Tolbooth (No.27) had its 'Gentlemen's Chamber', and Glasgow (No.34) had two rooms for 'prisoners of note and distinction'. During the 18th century it became common to provide separate and better-ventilated accommodation (cf. Selkirk, No.77), or the use of one of the business-rooms (e.g.

B. **Pittenweem** *(No.71), tolbooth steeple from N   (B39399)*

ARCHITECTURAL INTRODUCTION

SCOTLAND AND EUROPE

The revival or creation of urban communities occurred throughout Western Europe from the 12th century onwards, and civic buildings became an essential feature of these towns.[79] Scottish examples cannot match the scale, elaboration and antiquity of those in the great commercial centres of Europe, such as the civic *palazzi* of Florence and Siena; the 15th-century town hall of Brussels with its 115m belfry, or that of 1667 at Amsterdam (built partly with stone from Culross[80]) which became a royal palace; and the classical *hotels de ville* of France. In scale most of them are nearer to those in Scandinavia and the smaller towns of the Netherlands, the areas with which Scotland had its closest trading links. The prevalence of steeples in Scottish tolbooths, in contrast with the design of English town halls, may reflect their popularity in the Low Countries. Specific comparisons may be made, such as that between the hexagonal entrance-tower at Dunbar (No.24) and the corresponding feature at 's-Heerenberg (Gelderland, Netherlands).[81] The gableted crowsteps seen at Dunbar may have a similar source.[82] Leith Tolbooth of 1563-5 (No.53), with its flamboyant oriel-window and stepped string-courses, is unusual in showing French stylistic influence, which may be explained by the port's close connection with Queen Mary and her mother, Mary of Guise. The simple rectangular town-house with a small belfry surmounting the centre of the roof-ridge, seen at Lerwick and North Berwick (Nos.54, 67), is also found in Scandinavia, as at Sigtuna (Sweden) in 1744.

However, Scottish tolbooths had strong native roots, with the tower-house tradition influencing the design of early buildings, and later town-houses continued to show close links with domestic architecture in the use of features such as forestairs. The significance placed on the town steeple, often in preference to the burgh church, produced several fine spires which are indistinguishable from those of contemporary churches (cf. Nos.28, 73). The requirement for Scottish tolbooths and town-houses to include prison-accommodation, in contrast to England and France where such provision was normally made in purpose-built structures, had an obvious effect on internal planning. The use of the ground storeys of many civic buildings for market purposes is comparable with English tradition, whereas in France separate covered market-halls were common from the medieval period onwards. However, during the medieval period the halls of the merchant guilds in many English towns came to equal or surpass their municipal buildings (indeed the Guildhall of London became its civic headquarters), whereas in Scotland, where guild organisation was generally later and less elaborate,[83] the tolbooths retained a wider range of civic functions.

LOCATION

The Scottish burgh was primarily a trading community with the market-area as its focal point, whether this took the form of a rectangular or square market-place, as at Aberdeen and Kelso (Nos.1, 42); a linear street, perhaps with a central expansion, as at Arbroath (No.4); or a combination of both as at Edinburgh (No.27). In 1625 the council of Kirkcudbright (No.48) sought for a site 'within the hairt and bodie of thair toun'. The early tolbooths were commonly situated in this central area, and usually close to those other symbols of burgh status, the mercat cross (e.g. Stirling; No.79) and the 'tron' or weighing-machine.[84] The close relationship with the burgh church, most memorably expressed at Edinburgh (No.27) in the juxtaposition of the Old Tolbooth with St Giles's Church, is also seen at Lanark and Lauder (Nos.50, 52), and in some cases burghs made use of church steeples (*infra, p.12*). With the greater scale of civic buildings in the early 19th century, and requirements such as that of exercise-space for prisons, it became increasingly difficult to find adequate sites in town centres, which in some cases had suffered social decline. Prisons or Town and County Buildings of this period were often built in new suburbs or peripheral locations (e.g. Ayr,

A. **Port Glasgow** *(No.73), Town Buildings and harbour from N, c.1890 (C 54996)*

B. **Perth** *(appendix, no.16), Council-house and quay from N, c.1798 (C 62915)*

C. **Dumfries** *(No.23), Midsteeple and market-place from S, c.1835 (DFD/113/2)*

Dumbarton; Nos.6, 22).

Although many of the burghs were sea-ports, it was unusual for the market-place and tolbooth to be in immediate proximity to the harbour, the re-used warehouse at Stonehaven (No.80) being an exceptional case.[85] At Anstruther Wester (No.3) an early tolbooth in the harbour area was swept away in a storm during the 17th century. The close connection of harbour and tolbooth at Leith was expressed in 1656 by the traveller Richard Franck, who observed: 'the pier like a gnomon directs to the tolbooth'.[86] The most impressive monument of the association of the town-house with overseas trade is seen at Port Glasgow (No.73), where the Town Buildings tower above the now partly-infilled harbour, and in the 19th century were used to house mercantile offices. At Perth (appendix, no.16) the tolbooth stood beside a bridge over the River Tay which was demolished in 1621, and a pend adjoining the 17th-century council-house led to a quay on the river-bank.

The royal grant of 1393 to Aberdeen (No.1), authorising the citizens to build their town-house anywhere in the burgh 'except in the centre of the market-place', implies that this was a common position for such buildings. The burgesses of Aberdeen responded with a site at the N edge of the market-place and intruding into it, but free-standing island sites were used by other recipients of 14th-century charters, at Edinburgh (No.27), Irvine (appendix, no.12) and Montrose (No.59). All three were demolished in the 19th century, as were other ancient tolbooths in similar locations such as Ayr (No.6), Elgin and St Andrews (appendix, nos.8,20). The justification given was often that of the magistrates of Cupar (No.19) in 1810: 'it is situated in the middle of the principal street and greatly obstructs the entry and passage'.

Despite this vulnerable position, several tolbooths survive on island-sites, including Crail, Forfar, Kilmaurs, Lochmaben and Sanquhar (Nos.15, 31, 44, 56, 76). Others such as Kelso, Kintore and Tain (Nos. 42, 47, 84), project fully into the market-place, as originally did Aberdeen and Linlithgow (Nos.1, 55). One of the most impressively situated, Dumfries Midsteeple (No.23), occupies an area which in 1703 was still open market-space, and the council were able to choose between building it above or below the mercat cross. At Haddington and Lauder (Nos.36, 52) the town-house is prominently set at the end of a 'mid-raw', a row of buildings which may have encroached on an original larger market-place, and it is possible that the predecessor of the latter was originally free-standing. Old Aberdeen Town-house (No.68) only acquired its island site in the 1920s when older buildings adjoining it to the N were demolished for road-construction.

In many other burghs the tolbooth was situated on the street-front of the high street or market-place, sometimes gaining greater prominence by the setting-back of the adjacent house-line (e.g. Newmilns; No.64) or recessing of the tolbooth itself, as at Dingwall and Nairn (Nos.21, 61). Particularly favoured were corner-sites at the junction of a street with the market-place (e.g. Brechin, Cullen, Montrose, Musselburgh, Stirling; Nos.9, 17, 59, 60, 79) or with another street (e.g. Ayr Steeple, Dysart, Falkland; Nos.6, 25, 29), which allowed two fronts to be seen. At Glasgow (No.34) from the 15th century the tolbooth stood at the principal crossroads of the burgh, and its steeple still survives at 'Glasgow Cross', isolated on a traffic-island. The preference was for the axis of the building to be placed parallel to the street, as at Canongate and Kirkcudbright (Nos.11, 48). For lack of space it was sometimes necessary to present a gable to the street, as at the site acquired for Strathmiglo Town-house (No.82) about 1730, which was however given emphasis by a substantial steeple.

The building or enlargement of street-frontages in the congested conditions of the Scottish burgh were bound to conflict with the network of small wynds and closes that gave access to 'backlands' or arable plots. Successive additions to Edinburgh City Chambers (No.27) led to the absorption or disappearance of several adjacent closes, including the celebrated Mary King's Close. Such pre-existing rights of way were sometimes maintained by pends or passageways running through the tolbooth. A pend below the tower of Canongate Tolbooth (No.11) gives access to Tolbooth Wynd, which was one of the main routes leading N from the burgh, and at Dunfermline (appendix, no.7) the tolbooth spanned the principal street that led S from the high street. At Aberdeen in 1750 the town-house (No.1) was extended by a record-room built above a pend at the entrance to Lodge Walk, which was further heightened in 1839. A well-documented example of a passage-way which preserved the traditional access to a parish churchyard is the 'deid arch' of 1763 in the rear wall of Montrose Town-house (No.59). Central archways having spires above also led to churchyards at Jedburgh and Newton on Ayr (Nos.41, 65). Pends could also give access to enclosed yards or to public services situated behind the tolbooth, as at Girvan (No.33) and at Leith Tolbooth (No.53), where a fleshmarket in this position was established in 1569.

Some town-houses were original features of the planned new towns of the 18th and early 19th century. That at Inveraray (No.37) was prominent in the show front designed by John Adam for the 3rd Duke of Argyll, symmetrical with the 'great inn' built for the convenience of the visiting judges. At Fochabers (No.30) the town-house and an identical house intended for the baron-bailie flank the slightly later parish church, all designed for the 4th Duke of Gordon by John Baxter. The town-house of Cullen (No.17), part of the burgh relocated by the 4th Earl of Seafield, occupies a conspicuous corner-site at the upper side of the great central square. Elsewhere, the town-house of Strichen (No.83) was erected in 1816 at the centre of the 18th-century planned village. In another scheme of urban improvement, Cupar Burgh Chambers (No.19) of 1815-18 occupy a prominent position at the junction of the newly-created St Catherine Street with Crossgate, the traditional market-area.

ADAPTATION AND RE-USE

In some burghs existing buildings were adapted for use as tolbooths or town-houses, such as the warehouse at Stonehaven (No.80) which was converted into a tolbooth about 1600. At Maybole (No.57) the late 16th-century tower-house of the laird of Blairquhan was bought for this purpose in 1673. The 16th-century Bishop's Castle at Dornoch (appendix, no.5) was refurbished in 1813 for use as a court-house and prison. A more complete 16th-century tower-house, the 'Castle of St John' at Stranraer (No.81), was restored as a prison in 1820-2, following the model provided by the adaptation of Portchester Castle (Hampshire) for French prisoners. At Edinburgh (No.27) the city council in 1811 established their City Chambers in the former Royal Exchange, which had been built in the 1750s as a municipal 'improvement'.

The use of former or active ecclesiastical buildings was common. The medieval N range of Fortrose Cathedral (No.32) became the burgh tolbooth after the Reformation, with a prison in the vaulted chapter-house and a council-chamber above. The most celebrated example of shared use was at Edinburgh (No.27), where in the 1560s council- and court-rooms were inserted in the W part of St Giles's Church, which later became the 'Tolbooth Church'. Perth town council met in 'a housse' within St John's Church until 1696-7, and the town records were still being kept there in 1767. At Dundee the magistrates made occasional use of the fine medieval tower of St Mary's Church as a prison as late as 1837.[87] Several other church towers were also used for prisons, as at Anstruther Wester, Greenlaw and Pittenweem (Nos.3, 35, 71) and at the first of these a cell in the tower was linked by a passage to the town hall built in 1794-5.[88]

BUILDING-MATERIALS

All of the surviving buildings included in this survey are built of stone, although timber was widely used in earlier periods, as in the 'hous biggit of tymmer' added to the W gable of Aberdeen Tolbooth (No.1) in 1597 to house the town clerk's office. However, the type of masonry employed varied widely, depending on the location of quarries and the financial resources available. At Glasgow in 1626-7 it was possible to face all of the visible frontages with ashlar, whereas most burghs even in the following century could aspire only to a principal front of ashlar (e.g. Old Aberdeen, No.68), and in other cases rubble was used throughout.

Some burghs, including Dundee, Edinburgh and Glasgow, had excellent local quarries and a thriving building-industry, and as at Dumfries (No.23) they might own a town quarry, which would be leased out but on which they had an over-riding claim. One of the earliest recorded Scottish building-contracts was for the quarrying, hewing and laying of ashlar in 1501 for Edinburgh Tolbooth (No.27), and in 1668 a detailed contract was made for the supply of shaped stones to Linlithgow Town-house (No.55) from the nearby quarry at Kingscavil. Where suitable stone for dressings was not available locally it might be imported over long distances, and at Lerwick (No.54) payment was made in 1770 'for free stone brought from Leith and Orkney'. At Aberdeen (No.1) sandstone for the dressings of the tolbooth steeple was imported in the 1620s from the Mylne family quarry at Kingoodie near Dundee. During the extension of this building in 1704, dressed stone from the older work was carefully set aside and re-used. Such re-use was an important source of stone and timber in all periods, and in addition to the fabric of previous tolbooths (e.g. Pittenweem, No.71) material was often removed from abandoned abbeys and churches, as at Arbroath, Kirkcudbright and Musselburgh (Nos.4, 48, 60), or castles and forts, at Ayr (No.6), Kirkwall (appendix, no.15) and Sanquhar (No.76).

The supply of large timbers for major works, for scaffolding as well as structural use, was a persistent problem for civic and private patrons,[89] and suitable Scottish timber was rarely available except in the Highlands, the main source of supply being the Baltic. However, the building-committee for Dumfries Midsteeple (No.23) was unsuccessful in its efforts in 1704 'to fraught (freight) a free Danish or Swedish bottom (vessel) to go to Norway for timber and dales (boards)'. Following a lengthy search for suitable native timber, trees were purchased and transported from Garlieswood, some 90km distant. 'Hyeland oak trees' were used at Stirling (No.79) in 1703, and at Banff (No.7) in 1798 timber from Speyside and the Baltic was used. At Cullen (No.17) in 1822 the choice was extended to include American timber as well as that from Abernethy Forest or Norway.

Slate was the most commonly used roofing-material, obtained either from local sources or from the celebrated Argyll quarries of Easdale and Ballachulish which, from the middle of the 18th century, shipped much of their production to East Coast ports. Slate from either of these quarries was specified for Kinghorn Town-house (No.45) in 1829, but at Cullen (No.17) in 1822 it was obtained from local quarries at Rannas and Darbreich.

In earlier buildings other materials were used as roof-coverings. Oak shingles remained on the turrets of Canongate Tolbooth (No.11) until 1871, and an example is preserved in Huntly House Museum. Heather thatch at Fortrose (No.32) was replaced in 1721 by slates, and similar thatch was used in demolished tolbooths, at Tain (No.84) in the 17th century and at Sanquhar (No.76) until 1731. Stone slabs were also used, mainly for roofing steeples or areas where additional security was required, as at Pittenweem Steeple (No.71) and the exercise-corridor of Cromarty Court-house (No.16).

ARCHITECTS, MASONS AND CRAFTSMEN

One of the main principles of the organisation of the Scottish burgh was the protection of its own merchants and craftsmen, including masons, wrights or carpenters, and hammermen (smiths). Those who were deacons (heads of the various trades) or members of the burgh council were especially favoured in the award of contracts for building-work. This practice is seen in an extreme form at Airdrie (No.2), where in 1825 a design by the burgh treasurer for the town-house was chosen in preference to one by a former councillor, and the successful contractor, as well as his three rivals, were also members of the council. The most distinguished such beneficiary was the Glasgow wright and architect Allan Dreghorn, who served as city treasurer in the late 1730s when he was engaged on the new town hall attached to Glasgow Tolbooth (No.34). At Edinburgh in 1785 another wright and councillor, Deacon William Brodie, was employed to supervise the construction of a door to the new execution-area at the tolbooth (No.27), and to devise the drop-mechanism on which he was himself executed for burglary three years later.

In some of the larger burghs a 'master of works' was retained, one of whose duties was to design and supervise the construction or alteration of civic buildings. At Glasgow (No.34), John Boyd received special payment in 1627 'for his

diligens in building the Tolbuithe', and at Aberdeen (No.1) in the early 19th century the post of master of works was held by the local architect and contractor John Smith.

As standards of scale and elaboration developed it became increasingly difficult for small burghs to undertake ambitious projects using local expertise and manpower. The custom of employing an expert master-mason or architect from outside the burgh became common in the 17th century. In the case of Lochmaben (No.56), where courts were held by the Warden of the West March, James VI and I himself sent his master of works to choose a site and build a tolbooth. John Mylne, master-mason to Charles II, supplied designs to rebuild Linlithgow Town-house (No.55) in 1667, just before his death, although the work was carried out in amended form by a master-mason named John Smith.

The degree of an architect's involvement could vary greatly, from advice by correspondence to repeated site visits or execution of the contract itself. At Stirling (No.79) a local mason was sent to consult Sir William Bruce at his home in Kinross, taking with him the dimensions of the ground available for a new town-house and steeple, from which Bruce prepared a 'draught or sceme of the work'. The building-committee at Dumfries (No.23) in 1703 looked to Edinburgh, attempting in vain to employ 'Mr James Smith, James Smith his nevoy, or any other Architect'. Their eventual choice, reflecting the trading-contacts of the burgh, was a Liverpool architect, John Moffat, who was unable because of other work to undertake the building-contract. His design was modified under the committee's direction by the contractor, Tobias Bachup from Alloa, who was appointed in preference to a local bailie. Meanwhile, in 1704 the council of Aberdeen (No.1) gave twenty guineas 'to Mr James Smith, Architect, for comeing north to give his advice anent the said Tolbooth', and Smith also wrote at least two letters about the extension of the wardhouse.

In some cases, as had been common since medieval times, existing buildings were chosen as models. Thus at Dumfries (No.23) in 1704, John Moffat was sent to Glasgow to view the steeple of the Old College, and subsequently the deacon of the wrights was paid 'for going to see other steeples that he might know how to make the spire of the Steeple'. At Dingwall (No.21) the architect, wright and mason involved in building a new belfry were sent in 1773 to Forres 'to view the stiple, clock and bells there', and the architect was paid 'to meke a modell thence as a plan for the proposed operations'.

The list of architects employed on Scottish town-houses (see index, s.v. 'architects') includes many of the most distinguished native members of the profession, from Sir William Bruce, James Smith, and William Adam and his sons, to David and Thomas Hamilton at the end of the period.[90] Architects were often chosen on the basis of their reputation, but in some cases they were known to councils through other work in the area. Thus, John Adam's employment for Banff Steeple (No.7) followed work at nearby Cullen House, and Thomas Hamilton was well-known in Ayr (No.6) for the design of the Burns Monument at Alloway.

Some architects also supplied building-materials and fittings, as William Adam did at Aberdeen Town-house (No.1), where he provided a marble chimneypiece in 1731, and at Sanquhar (No.76) in 1735. This practice, and that of architects acting as building-contractors, continued into the 19th century although increasingly disapproved of by many members of the profession as it became more formally organised.[91] John Smith executed his own designs at Aberdeen (No.1) as did Richard Crichton at Kirkcudbright Jail (No.48) and Stirling Court-house and prison (No.79). In smaller burghs the older tradition of the master-mason or 'builder-architect' also continued, producing accomplished designs such as the town-houses at Falkland (No.29) by Thomas Barclay, 'mason at Balbirnie', and Newburgh (No.62) by the local mason John Speed.

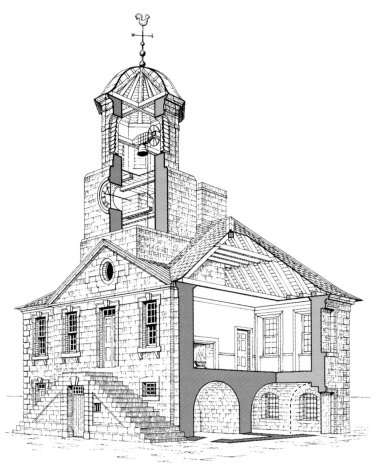

A. Sanquhar Town-house (No.76), perspective section from NE

B. Ayr (No.6), Town Steeple and New Bridge from N, 1859   *(B 63848)*

OVERALL DESIGN AND STYLE

The size of a tolbooth or town-house was generally related to the resources available for its construction. The largest and most complex buildings were found in major burghs such as Edinburgh, Glasgow, Aberdeen, Dundee and Stirling. Such buildings commonly evolved over centuries, often with a small core being augmented and rebuilt as resources and necessity dictated. Aberdeen (No.1) demonstrates the development from a semi-fortified structure into an edifice appropriate for grand civic display, while on a smaller scale South Queensferry (No.78) shows a similar complexity.

This class of building normally had a main block of two or three storeys, although Edinburgh Tolbooth (No.27) had four storeys and that built at Glasgow in 1626-7 (No.34) was five-storeyed. The roof-line would originally be of consistent height, but later alterations and additions brought much diversity of scale and style. In most cases there was a steeple set either centrally or at one end, or else a bellcot on the gable or roof-ridge.

The ground storey was often used for storage and prison-accommodation, and part of it might be rented out as tradesmen's booths or shops. Open arcades giving access to market-space, which are best preserved at Montrose (No.59), were a feature of many of these buildings. The principal rooms, the council-chamber and court-room, were almost always at first-floor level and often entered from a forestair, although ground-floor entrances became normal in the second half of the 18th century. Offices for clerks and other officials tended to be placed on the same floor as the principal rooms, as at Sanquhar (No.76). Subordinate meeting-rooms were often placed above the principal rooms as in Old Aberdeen Town-house (No.68), which has a Masonic Hall on the second floor. The top floor might also be used to hold prisoners, as at Kirkcudbright and Musselburgh Tolbooths (Nos.48, 60), and was particularly favoured for debtors.

The architectural styles adopted range from the semi-fortified tolbooths and massive steeples of the late 16th century (Nos.11, 15, 25, 60) to the castellated revival seen at Rothesay (No.74) in 1833-5. Glasgow Tolbooth of 1626-7 (No.34) compared closely with the court architecture of the period in its Renaissance style, regular fenestration, sculptured pediments and systematic use of string-courses, although it retained castellated turrets. At Linlithgow (No.55) in 1668-70 a strictly symmetrical main elevation was adopted for the first time, and further Renaissance features were introduced at Dumfries and Stirling (Nos.23, 79) in the first decade of the 18th century. Classical styles, often related to neo-Palladian domestic design, were widely used in the 18th and early 19th centuries, on a grand scale at Dundee (appendix, no.6) but also in such small burghs as Falkland (No.29). A simpler domestic style, sometimes embellished by a steeple or bellcot, was adopted in many other small burghs, as at Anstruther Wester, North Berwick and Whithorn (Nos.3, 67, 86).

The late 18th and early 19th centuries saw the erection of several classical spires of great sophistication, at Falkirk, Inverness and Port Glasgow (Nos.28, 40, 73), which were closely related to contemporary church spires. The tallest of all, at Ayr (No.6), introduced some baroque elements, and the influence of this style is also seen in the design of Leith Town Hall (No.53). The much-altered Glasgow Green Court-house (No.34) was one of the first major works of the Greek Revival in Scotland. The castellated style, in a strictly symmetrical presentation, was used at Kinghorn (No.45) as well as Rothesay, and also in the rebuilding in 1820 of the main front of Aberdeen Tolbooth (No.1). Castellated features also occur in the Gothic steeple of the town-house at Strichen (No.83), but Gillespie Graham used the Perpendicular ecclesiastical style for the demolished town hall of 1816 in Duns (appendix, no.37).[92]

During the second half of the 19th century, the heyday of 'national romanticism',[93] many of the buildings dealt with in this survey were extended, or partially replaced, in the baronial style that was also commonly used for new town halls. The outstanding example is the rebuilding of Aberdeen Town-house (No.1), to designs by Peddie and Kinnear, in 1867-74, and the style is also found in smaller burghs such as Maybole (1887; No.57), Dunfermline, Lockerbie and Portobello. The adoption of continental Renaissance motifs, equally fashionable in urban contexts, is seen at its most sumptuous in William Young's Municipal Buildings of 1883-8 in Glasgow.

3A

3B

STEEPLES

The tolbooth steeple was often a conspicuous local landmark and demonstration of civic pride and authority, rising above the low buildings of the pre-industrial Scottish burgh to dominate the surrounding countryside. Over half of the buildings included in this study have steeples while others have clock-towers or bellcots on the gable or roof-ridge. Outstanding examples range in time from Aberdeen and Glasgow (Nos.1, 34) in the early 17th century and Tain (No.84) after 1708 to the classical spires of Ayr, Falkirk and Port Glasgow (Nos.6, 28, 73) in the early 19th century.

Their main practical function was to house the burgh clock and bell (*infra*), and at Kirkcudbright (No.48) the town council recorded in 1642: 'the necessitie of ane steiple and bel house to keip their knok and bel, quhilk is ane speciall ornament belanging to every burgh, and quhilk they are bund be the antient laws of the burrows of this kingdome to mantein and uphauld'.[94] The steeple was often used to provide internal stair-access with minimal loss of space in the main block, as at Cromarty and Glasgow (Nos.16, 34). At Banff (No.7), where the steeple was originally self-contained, John Adam in 1767 designed an unusual spiral stair with an open cavity (perhaps intended to house the weights of the clock) instead of a central newel. In providing confined spaces to which there was usually only one means of access, they were particularly suitable for prison cells or lock-ups, and free-standing steeples formed the only prison-accommodation at Coupar Angus and Falkirk (Nos.14, 28). At South Queensferry (No.78) the first floor housed a small court-room, and this may also have been the case at Coupar Angus. At Kirkcudbright and Stonehaven (Nos.48, 80) the ground storeys were adapted to hold water-cisterns.

Typically, steeples were set either at the centre of the main elevation or at one of the gable-ends. In the latter case the steeple might extend the length of the main front, as at Inverness, Kirkcudbright and Stirling (Nos.40, 48, 79), or occupy the centre of the gable, as at Clackmannan and Kilmaurs (Nos.13, 44). Centrally-placed steeples commonly enclosed the principal entrance to the building, often with a stair rising through the lower storey (e.g. Auchtermuchty, Selkirk; Nos.5, 77), and the same arrangement is found at Stirling. At Jedburgh and Newton on Ayr (Nos.41, 65) they were built above central pends, while a pend in the steeple at the W end of Canongate Tolbooth (No.11) gives access to Tolbooth Wynd. Steeples which occupy exceptional positions include those at Falkland (No.29), which is set on a side-elevation, and Linlithgow and Whithorn (Nos.55, 86) which are placed at the rear, an arrangement also found in the Netherlands.[95] At Dundee (appendix, no.6) and Port Glasgow (No.73) they rose from the centres of the buildings.

Most steeples are square on plan, ranging in area from 2.6m and 2.8m square at Earlsferry and Kilmaurs (Nos.26, 44) to almost 8m square at Tain (No.84). However, that at Dunbar (No.24) is of irregular semi-hexagonal form and that of Campbeltown (No.10) is semi-octagonal. In height they vary from 13m at Clackmannan (No.13) to 48m and 64m in the spires of Port Glasgow (No.73) and Ayr (No.6). Some steeples project almost totally from the adjoining frontage while others are advanced only slightly, if at all, rising above a pediment (e.g. Peterhead, No.70) or direct from the wall-head (e.g.

Culross, No.18). Even in these cases, however, the base of the steeple is often emphasised on the façade by distinctive quoins. The steeple at Culross was an addition of 1783, supported within the building by an inserted arch. The thick internal walls required to carry central steeples are a feature of many town-house plans, often enclosing arched vestibules or stairs.

A. *Stirling Town-house* (ST/668)
(No.79), upper part of steeple

The earliest surviving tolbooth steeples belong to the second half of the 16th, when very few churches were built, and the influence of the tower-house may be seen in the robust towers at Dysart (1576, No.25) and Crail (No.15). The upper stages of both were rebuilt in the 18th century, but an array of angle-turrets and other fortified features are preserved at Canongate (1591, No.11), and a late example of the style is the steeple at Tain (post 1708; No.84). Over half of the recorded steeples belong to a traditional type, familiar also in church architecture,[96] whose origins may be traced to medieval examples such as the 15th-century tower of St Salvator's College at St Andrews. This type has a tower rising through several stages, sometimes defined by string-courses, to a parapet or balustrade. This may enclose a spire or else a belfry, itself terminating in a cupola or a spire. The style of these steeples was modified by Renaissance features such as rusticated or pilastered quoins, but traceried belfry-windows of medieval character were used at Maybole (No.57) about

B. *Dingwall Town-house* (No.21), reconstruction-drawing from SE

15

1680, and paired lancets at Strathmiglo (No.82) in 1734. Wall-heads were often decorated with features of defensive origin such as corbelling and crenellation, and at Pittenweem (No.71) the water-spouts of the parapet take the form of mock gun-barrels.

In the 17th and 18th centuries belfry roofs were often of ogee form, but a type of spire which was probably derived from the Low Countries was favoured for important buildings.[97] This had a lead-covered lower part of concave profile and a small ogival upper section, although in the demolished steeple of 1697 at Falkirk (No.28) the latter was of double-ogee form. The demolished spire of Linlithgow Town-house (No.55), with those of the Tron Kirk, Edinburgh, and the Old College of Glasgow, belonged to the third quarter of the 17th century. The surviving examples at Dumfries and Stirling (Nos.23, 79) are of the first decade of the following century, and with their elaborate cresting they closely resemble that of St Ninian's Manse, Leith.[98] The 'imperial crown' on the steeple at Glasgow (No.34) is a unique secular example of a late-medieval form, but low stone spires, often of circular plan, are common in the 18th century. The 18th-century slated spire at Crail (No.15) is of unusual pagoda-like form.

In the first half of the 18th century classical steeples became common in civic and church architecture, often rising from a square base through several diminishing stages to a cupola or an octagonal stone spire.[99] The earliest example in a town-house was that designed by William Adam for Dundee in 1731, a reduced and less ornate version of James Gibbs's celebrated steeple of 1721-7 at St Martin's in the Fields, London.[100] Palladian features including Venetian and thermal windows were used in simple spired steeples such as Lochmaben (1743; No.56) and Banff (1767; No.7). The full classical repertoire of pedimented aedicules, angle-columns and pilasters, decorative vases and ornamental sculpture, is first seen at Inverness (No.40) in 1789-91, and developed at Ayr, Falkirk, Haddington and Port Glasgow (Nos.6, 28, 36, 73). The octagonal belfry with a domed or ogival cupola, set above a pediment by William Adam at Sanquhar (No.76) in 1735, is a common termination of 18th-century steeples, or an addition to an older one (e.g. Inverkeithing, No.39; Dysart, No.25). A number of small town-houses had simple clock-towers (e.g. Moffat, No.58) or open bellcots, set on the gable or, at Lerwick and North Berwick (Nos.54, 67), on the roof-ridge. Although bellcots were used on Scottish churches from the medieval period,[101] the earliest surviving example on a town-house is probably that at Newmilns (No.64), whose weather-vane is dated 1739.

FORESTAIRS

The forestair was a familiar feature of Scottish urban domestic architecture from the medieval period onwards, and in a poem of about 1500 William Dunbar complained to the merchants of Edinburgh that 'Your foirstairis makis your housis mirk (dark)'.[102] They were also used in about two-thirds of the pre-1740 buildings included in the gazetteer, whereas only eight examples are recorded thereafter, and only two of these after 1800. Changing fashions were exemplified at Aberdeen Tolbooth (No.1), where a simple 17th-century forestair on the E wall was replaced in 1750 by a double forestair at the main (S) front, and this in turn by a ground-floor entrance of 1820.

Forestairs afforded direct access to the first floor of a building without using up internal space. They were also used for proclamations and election-declarations and other ceremonies. At Cupar in 1516, for example, a legal notice was 'maid publict at the tolboith stare as the Maner is', and at Kilmarnock the forestair was used by the town council to celebrate public occasions such as the King's birthday.[103] At Kirkcudbright (No.48) the mercat cross was re-erected on the platform of the forestair in 1760.

Most forestairs are simple straight flights of stone steps, as at Stonehaven Tolbooth (No.80). These may run parallel to the wall they abut, as at Canongate and Kirkcudbright (Nos.11,

48), or project at right angles, as at Lauder and Newmilns (Nos.52, 64). Greater elaboration might be provided by a wall-balustrade, as at Dysart and North Berwick (Nos.25, 67). Balustrading could also be very elaborate, as in the case of the wrought-iron 'ravel' at Dumfries Midsteeple (No.23), which was made by Patrick Sibbald at Edinburgh in 1709. Use was sometimes made of the space below a forestair to house a small cell, as at Lauder (No.52) At Dingwall and Kirkcudbright (Nos.21, 48) access to cells in the ground storey of the steeple was originally through a doorway in the forestair. Those at Kirkcudbright and South Queensferry (No.78) also incorporated pumps for the public water-supply.

Double forestairs, which offered greater dignity, were provided in six buildings, of which only Linlithgow (1668-70; No.55) was earlier than the 1730s. That at Kintore (No.47) is a relatively simple example, whereas at Sanquhar (No.76) at the same period the double forestair encloses an access-doorway to cells at ground-floor level. The example at Culross (No.18), which is an addition of 1783 to the original building, has an oculus in the centre of its main face. The demolished tolbooth of Irvine (appendix no.12) had a double forestair of unusual reversed type.

COUNCIL-CHAMBERS AND COURT-ROOMS

The council-chamber was an essential element in the tolbooths and town-houses of all royal burghs, and in some burghs of barony and regality. In the smaller burghs it often served also as the court-room, but in larger buildings separate rooms were provided. Both rooms were normally situated on the first floor, entered from a vestibule which at Sanquhar (No.76) contained recesses for seats. The vestibule of about 1616 at Aberdeen Tolbooth (No.1) was divided from the court-room by an elaborate triple arcade which was rediscovered in 1993.

At Culross (No.18), as altered in the 18th century, the two rooms were almost equal in size, whereas at Aberdeen (No.1) after 1730 the council-chamber was much the smaller. William Adam's plan of 1731 for Dundee Town-house,[104] in contrast, shows a large council-chamber running through the depth of the building and a small court-room at the centre of

 203A

Rothesay Town Hall and County Buildings (No.74)   *(C 48545)*
declaration of Parliamentary election result from forestair, 1865

A. **Canongate Tolbooth** (No. 11), court-room, from a series of pro-reform cartoons showing the installation of an ass as burgess

(C 65768)

the main front, but the Guildry room, equal in size with the council-chamber, came to be used for courts. One of the smallest council-chambers occupies the upper storey of Newmilns Town-house (No.64), a rectangle some 5.2m in length, whereas a more typical example, at Dunbar (No.24), is twice as long. They were normally rectangular in plan, a rare exception being the circular example of 1822 at Cullen (No.17). Typically a rectangular room would have a council-table at whose upper end or centre the provost and bailies would be seated, often with their backs to the principal fireplace. The council-chamber would often be the most elaborately furnished and decorated room in the building (*infra*, pp. 18-19).

The judges' bench, bar and table, and a 'lang bynk (bench)' on which eight or nine spectators could sit, are mentioned in early 16th-century instructions for the holding of royal courts in Edinburgh Tolbooth (No.27).[105] At Leith (No.53), later in the same century, a court officer was required to escort the magistrates 'up stairs to the bench within the court place'. Where separate court-rooms existed, as at Cromarty (No.16), their permanent furnishings would include a raised and enclosed magistrate's bench, separate enclosures for the accused, the jury, witnesses, court officials and lawyers, and public seating. The specialised court-houses of the 19th century include well-preserved court-rooms at Ayr and Dumbarton (Nos.6, 22). They also had a variety of ancillary rooms for the judges, jury and witnesses, often with separate access to the court-room, and the need for such facilities was instrumental in the erection of new court-houses in the early 19th century.

ASSEMBLY-ROOMS

Rooms for holding balls and public meetings became popular in the middle of the 18th century and often attracted the financial support of institutions or groups of individuals (*supra,* p.7).[106] One of the earliest was the Guildry room in William Adam's Dundee Town-house (begun 1732; appendix, 6), which measured 11m by 6.9m. At Glasgow (No.34) in 1735-40, a town hall for civic functions was built in Palladian style adjoining the tolbooth, and twenty years later it was doubled in length, in the same style, to house an assembly-room. At Montrose (No.59) the building of the town-house originated in 1759 with a public subscription for an assembly-room, which was placed at the centre of the main front. The suite of rooms in the added second floor of 1819 included a large ball-room (which gave the building its local name, 'the ba' hoose'), with an adjacent 'card-room and a 'supper-room'.

B. **Aberdeen** (No.1), interior of 'Great Room' by Longmuir, 1871

(C 17905)

17

The appearance of this and other examples has been altered by the removal or insertion of partition-walls (e.g. Forfar, No.31), but at Haddington (No.36) the assembly-room of 1788 remains intact and is still used for dances. The most sumptuous set of assembly-rooms was that built in 1828-30 at Ayr (No.6), with its domed ball-room, 14.2m by 8.2m, having a steel-sprung wooden floor 'which takes away that hardness usually felt by people dancing upon a floor strongly supported upon beams'. The connecting doors to the supper-room and ante-room could be opened to allow a continuous dining-table over 30m in length.[107] A common feature of these rooms was the musicians' gallery, variously known as the 'orchestra' or 'fiddle-box', usually housed in an end-wall but in the large rooms at Arbroath and Ayr (Nos.4, 6) at the centre of a side wall. The latter (removed in 1878), which was entered from outside the building, had a balcony supported by caryatids.

INTERIOR DECORATION AND FURNISHINGS

Few tolbooth interiors of pre-19th-century date survive in unaltered form, because of continuing changes in response to new functions and styles, and in particular the increasing demands of space for prisoners. However, there is a wealth of documentation for many features of these buildings, and civic records for Perth and Aberdeen give particularly detailed descriptions of two notable vanished interiors.

Perth and Aberdeen
The new council-house and town clerk's office at Perth (which were to be demolished in 1839), were completed in 1696. In May of that year three dozen 'good rushie (Russian) leather chairs' and a large table were purchased for the council-house.[108] A few months later an act was passed 'for purchasing in Edinburgh, and if it cannot be had there, in London, a good fashionable carpet for the council table'.[109] Moulded frames were made for four maps, and an artist, Henry Reid, was employed to paint the chimneypiece and 'furnish a landscape'. He also painted the chimneypiece in the clerk's office, which was furnished with a smaller table.[110]

17B The top floor of Aberdeen Town-house (No.1), as remodelled in 1750, was fitted up as the 'Great Room' or 'Town Hall' for civic functions. In that year the council agreed that laying the floor-boards transversely, as in the old room, would be 'a great Eye Sore', and that the new floor should be laid with 'dales [boards] along the length of the room, which will greatly add to the beauty thereof'. The walls were to be finished 'with the best firr boxing, and to have a marble chimney from Holland, and that the space above the chimney be finished with the Town's Arms in Stucco work and ornament ... in as genteel but easy a manner as possible'.[111] Following the decision that 'the second draught of the chimneypiece ... containing a landskip was prettiest', a 'perspective of the southside of the town and harbour' was drawn with a camera obscura, to judge its suitability for the position.[112] A large 'crystall lustre, with tossles, ballances & ca.' was obtained from London in 1751 at a cost, including freight, of £64, and two smaller lustres were subsequently ordered, as well as four large and eight small wall-sconces.[113] The 'Town Hall' was opened in 1753 with a grand charity concert in aid of the infirmary.[114]

The overmantel painting of the town was finally executed by William Mossman in 1756, at a cost of twenty guineas, after 'a draught thereof in miniature' had been approved.[115] The burgh already owned several large paintings, including a portrait of Queen Anne by Kneller. In 1755 Cosmo Alexander, a Scottish-born 'limner' with a studio in London, was commissioned to paint portraits of the Earl and Countess of Findlater, who agreed to sit for them after assurances that they would be hung in a favourable position in the room.[116] These portraits are prominent in the watercolour of the 'Great Room' that was painted by A D Longmuir shortly before its demolition in 1871. The collection of portraits and Mossman's landscape, with the lustres and several of the sconces, are now

displayed in the Town and County Hall and adjacent rooms on the top floor of the new building.

Floor-coverings
An early reference to floor-covering is contained in the treasurer's accounts for Lanark for 1507, when meadow-sweet was purchased for strewing on the floor of the tolbooth.[117] These sweet-smelling herbs were presumably strewn over stone floors which remained common in tolbooths, for security and fire-proofing, throughout the period of this study. Floor-carpets (as opposed to table-carpets) became popular in the 18th century, and Edinburgh council bought one for the council-house in 1704.[118] In 1768 the Magistrates and Council of Glasgow purchased 62 3/4 square yards of carpet from Robert Hannah and Company, carpet-makers in Glasgow, for the 'town's hall'.[119]

Walls
Interior walls were commonly plastered, and at Edinburgh and Glasgow in the 16th and 17th centuries they were painted or whitewashed, while instructions for regular whitewashing were given by the prison inspectors in the 1830s.[120] A simple painted scheme of the mid 18th century, of two colours separated by a black horizontal band, is preserved in the former vestibule at Aberdeen Tolbooth (No.1).

Council-chambers and court-rooms were often 'wainscotted' or panelled. The earliest surviving example of this is at Stirling Town-house (No.79), which has a pilastered chimney-breast and heavy cornices of early-18th-century character. Other 18th-century panelling is preserved at Culross and Dunbar (Nos.18, 24). A drawing of 1731 survives for the panelling of the principal room in the new extension of Aberdeen Town-house (No.1), and the 'Great Room' of the 1750s was fitted with 'the best firr boxing' (*supra*). From this period onwards, it was common for panelling to be restricted to the dado. An interesting use of lath-and-plaster to create regular walls and vaults within an earlier structure was provided by John Smith's remodelling of the lower storeys of Aberdeen Tolbooth in 1820.

30B

Chimneypieces
Three 17th-century stone chimneypieces with floral swags are preserved at Linlithgow Town-house (No.55), and an early 18th-century one with an overmantel painting at Stirling (No.79). A marble chimneypiece was supplied by William Adam for the town-house extension at Aberdeen (No.1) in 1731, whereas the large one for the new town hall at Glasgow (No.34) was carved by a local craftsman in 1742.[120] Few ornate chimneypieces have remained *in situ* in town-houses, and that of about 1800 at Falkland (No.29) is a recent import. An interesting example of the 1820s, with a cast-iron inner surround bearing figures in Egyptian style, is preserved at Pittenweem (No.71).

Ceilings
In the late 16th and early 17th centuries domestic ceilings in Scotland were often elaborately painted, and it is likely that council- and court-room ceilings were commonly decorated in the same way. Fragments of two open-beam ceilings of this period, one of which is of unique type, survive in the first-floor rooms of Culross Town-house (No.18). The ceilings in Canongate Tolbooth (No.11), however, belong to an adjacent house of early 17th-century date. There are no surviving ceilings of the late 17th century, but that of the 'upper inner room' at Banff (No.7) is said to have been decorated in 1686 with the arms of Sir George Gordon of Edinglassie, the sheriff-principal.[121]

In the 18th and early 19th centuries decorative plaster ceilings were fashionable, and Thomas Clayton, 'stucatorian', was employed to decorate the town hall at Glasgow (No.34) in 1766. Contemporary plasterwork ceilings with enriched cornices and coving are preserved, for example, at Banff and

Falkland (Nos.7, 29). Elaborate coffered ceilings of early 19th-century date are preserved at Ayr County Buildings (No.6), and decorative vaults and cupolas at Ayr Assembly Rooms and Port Glasgow (Nos.6, 73).

Furniture
The continuing popularity of Russia leather for council-chamber chairs (cf. Perth, *supra* p.18), and the measures taken to procure it, are illustrated at Elgin in 1728: 'The Counsell considering that it is absolutely necessary for fitting up the new councill chamber to provide at the publick charge two dozen of chairs of Russia leather one of each dozen to be an elbow chair and that the wood for strength and durableness in the frame of the chairs be of oake and considering that there is shortly ane opportunity for a ship going from the Murray Firth to Dantzick, Doe impower the Magistrates to commission for as much hydes of Russia leather as will cover the said chairs and as much oake or knappell wood as will make the frames thereof'.[122]

Glasgow Tolbooth (No.34) contained 'a fine large oval table' of mahogany for the town council, at which the town clerk was seated when he was murdered in 1674. However, oak furniture continued to be popular in the 18th century. In 1765 Montrose Town Council commissioned William Strachan junior, wright, 'to make for the use of the Town Hall, three square wainscot tables five feet in breadth and six feet in length each of them so that when joined together they will make one table of eighteen feet in length'.[123] The council evidently required a further section since in 1767 Strachan was paid £4 10s for 'four square folding oak tables lately furnished by him for the use of the Council in the Town Hall'.[124] Sets of chairs were often ordered, and normally, as at Elgin, included an armchair for the provost.

Other items of furniture for council-chambers included hour-glasses, for timing speeches, or clocks. Stirling (No.79) had a particularly fine long-case clock by Andrew Dunlop of London (1710-15); the marquetry pattern is both geometric and floral and includes birds and butterflies.[125] Many councils also had a box for the reception of fines imposed upon councillors for being late or absent, which often stood on the table in the council-chamber. At Dundee this 'pirlie pig' or money-box took the form of a pewter pig dated 1602, while at Edinburgh in 1597-8 a green iron box was bought for this purpose, 'to be putt in the counsallhous almery'.[126]

Paintings and sculpture
The earliest record of an individual painting in a tolbooth is at Edinburgh in 1677, when payment was made to James Alexander 'for helping and painting of the great draught of the good toun presentlie hanging in the laich council hous'.[127] Except for armorial paintings, an important class which is dealt with separately, the earliest surviving painting is a classical overmantel in the council-room of 1703 at Stirling (No.79). Large portraits formed an important part of the decoration of the new town halls at Glasgow and Aberdeen in the 1730s and 1750s, and other notable collections include that at Forfar (No.31). Commemorative paintings include that of the landing of George IV at Leith in 1822, which has hung in Leith Town Hall (No.53) since its opening in 1829.

Portrait sculpture was not a common feature of Scottish town-houses before the 19th century, when Glasgow obtained for the town hall a figure of William Pitt the Younger by Flaxman.[128] The bust of Dr John Wyllie by the great Danish sculptor Thorwaldsen was a later gift to Forfar (No.31), and a bronze figure of 17th- or early 18th-century date at Edinburgh (No.27) is of mysterious provenance. The upper half of a wooden figure of the local piper Habbie Simpson, executed by a Greenock figurehead-carver in 1822, is preserved at Kilbarchan (No.43).

CELLS AND PRISONS
About half of the buildings in the survey retain cells or lock-ups. Their entrances are normally, but not always, placed away from public areas. Nevertheless a solitary cell, often referred to as a 'black hole', 'nether hole' or 'thieves' hole', might be contained within the space below a forestair, as at Lauder (No.52), or entered through the forestair as at Dingwall and Kirkcudbright (Nos.21, 48). Another restricted area, below an internal staircase, was used for small cells at Newton Stewart and Peterhead (Nos. 66, 70).

An advantage of placing cells on the ground storey was that stone vaulting, an obvious security and fire-proof element, could be employed without placing undue stress on the structure. Barrel-vaulted ground-floor cells are found, for example, at Coupar Angus, Maybole, Newmilns and Pittenweem Steeple (Nos.14, 57, 64, 71). At Kilmaurs Town-house (No.44) the ground floor is occupied by two parallel barrel-vaulted cells with external entrances in opposite side-walls. However, at Tain Tolbooth (No.84) the thick walls allowed a barrel-vaulted cell on the second floor of the steeple. A vertical sequence of barrel-vaulted cells was used on the lower floors of the steeple at Kirkcudbright (No.48) and, in a more complex and sophisticated form, at Aberdeen (No.1) in 1616. At Falkirk Steeple (No.28) in 1813-14 and at Girvan (No.33) in 1825-7 a vertical sequence of cells was employed, entirely contained within the space of the steeple. Barrel-vaulted cells continued to be used in the 'improved' mid-19th-century prisons, and a ground-floor range of cells entered from

A. **Kirkcudbright** *(No.48), padlock dated 1754* (B 70328)
and key from tolbooth

B. **Kirkcudbright** *(No.48), lock and key from tolbooth* (B 70325)

19

A. *Aberdeen Tolbooth (No.1), prisoners' bed in third-floor cell*   (A 74776)

heavy grille. The small prison-wing added to Cromarty Court-house (No.16) in the 1840s has an external exercise-corridor, with large barred openings on three sides.

ARMORIALS AND INSCRIPTIONS

Royal and burgh armorials and other emblematic devices were widely employed to display the status of burghs and the source of their authority, while didactic inscriptions emphasised the gravity of their judicial functions and the responsibilities placed on magistrates. They are found on both the exteriors and interiors of tolbooths and town-houses of all periods, commonly in the form of carved stone panels, lintels and window- or dormer-pediments. Armorials are also found painted on boards, canvas and wall-plaster, and the arms of George IV in stained glass are set above the magistrate's bench at Ayr County Buildings (No.6).

Scottish landowners holding directly from the crown were entitled to display the royal arms above their own on the forefronts of their castles or houses, as seen most memorably at Huntly Castle. Royal burghs enjoyed the same legal status, and at Aberdeen (No.1) in 1569 the royal and burgh arms were set into two blank 'housines' (frames) in the principal front of the town-house, while the royal arms were displayed on the main front of Glasgow Tolbooth (No.34). The panels built into the S front of Dumfries Midsteeple (No.23), which show the royal arms and St Michael, patron of the burgh, are probably

a corridor was added in 1844 at the rear of Nairn Town and County Buildings (No.61).

Cells were also formed out of basement space, as at Dalkeith (No.20), where there is a flat-ceiled pit known as the 'black hole'. The basement of Ceres Weigh-house (No.12) was also used as a prison. Flat-ceiled cells were not uncommon, but as their ceilings were usually of timber they afforded less security and tend to be found in the upper floors of steeples, as at Coupar Angus (No.14). Such cells were often used for the incarceration of debtors rather than criminals, as at Dunbar (No.24). The main cell at Auchtermuchty (No.5), which is a flat-ceiled room on the ground floor, has a ceiling reinforced with metal sheeting. Similar reinforcement was used at Stranraer Castle (No.81) in cells where wall-thicknesses were reduced by chimney-flues. A number of early nail-studded and iron-bound doors survive, some with elaborate chains and padlocks (e.g. Aberdeen, No.1) as well as internal yetts and heavy window-grilles. Other padlocks and keys are preserved in museum collections, as well as fittings such as manacles, stocks, jougs, branks, and thumbscrews.

The special provision made for wealthy prisoners and debtors has been referred to (*supra*, p.10). The fittings of cells for other prisoners were usually sparse, but in general the later buildings were better equipped in this respect, if only because they tended to have flagstone rather than earthen floors. The wooden cell-beds at Aberdeen (No.1) are a rare survival, and hammocks were often used in the 19th century.[129]

A small number of tolbooths and town-houses allowed direct communication between the prison-area and the court-room. Saltcoats Town-house (No.75) has a cell at first-floor level within the steeple, which gives directly onto the court-room. A similar arrangement was employed in 1794 at Anstruther Wester (No.3), where there was access by a passage to a cell in the 16th-century church steeple. At Kinghorn (No.45) a ground-floor cell-block is linked to the first-floor court-room by a spiral stair independent of the main staircase.

The lack of exercise-facilities and 'airing-grounds' in Scottish prisons, because of restricted sites or fears over security, was a frequent complaint of reformers and inspectors. The new prisons built in the 19th century normally had such facilities, although in the adaptation of Stranraer Castle (No.81) for prison use in 1820-2 the only space available for exercise was a corridor outside the cells, fitted with its own

B. *Falkland Town-house (No.29), burgh armorial, 1618*   (B 58189)

C. *Cupar (No.19)*   (A 80322)
royal armorial from tolbooth, built into former academy

D. *Dumbarton (No.22)*   (DB/305)
burgh armorial above prison gateway

A. *Montrose Town-house* (No.59)　　　　　　　(B 47601)
　burgh armorial in W pediment

B. *St Andrews* (appendix, no.20)
　armorials of provost Sir Patrick
　Learmonth and of burgh, 1565,
　from tolbooth

(C65074)

of mid-17th-century date and re-used from the older tolbooth or prison. Such re-use was common, and in 1789 the council of Old Aberdeen (No.68) ordered the alteration of the 1721 date on a panel bearing the burgh arms, which nevertheless survives in its original state. As in many other cases this panel was to be 'painted and gilded', and armorials were often refurbished in advance of special occasions such as royal visits. Surviving stone panels from demolished tolbooths include a vigorous rendering of the arms of Queen Mary, dated 1565, from Leith Tolbooth (No.53); a reset panel of 160[-] bearing the arms of Crail (No.15); royal and burgh armorials of 17th-century character at Cupar (No.19); burgh arms of 1618 and 1715 at Falkland (No.29); and late 17th-century examples at Irvine (appendix, no.12).

Burgh arms were normally represented in the form shown on the burgh seal, and are sometimes identified as such, as on the early 17th-century dormer-pediment inscribed SIGILLUM BURGI DE CULROSS ('Seal of the burgh of Culross') in the town-house there (No.18). In the immediate aftermath of the Reformation, however, a panel dated 1565 at the tolbooth of St Andrews bore the arms of the provost and of the burgh, with the notable omission of the patron saint himself.[130] With the advent of classical town-house designs it became common to place the burgh arms in a wall-head pediment, as at Dundee (1732-4; appendix, no. 6), Peebles (1753; No.69), and Montrose (1819; No.59). At Inverkeithing (No.39) the armorial is enclosed within a pediment set against the main front of the steeple of 1754-5.

Within the tolbooth, burgh arms had an obvious association with the council-chamber and royal arms, as representing the fount of justice, with the court-room. Anstruther Wester Town

Hall (No.3), and nearby Pittenweem Town Hall of 1821-2 (No.71), have remarkable burgh armorials painted on plaster in grisaille over the fireplaces in their council-chambers. They are evidently the work of the same accomplished but unidentified artist. Notable among the painted royal armorials are those of Charles I, dated 1637 and with the motto UNIONUM UNIO ('A union of unions') at Culross (No.18), and the 1686 armorial of James VII and II, and that of one of his Hanoverian successors, at Dunbar (No.24). The latter burgh also commissioned in 1686 a 'broad' or panel bearing the burgh arms and the words 'Justice seat for the Magistrates and Councill', but this does not survive.

Armorial panels might also record benefactors of the burgh, or individual magistrates. The stone panel at Culross (No.18), which names Sir George Bruce of Carnock, bears the date 1628, three years after his death, and is closely related to the armorial on his splendid tomb in Culross Abbey. At Aberdeen (No.1) armorials accompany many of the names painted on the 'mortification boards', and the shield of Provost Paul Menzies appears on a lead plaque of 1630 marking the completion of the tolbooth steeple. A painted iron plaque of 1817 attached to the forestair of South Queensferry Tolbooth (No.78) bears the burgh arms and the crest of the 4th Earl of Rosebery, then provost, who donated a public water-supply. The arms of donors also appeared on bells, such as that of 1711 at New Galloway (No.63) which bears the arms of the burgh and of the 6th Viscount Kenmure, later to be executed for his leading rôle in the Jacobite rising of 1715. At Cullen, where the Earl of Seafield paid for the new town-house of 1822 (No.17), his arms are prominently displayed on its wall-head. The arms of Bishop Kennedy of St Andrews (d.1465), set upside-down in a gable of Pittenweem Town Hall (No.71), appear to be an accidental re-use derived from the adjacent priory.

In burghs of regality and barony the arms or initials of the superior often appeared, such as the Buccleuch panel of 1648 at Dalkeith (No.20) and that of 1734, bearing the arms and name of the Hon. Margaret Balfour of Burleigh, at Strathmiglo (No.82). At Canongate (No.11) the arms of the burgh are displayed, as well as a pediment bearing a crown and the initials of James VI with a pious motto (*infra*). Crowns and thistles are frequent, especially on window-pediments, and in Glasgow Tolbooth Steeple (No.34) a crown is carved in relief above the door that led from the stair to the 'King's Hall'. An unusual emblem is the panel above the entrance to Ceres Weigh-house (No.12), which shows a balance or tron, with the motto: GOD BLESS THE JUST. At Maybole (No.57) the old tolbooth itself appeared on the burgh seal, and it is represented on a gable panel of the 1887 town hall that partly replaced it.

Moralistic and pious inscriptions were a familiar feature of Scottish domestic architecture in the 16th and 17th centuries, especially in the burghs. A notable example displaying several inscribed panels of 1570 is Huntly House,[131] situated opposite the Canongate Tolbooth of 1591 (No.11). The tolbooth itself bears the initials of James VI, with a motto meaning 'Justice and piety are truly the bulwarks of a prince', and the initials of the superior are accompanied by 'For native land and posterity'. The lintel of the inner door to the stair is inscribed ESTO FIDUS ('Be faithful'), and such moral injunctions to magistrates were especially common. At Musselburgh, a lintel of 1773 bears the burgh arms between the texts 'Magistrates do justice in the fear of God' and 'He that God doth fear, will not to falsehood lend an ear'. A Latin inscription,[132] preserved in the New Tolbooth of Edinburgh (No.27) in the early 19th century, exhorted: 'Any judge (*senator*) who enters this court in the cause of duty, before this door cast away all emotions — anger, hatred, friendship — for as you do justice to others impartially or unfairly, so you will await and undergo the judgement of God'. This was probably addressed to the Senators of the College of Justice, who held their courts in the New Tolbooth before the completion of Parliament House in 1639, and the latter building was to be adorned with statues of Justice and Mercy.[133] A board bearing the Ten

Commandments was gifted by 'a stranger' for display in the council-house at Edinburgh in 1675.[134]

Other inscriptions emphasised the punitive as well as the judicial and ceremonial functions of tolbooths. At the entrance to Glasgow Tolbooth of 1626-7 (No.34) there was a panel bearing a Latin couplet, which appears in translation on an 18th-century lintel[135] at Perth:

HAEC DOMUS ODIT, AMAT, PUNIT, CONSERVAT, HONORAT
NEQUITIAM, PACEM, CRIMINA, JURA, PROBOS.[136]

THIS HOUSE LOVES PEACE, HATES KNAVES, CRIMES PUNISHETH,
PRESERVES THE LAWS AND GOOD MEN HONOURETH.

The Perth inscription probably came from the same building as the panel with verses warning debtors to settle with their creditors (*supra*, p.10). Of more general application was the comfortless verse on a panel hung in the hall of Edinburgh Tolbooth (No.27):

A PRISON IS A PLACE OF CARE,
A PLACE WHERE NONE CAN THRIVE,
A TOUCHSTONE TRUE TO TRY A FRIEND,
A GRAVE FOR MEN ALIVE.

Commemorative inscriptions recording donations include those at Culross and South Queensferry (*supra*, pp.7,21), and a plaque of 1712 marks the erection of the burgh court-house at Greenlaw (No.35) by the 1st Earl of Marchmont. A renewed panel of 1763 marking the introduction of a public water-supply at Kirkcudbright (No.48) records that 'Posterity must surely bless, Saint Cuthbert's sons who purchas'd this'.

A. **Leith Town Hall** (No.53), S pediment   (C 65073)

Inscriptions recording the names of builders or magistrates are found on the steeples at Lochmaben (No.56) in 1743 and Inverness (No.40) in 1791. An armorial of 1819 in the pediment of Montrose Town-house (No.59) was signed by the Edinburgh sculptors, D Ness and Co., and by the stone-carver. The most prominent of such inscriptions, on the wall-head of Leith Town Hall (No.53), recorded its erection by the 'Magistrates and Masters' in 1828, with the names of the architects R and R Dickson.

Graffiti are a common feature of prisons, and those in the medieval chapter-house at Fortrose (No.32) include examples of the 1650s with decorated incised frames and the MacKenzie crest. A remarkable poem, which was formerly scratched on a window-pane in Edinburgh Tolbooth (No.27), was believed to be by the Marquis of Montrose, and referred to the dismemberment of his body after his impending execution.[137]

BELLS
Tolbooths and town-houses were normally fitted with a bell to mark the times of rising and curfew, council-meetings and other public events, often including church-services. Many of them remain in use in connection with clocks, and at Montrose and Selkirk (Nos.59, 77) the curfew-bell is rung by hand

nightly. Most of the buildings included in this study have had one or more bells, with a wide variety of origins, dates, and sizes. In general they show a similar development to church bells in Scotland, with an early reliance on imports, but with native bell-foundries emerging in the early 18th century.[138]

The earliest bells recorded here were indeed of ecclesiastical origin, at Jedburgh and Crail (Nos.15, 41). Other pre-Reformation bells, bearing a possible reference to John the Baptist and the name of St Catherine respectively, are preserved at Dysart and Glasgow (Nos.25, 34). The Crail bell of 1520 hung in the parish church until 1702, when it was transferred to the tolbooth in exchange for its smaller bell. In some burghs, such as Lanark, Montrose and Peebles (Nos.50,59,69), town bells were hung in church steeples, while tolbooth bells were often used to mark church services, that of Old Aberdeen (No.68) being inscribed in 1713: AD SACRA ET CONCILIA VOCAMUS ('We summon to sacred rites and councils').[139]

The ornate Crail bell of 1520 was probably cast in the van den Ghein foundry at Mechelen (Malines), Belgium, and the Glasgow bell of 1554 was by Jacob Waghevens of the same

B. **Falkland Town-house** (No.29)   (B 70231)
detail of bell by Michael Burgerhuys, 1630

town. Many other bells of the 16th and 17th centuries were also imported from the Low Countries.[140] The Burgerhuys foundry in Middelburg, close to the Scottish staple port of (Camp)veere, was especially favoured. There are bells with characteristic ornament by Michael Burgerhuys at Falkland and Tain (both dated 1630; Nos.29, 84) and Kirkcudbright (1646; No.48). Other foreign bells include a Swedish one of 1663 at Pittenweem (No.71), and one of probable Spanish origin, dated 1771, at Cromarty (No.16).

As late as 1724 a small bell damaged by fire at Kirkcudbright was sent to Rotterdam for recasting, but by that time there was a well-established native industry. Numerous bells were cast for civic use by the Edinburgh founders John Meikle, Robert Maxwell, George Barclay and George Watt. Bells were also cast for Elgin (appendix, no.8) and Old Aberdeen (No.68) in 1713 at the Old Aberdeen foundry of 'Albert Danel Geli, a Frenchman'. Gely thus designated himself on his 1696 Maybole bell (No.57), which was 'founded at Maiboll'.

A feature of the larger Scottish burghs, which visitors compared with continental practice, was the use of carillons. That of Edinburgh, cast by Meikle in 1698-9,[141] although paid for by the city, was housed in the steeple of St Giles. The carillon at Stirling Town-house (No.79), which is still played regularly, has sixteen 'musick bells', two of which are dated 1729. At Glasgow a set of 'tuneable bells' was installed in the 1730s, and their replacements of 1881 still hang in the crown of the Tolbooth Steeple (No.34).

Bells were not always found to be satisfactory by their purchasers, and successive recastings were often required, as at Kirkintilloch (No.49), where the bell of 1829 cracked and was recast in 1835 and again in 1849. Over-enthusiastic ringing sometimes caused bells to crack, as at Kinross (No.46) during the Napoleonic wars and at Irvine when the Reform Act was passed in 1832.[142] The town council of Dumfries complained in 1708 that the smallest of the three bells supplied by George Barclay for the Midsteeple (No.23) was 'small and short' in tone, but it is the only one to survive without recasting. At Leith (No.55) in 1665 the kirk-session complained of the 'naughtiness' of the tolbooth bell, 'that cannot be heard be the halfe of the toun'. Similar fears about the low site chosen for Ayr Steeple (No.6) were answered by the elevation of the belfry and the size of the bell supplied in 1830. For reasons of central location and audibility the church bell was placed in the tolbooth steeple at Dysart (No.25) as well as Crail (*supra*, p.22). In an extreme case, at Jedburgh (No.41) in 1779 a bell provided by the Mines Royal Company of London was returned for replacement after it 'had entirely lost its sound'.

Another London bell, by Lester and Pack, was presumably supplied from existing stock for the new steeple at Banff (No.7), since the incised inscription of 1767 naming the burgh appears to be an addition, although the bell exactly matches the maximum dimension specified by John Adam as suitable for the belfry. The London (Whitechapel) foundry of Thomas Mears and his successors supplied many bells for Scottish burghs in the 19th century, including the 1.25m bell of 1830 at Ayr (No.6). However, several bells were cast by Stephen Miller of Glasgow, and the principal Scottish manufacturer in the second half of the century was the Gorbals foundry of John C Wilson.

It was fairly common for bells to be donated by local landowners or political figures. The bell of Kilmarnock Council-house (appendix, no.51) was given by the Earl of

A. **Culross Town-house** *(No.18)*   *(C 23788)*
   clock-mechanism by Laurence Dalgleish, 1783

Kilmarnock in 1711, and one for Clackmannan Tolbooth (No.13) was given by Sir Lawrence Dundas in 1765. The inscription on the 1724 bell at North Berwick (No.67) claimed it to be a gift from Sir James Dalrymple of Hailes, but the cost was paid by the burgh after a legal action for payment brought by the bell-founder, Robert Maxwell. At South Queensferry (No.78) in 1694 'the seamen of Queensferrie did gift this bell to the towne', while a larger bell was donated in 1723 by the local member of parliament.

CLOCKS

As early as the 17th century it was considered an obligation of every burgh to have a clock (*supra*, p.15). Aberdeen Tolbooth (No.1) had a clock by the mid 15th century, which was taken to Flanders in the early 16th century for repairs. One of the earliest surviving burgh clocks is a single-hand mechanism from Kirkcudbright Tolbooth (No.48), which may date from the late 16th century. Made of malleable iron, it is believed to have been imported from the Low Countries. A clock at Musselburgh Tolbooth (No.60) is reputed to have been given to the burgh in 1496 by the Dutch. Some tolbooths, such as Dunbar (No.24), had sundials as well as clocks, and a square dial, probably of 1733-4, is preserved at Aberdeen (No.1), while at Old Aberdeen (No.68) a 'globe for the moon's age' was set up when a new clock was supplied in 1719-20.

During the 18th century many tolbooths and town-houses had clocks of local manufacture, and some, as at Auchtermuchty (No.5), bear engraved plates recording their construction or repair.[143] That at Kintore (No.47) was made in Aberdeen in 1774, and that at Cromarty (No.16) was made in Tain in 1782. Some were still obtained from further afield, usually England, and the clock of Dumfries Midsteeple (No.23) was made in Stockport in 1708. In the 19th century an increasing number of burgh clocks were made in Scotland, and many were made or repaired by the Edinburgh firm James Ritchie and Sons. In the 20th century many clock-mechanisms have been replaced or adapted to electric drives.

B. **Dysart Tolbooth** *(No.25), interior of clock-stage*   *(B 39474)*

1 ABERDEEN TOLBOOTH
City of Aberdeen
NJ 9440 0635

The 17th-century 'wardhouse' or prison-tower, with its elaborate spire, rises at the E end of the massive Municipal Buildings of 1867-74. These replaced a tolbooth or town-house which since the late 14th century had occupied this same site on the N side of Castlegate (Castle Street), the main market-area of the burgh. In 1393 Robert III granted the burgesses permission to build a *pretorium* measuring 24.4m by 9.1m, anywhere in the burgh 'except in the middle of the market-place'.[1] Early views show that until the 18th century the building occupied what was virtually an island site.[2]

SUMMARY

In 1616 the town council employed Thomas Watson, mason, to build a wardhouse 'within the tolbuith ... in the east end thairof', and the contract describes in detail many features which are still identifiable, despite numerous later alterations.[3] The tower was formed by building a massive internal cross-wall, and part of the E end-wall of the earlier building is preserved. The most substantial addition, undertaken in 1704-6 after a visit by the Edinburgh architect James Smith, was the extension of the tower to the N to provide an extra cell at each level. In 1756 the main entrance was moved from the E to the S side, and a new entrance-façade with a forestair was created facing Castle Street. At the same time a charter-room and additional cells were provided in a two-storeyed addition above a pend to the E, at the entrance to Lodge Walk. The S front was rebuilt in 1820 by the local architect John Smith, who transferred the entrance to ground-level and removed the lowest internal vaults to form a high entrance-corridor to the new court-house, adjacent to the N. Smith's S front was in turn rebuilt in Kemnay granite by Peddie and Kinnear in 1871, matching the baronial style of their Municipal Buildings. An extensive renovation was carried out in 1992-4, and the accompanying drawings and description incorporate information revealed by the removal of later plaster and wall-linings.

2A, 31A

3A, 31B

DESCRIPTION

In its present form the wardhouse comprises a rectangular tower some 15.8m from N to S by 7.2m and rising to a battlemented parapet at a height of 15m. This encloses a square belfry carrying an elaborate lead-covered spire 35m in overall height. Except for the rebuilt S front the external wall-faces are wholly or partly abutted by later buildings, and the only visible areas of early masonry are the NE angle and the upper parts of the N and E walls, while the E wall-face is also exposed in the room above the pend.[4]

26

27A, B,

The contract of 1616 required Watson to incorporate substantial parts of three walls of the earlier tolbooth, including the E gable-wall up to a 'tabling' or string-course which survives at a height of 11m.[5] The masonry visible below this string-course in the room over the pend is random rubble of moderate size, while larger and more regular dark rubble is used in the upper part of the same wall. The N end of this E wall, however, and the whole of the N wall, are built of irregular blocks of red granite and evidently represent the addition of 1704. It is also clear that the earlier N wall, which contained the garderobe-chutes,[6] was completely removed at this time, and the surviving cross-walls in the second and third floors were probably inserted, before its demolition, to support the steeple above. A change of alignment, most clearly identifiable in the W wall at second-floor level, is close to the recorded position of the N wall of the pre-1871 town-house.[7] This suggests that the length of the original tower was about 11.3m, and that the addition of 1704 extended it by about 4m. The series of rectangular slits in the E wall, which light an internal newel-stair, is probably at the junction of the two phases. These and the other openings in the N extension have plain surrounds, while the few surviving earlier openings are narrow slits with rounded arrises. At first-floor level in the E wall of the extension there are remains of a roll-moulded doorway, later contracted to a window, which gave access to a newel stair.

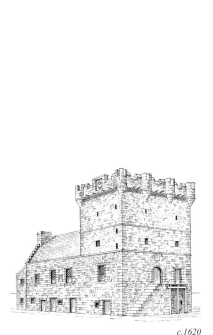

c.1620

c. 1630

c. 1706

Aberdeen Tolbooth (No.1) , conjectural reconstructions

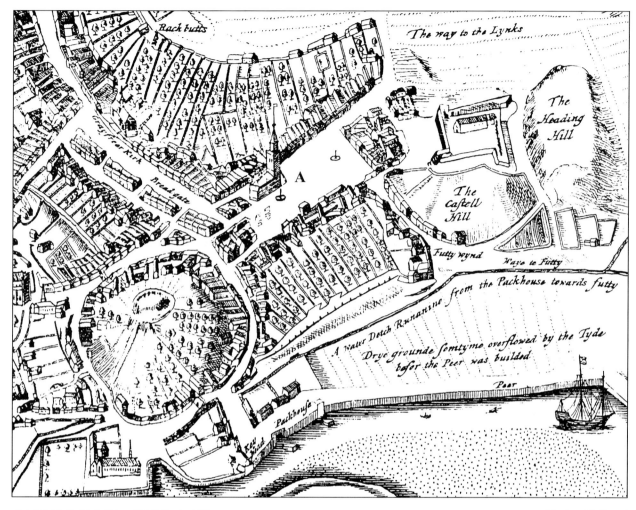

Aberdeen (No.1), detail of view, 1661 (tolbooth at 'A')

(Gordon of Rothiemay)

c.1751

c.1760

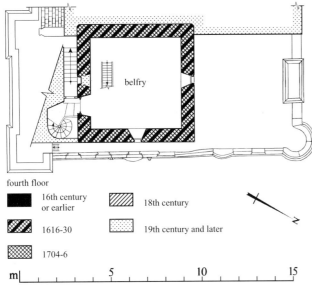

fourth floor

- ■ 16th century or earlier
- ▨ 1616-30
- ▨ 1704-6
- ▨ 18th century
- ▨ 19th century and later

m | 5 | 10 | 15

Aberdeen Tolbooth (No.1), plans and elevations

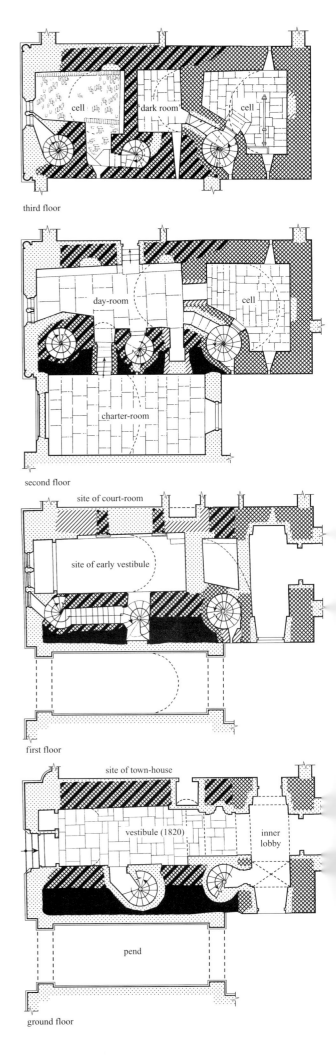

third floor

second floor

first floor

ground floor

The corbelled and crenellated parapet at the E wall-head is partly of sandstone ashlar, as specified in 1616, although the S part was rebuilt in granite in 1871. It incorporates remains of original spouts 'to convoy the watter off the platforme', and the bases of two mid-wall turrets (that to the N being at the original NE angle) whose upper masonry was probably re-used in the NE angle-turret of the 1704 addition. The parapet of the extension shows a polychrome mixture of grey granite and sandstone, probably made necessary by the scarcity of the latter, but preserves a panelled treatment of vertical ribs which is also seen in pre-1820 views of the S wall-head.[8] The parapet encloses an ashlar-built belfry, 6.4m square, which is entered from a newel-stair at the S wall-head and has large double-lancet louvred openings of Gothic character, linked by two string-courses. A corbelled balustrade with angle-finials, much restored in 1840 and incorporating central clock-faces, surrounds a slightly intaken stage, 2m in height, which carries the spire. This has a broad lead-covered ogival lower stage, and an arcaded timber octagon below the concave two-stage flèche. Set in the E recess of the octagon there is a lead plaque bearing the date 1630 and a shield: on a field vair, a chief. This is a variant of the Menzies arms and evidently for Paul Menzies of Kinmundy, provost of Aberdeen when the steeple was completed in that year. A plaque to the NW names the plumber John Blaikie, who repaired the leadwork in 1839.[9]

The 1616 contract was for a wardhouse containing five vaulted storeys, but in 1618 Watson offered a deduction from his contract-price since the fifth vault was 'unbiggit'.[10] The main tower remained four-storeyed, and with a first-floor entrance, until Smith's alterations of 1820. The most remarkable features of the interior are the immense E wall, which contains three newel stairs, and the consequent restricted width, of only 3m in the lower storeys rather than the 4.6m of the contract. The N stair, with its original external doorway, was presumably built in 1704-6 to serve the new N cells,[11] and about 1820, after the prison was removed, it was extended down to ground-floor level as well as being linked with other upper-floor rooms. The two original stairs were distinct in function, that 'in the southeast nuik' rising direct from the first floor to the wall-head and steeple without any communication with the prison-rooms on the upper floors. The position of its doorway, either inside or outside the building, was left undecided in the 1616 contract. It is now reached by a straight flight of steps, possibly original, rising from the S wall of the main entrance-passage. This served an original central doorway, now blocked by the pend, in the E wall of the tolbooth, and has a vaulted roof reinforced with a metal grille.[12]

*A. **Aberdeen Tolbooth** (No.1) from N*   *(A 74763)*

B. S windows of belfry   *(A 74796)*
C. NE angle-turret and steeple   *(A 74805)*

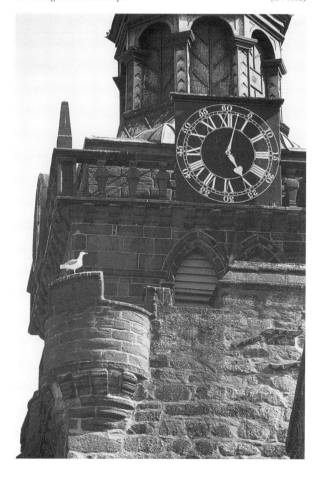

    To the N of the main door there was to be a door to the jailer's house and prison, reached from an extension of the pre-1616 forestair.[13] This door was associated with an access to the ground storey,[14] and with a stair, either straight or spiral, to the jailer's house on the second floor. From here a narrow spiral stair, built, as was specified, on the crown of the vault of the entrance-passage, rises to the third floor. In 1820 an additional newel-stair linking the ground floor to the steeple stair was built, in the floor of the former main entrance-passage.

    The first floor was the vestibule for the court-room in the town-house, to which it opened through an elaborate arcade. Watson's contract specified that the vaulted entrance-passage in the E wall was to be flanked by two small chambers,

A. **Aberdeen Tolbooth** (No.1), first floor, arcade in W wall (scale, 1:40)

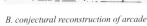

B. conjectural reconstruction of arcade

C. manacles   (A 74779)

continuing a similar earlier arrangement of timber 'houses'. These chambers may have been infilled to produce the existing thick E wall, but it is more probable that the final location of the stairs caused a change of plan. To the W, where there was no older work to incorporate, Watson was required 'to big ane massie wall of fyve futes (1.5m) in thiknes' at ground level, and upon it to build a first-floor arcade 'of hewin wark, twa pileris and thrie bowis (arches), fynelie wrocht with chapture heidis (capitals)', with arch-mouldings and decorated spandrels. All of these features are visible in the E face of the infilled arcade, as partly exposed in

1993, along with sub-classical bases and fluted faces on the slab-like pillars, which penetrate the thickness of the wall.[15] A vault of three compartments was to spring from above the arcade, but the existing axial barrel-vault again probably represents an early change of plan. In 1820 the lower part of the cross-wall between the vestibule and the lowest of the three cells of 1704 was removed, and a brick arch formed to support the remainder of it. At the same time the ground floor of the N extension of 1704 was converted into an inner lobby, and it retains most of its groined plaster vault springing from moulded corbels.

30B

A. **Aberdeen Tolbooth** (No.1), first floor, arcade in W wall   (C 45429)

B. third floor, N room showing iron 'gad'   (A 74775)

C. iron-bound door   (A 74781)

29

The large room in the S half of the second floor was intended in 1616 to be the jailer's dwelling, but after the failure to build the fifth storey it is probable that it was adapted for prison use, and by 1782 it served as a day exercise-room.[16] It has a blocked fireplace with roll-moulded jambs, and remains of another, both in the W wall. The criminal cell of 1704 to the N has splayed slits in E and W walls, as does the cell above where a blocked fireplace was formerly visible in the N wall. Fixed to the floor of the latter room there is an iron 'gad' or bar to which prisoners were chained, and manacles are fixed to the walls of all three rooms at this level. The central room was probably contracted in size in 1704, and was described in the late 18th century as the 'dark room' or dungeon.[17] These second- and third-floor rooms have stone-flagged floors, iron-bound timber doors with elaborate bolts and padlocks, and narrow windows which in several cases have yett-like inner as well as outer grilles.

29B

20A, 29C

The interior of the steeple contains a heavy timber bell-frame which, like the timberwork of the spire, was extensively renewed in 1839 and subsequently. The bell, which is 0.9m in diameter, was recast by Thomas Mears in 1799.[18] The tolbooth clock was sent to Flanders for repair as early as 1535. In 1616 it was specified that the clock was to be erected on the S wall-head of the wardhouse, and a passage for the weights was to be provided near the SE newel-stair. It was subsequently set up in the intaken stage above the belfry, and the existing clock is of early 20th-century date.[19]

When the New Inn was built to the E in 1756, the original first-floor entrance-passage remained in use for access to a charter-room above the pend that abutted the wardhouse. Two cells at second-floor level were entered by separate doorways from the day-room, and one of these entrances was retained in 1841 when a brick-vaulted charter-room was formed above the much-heightened pend as part of the new bank designed by Archibald Simpson.

A sundial was provided for the town-house in 1598, and in 1733-4 payment was made 'for a fine peuther Dial and for cutting, calculating, painting and gilding the same'. This may be the square dial, with the motto: UT UMBRA SIC FUGIT VITA ('As flies the shadow, so does life'), that is now built into the S front of the wardhouse at second-floor level.[20]

A. *Aberdeen Tolbooth (No.1)*
sundial (C 45439)

HISTORY

In 1317 the burgh court was held in the *tolloneum*, but the site of this early tolbooth is not known, although it has been assumed that it stood close to the harbour.[21] In or shortly before 1358 the sheriff was allowed £4 for the cost of building the prison (*carcer*) of Aberdeen.[22] Following the grant of a site by Robert III in 1393 (*supra,p.24*), courts were regularly held in the *pretorium* and burgesses were imprisoned there, although labour services 'until the *pretorium* will be completed' were still being required in 1407.[23] Between 1507 and 1596 various repairs were carried out to tolbooth and steeple, including in 1569 the addition of royal and burgh arms to two blank 'housines' (frames) in the S wall. At this period the building contained six booths on the ground floor with a court-room above.[24] In 1597 alterations were made to

B. *ground-floor vestibule from N, 1988*   (A 74764)

prison doors, and in the same year the tolbooth was extended by 'ane hous biggit of tymmer, on the wast gavill of the tolbuyth, tua stair hicht, and [ten] futtis in breid'. This was to contain, on the first floor, the town clerk's offices and a charter-room, with access to the council-house, and on the upper floor a room where the magistrates could discuss cases and the council could hold occasional meetings. The ground floor was also to provide shelter for the flesh-market, but in 1628 this was replaced by four shops.[25]

It was decided in 1612 to build 'ane ward and jealhous for resett of his Maiesties rebellis, and all sic transgressours of his laws', but the contract with Thomas Watson, mason in Auldrayne, was not drawn up until 1616. Watson was to be paid 5,000 merks for the work, which was financed from a variety of sources including the Common Good, various loans and a tax levied on the inhabitants of Aberdeen in 1619.[26] An approach was also made to the Marquis of Huntly, as sheriff, since the wardhouse would be 'for the gude and benefitt of the whole shyre', but no aid seems to have been obtained.[27] The contract specified that freestone from Kingoodie (near Dundee) or Stonehaven was to be used, and partially-dressed stone from John Mylne's Kingoodie quarry was ordered in 1619 and in 1622, when Watson was employed on 'the wark of the tolbuith steppill'. In the following year 40 merks were paid to John Bla(c)k, wright in Dundee, 'for coming to advise about the timber work for the tolbooth'. Instructions were given to build the 'pricket' of the steeple in 1629, and the lead plaque dated 1630 (*supra*) probably marks its completion.[28]

The decision not to build the fifth vaulted storey limited the space available for prison use, and it is likely that the payment to a mason working in 1627-8 in the 'new laigh prison house' referred to the adaptation of the ground storey for that purpose.[29] The proposed jailer's house on the second floor was also used as a prison by 1673, when Francis Irvine and others broke through the floor and escaped by the town-house.[30]

The wardhouse was extended to the N in 1704, when 20 guineas were 'given to Mr James Smith, Architect, for

A. **Aberdeen Tolbooth** (No.1) from SE by Irvine, 1812   (ABD/518/1)

comeing north to give his advice anent the said Tolbooth'.[31]
The surviving accounts are copious, listing such items as the
bringing of the great windlass from King's College, but not
specific. It is possible that other work was carried out as well
as the N addition, but the amount paid, £8,087, is impressive.[32]

In 1730-1 a higher two-bay block, containing a council-
room and staircase, replaced the timber structure at the W end
of the tolbooth, after a plan by William Adam for a wider
addition was rejected as too elaborate. Adam supplied the
marble chimneypiece for the principal room, which was
panelled throughout.[33] In 1750 the rest of the tolbooth was in
a poor condition, and it was decided to rebuild the frontage
and heighten it to a design by Patrick Barron, producing a
uniform three-storeyed seven-bay front to the W of the
wardhouse. The second floor of the five-bay main section
contained the elaborately furnished 'Great Room'
(Introduction, p.18), with the court-room below it and the
council-chamber in the W block.[34]

The main entrance to the court-room remained through the
E wall of the wardhouse, but in 1756 the Society of Free
Masons proposed to replace this with a new S entrance since
they were building a tenement to the E to accommodate the
lodge and the New Inn. The E forestair was removed and a
pend was created into what is still known as Lodge Walk. The
new tenement completed an impressive fifteen-bay front with
the wardhouse at the centre. Its first-floor S entrance was
reached by a double forestair which also incorporated a
ground-floor doorway, and the tall doorway with fanlight was
set in a pedimented projection.[35] Since 1734 part of the first
floor of the wardhouse had been used as a charter-room,[36] and
this function was transferred to one of the new rooms above
the pend.

In 1818-20 a new court-house was built to John Smith's
designs, on the W side of Lodge Walk to the N of the town-
house. This involved massive reconstruction of the interior of
the wardhouse as an entrance-lobby to the new building, and
Smith rebuilt the S front in granite, in Tudor style.[37] At this
time the prisoners were rehoused in the Bridewell until the
completion of a new prison to the N of the court-house, again
to Smith's designs, in 1831.[38] Part of the second floor of the
wardhouse was converted into a record-room, and the charter-
room above the pend was enlarged in 1841 when Archibald
Simpson heightened the arch to match his new Town and
County Bank (later Clydesdale Bank) on the site of the New
Inn. The masonry and leadwork of the steeple were
extensively repaired at this time under Smith's direction.[39]

17B

2A

B. view from E, c.1920   (AB/3995)

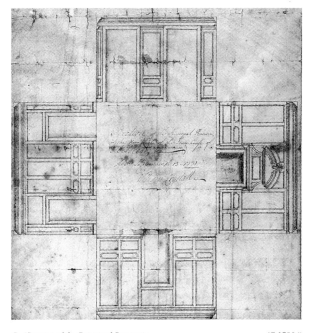

C. 'Section of the Principal Roome in   (C 17904)
   the New Worke of the Toun House' by Crystall, 1731

The erection of new County and Municipal Buildings was
under discussion from 1862, and after a limited competition
the elaborate baronial design by Peddie and Kinnear was
chosen. The new building was to replace, and extend W of,
the old town-house, only the wardhouse being preserved.
Even there, although the building committee wished to retain
Smith's S front, the architects argued that the façade was
splitting from the adjoining walls, and their own design was
accepted in 1871.[40] The town-house was demolished in the
same year, after alternative accommodation for the council,
including a high clock-tower, had been completed at the W
end of the site. The wardhouse was opened as the Tolbooth
Museum in 1995.

2 AIRDRIE TOWN-HOUSE
North Lanarkshire
NS 7596 6535

Situated on the E side of Bank Street, this two-storeyed late-Georgian building has a six-stage steeple some 30.8m high rising above the central bay of the main (W) front. It originally measured 13.3m across the W front by about 10m in depth, but was extended in depth to 19.5m in 1948 when a new council-chamber was built at the rear.[1] The three-bayed main front, which has angle-pilasters, has channelled masonry at ground-floor level, and the upper stages of the steeple are of ashlar. The remaining masonry is rendered, and the double-hipped roof is slated.

The central bay of the W front, at the base of the steeple, is slightly advanced and encloses a doorway framed by twin engaged Tuscan columns on raised plinths. The third principal stage of the steeple, which stands on a square double-stepped pedestal, has recessed Tuscan columns at the angles and a pedimented window in each face. This stage is surmounted by an entablature with a heavy cornice. At the next level there are clock-faces within square surrounds in the principal faces, and recessed panels in the narrow oblique ones. The belfry has round-headed openings within Tuscan columns supporting an emphatic entablature which steps in at the angles and is surmounted by an octagonal spire.

When built, the town-house had a police office and cells on the ground floor and a court-room, also used as the council-chamber, on the first floor.[2] Few original internal features survive since both floors have undergone extensive reworking from the late 19th century onwards.

HISTORY
The decision to build 'a small Town House and a jail' in Airdrie was taken in 1822, a year after the town had become a burgh of barony. Previously, courts and council meetings had been held in the masonic lodge.[3] Following a dispute between the Town Council and local heritors regarding the site first proposed,[4] the present building was begun in June 1825 and completed eighteen months later to the designs of Alexander Baird, the burgh treasurer. His plans were chosen in preference to those of George Waddell, a former councillor, and the contract for £1,075 was awarded to James Orr, who was also a member of the council as were the three unsuccessful tenderers.[5] A further public subscription allowed the addition in 1828 of a bell cast by Stephen Miller, Glasgow, and a clock which was replaced in 1954.[6]

A. *Airdrie Town-house* (No.2)
view from NW   (B 39144)

B. *Anstruther Wester Town Hall* (No.3)
view from SE   (C 42741)

3 ANSTRUTHER WESTER TOWN HALL
Fife

NO 5643 0351

The town hall, which was built in 1794-5, is situated at the NE angle of High Street and Elizabeth Place, adjoining the graveyard of the former parish church. Its N gable abuts the S wall of the 16th-century church tower,[1] which was used as a prison and housed the burgh clock. It is a two-storeyed gabled building of harled rubble, measuring 15.4 from N to S by 6.5m.

The building preserves original crowsteps at the N gable, but the skews of the S gable have been renewed. Towards the S end there is a chimneystack marking the principal internal dividing-wall, and immediately S of it in the W wall there is a doorway giving access to the stair. This opening has a quirked rounded arris and is surmounted by a pedimented over-lintel of 1911, inscribed 'Town Hall'.[2] The first-floor windows at the N and S ends of the main front have been enlarged, and it is possible that there were further windows in the E and S walls which have been blocked. The window-surrounds have straight arrises except for one small opening in the rear wall which is chamfered.

The ground floor is entered by three modern doorways, including one that connects it, through the tower, to the former parish church, which was largely rebuilt in 1846.[3] The original large room N of the dividing-wall was used as the school-room until about 1827, but it has been sub-divided and this floor retains no early features. The straight stone stair to the first floor, however, gives access on the N to the main council-room, which remains largely unaltered. It retains doors and shutters with fielded panels, a coombed ceiling with an emphatic wall-head cornice, and an elaborate plaster ceiling-rose. Painted in grisaille on the wall-plaster above the former chimneypiece in the S wall there is a lively rendering of the burgh arms, probably by the same artist as the larger armorial in Pittenweem Town Hall of about 1820 (No.71). In the former committee-room to the S, now divided, there is a lugged wooden panel-surround of 18th- or early 19th-century date.

From an early date the church tower, which measures about 6m square, was used for burgh purposes, including use as a prison. Access to the upper floors is by a newel-stair in the NE angle, but an additional doorway was slapped through the S wall at first-floor level, probably in the 17th or early 18th century, and it retains an original nail-studded timber door. It was evidently approached from the churchyard by a forestair carried on a half-barrel vault which survives in a small chamber in the re-entrant between the tower and the original W wall of the church. This doorway continued in use after the building of the present town hall in 1794-5. At that time a connecting first-floor lobby was contrived in the SE angle of the tower and the hall, supported by the vaulted chamber and entered by a doorway at the NE angle of the council-room.

The town council carried out repairs to the church steeple at various times, and in 1827 they defended their ownership of the bell and clock against the claims of the kirk-session.[4] The bell, which hangs in the lower part of the spire on the tower, is 0.55m in diameter and is inscribed: GEORGE WATT ME FECIT ST NINIANS ROW ED(I)N(BU)R(GH) 1789. The clock-mechanism by Ritchies of Edinburgh dates from 1868.

HISTORY
A tolbooth was in existence in the harbour area of Anstruther Wester by the 17th century, but it is said to have been swept away in a storm, along with several houses, so that the site became a rock 'covered by the sea every spring tide'.[5] In 1741 the town council met in a bailie's house, 'because a prisoner [is] in their Tolbooth where they usually sit', but nothing is known of this building. In 1794, 'considering that they are in much need of a Town house', the council discussed a possible

A. Anstruther Wester Town Hall (No.3) from SE   *(C 42741)*

B. armorial painting   *(C 42745)*

site, and the present building is said to have been built soon after.[6]

The ground floor was evidently used from the first as a school-room, and in 1798 the parish heritors agreed to enlarge it to 9.1m in length (the same as the council-room above) by removing a partition-wall. Repairs were carried out in 1812, but the school is said to have moved elsewhere about 1827.[7] The 'very old' building that was in use as a prison in 1836 was presumably the church tower, but part of the ground floor of the town hall came to be used as a lock-up, and part as a shop.[8]

4 ARBROATH TOWN BUILDINGS
Angus

NO 6430 4088

The Town Buildings of 1808, now occupied by the Sheriff Court, are situated on the W side of High Street, backing on to the Market Place. They stand directly opposite the site of the late 17th-century tolbooth, which survived until 1864 but ceased to be used for civic purposes in 1780.[1] In that year a plain three-storeyed building designed by Andrew Smith, wright, was erected almost immediately N of the site of the 1808 town-house, for use both by the burgh and by the guildry, a body which had been incorporated in 1725.[2] This building, which was rebuilt by the guildry after a fire in 1880, was vacated by the town council in favour of the new town-house begun in 1808 to designs by David Logan, a Montrose architect.[3]

Like its predecessors, the new building included prison-accommodation until about 1842, when a new prison was built on a separate site.[4] Following the removal of the cells, internal alterations were carried out in 1844 to plans by David Smith, a Dundee architect, but a public outcry forced the council to abandon a proposal to lease out the ground floor for shops.[5] At that time a single-bay wing was built over the alley separating the town-house from the guildry building, which had been linked by an arched bridge in 1820.[6]

The building is a three-storeyed block, 15m square, with a hipped and slated roof. Its three-bay main (E) front is little altered except for the installation of the consoled central doorcase in 1844. The ground storey is rusticated, and its windows are recessed between the advanced centrepiece and angle-piers carrying the paired pilasters of the upper storeys. At first-floor level the centrepiece has a large tripartite window in a round-headed recess, between pairs of Tuscan columns which support a fluted frieze and a high entablature containing a clock-face draped with swags. The side-bays have rectangular windows with balustraded aprons, and above there are horizontal blind panels, while the corresponding sections of the parapet are also balustraded.

The alley between the town buildings and the rebuilt guildry building is spanned by a shallow segmental arch supporting the plain two-storeyed addition of 1844. The rear elevation to Market Place was much altered in 1844 after the building ceased to be used as a prison, and there are several tripartite windows which are probably of that date.

Originally most of the rooms at the rear of the building were given up to prison use, with criminal cells on the ground floor and debtors' rooms on the second floor, but it also housed the council offices and a large first-floor hall whose roof rises through the next storey. The ground-floor space N of the central corridor was fitted up in 1844 as a court-room, but it was converted into two offices about 1900.[7] The timber staircase has been rebuilt, but occupies its original central position at the rear of the building.

The hall, which was used for assemblies as well as courts, ballots and public meetings, retains a small balcony above the main door from the stair-landing, in the position of the 'orchestra' or 'fiddlers' gallery' which was an original feature.[8] It has panelled door- and window-architraves, dado, doors and shutters, with two chimneypieces of dark grey marble in the end-walls, and a coombed and decorated ceiling. The SW room on the first floor was used as a retiring room during assemblies, and also as the council-chamber, but retains no early features except for a moulded cornice. One of the rooms added in 1844 above the alley to the N, which have stone-vaulted floors and roofs, was used as a store for the burgh records.[9]

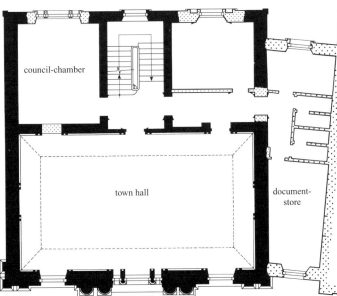

first floor

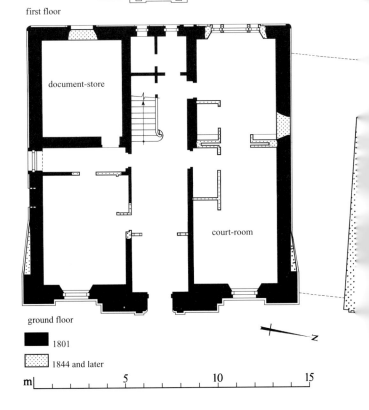

ground floor

■ 1801

▨ 1844 and later

Arbroath Town Buildings (No.4)
E elevation and plans

*A. **Arbroath Town Buildings** (No.4) from NE*　　　　　　　　　　　　　　　　　　　*(C 17199)*

B. first floor, hall from S　　　　　　　　　　　　　　　　　　　　　　　　*(C 17202)*

5 AUCHTERMUCHTY TOWN-HOUSE
Fife

NO 2380 1184

Although the burgh of Auchtermuchty was granted the right to hold a court and collect tolls in its royal charter of 1517,[1] the oldest part of the present town-house was built in 1728, the date carved on a panel set into the N wall of the steeple. In the previous year the town council had considered 'how uneasie and troublesome' was 'the want of a good tolbooth with a clock and bell and steeple for containing the same'. A committee was appointed to make contracts with tradesmen, and money for the building-fund was borrowed from local residents and from the kirk-session. The work was completed in 1729.[2]

The town-house stands in a prominent position on the S side of High Street at its broadest part, apparently on a different site from its predecessor.[3] It originally comprised a two-storeyed block measuring 17.9m across its main (N) front, with a single-storeyed cell extension at the rear which in the 19th century was encased in a larger SE wing. The building is constructed of rubble with dressed margins and the N front of the ground storey is rendered and painted. The gables of the main block are crow-stepped and the roofs are slated, that of the added wing being hipped above its faceted S end.

A steeple some 4.1m square rises above the main block to a balustraded parapet at a height of 16m enclosing a pyramidal stone spire. The base of the N wall of the steeple is corbelled out slightly from the centre of the N front a little below present wall-head level, and it rises, with pairs of slit-windows in the lower part, to square clock-faces of 1897 and round-headed louvred belfry-openings below the balustrade.

The fenestration of the N front is regular, with three-bay ground-floor frontages flanking the steeple. The main ground-floor rooms were functioning as shops by 1840,[4] and probably served to raise revenue for the burgh. While the steeple has remained unaltered, the main block was extensively re-worked in the second half of the 19th century when the first-floor windows were enlarged and given prominent dormer gablets. A surround with similar detail was added to the main doorway, which gives access by steps rising through the solid base of the steeple to the first-floor rooms that were formerly used by the town council. The ground- and first-floor rooms in the SE addition of this period are bow-ended internally, the latter extending through the whole depth of the original block and the extension.

The surviving cell at the rear of the main block is rectangular on plan and retains a timber door and iron yett set within re-worked jambs, while its flat ceiling is reinforced with metal sheeting. Immediately to the W there was a smaller cell,[5] through which a modern passage has been formed. The continuation of the splayed W wall of this cell to the SE may have belonged to an original enclosing-wall for a rear courtyard. It is possible that another small cell was fitted into the base of the steeple below the main stair, but later re-working of the interior has obscured any evidence of this. In 1840 the cells were 'very seldom used'.[6]

A new clock was ordered in 1728, and the existing mechanism incorporates a metal plate recording its repair in 1740 and 1841.[7] A bell weighing seven hundredweight was ordered at London in 1728, but split in 1740 and was shipped back there for recasting to eleven hundredweight.[8] The present bell was cast in 1874 by John Warner and Sons of London.

A. **Auchtermuchty Town-house** (No.5), conjectural reconstruction
B. plans

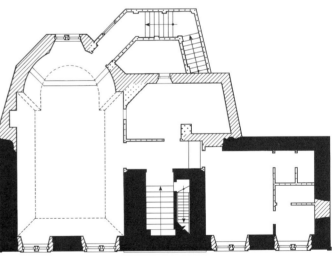

first floor

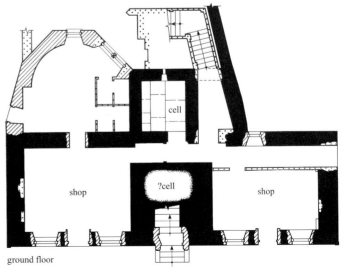

cell

?cell

shop   shop

ground floor

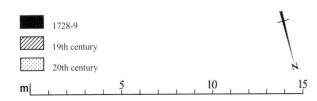

■ 1728-9

▨ 19th century

▦ 20th century

m | 5 | 10 | 15

N

A. **Auchtermuchty Town-house** *(No.5) from NW* (B 39403)

B. cell door and yett (B 39457)

C. inscribed plate on (B 39461)
clock-mechanism

D. clock-mechanism (B 39459)

6 AYR
South Ayrshire

The earliest known tolbooth in Ayr, first recorded in 1427, stood in the market area in High Street (NS 3379 2199). A new 'High Tolbooth' on an island site at the N end of Sandgate was built in 1575-8, and a timber belfry with a spire was added to it in 1615-17.[1] A massive N tower with a belfry was added in 1722-6, incorporating re-used masonry from St John's Church and the Cromwellian fort, and the main block was rebuilt in 1754-5,[2] but both became ruinous and were demolished in 1825. The council offices were moved to new Town and County Buildings which, with an adjacent jail, had been built near the sea-front to the SW of the town. A steeple of great height was incorporated in the new Assembly Rooms that were built in 1828-30 on a site close to that of the High Tolbooth.

The burgh also acquired in 1673 the 'Auld Tour' or Wallace Tower on the E side of High Street (NS 3385 2179), and in 1731 added a belfry for the benefit of local residents, as well as later using it as a prison. Attempts to repair the tower in 1830 were unsuccessful, and it was rebuilt in 1831-2 to a Gothic design by Thomas Hamilton.[3]

THE HIGH TOLBOOTH (NS 3366 2206)
This building, also known as the 'Dungeon Clock', is recorded in several early views and in floor-plans of 1754, which correspond closely with a description of 1812.[4] The steeple was a prominent feature on the axis of Robert Adam's New Bridge, and in 1785 Adam drew elevations as it existed, and with proposed classical embellishments. It comprised a six-stage tower 8.2m square and 25m high, carrying a tall square belfry whose ogival roof supported an open pillared octagon with a small ogival spire, 40m in overall height. A straight forestair and balustraded platform, on which executions were

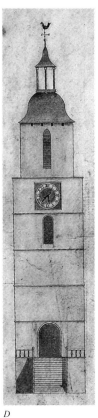

Ayr (No.6)
A. *High Tolbooth and New Bridge from N, c.1800 (AY/1860)*
B. *Town Steeple and Old Bridge from NE, 1859 (AY/2420)*
C. *High Tolbooth from S, c.1800 (C 39494)*
D,E. *High Tolbooth steeple, survey drawing and proposed alterations by Robert Adam, 1785 (AYD/37/2 and 1)*

A

Ayr County Buildings (No.6)
A. proposed elevation by David Hamilton,
   1816 (AYD/124/3)
B. view from E (C 66512)

B

held, gave access to the first-floor entrance, and two of the upper floors contained prison-cells.

The three-storeyed main block was of the same width as the steeple and 16.5m long, with a lower three-storeyed annexe against the S gable. The ground floor was divided into four vaulted rooms, probably let as shops, and the first floor contained a stair-lobby entered through the tower, and two vaulted cells adjoining a vaulted corridor which led to the debtors' room at the S end. The court-room occupied the main part of the second floor, with a room having a fireplace in the S annexe, whose lower floors had no communication with the main block.

AYR COUNTY BUILDINGS (NS 3330 2174)

This classical building occupies a site on the W side of Wellington Square, which in 1815 was given by Ayr town council to commissioners for erecting a new jail, court-house and county offices.[5] Designs were obtained from David Hamilton and from Robert Wallace, a London architect whose 'elegant plans' were preferred despite their greater cost.[6] The foundation stone was laid in 1818 and the buildings were completed in 1822 at a total cost, including the jail, of over £30,000.[7] Ayr town council offered the materials of their old tolbooth and a subscription of £500, on condition that a council-room, town clerk's office and record-room were provided in the new building, and the burgh retained these rooms until 1889.[8] The extensive jail occupying the W part of the site was replaced in the 1930s by new County Buildings in neo-classical style, and the original building is now occupied by Ayr Sheriff Court.

The two-storeyed main block is rectangular, measuring 58m

by 19m, and the addition of two lower wings overlapping the rear (W) wall was decided upon before the building was completed.[9] The principal (E) front is of eleven bays, including a central three-bay Ionic portico having an inner row of two columns *in antis*. The lower storeys of the three-bay-link sections flanking the portico, and the slightly advanced end-bays, are of channelled ashlar and have round-headed sash-windows, or blind niches in the end-bays, in matching recesses. The upper storey is of polished ashlar and has rectangular windows with moulded architraves and entablatures, and consoles in the end-bays only. At parapet-level there are sections of blind balustrade corresponding to the window-bays below. Behind the central pediment a dome rises from a low drum and carries a side-lit cupola, while two large rectangular cupolas light the court-rooms to N and S. The five-bay end-elevations are of similar character, but with central ground-floor doorways, and the same treatment is continued in the projecting wings at the rear. The masonry throughout is white sandstone ashlar quarried at Corrie in Arran, whose colour variations caused much anxiety to the architect.[10]

Wallace designed the building round a central rotunda enclosing an elaborate spiral stair and a domed first-floor landing which was flanked on the S by the justiciary court and on the N by the county hall, now also used as a court-room. The stair-treads are supported by a peripheral ring of eight Doric columns, and they spring from a massive newel-pillar which continues at first-floor level as the pedestal for a bronze tripod.[11] Axial groin-vaulted corridors on the ground floor give access to offices and strong-rooms, and to entrance-lobbies which include staircases. Three of the

*A. **Ayr Assembly Rooms, Steeple and Town-house** (No.6) from S*   *(C 42620)*

B. perspective design by Thomas Hamilton (AYD/113/38)
C. view from NW (C 42624)

rooms in the end-bays have groined vaults springing from rectangular central pillars, while the NE room, which was probably one of those used by the town council, has two blind recesses in the E wall echoing the round-headed windows in the N wall. An extensive basement provided storage space.

The wall of the first-floor rotunda is divided into eight bays by pilasters carrying an entablature below the coffered top-lit dome. Alternate bays contain doors and a window with elaborate carved consoles and architraves, and round-headed niches of which one retains a neo-classical iron stove. The original justiciary court-room, three window-bays in width and occupying the entire depth of the building, has a two-stage elevation with vertical timber panelling below, incorporating two elaborate timber doorcases. Its upper stage comprises, in the side-walls, seven bays divided by engaged Ionic columns, and in the end-walls three bays with paired pilasters, all carrying a full entablature and a coffered ceiling with a central rectangular clerestory. The judge's bench in the W wall is set in a round-headed panelled recess enclosing a lunette with the royal arms of George IV in painted glass. The former County Hall to the N is similar in arrangement, with a large radially-glazed lunette in the W wall and a clerestory-lit coffered ceiling having neo-classical detail, but most of its ornament is of late 19th-century character.

AYR ASSEMBLY ROOMS, STEEPLE AND TOWN-HOUSE (NS 3370 2208)

The 'Town's New Buildings', erected to the designs of the Edinburgh architect Thomas Hamilton in 1828-30, are situated in the SE angle of High Street and New Bridge Street, a few metres NE of the site of the 'High Tolbooth'. The original building was a two-storeyed L-plan block, 33.7m along the New Bridge Street (NW) front and 11m along the

14B, 38B

NE front, but with the SW wing, which contained the main assembly-room, extending a further 5m to the rear. The NW gable of this wing exploits the sloping site and rises above the remainder of the New Bridge Street front, which is also divided asymmetrically by the massive base of the steeple. In

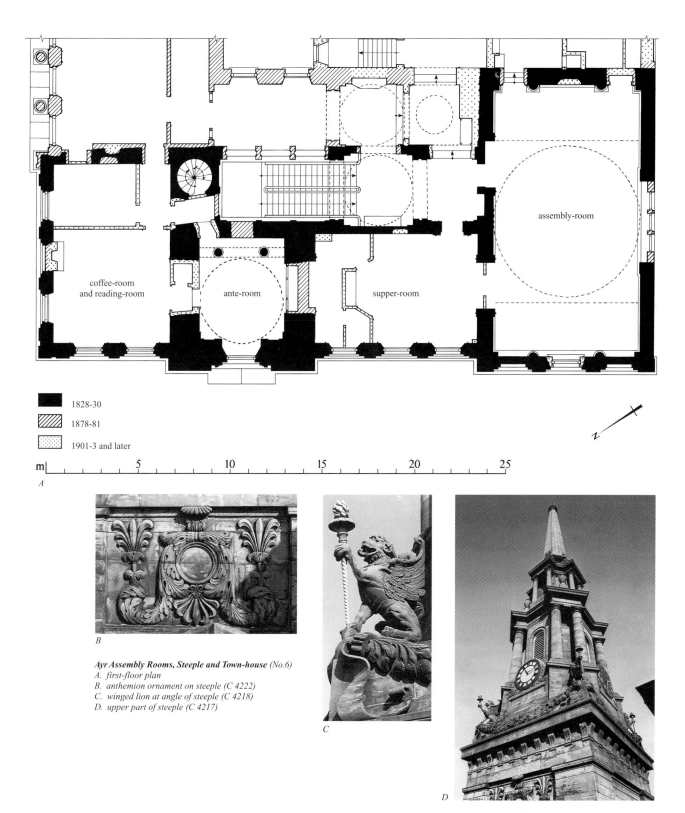

1828-30

1878-81

1901-3 and later

m | 5 10 15 20 25

A

Ayr Assembly Rooms, Steeple and Town-house (No.6)
A. *first-floor plan*
B. *anthemion ornament on steeple (C 4222)*
C. *winged lion at angle of steeple (C 4218)*
D. *upper part of steeple (C 4217)*

B

C

D

1878-81 the buildings were extended to the SE, and 24m added in matching style to the High Street frontage, to designs by James Sellars of the Glasgow firm, Campbell Douglas and Sellars. In 1901-3, following fire-damage to the main hall added by Sellars, further internal alterations were supervised by the local architect J K Hunter.[12]

The original building is faced throughout with white sandstone ashlar from the Cullaloe quarry in Fife, for which a reduced freight charge through the Forth and Clyde Canal was negotiated.[13] The main frontages, except for the steeple, are in a simple neo-classical style, with ground-floor shop-fronts and a high first floor articulated by shallow pilasters with simple bases and capitals framing tall round-headed windows. The

entablature terminated in a flat parapet, replaced by Sellars with a balustrade except in the pedimented gable of the SW wing.

Hamilton responded to local criticism that the site was too low-lying, and that the bells would be inaudible, by designing a monumental steeple in baroque style, 8m square at base and 64m in height, which dominates the town and the surrounding countryside.[14] Its NW front, slightly advanced from the flanking wings, has a rusticated ground storey with a pedimented entrance-doorway, above which massive angle-pilasters frame a tall round-headed window and rise to an entablature with a bold cornice carried on scrolled triglyphs. In three faces of the tower below the entablature there are large

3C

A

B

Ayr Assembly Rooms,
Steeple and
Town-house *(No.6)*
A. *staircase and first-floor*
   vestibule (C 4202)
B. *first-floor ante-room*
   in steeple (C 4206)
C. *bell (C4229)*

C

41B
41C
41D

boldly-carved panels of anthemion-ornament, and at the angles above the cornice there are winged lions holding torches, linked by rich festoons which enclose the octagonal upper stages.[15] The belfry-stage has projecting paired Tuscan pillars set on the oblique faces, and clock-faces below round-headed louvred openings in the principal ones. In the next stage pillars with distinctive Corinthian capitals, based on those of the Tower of the Winds in Athens, frame the openings in the principal faces, while at the angles, which were originally intended as the location for the clock-faces, there are urns on tall plinths. Above the entablature eight scrolled trusses support a thin octagonal spire or obelisk with recessed panelled sides, terminating in a capital which is a simplified version of those from the Tower of the Winds. For a few years this carried a copper figure of Triton, based on the finial of the same monument, but following lightning-damage in 1836 this was replaced by a simpler vane to Hamilton's design.[16]

A vestibule in the base of the steeple, ornamented with pilasters and tall round-headed niches in the side-walls, leads to the main staircase, which was designed as a series of short flights and landings but replaced by Sellars with a single broad flight. The elliptical-vaulted coffered ceilings of the staircase and inner vestibule correspond to Hamilton's design-drawings although the top-lit cupola of the main landing differs in the number of panels.

The first-floor rooms comprised a suite of assembly-rooms – hall to the SW, supper-room and an ante-room in the steeple – and a coffee-room and reading-room to the NE.[17] In 1878-81 these were adapted as council-chamber, committee-room, strong-room in the steeple and town clerk's office. Hamilton also provided a four-storeyed block of offices in the rear re-entrant, but in 1878 these were replaced by a link-area to the new main hall. The principal assembly-room, some 14.5m by 8.3m, retains the main features of Hamilton's design, but the coffered ceiling with central domed cupola was altered by Sellars, who raised the wall-head by about 1.4m. At the same time, the pairs of timber Corinthian pillars in the end-walls, and the simpler pilasters in the angles, were raised above a dado. Here and elsewhere, several of the original fine mahogany doors, with rich consoles, have been preserved, although the marble fireplaces in both end-walls have been

removed. A three-light stained-glass window of 1881 in the SW wall replaced the 'orchestra' or musicians' gallery, which is shown in Hamilton's drawing as having a metal balustrade supported by two caryatids.

The former supper-room retains its coffered ceiling and windows intact, while the square ante-room in the steeple preserves much of its ornament, although the entrance-doorway from a former stair-landing on the SE has been removed. It was entered through a screen with two Greek Doric columns supporting a deep entablature, which continues round the room to the pilastered window-surround, and the ceiling is a shallow dome.

The three lower stages of the steeple are linked by a newel-stair projecting at the NE angle, above which step-ladders continue through apertures in the groin-vaulted roofs of the main stages to the base of the spire. The clock-mechanism was made by Mitchell and Son, Glasgow, in 1830 and retains a pendulum in a long timber case. A massive framework supports the principal bell, 1.25m in diameter and 1.18 tonnes in weight, which was supplied by Thomas Mears in 1830 and recast by Mears and Stainbank in 1897. A smaller bell hung at a higher level bears the inscription: SOLI DEO GLORIA DALMAHOY 1700.[18]

HISTORY

The town council asked Hamilton to consider possible locations for a new steeple in 1824, when it was clear that the old tolbooth in Sandgate would have to be demolished, and it was decided that the site of the old assembly rooms would be most convenient.[19] The council offices were moved to the new Town and County Buildings, but in 1827 the inhabitants petitioned for the new steeple to be erected, and Hamilton produced a full set of drawings for which he received £150. The contractor, Archibald Johnston, began work in 1828 and completed the building, at a total cost of £9,965, in time for the inaugural ball to be held in November 1830.[20]

7 BANFF TOWN-HOUSE
Aberdeenshire

NJ 6899 6395

The town-house stands at the N end of Low Street fronting the raised paved area known as the Plainstanes. It comprises a steeple, originally self-contained, which was completed in 1767, and to the N a three-storeyed main block of 1796-7.

Although the following description was written in 1842, the building remains unchanged in external appearance: 'The town-house, built about forty years ago, is a very large, but entirely plain building, forming two sides of a square, with a spire rising from the external angle. The spire, which is much older than the house, is a sort of fluted cone, of very graceful proportions, rising from a square tower. The whole height of the spire is 100 feet. The tower, spire, and front of the house are built of dressed freestone. The house is of three very lofty stories. It contains a hall, two large drawing-rooms, Town-council Chamber, Sheriff-court Room, Town Chamberlain's and Sheriff Clerk's offices, and prisons. The staircase and landing-places are spacious'.[1]

44A,B The main block is of T-plan, measuring 16.2m across its principal (W) front by 23.7m in depth, and is built of sandstone rubble, some of which was probably re-used from the previous tolbooth. The five-bay main front is faced with sandstone ashlar, with channelled blocks in the ground storey and the quoins. The square-headed entrance-doorway is placed centrally, and the fenestration is regular. The roof is gabled, with a flat apex, and is slated. The town council gave much consideration to the best form of roof-structure, but having seen a model prepared by the wright John Smith, they concluded that 'the flat roof, tho' more expensive is ... by far the most substantial and proper'.[2] It survives largely unaltered, some of the original assembly-marks still being visible.

The steeple, which is partly enclosed on the N and E by the later building, is square on plan and measures some 5.5m across its exposed S front. Its four-storeyed tower carries a spire 29m in overall height, and both are faced with sandstone ashlar. At ground-floor level the W front has a heavily-moulded square-headed doorway below a blind oculus, both recessed within a round-headed arch. At the next level the visible faces display blind thermal windows, while the clock-stage above is intaken by a concave course. The clock-faces, which have been renewed, are surmounted by broken gablets supported by consoles and linked at cornice-level by a continuous string-course. The belfry stage has a round-headed

A

B

Banff Town-house (No.7)
A. plaster corbel (C 4024)
B. bell (C 4037)
C. W elevation

C

43

louvred opening in each face, and the tower terminates in a heavily-moulded corbelled cornice surmounted at each angle by a ball-and-square finial. The stone spire is octagonal, each facet being concave and pierced by oval vents, and is terminated by a small stone drum surmounted by a ball and weathervane.

Internally, much of the original character of the building has been lost in modern alterations, but a musicians' gallery and the coving of the ceiling of the original ballroom survive above an inserted ceiling on the second floor. The cells, situated in the vaulted rear block, remain largely unaltered, the two in the SE angle retaining early strengthened doors.

The steeple contains a cantilevered newel-less stair to second-floor level. In the belfry there is a bell 0.6m in height and 0.76m in diameter at the mouth, which bears the cast

43B

inscription: LESTER AND PACK LONDON FECIT, and the incised one: THE BURGH OF BANFF 1767. The disused clock-mechanism is presumably the one which was ordered in London, at the same time as the bell, in February 1767.[3]

HISTORY

Banff had a tolbooth in 1501[4] which probably stood in the SW angle of Low Street and Strait Path, on the site occupied since 1801 by the Tolbooth Hotel. Rebuilding took place in the early 18th century, when financial assistance was provided by the Convention of Royal Burghs.[5] In 1762, following the demolition of the ruinous steeple, the town council resumed possession of part of a house at the Plainstanes as a site for the present steeple, which was completed in 1767.[6] Plans were provided by 'Mr Adam' (almost certainly John Adam), and the mason contractor was John Marr.[7] The erection of the steeple was resisted by the owner of the property to the S, Admiral Gordon, who expressed fear 'of the spire falling on the roof of my house, or if it stand, which will be a miracle, a continual alarm of bees'. Adam reported that there was 'no risk of falling, except from an earthquake or lightning'.[8]

In 1794 the old tolbooth was described as ruinous and dangerous, and a year later the council obtained plans from James Reid, wright, for a new building to adjoin the steeple. The length of the site, which was burgh property, was subsequently increased by the partial demolition of an adjacent house, 'for making a handsome front, and giving proper accommodation to the town and county'. Construction began in 1796 and was largely completed in the following year. The county authorities offered £700 of the estimated cost of £1700, and subscriptions included 100 guineas from Sir William Grant, MP.[9]

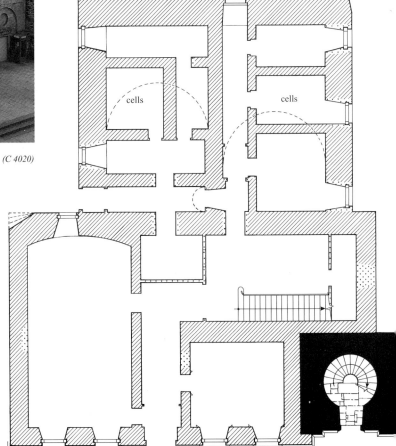

A. **Banff Town-house** (No.7) from NW   (C 4020)
B. ground-plan

■ 1766-7
▨ 1796-7
⬚ 20th century

N

m | 5 | 10

Banff Town-house (No.7)
cantilevered stair in steeple
    A. *view from above (C 4031)*
    B. *lower flight (C 4029)*
C. *cell door (C 4022)*

A

B

C

45

8   BEITH TOWN-HOUSE
North Ayrshire
NS 3476 5384

Situated at the corner of Strand and Eglinton Street in the centre of Beith, the town-house was constructed in 1817 by public subscription, and was owned by the subscribers until 1838.[1] It is said to occupy the site of a tolbooth of 17th-century date which housed the parish school on the upper floor but was abandoned about 1768.[2]

The town-house is two-storeyed and rectangular on plan, measuring 13m from E-W by 7.1m, and is constructed of sandstone ashlar. Its main (E) front is a pedimented design of three bays while the N front to Eglinton Street is of four bays. The angles of the building are marked by pilasters. While the ground-floor windows and doorways are unmoulded but have segmental heads, the first-floor windows are rectangular and have moulded surrounds rising from continuous sill-courses. The E pediment is surmounted by a round-arched bellcot, capped by an ogival dome and containing a bell 0.51m in diameter which was gifted in 1823 and cast by Thomas Mears.[3]

Originally the ground floor contained a small cell and shops which provided public revenue from their rents. The first floor, consisting of a large hall, was used as a court-room and a public reading-room.[4] The building retains no early internal features.

Beith Town-house (No.8) from NE   (B 39148)

9 BRECHIN TOWN-HOUSE
Angus
NO 5969 6018

The two-storeyed town-house is set in the NW angle of
Church Street and High Street, which here broadened out for
use as a market-place. It is rectangular on plan, measuring
14.5m across its S front by 7.7m, and is constructed of grey-
brown sandstone ashlar with rusticated quoins. The S front is
of four regular bays, with a ground-floor doorway in the W
bay giving access to the staircase, and a central gablet
incorporates a renewed date-stone inscribed '1789'. A modern
shop-front in the ground floor of the E wall replaces three
square-headed lights visible in early photographs, but at first-
floor level there is an original Venetian window and in the E
gable there is a clock-face surmounted by an open bellcot with
an ogee-shaped roof.

Some internal alterations were carried out in 1855-6,[1]
notably to the staircase and the ground-floor rooms, while the
main first-floor room has been partitioned during modern
alterations. This room, which has a coombed ceiling, had two
fireplaces in the N wall and is overlooked by a W gallery
framed by wooden pilasters and surmounted by a plaster
cornice decorated with swags. A small recess to the N of the
Venetian window evidently contained a rope which enabled the
bell to be rung from inside the building.

HISTORY

While Brechin possessed a *pretorium* (court-house) where a
sheriff's inquisition into market-privileges was held in 1450,
the present town-house replaces one of late 17th-century date
which by 1789 was in 'great disrepair'.[2] The new building was
begun in that year and completed in 1790. It was agreed that
John Gourlay, mason, should 'oversee the carrying on the
whole work of that building', while the mason-contractor was
George Scott.[3] The town council agreed to fund the new
building by public subscription, and contributions were
received from the guildry and from the local Member of
Parliament, Sir David Carnegie. For their contribution, the
guildry received the right to call the main first-floor room,
which was also used as the council-chamber, 'The Guild Hall
of Brechin'.[4]

The ground storey originally contained a shop, court-room,
debtors' prison and two cells for criminals, one of them a
'black hole'. Gurney in 1819 described 'a tolerably decent
apartment for debtors, and two wretched, dirty cells for
criminals', one of which allowed communication by a grating
with passers-by. The prison inspector in 1835 considered that
it was 'one of the worst prisons I have visited', and despite
subsequent repairs a new prison was built on the edge of the
town in 1844. Part of the ground storey was subsequently
used as a police-station.[5]

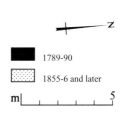

A. *Brechin Town-house* (No.9)
*E elevation (partially
reconstructed) and plans*

1789-90

1855-6 and later

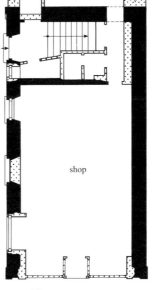
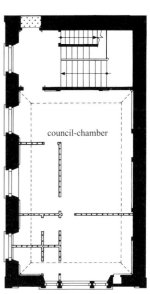

ground floor

shop

first floor

council-chamber

B. *view from SE, c.1900* (C 39497)

C. *view from SE* (B 39151)

10 CAMPBELTOWN TOWN-HOUSE
Argyll and Bute
NR 7191 2036

This building,[1] which stands midway along the NW side of Main Street, was erected in 1758-60 on the site of an earlier tolbooth. It consists of a rectangular main block fronted by a projecting octagonal steeple, a conspicuous classical landmark in the centre of Campbeltown. The all-stone upperworks of the steeple, which replaced an original timber spire, were designed and built in 1778 by John Brown, an Inveraray mason-architect.[2] The SW bay containing the present main entrance was added in 1866, and the interior extensively remodelled, to designs by the Glasgow architect, Campbell Douglas.[3]

50A   The original two-storeyed main block measures 16.2m from NE to SW by 13m, the length being extended to the SW by 5.6m in 1866. The steeple projects some 3.7m from the centre of the original symmetrical SE front. The masonry is of stuccoed rubble with some painted freestone dressings, and the roof is gabled and slated.

The steeple incorporates three tiers of openings below wall-head level, the inner ones being of blind, alcoved form. The entrance-doorway has a Gibbs-surround, and the other openings on the two lower storeys are semicircular-headed and have moulded architraves with projecting keystones and imposts, the imposts of the ground-floor openings being extended to form a continuous string-course. The openings of the upper stage are circular and have Gibbsian architraves. Above a prominent cornice at wall-head level the steeple rises in two main stages, surmounted by a spire. The lower stage incorporates a series of square lug-moulded panels and the upper a range of blind niches, three of which contain clock-faces. The spire itself incorporates a tier of round-headed louvred openings alternating with circular recesses, and two more tiers of circles of diminishing size.[4]

The flanking bays of the main block contain round-headed windows at both levels, similar in character to the corresponding openings in the steeple. There are well-defined rusticated quoins and a moulded eaves-cornice.

The general design and detail of the SW extension of 1866 harmonise with the original work. The two-leaf principal doorway is framed within a colonnaded porch of the Roman Doric order, and the tympanum of the first-floor window bears in relief the arms and motto of the burgh.[5] The pedimented dormer above bears the date 1866.

The interior survives substantially in its remodelled mid-Victorian form and possesses few features of special interest. Until the 1850s the ground storey contained criminal cells and the garret two debtors' rooms with fireplaces. The NE half of the ground floor was later adapted as the council-chamber, which is lined with modern panelling. The first floor of the original block was divided into a hall in the NE half, and two rooms and a lobby to the SW.[6] In 1866 the entire space was given over to the town hall, which is ceiled with a segmental and coffered plaster vault. It is entered through a large SW doorway with a segmental armorial pediment. This is reached by a wide scale-and-platt stair in the 1866 extension, which replaced the original newel-stair within the steeple.

50C

The steeple bell is inscribed in relief: THE TOWN OF CAMPBELTOUN: A C PRO(VOS)T: D B & R O BAILIES: 1779. These initials commemorate Alexander Campbell, Duncan Ballantine and Robert Orr, all of whom were elected to office in 1778. Instructions were given in 1779 to purchase a bell of suitable dimensions at Bristol, while a clock, which has been replaced, was commissioned from 'Mr Townsend' of Greenock at an estimated cost of £50.[7]

Campbeltown Town-house (No.10), view from E by MacKinnon, 1886

(C 4241)

Campbeltown Town-house (No.10)
SE elevation and strip-plan

m| 5   10   15   20

HISTORY

Originally known as Kilkerran or Lochhead, Campbeltown was erected into a burgh of barony for the 9th Earl of Argyll in 1667 and became a royal burgh in 1700. The old tolbooth is said to have been built 'long before' 1700 and to have comprised a first-floor hall above a prison on the ground floor.[8] By the middle of the 18th century its condition was a matter of serious concern, and in 1745 the town council accepted the 3rd Duke of Argyll's offer to build and pay for a new tolbooth, but nothing came of the scheme. They again expressed their disquiet in 1754.[9]

In 1757 the council recorded that 'the Town House or Tolbooth ... is and for a considerable time past has been in so ruinous condition that a criminal cannot be secured in it, nor any other prisoner legally confined to it'. They resolved to impose an annual tax of between £20 and £22 upon the inhabitants of the burgh (later excepting those who made voluntary contributions) and to borrow up to £300 for the building of a new tolbooth.[10] A further sum of £100, payable in three yearly instalments, was secured from the Commissioners of Supply in May 1758. By that date the old town-house and prison had been taken down, and an un-named contractor was engaged to build a new one 'according to a plan seen and approved by His Grace the Duke of Argyll'.[11] Having made a donation to the cost of a bell in the steeple and supplied furniture for the town hall, the Freemasons' Lodge of Campbeltown was in 1767 granted permission to use the hall and an adjacent room, and it was agreed that these rooms would also be made available for a proposed monthly assembly.[12]

The work authorised in 1778 was for 'building a steeple on the townhouse or an addition to the present steeple in place of the timber work now standing thereon', at an estimated cost of £50 3s 6d. Some modifications to the original specification of the clock were also made in 1779, partly because the steeple was 'not so properly adapted for a clock as it ought to have been'.[13]

Sixty years later, physical conditions had again degenerated so far as prison accommodation was concerned. In 1835 the sheriff was quoted as considering it 'perhaps the worst gaol in Scotland, after the old gaol at Roth[e]say', and an official report of 1838 confirmed the prison as 'one of the worst in Scotland'.[14] A further inspection in 1844 revealed some minor improvements, but a new prison was still 'much wanted'. A new building adjoining Castlehill Church was finally opened about 1856.[15]

A scheme for remodelling and extending the town buildings was initiated in 1865, and it was proposed that the extension to the SW would embrace a close which was part of the adjacent house occupied by the Town Officer. The principal contractors for this work were Robert Weir, builder, William Stewart, joiner, and Robert Armour, plumber and gas-fitter. The sculptor James Mossman was employed, perhaps for the armorial panel, while James Steel modelled the ornamented tympanum of the hall door and Galbraith and Winton supplied the marble mantlepieces. The architect Campbell Douglas received £170 11s 3d for drawings and 'outlay'.[16]

A. *Campbeltown Town-house* (No.10) from E   (C 4237)

B. *vestibule in steeple*   (C 4247)   C. *first-floor hall*   (C 4252)

11   CANONGATE TOLBOOTH
City of Edinburgh
NT 2641 7379

An archetypal tolbooth in the external appearance of its tower and council-chamber block, this building[1] stands on the N side of the Canongate opposite Huntly House. To the W it adjoins a 17th-century house whose upper storeys are now incorporated in the Tolbooth museum, and its E gable was formerly abutted by a lower three-storeyed building which was removed about 1689 to create the Canongate churchyard.[2]

3B, C The projecting belfry-tower at the W end, which is dated 1591, contains an arched pend opening into Tolbooth Wynd and is capped by a broached spire. The three-storeyed main block
52A contains a first-floor hall, which served as council-room and
17A court-house, over an undercroft which is itself partly built above a cellar. A three-storeyed wing, gabled to the N, was built N of the tower, 'be way of addition to the tolbuith', in 1677.[3] The council-chamber block was extensively restored and altered in 1875 by R H Morham, City Superintendent of Works. The interior underwent further alterations in 1908, in 1952-4 when it was adapted as a museum, and again in 1988, and it retains few early features.[4]

The S front of the main block measures 17.3m from E to W and it is 7.6m wide, while the tower, which projects 1.5m to the S, extends the frontage a further 4.7m to the W. The tower is, however, of L-plan, with an E wing which is encased in the main block, and its N wall is 7.2m long. The masonry of the S wall of the main block is not bonded with that of the tower, and its thickness is less than 0.8m, compared with 1m in the N wall and 1.1m in the tower itself. It is possible that the stair-doorway in the SE re-entrant of the tower was intended to be an external one, and that the S front, on its present alignment, represents a change of plan, but the stylistic character of both

parts, and their identical masons' marks, indicate that only a short space of time can have intervened. The tower and main block are ashlar-fronted, whereas the rear wall and the E gable, which was probably extensively rebuilt in 1690,[5] are of rubble.

The tower rises through four storeys above the pend, the uppermost being the bell-chamber, and most of its windows have rounded arrises, although a small ground-floor opening and the much-renewed third-floor one have quirked edge-rolls. The barrel-vaulted pend has an inner arch, rebated for two-leaf doors, 2.2m from the street-frontage, and a wide relieving-arch in the E wall. It was extended in 1677, with a shallower vault, through the ground floor of the added N wing. Over the entry to the pend there is a panel bearing the inscription: SLB / PATRIAE / ET POSTERIS / 1591 ('S(ir) L(ewis) B(ellenden), For Native Land and Posterity'), set between an index hand and three conventional flowers in the angles. The window immediately above has a lintel which was moved from the main block in 1875[6] and is carved with a shield bearing the burgh crest, a stag's head erased with a cross between the tines. A vertical sundial below the second-floor window was removed some time before 1936.[7] An ogival-roofed clock projects on a cantilevered platform reached from the bell-chamber and supported on long double-curved iron brackets of about 1820. The present clock-casing is dated 1884 as is the mechanism, by James Ritchie and Son, which is housed in the belfry, but the clock replaces an 'orlech' or 'knock', dating from the 17th century.[8]

At the SE and SW angles of the bell-chamber there are angle-rounds, with cable-mouldings in the highest courses of corbelling. These turrets and the bell-chamber are equipped

Canongate Tolbooth (No.11) from SE, c.1900 (ED/9478)

51

with quatrefoil and plain gun-ports, presumably ornamental in function, and they have conical slated roofs which were originally laid with oak shingles.[9] The spire, which was also shingled, has four small timber lucarnes at the base. The E wing of the tower was originally gabled, and the crow-steps of the N half-gable remain, while a cavetto skewputt from the former S half survives at the third stage above the entrance-doorway. The small lean-to room above this level probably dates from 1698, when a stair to the bell-chamber was constructed in this area (*infra*). The main newel-stair, immediately to the N, had a rectangular cap-house which is partly preserved at the E wall-head of the tower and appears also to have been an addition.[10]

The original appearance of the main block is shown in Gordon of Rothiemay's map of 1647. A forestair rose at right angles to a door in the SE re-entrant of the tower; the lowest floor was lit by four windows and had two entrances; the principal or first floor, which was defined by a string-course, had five windows, the easternmost being an oriel; and the attic was lit by four triangular-pedimented dormer-windows.

Externally, the 1875 restoration of the upper levels involved the creation of a new steeply-pitched roof, a corbelled parapet and four pedimented dormers in place of three hipped ones. The large first-floor windows were extensively renewed at the same period, although early photographs show that the double-saw-tooth frame and the roll-moulded daylight of the oriel, and the broad hollow chamfers of the other windows, reproduce their original forms. Between the two central windows there is a moulded frame containing a panel (renewed in metal) with the arms and motto of the burgh and the date 1128, the foundation-date of Holyrood Abbey. The pediment above the frame has thistle-shaped finials and contains a crown above the inscription: I(ACOBUS) R(EX) 6 IVSTICIA ET / PIETAS VALIDE / SVNT PRINCIPIS ARCES ('Justice and piety are truly the bulwarks of a prince'). The forestair now rises along the S wall to a doorway whose chamfered jambs have been heavily renewed but retain some early sharpening-marks. At ground-floor level a pedimented porch of early 19th-century date below the oriel window, and a doorway at the E end, were replaced in 1875 by an archway for the 'fire engine station', and this in turn by a segmental-headed doorway in 1954. The two windows and adjacent doorway at the W end probably occupy original positions, but have been renewed.

None of the openings in the back wall is original, but the W jamb of a tall blocked opening is visible E of the first-floor E window, and the relieving-arch of a former doorway survives above the ground-floor E window. The E gable-wall, which was at first a mutual wall with the adjacent property, contains no original openings, but there is a blocked one at the centre at ground-level. The mural monument of Lord Provost George Drummond (d.1766) is built into this wall, and the reredos monument of the economist Adam Smith (d.1790) is set against the N wall.

Internally, except for a vaulted cell in the S part of the tower, the ground floor has been modernised. A subterranean cellar underlies the W end of the main block and is lit by a small grated window at street-level. An excavation in this area revealed remains of a shallow, stone-built drain.[11] The first-floor entrance-doorway opens into a small lobby, from which the council-room and the newel-stair to the upper levels of the tower are both entered. The stair-doorway bears an index hand and the inscribed legend ESTO FIDUS ('Be faithful') on the stone above the lintel. The door itself is nail-studded and retains a wrought-iron risp and escutcheon plate. The attic floor of the main block was removed in 1875 to form a heightened first-floor room whose inserted W gallery has itself subsequently been removed. The pine panelling in this main hall, which was installed in 1954, came from demolished houses in the area, and the 18th-century fireplace with elaborate plaster overmantel, concealed behind modern panelling in the E wall, came from Craig's Close. The upper rooms in the adjacent house, which are entered from the tower, contain a poorly-preserved early 17th-century ceiling with

B. detail of plan of Edinburgh by Gordon of Rothiemay, 1647 (C 48619)

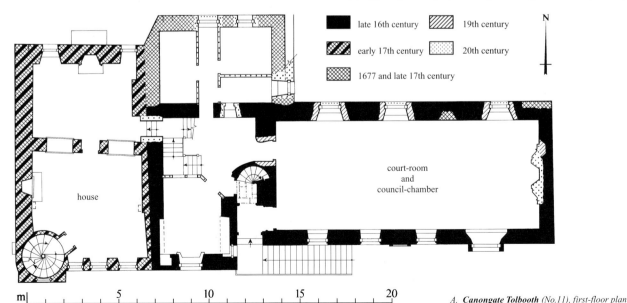

■ late 16th century		▨ 19th century	
▨ early 17th century		▨ 20th century	
▨ 1677 and late 17th century			

N

*A. **Canongate Tolbooth** (No.11), first-floor plan*

painted beams, and fireplaces of 18th-century character.

With the exception of the bell-chamber, the main rooms in the tower, which contained prison-accommodation, have also been modernised. In 1698 Edinburgh town council ordered 'that a trap stair be made throw the two studies at the tolbooth yeat (entrance) for ringing the bells that the prison may not therby be troubled or endangered'.[12] This appears to refer to the small rooms in the two storeys above the main entrance, and these rooms, with an upper storey which was probably added at this time (*supra*), retain traces of the newel-stair that was then inserted. The spire and bell-chamber retain early timbers in the roof-structure and the two superimposed bell-frames. The larger of the two bells, measuring 1.11m in diameter and 0.86m in height, was recast in 1847. The smaller one, 0.58m in diameter and 0.51m in height, bears the inscription: IAN BVRGERHVYS ME FECIT SOLI DEO GLORIA 1608 ('Jan Burgerhuys made me. Glory to God alone').

HISTORY

The burgh of Canongate was originally dependent on the abbey of Holyrood, by a grant from the founder, David I (d.1153).[13] The earlier tolbooth, which probably occupied the same site, was referred to in 1477 and was repaired in 1572-4.[14] Plans for funding the building of the existing structure were in hand even before Canongate's erection in 1587 into a burgh of regality under Sir Lewis Bellenden, the justice-clerk. In 1590 Sir Lewis and the burgh council represented to the Privy Council (of which he was a member) that 'the hous of justice, uthirwayes callit the tolbuith of the Cannogait, is altogidder becum ruynous', and that they had begun a sufficient house 'with strong wardis', which was 'grite and sumptuus'. A tax of 2,000 merks was granted, to be levied equally on the burgh and the associated barony of Broughton, and the burgh and barony courts continued to be held in the tolbooth until the 19th century.[15] The superiority was acquired by the City of Edinburgh in 1639, and Canongate was finally amalgamated with the city in 1856.[16]

The wing to the N of the tower was added in 1677, and throughout the late 17th and 18th centuries repairs of varying extent were undertaken. Specific mention was made of repairs to the stair in 1678, to windows and roof in 1689, to the gable-wall 'lately fallen' in 1690, to the area around the caphouse on the N side in 1694, to the stair, chimney-heads, hearths in the 'woman house', toilets, roof-coverings, belfry trap-stair, and the causeway of the close in 1698.[17]

At first the tower alone served as the prison, but by 1689 it appears that part of the top floor of the main block housed female prisoners.[18] As described in 1837, the prison-accommodation was spread through eight heated rooms, one 'large' and the others 'small'. By this period, its use was confined to debtors and, after a period of disuse, the building was re-opened as a debtors' prison for the whole of Edinburgh in 1842, continuing as such until 1848.[19]

After the end of the burgh's separate status in 1856 parts of the building continued to serve local government functions, and the ground floor housed a police station and the local fire engine. The main hall became a literary institute, with a library in adjacent rooms, and a gallery was installed in the hall in 1908. The tolbooth was adapted by A G Forgie, city architect, in 1952-4, for exhibition use by Edinburgh City Museums, and in 1989 the Peoples' Story Museum was opened.

A. **Canongate Tolbooth** (*No.11*)   (B 24821)
   bell-frame

B. *view from SW by Storer, 1820*   (C 62956)

C. *view from SW*   (B 39269)

12 CERES WEIGH-HOUSE
Fife
NO 4002 1153

Situated on the W side of the High Street, the Weigh House stands on ground which falls steeply to the E bank of Ceres Burn, allowing the construction at the rear of an additional basement storey. The building is only one bay in length, but the N gable, which abuts the Inn, may have been rebuilt. Set against the S gable, and stepped down from it, there is a single-storey cottage with a re-used door-lintel inscribed '17 AB MB 10'. The basement of the weigh-house, which intercommunicates with this cottage, was originally used as a prison, and the rear wall has a small window with iron bars.

The building is constructed of rubble with dressed margins, and measures some 3.7m across its main front by 6.9m. Its roof is slated and it has rebuilt gable chimney-stacks. Although simple in form, it has scrolled skewputts to its S gable and a carved panel over the doorway. This is inscribed: GOD BLESS THE JUST, and is carved with a set of scales having a weight on one side and a bale on the other. Fixed to the front wall to the N of the doorway there is a pair of jougs.

The skewputts of the S gable are matched by similar skewputts to the N gable of the Inn, which maintains the same wall-height. It is possible that the weigh-house and the Inn originally formed a single building. The weigh-house may be ascribed to the early 18th century, although Ceres was made a burgh of barony for the Hopes of Craighall in 1620.[1]

B. carved panel (B 47699)

A. Ceres Weigh-house (No.12) from SE (B 39393)

13 CLACKMANNAN TOLBOOTH
Clackmannan
NS 9111 9189

The surviving remains of the tolbooth, which stand on an island site at the W end of Main Street, consist of the W bell-tower and the adjacent gable-wall of the two-storeyed main block. The walls are constructed of sandstone rubble and the gable has crowsteps and off-set quoins, while the quoins of the tower are channelled. The main block measured 5.8m in width and was probably about 16m in length, while the tower, which carries an ogival slated spire, is 2.7m wide and projects 2.2m from the gable. The detail of the building suggests a late 17th-century date and the spire is similar to that of the old parish church at Alloa.[1]

HISTORY

Until 1592 no provision was made for a tolbooth at Clackmannan, the sheriff having been 'compellit to hald courts opinlie at the mercat croce ... and to keep in ward the transgressouris and malefactors within his dwelling hous'. In that year Parliament ordered 'ane tolbuith to be biggit ... upoun the commoun hie street thairof be wast [west of] the croce where the samyn may maist commodiouslie serve and be best sparit'.[2] In 1765 Sir Lawrence Dundas gifted a new bell to the burgh, and a new clock was donated in 1865.[3] By 1792 the tolbooth was described as 'a heap of ruins', although courts and elections were still held there, and in 1822 it was abandoned, only the bell-tower being retained.[4]

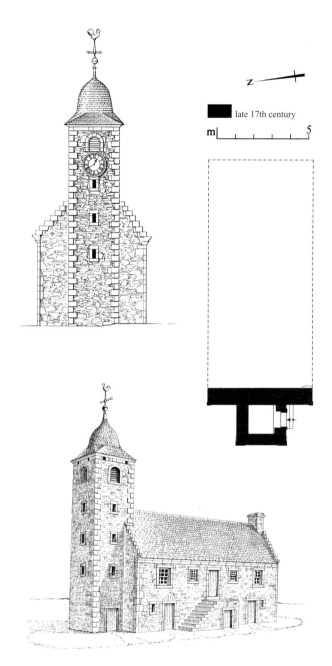

late 17th century

m |_____|_____|_____|_____|_____| 5

*A. **Clackmannan Tolbooth** (No.13)*   *(B 39156)*
    tolbooth and mercat cross from W

B. W elevation, ground-plan and conjectural reconstruction

MERCAT CROSS

Immediately SW of the tolbooth there stands the mercat cross, whose shaft is decorated with the Bruce arms, having been donated by Sir Henry Bruce in the 17th century. The ball-finial and steps have been renewed, but the lower part of the shaft still shows wear, possibly caused by prisoners' chains. In 1833 the ancient 'stone of Manau' (which gave its name to Clackmannan), a massive tapered block with round capstone, was moved to its present site S of the tolbooth.[5]

14   COUPAR ANGUS STEEPLE
Perthshire and Kinross
NO 2223 3990

This six-storeyed building is a conspicuous landmark on the W side of Queen Street to the S of the town centre. It is believed to occupy the site of the prison of the regality of Coupar Angus, held originally by the Cistercian abbey and granted in 1607 to the ancestor of the Lords Balmerino. While there are some areas of later infilling, the steeple remains largely unaltered from the time of its construction in 1762.[1] Until the middle of the 19th century the ground floor was used as an occasional prison, and it is possible that local courts were also held in the steeple.[2]

Constructed of red-brown sandstone rubble with dressed margins, the steeple measures 6.3m square on plan and is some 24m in overall height. There are pronounced set-backs at the second and fourth floors, and the slated spire has four faces of convex profile, each containing a small louvred belfry-opening. At the fifth floor each face of the steeple has two windows, each comprising a roundel above a round-headed light and set within a projecting surround, and clock-faces are placed between these windows in the N and S walls.

In the SE angle there is a newel-stair which gives access to all floors, and a vaulted cell with a blocked fireplace occupies the W half of the ground floor. The internal stone wall enclosing this 'small dark cell' on the E was built about 1828 to replace a timber partition.[3] The clock was installed in 1865, and the bell, which is 0.68m in diameter, was donated by the Earl of Moray in 1767 and cast by John Milne and Son, Edinburgh.[4]

A. *Coupar Angus Steeple (No.14) and abbey from S, c.1850*   (B 14995)

B. view from S (B 58264)
C. S elevation and plans

B

C

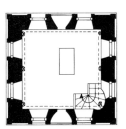

clock stage

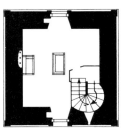

first floor

cell

ground floor

N

■ 1762

▒ 19th century and later

m |___|___|___|___|___| 5

15 CRAIL TOLBOOTH
Fife
NO 6131 0777

58A

Crail Tolbooth is situated on an island site at the SW end of Marketgate, which originally formed a broad market-place. The rectangular main block, 11.8m in length by 7.9m, is two-storeyed and has a gabled and slated roof. The steeple, situated at the SW end, is 6.2m square and has five storeys, with a distinctive pagoda-like spire 18.3m in overall height.

Although a date of 1517 has been claimed for the rubble-built lower portion of the steeple, this part of the building may equally correspond with the 'bigging off ane towbuth' ordered by the burgh council in 1598.[1] To supplement local funds the council applied in 1607 for assistance from the Convention of Royal Burghs.[2] An armorial panel dated 160[-], now built into the NW wall of the main block, may mark the completion of a substantial portion of the building.[3]

Minor alterations were carried out in the mid 18th century, including the insertion of a doorway in the SE front. This was subsequently obstructed by a forestair and reduced to a window, but it retains a lintel inscribed 1754. In 1776 the Council approved the repairing of the spire 'either by wright or mason work'.[4] This involved the insertion of ocular windows at the third stage of the steeple, and the rebuilding in sandstone ashlar of the upper two storeys, which are slightly intaken. The

existing slated spire with its dormer belfry-openings was probably built at the same time.

The main block itself, which had become 'old and ruinous' and was of 'limited demensions', was extensively rebuilt in ashlar in 1814-15, the former date being inscribed on its NE gable.[5] The windows, which have off-set margins, are disposed symmetrically, but those at first-floor level are markedly larger than those below. The SE one in the NE wall has been blocked, probably following litigation with a neighbouring householder which delayed the rebuilding.[6] The council-chamber, which occupies the whole of the first floor, has a coombed ceiling and a SW gallery supported on cast-iron columns. In the NE wall there is a blocked fireplace with a simple moulded surround.

Although the work carried out in 1776 and 1814 removed much of the early structure, a surviving slit-window between first and second floors at the NE end of the NW face of the steeple may indicate the position of an original staircase. At ground-floor level there has been access from the N angle of the steeple to the main block, at least since 1814, and the original building probably had a doorway in this position.

In 1866 consideration was given to raising the height of the

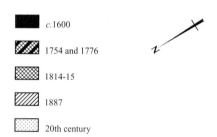

- ■ *c.*1600
- ▨ 1754 and 1776
- ▧ 1814-15
- ▨ 1887
- ▨ 20th century

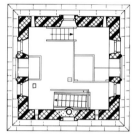

clock stage

Crail Tolbooth (No.15)
plans and SW elevation

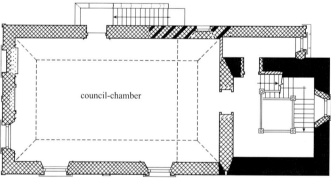

council-chamber

first floor

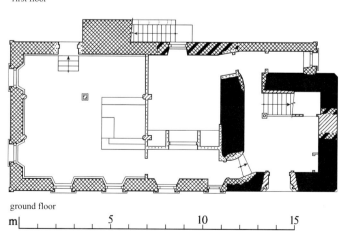

ground floor

m | 5 | 10 | 15

*A. **Crail Tolbooth** (No.15) from W*   (B 39405)

steeple to make the faces of the new clock more visible, but
'the Council did not feel warranted in expending such a sum
[£180]'.[7] A local architect, John Currie of Elie, was employed
in 1887 on alterations which included building a new NW
doorway in the steeple and installing a large staircase in its
lower storeys. Previously these had been used as cells.[8]
Modern fitting out of the ground floor as a library has
involved alterations including the insertion of a doorway in the
NE end of the SE wall, and a fireplace in the NE wall has been
blocked.

The steeple houses a fine Flemish bell which in 1702 was
removed from the parish church in exchange for the smaller
town bell of 1614, because of the more central position of the
tolbooth.[9] It measures 0.66m in diameter and is inscribed: IC
BEN GHEGOTEN INT IAER ONS HEEREN MCCCCCXX
('I was cast in the year of our Lord 1520'), between borders of
scrolled decoration. Beneath the inscription there are three
medallions, one bearing the arms of Mechelen (Belgium),
where the bell was probably cast by Willem van den Ghein.
The others show the Saviour as a seated child holding a cross,
and the Virgin and Child, an appropriate subject for a bell
which originally hung in a church dedicated to St Mary.[10]

A 12th-century scalloped capital and base are built into a
lean-to annexe added to the SE wall of the steeple in 1814-15,
at a time when the nearby parish church was itself undergoing
repairs.[11] There is a plain angular sundial at the E angle of the
tower.

B. ornament on bell (scale, 1:7.5)

C. detail of bell   (B 58219)

16 CROMARTY COURT-HOUSE
Highland
NH 7898 6739

This court-house,[1] which dates from 1773 and was evidently designed to serve both county and burgh, stands within an enclosed courtyard mid-way along the S side of Church Street, a short distance to the W of the foot of The Paye. Described in 1845 as 'a neat substantial edifice'[2] and recently restored as a museum, it comprises a two-storeyed main block whose five-bay principal (NE) front is dominated by a central projecting

*A. **Cromarty Court-house** (No.16)*
NE elevation and plans

B. view from NE (B 57181)

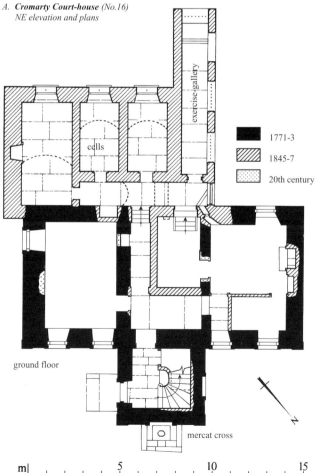

cells

exercise-gallery

■ 1771-3
▨ 1845-7
▧ 20th century

ground floor

mercat cross

m   5   10   15

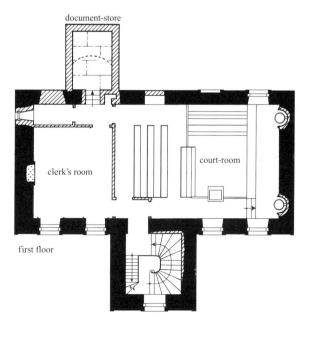

document-store

clerk's room

court-room

first floor

A. **Cromarty Court-house** (No.16), court-room   (C 4056)   C. cell   (C 4062)

B. cell-block and exercise-gallery from W   (C 4050)   D. exercise-gallery   (C 4055)

stair-tower surmounted by an octagonal clock-stage and cupola. Attached to the rear wall there is a single-storeyed L-plan range dating from 1845-7, which contains three prison-cells and an arcaded exercise-gallery.

The main block of the court-house measures 15.4m from NW to SE by 7.6m over walls about 1m in average thickness. The tower measures 4.8m by 4.1m over 0.8m walls, while the prison extension measures 11.6m by 7m, with a short projecting gallery-wing at the SW angle. The building is constructed mainly of harled rubble, but the dressed margins, the drum of the clock-tower, and the rear extension are built of coursed red sandstone. The slated roofs of the main block and extension are gable-ended with plain copes, and the cupola was originally lead-covered.

The quoins of the main elevation and the tower are banded to a height of just over 2m, above which they are reduced to plain off-set margins like those of the windows and doorways. In the symmetrical fenestration, the ground-floor windows are square whereas the large first-floor ones are semicircular-headed, as are the SE doorway and matching blind openings in the tower. At the third stage of the tower there is a blind

tripartite lunette. Four obelisks are set at the angles of the tower, below the octagonal clock-stage which has a dial in the NE face and louvred oculi to the sides and rear. Panelled chimney-stacks are set on both gables, but that on the rear wall of the main building serves the prison-block, as does another on its own SE gable.

The cells in the prison-block are lit by narrow oblong iron-barred windows in the rear (SW) wall. The exercise-gallery is slab-ceiled and three of the four main openings, which in the NW wall are segmental-headed, also retain iron grilles.

The interior survives substantially as remodelled and extended in the mid-1840s. The stair-lobby in the tower opens into an inner lobby giving access to two principal rooms in the ends of the ground storey, both of which have been modernised and re-decorated. In the original arrangement, the small central room was used to house prisoners, and the others were used by the jailer, who was also 'keeper of the County Road Tools'.[3] By 1836, one of the larger rooms housed debtors and the other criminals, and the small room was a cell 'used chiefly for drunken men'.[4] It was altered in 1845-7 by the creation of doorways and a transverse corridor giving

A. *Cromarty Court-house (No.16), bell* (C 4077)

access to the prison-block. The larger rooms were again used by the jailer, and the NW one, although sub-divided, retains a fireplace with basket-grate and cast-iron oven-range.

An open-well stone stair rises within the tower to the first floor. The court-room, as re-fitted in the 1840s, occupies about two-thirds of this storey, measuring 9m in length and retaining most of its furnishings: at the NW end a raised bench for the sheriff, heated by cast-iron stoves set in flanking mural niches; in the centre, boxes for the accused, jury and witnesses; and at the lower end, three rows of public benches entered from the box-porch in the E corner. The SE end of this floor is taken up by the former clerk's room and a corridor on the SW, which gives access to a document-store within the roof-space of the prison-block. It has a plated iron door, and hooks set into the segmental vault allowed documents to be suspended, reducing the risks of dampness and rodent-damage.

The prison-block of 1845-7 contains three segmentally-vaulted and slab-floored cells linked by a vaulted corridor, which stands slightly above the ground-level of the main block and extends NW to the entrance of the exercise-gallery. At the angle of the corridor and gallery a small squint with splayed reveals opens from the NW room in the main block. Originally equipped with slab beds, one of the two smaller criminal cells retains a curved wooden corner seat. The easternmost and largest of the cells, which has a fireplace, was designed for debtors and used as a day-room. All three cells have studded, metal-plated doors.

The 1845-7 works included the introduction into the court-house and prison of a heating- and ventilation-system, which was ducted through flues and vents from a stove on the NE side of the prison corridor, and controlled from a brazier within a mural chamber in the first-floor corridor, NW of the entrance to the document-store.

The clock-mechanism in the tower bears a plate recording that it was made by John Ross of Tain in 1782, and it was restored in 1990. The bell above, complete with its wooden stock and wheel, measures 0.45m in height and 0.50m in diameter. It bears an ornate cross and the inscription: S DIMAS CARRACA AN(N)O D(OMIN)I 1771, and was probably a ship's bell from a Spanish carrack or trading-vessel named 'St Damasus'.

A mercat cross, evidently re-assembled from a number of fragments, stands on a simple stepped base immediately in front of the clock-tower. Its uppermost section, comprising a stubby cross-finial and a cubical capital bearing a lozenge pattern, may in part be of medieval origin, whilst the main shaft, which is made up of three pieces of varying profile,[5] is

B. *clock-mechanism* (C 4073)

probably of 17th- and 18th-century date. The cross bears the dates 1378[6] and 177(?3/8) and the initials G R for George Ross, the builder of the court-house, who was also responsible for the transfer of the cross from the old tolbooth.

HISTORY
Cromarty was a royal burgh as early as the 13th century, but was reduced to the status of burgh of barony in 1685.[7] Early courts were held at the castle or the court hill, but there was also a tolbooth, which stood on the E side of the Causeway, close to Clunes House. The new court-house was one of the developments initiated in the burgh in the 1770s by the vigorous owner of the forfeited Cromarty estate, George Ross.

The building of the court-house commenced some time after July 1771, in accordance with plans and a £350 estimate forwarded to the Commissioners of Forfeited Estates by the sheriff-depute, Hugh Rose of Kilravock.[8] By June 1772 Ross was reported to have begun the building 'some time ago', and by mid-February 1773 it was described as 'almost finished'. Payment of a grant of £350 was authorised by the commissioners in July 1773, when Ross was claiming an actual final cost of between £400 and £500.[9]

First advertised in 1843, work on the prison extension, together with the building of the perimeter-wall and courtyard, was begun in 1845 and the cells were authorised for use in 1847, the architect for these operations being Thomas Brown.[10] The ground floor of the main block was converted into a suite of rooms for the jail-keeper, with a small bathroom and a lock-up cell for vagrants. Never fully utilised and expensive to maintain, the prison was closed in 1872, to be used as a lock-up by the police and later still by naval authorities.

17 CULLEN TOWN HALL
Aberdeenshire

NJ 5128 6711

The new town of Cullen was begun in 1821 to replace the old burgh situated near Cullen House, 0.9km to the SW. The town hall, which was built in 1822-3 at the expense of the Seafield estate, occupies a prominent corner-site on the upper (E) side of the large central square. It forms part of a complex which originally included a council-room, assembly-room, post-office, inn and stables. In common with many of the buildings in the town it was designed by the Elgin architect, William Robertson, but it was given special emphasis by its sophisticated architectural details.

The building is two-storeyed and of L-plan, with a three-bay quadrant at the W angle. A rectangular outshot projects to the NE in the re-entrant angle. The NE wing measures 42m along its principal front and is 10.4m in width, while the SE wing is 23m in length, and a detached former stable-block continues its line to the SE. The NW and SW fronts are treated as five-bay frontages, with central doorways and projecting end-bays, while three of the four additional bays of the NW front retain matching openings. Whereas the ground-floor openings are segmental-headed, the first-floor windows are square-headed and those of the angle-quadrant and the projecting bays are recessed within round-headed arches. The others have entablatures, which in the SW front retain their original

consoles.[1] The angle-quadrant, which is recessed between the end-bays of the adjacent wings, is approached by a flight of steps and now contains three ground-floor doorways. Built into the parapet above there is an armorial panel bearing the Seafield arms, which is believed to have been re-used from a gateway at Cullen House.[2]

The building is mainly constructed of harled rubble, which in the building-contract was specified 'on the two principal fronts to be washed over the colour of the freestone'.[3] The whole of the angle-quadrant, the first-floor sill-course and the margins are of freestone, as specified: 'the bow upon the corner to be wholly of freestone polished, as also the four recesses in the projections, the corners of these projections also'. The chimneypieces in the main rooms were to be 'of Turin stone ... of neat patterns & well polished'. The walls of the vestibule and the inn lobby and passages were 'to be finished, lined & coloured in imitation of freestone'. Timber from Abernethy forest was to be used generally, with American or Norwegian red pine for the windows and American yellow pine for the doors and shutters.[4]

The most notable feature of the interior is the use of two circular spaces at the junction of the wings. The outer one, which is reflected in the external quadrant, is 7m in diameter

*A. **Cullen Town Hall** (No.17) from W*   *(B 39703)*

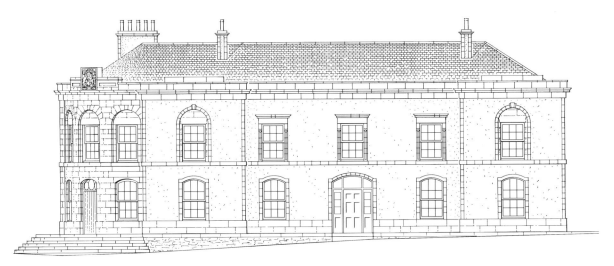

B. SW elevation

and houses a vestibule at ground-floor level and the council-chamber above. The vestibule gives access to the circular stair-hall, which retains a neo-classical statue in a niche at the half-landing, although the stair itself has been renewed. Part of the large room to the NE at first-floor level is believed to have been used as a court-room, while the equivalent room on the ground floor was an assembly-room, which originally had a musicians' gallery. [5] The interior has undergone extensive alterations, and many of the rooms have been divided by modern partitions. The hotel in the SE wing retains much of its original layout, and here and in the council-chamber there are panelled dados and shutters, doors with reeded architraves, and moulded cornices.

64A
64B

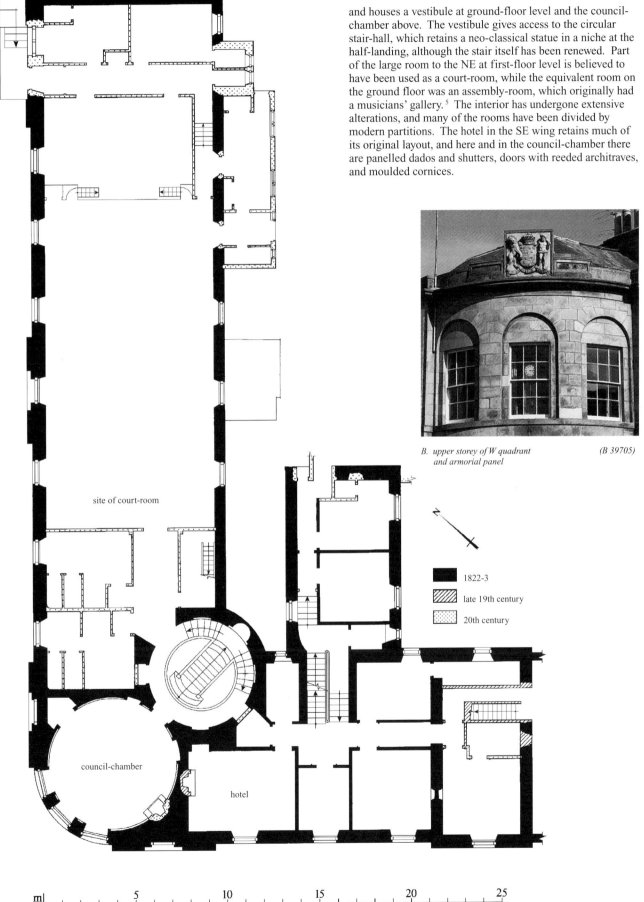

site of court-room

council-chamber

hotel

B. *upper storey of W quadrant and armorial panel*

(B 39705)

■ 1822-3

▨ late 19th century

▦ 20th century

m| 5   10   15   20   25

A. **Cullen Town Hall** *(No.17), ground-plan*

A. **Cullen Town Hall** *(No.17), council-chamber*   *(C 4081)*   B. *stair-hall*   *(C 4083)*

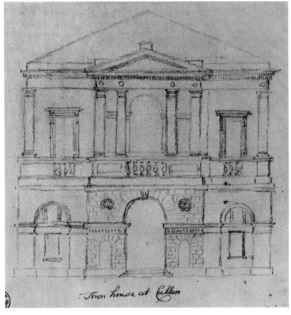

C. *proposed town-house by Robert Adam*   *(Soane Museum)*   D. *proposed town hall by James Playfair, 1788*   *(BND/7/7)*

HISTORY

Burgh courts were held in the tolbooth of Old Cullen in 1614, but a new building was begun in 1618, and the Convention of Royal Burghs was still demanding its completion or repair in 1624. [6] The roof was re-slated and other repairs were carried out in 1719, when a bell weighing 70kg was obtained from the Old Aberdeen founder, Albert Gely. [7] Council minutes for 1767, which report the insufficiency of the building's slender walls and decayed woodwork for a prison, describe it as having two ground-floor vaults, one a meal-house and the other a criminal prison. One of the upper rooms was used as a guard-room and the other as a debtors' prison. [8]

Several designs for the replacement of this building were procured in the late 18th century from architects who were engaged at Cullen House. An undated elevation by Robert Adam shows a three-bay façade with a pedimented centrepiece containing a round-arched doorway and a similar first-floor window framed by paired pillars. [9] In 1788 James Playfair produced drawings for a two-storeyed hip-roofed 'town hall', with a three-bay frontage having round-headed recessed openings. The ground storey was to contain a school-room in one side and a guard-room and debtors' prison in the other,

with a vaulted 'cell for criminals', partly housed in a projection at the rear, behind the central stair. On the upper floor there was to be a hall in one end, with a vaulted record-room behind the stair, while the other end was to form a two-room dwelling. [10] There is also documentary reference to a 'plan and estimate from Mr [?John] Baxter for a Church and Town House at Cullen'. [11]

The earliest plan for the new town, on paper watermarked '1811', shows a detached building in the NE part of the square, with the explanation 'the single building may be the Town House'. An expanded plan of 1817 by Peter Brown retains this caption, while showing a church in that position, but the stable-court attached to the inn is also indicated. [12] The contract of 1822 was for 'a new Town House, Inn, Post Office and relative accommodations ... conform to a plan, elevation and measurements designed ... by William Robertson Architect'. It included detailed specifications and stipulated that work was to be completed by Midsummer 1823. [13] The cost is said to have been £3,000. [14] In addition to 'an elegant ball-room' measuring 13.3m by 7m, and a 'commodious court-room, in which are held the sheriff and justice of peace courts', the building included three lock-up cells. [15]

18 CULROSS TOWN-HOUSE
Fife
NS 9857 8591

The town-house[1] stands at the NE side of Sandhaven, at the foot of the hill on which much of the burgh is built and facing the shore of the Forth across an open green. It comprises two storeys and a garret and has a steeply-pitched slated roof, with a crow-stepped W gable and straight skews to the E. The rectangular main block measures some 16m from E to W by 7.8m and the S front is faced with sandstone ashlar, the remainder being of coursed or random rubble. Its five-bay S front is distinguished by a three-stage central steeple added in 1783, and a double forestair of the same period, but the original building was probably erected in 1626.[2] It was renovated for the burgh by Ian G Lindsay and Partners in 1957-9[3] and is now maintained by the National Trust for Scotland. A tolbooth already existed in Culross by 1588, but its site is not known.[4]

The windows of the S front are disposed slightly off-centre. The ground-floor openings have rounded arrises, while those at first-floor level have roll-and-hollow mouldings. The ground floor is entered by doorways at both ends of the S front. Their masonry is disrupted, particularly that to the W, which had formerly been contracted to a window, and their surrounds appear to have been renewed. The W doorway has an over-lintel, probably re-used in its present position, inscribed ANNO DOMINI 1626. The first-floor windows and

66A (margin note)

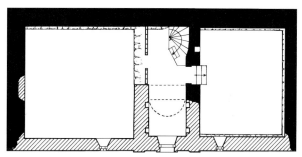

second floor

council-chamber   debtors' room

first floor

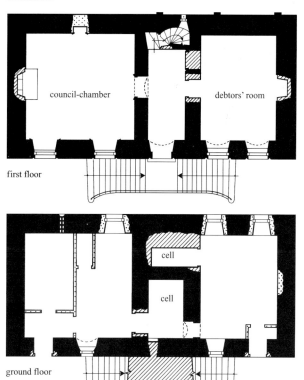

cell

cell

ground floor

■ early 17th century

▨ 1783

░ 19th century and later

m | 5 | 10 | 15

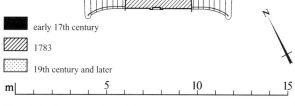

C. conjectural reconstruction and plans

*A. **Culross Town-house** (No.18) from SW*   (B 39164)

B. inscribed lintel in S wall   (B 39169)

A. **Culross Town-house** *(No.18), S elevation*

B. *first-floor vestibule* (C 23754)

C. *painted ceiling of first-floor E room* (C 23760)

D. *detail of painted ceiling* (C 23769)

E. *detail of painted ceiling* (C 23771)

A. **Culross Town-house** *(No.18), armorial of Sir George Bruce* (C 23766)

B. *painted armorial of King Charles I, 1637* (C 23764)

doorway appear to have been heightened, probably when the steeple and forestair were built, and the 1626 lintel may have been moved from an original position above the main doorway at this period. The stepped character of the stonework at the S wall-head suggests that there were originally dormer windows, which may have been removed when the steeple was built, and one dormer pediment, bearing the burgh seal, survives in re-use (*infra*).

The ashlar-built steeple, which is of more refined construction than the original block, is set slightly E of centre to correspond with the internal walls that support it. It has channelled angle-quoins rising to a fluted frieze and a bold cornice below the ogee-shaped roof. The lowest stage is marked by a round-headed S window with projecting springers and keystone, which is matched by similar belfry-openings below the cornice. In the S front, below the belfry-stage, there is a clock-face set in a circular recess.

The ground storey contains two large rooms and two smaller ones, set slightly to the E of centre. Until about the beginning of the 19th century one of the large rooms was used as a prison,[5] and the smaller rooms were presumably cells. The front one has an inserted doorway in its W wall, and a small window in its S wall has been blocked by the addition of the double forestair in 1783. The small cell to the N may originally have housed a straight stair to the vestibule above, where there is an original newel-stair.

Access to the centrally-placed main doorway is provided by the forestair. The first floor has two rooms divided by a narrow vestibule set slightly to the E of centre. Both rooms are now entered by doorways in the centre of the vestibule, but the E room had an earlier roll-moulded doorway to the N, which was blocked in the late 18th century. At this period the chimneypieces of both rooms were renewed and the walls of the council-room to the W were lined with raised and fielded panelling. Although the E room houses two inscribed panels (*infra*), it became 'the debtors' room', and in the early 19th century was also used for criminal prisoners.[6] Both rooms had original painted open-beam ceilings, although the surviving boards and beams from the W room have been re-set above the vestibule. They show a thin flowing arabesque pattern which is also found at Culross Palace and elsewhere. The ceiling of the E room has a unique pattern of repeated draped heads and cherubs' heads, stars and faceted rectangles.[7] To the rear of the vestibule there is a stone newel-

stair, partly contained in the thickness of the N wall and partly encroaching on the vestibule, which gives access to the garret.

The garret is laid out similarly, with two rooms, which are believed to have provided additional prison-accommodation,[8] flanking a slightly off-set vestibule. The only external openings are two small windows in the front wall, but a third below the steeple has been infilled. The side-walls of the vestibule support the steeple, whose rear wall is carried by a round-headed arch inscribed 1783. The roof-structure, which is largely intact, is of 17th-century type, with double-collared rafters having half-lapped joints and ashlared soles.

Above the fireplace of the first-floor E room there hangs a wooden panel painted with the arms of King Charles I, the date 1637 and the motto UNIONUM UNIO ('A union of unions'). Built into the same wall there is a stone panel bearing, within a heavy gadrooned margin, the date 1628 and the arms and name of Sir George Bruce, who died in 1625.[9] Another stone panel, built into the W wall of this room, records a benefaction to the burgh in 1721 by Sir George Preston of Valleyfield.[10] A damaged pediment, framed by raking volutes and showing a church and the inscription SIGILLVM BVRGI DE CV[LROSS] ('seal of the burgh of Culross'), is set into the W wall of the vestibule.[11]

The belfry contains a bell 0.58m in diameter, which is inscribed: THIS BELL IS FOR THE TOWN HOUSE OF CULROSS / GEORGE WATT FECET ST NINNANS EDIN(BU)R(GH) 1783.[12] The original clock-mechanism, which now stands in the garret vestibule, bears the maker's plate of Laurence Dalgleish, Edinburgh, 1783. A collection of weights and measures, including early 17th-century examples, is displayed in the E ground-floor room.

7

23A

6C, E

C. *pediment bearing burgh arms* (C 23768)

19 CUPAR BURGH CHAMBERS
Fife

NO 3755 1456

The Burgh Chambers occupy a prominent corner site to the E of the Cross, where Crossgate, St Catherine Street and Bonnygate meet opposite the re-erected mercat cross. It is a three-storeyed but relatively modest building of 1815-18, occupying the W end of a grand neo-classical terrace which forms the S side of St Catherine Street. This terrace also contains the County Buildings, the Sheriff Court and the Tontine Hotel, and was developed in the early 19th century to form the administrative and social centre of the town and county.

The principal feature of the building is the semicircular three-windowed bay overlooking the Cross, which is surmounted by a lead-covered dome carrying a tall thin octagonal belfry and cupola. The N elevation to St Catherine Street is of six uneven bays centred on a first-floor Venetian window.

The ground storey has always been occupied by shops, and the council-room is on the first floor, reached by a Roman Doric doorway and a straight flight of internal stairs. It is a double bow-ended room measuring 12.2m from E to W by 5.2m, and remains much as completed, save that the fireplace has been removed from the S wall. At the suggestion of the council, a musicians' gallery or orchestra, with a small retiring closet below, was installed at the E end, along with a safe in the S wall and an enriched cornice. [1]

After much negotiation the council secured access to the top floor by extending into part of the adjacent house to the E. [2] This floor was to be divided into two, the smaller E room being the town clerk's office with a safe, which was installed in a small outshot in the corridor. The larger W room was to be used for meetings and as a retiring-room when balls took place in the council-room. [3] It was subsequently offered on lease to the managers of the Library and is still lined with bookcases, although the town clerk's office and the library were subsequently moved to the guildry building in Castle Hill. [4]

HISTORY

The former tolbooth, which is mentioned in 1441, [5] occupied an island site now marked by the re-erected market cross, at the junction of Bonnygate and Crossgate. It was 'a quaint old-fashioned building of three flats, one of which was partially underground. The top-flat was used as a debtors' prison, the second as a public steel-yard, named, in consequence, the "Weigh-House," and the underground dungeon, then known as the "Black Hole" or "Iron House," served the purpose of a jail'. [6] The county gentlemen built an adjacent room about 1785, 'on a large scale, and in the modern taste ... for their use at head courts, for their accommodation and balls, etc.' [7] Two 17th-century armorial panels from the tolbooth, bearing the royal arms and those of the burgh, are built into the W wall of the former Cupar Academy in Castlehill.

Provost John Ferguson acquired extensive property to the E of the Cross in 1809 and proposed the building of a new street which would necessitate the removal of the tolbooth to improve the access. He laid before the council in 1810 'a Plan of the Improvements proposed by the removal of the old jail and the Town Council Room and other buildings attached to it', which was adopted. [8] A new county jail to the SE of the River Eden was designed by Gillespie Graham in 1810 and completed in 1813, with a contribution of £300 by the town council. [9] At the same time Ferguson commissioned from Graham designs for his proposed new street (St Catherine Street), including detailed plans of proposed County Rooms (now the County Buildings). [10]

In April 1815 the tolbooth was demolished 'under cloud of night', to the indignation of at least some of the council who claimed that the meeting which took this decision had been illegally called and that the hasty demolition had destroyed the building-materials. [11] This caused a fierce dispute between the council and Provost Ferguson, which was resolved by an agreement that 'a Council Room shall be built agreeable to Mr Hutchison's plan', with the town contributing £150 and Ferguson the balance of the cost, including the use of the remaining materials of the old council-house. Ferguson was also required 'to give the Town the first offer of the upper flatt above the Council Room'. [12] Robert Hutchison was later referred to as the contractor for building the house and stair. [13] The design may be based on Gillespie Graham's scheme of 1810, but the detail appears to be Hutchison's.

A belfry was proposed from the first, although in 1816 the roof was temporarily slated to allow for the plastering of the council-room. [14] The existing dome and belfry were built in 1819 by Thomas Middleton, [15] but the first meeting in the new council-room had been held in the previous year.

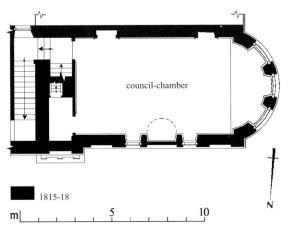

A. *Cupar Burgh Chambers (No.19), first-floor plan*

B. *view from NW*   *(B 58076)*

20   DALKEITH TOLBOOTH
Midlothian
NT 3332 6744

This two-storeyed building[1] stands on the E side of High Street, almost opposite the medieval parish church of St Nicholas and abutting the Cross Keys Hotel. It is rectangular on plan, measuring 16.3m by 6.5m, and is covered by a hipped and slated roof from which the chimney-stacks have been removed. The ashlar-built main (W) front has a central doorway and three bays of symmetrically-disposed windows to each side, but the ground-floor N window occupies the position of a former doorway.[2] The base-course is chamfered and there are rusticated angle-quoins and a moulded eaves-cornice. The S and E walls are of harled rubble. The building may be ascribed to the 17th century but it has undergone extensive later alterations.

The most distinctive feature of the main front is the doorway, which has a bolection-moulded surround and a pediment containing the arms of Scott of Buccleuch: on a bend a mullet between two crescents. Above the pediment there is a panel carved with two coronets above the initials E /

FB and C / MLB and the date 1648. The initials are those of Francis, 2nd Earl of Buccleuch, and his wife Margaret Leslie, and the panel is said to have been brought from the grounds of Dalkeith Palace in the late 18th or early 19th century.[3]

Internally the building is divided by a substantial cross-wall into a square S room and a larger rectangular N room on each floor. Against the N side of this wall a straight stair rises to the first-floor S room and continues with a dog-leg turn to the N room and a smaller room at the centre of the W front. While the moulded stone treads of its straight portion appear to be original, the wall abutting it to the N, and all the other internal walls with the exception of the cross-wall itself, appear to be additions to the original structure.

Beneath the S ground-floor room there is a flat-ceiled pit with earthen floor and rubble walls, some 2m square, known as the 'black hole'.[4] It is entered by a trap-door in the floor of the room above, which was previously used as a prison, as was the corresponding first-floor room. The main ground-floor room served as a weigh-house on market-days, and that at first-floor level as a court-room.[5] The interior of the building retains few early features, all fireplaces having been removed or blocked, and there have been various other modern alterations, notably to the openings of the rear (E) wall.

HISTORY
A tolbooth existed in Dalkeith in 1616,[6] and although the 1648 date-panel is apparently not *in situ*, the present building probably belongs to the second half of the 17th century. In 1759 it was considered 'to have been the private prison and court house of the Regality of Dalkeith and the property of the family of Buccleuch ... past all memory'.[7] The appearance of the main front suggests that extensive refacing has been undertaken, probably in the 19th century. In 1759 consideration was given to converting part of the tolbooth to a school,[8] but it continued to be used regularly as a jail until 1841.[9] From 1835 the tolbooth housed the meetings and library of the Dalkeith Scientific Association, and it came to be known as the 'Scientific Hall'.[10] In 1966 it was refurbished as a church hall by the Kirkcaldy architects Armstrong and Thomas.[11] In front of the building are stones marking the site of the burgh gibbet.

A. *Dalkeith Tolbooth (No.20), W elevation and ground-plan*

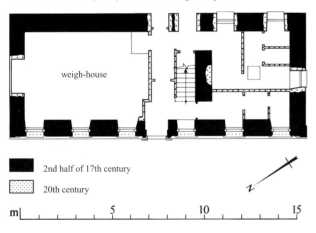

weigh-house

■ 2nd half of 17th century

▒ 20th century

m | 5 | 10 | 15

B. *view from W*   (B39172)

C. *pediment and armorial panel*   (B 39392)

21 DINGWALL TOWN-HOUSE
Highland
NH 5495 5876

This two-storeyed building stands on the N side of the High Street, its centrally-placed steeple surmounted by a distinctive timber clock-tower. The rubble-built steeple represents the core of the town-house begun in 1735, to which the clock-tower was added in 1773, but the dormered side-wings and the central balcony are work of 1902-5, to a design by W C Joass. The present length of the main (S) front is almost the same as the 19.4m of the original building, but the wings project about one metre beyond the original wall-line. [1]

The parapet of the steeple, which appears originally to have been crenellated, was constructed of 'hewn work finished with iron bars'. [2] It was later replaced with a timber parapet before the present stone one was added in 1902-5. The clock-tower of 1773 was rebuilt in 1902-5, but preserves the original octagonal form.

Despite its altered appearance, the early form of the town-house can be reconstructed from old views and descriptions. While the ground floor of the main block originally housed a school-room and two shops, the base of the steeple was used as a 'pit' for prisoners. [3] This prison accommodation proved insufficient, however, and the entire ground floor was converted to a jail in 1782. [4] The first floor was reached by a projecting forestair at the centre of the main front, replaced by a double forestair in the late 19th century. The council-chamber, furnished with 'proper seats and benches', occupied the largest space on the first floor and measured 4.9m square. This floor also incorporated a lobby area beyond the entrance-doorway, a 'retiring room for the council or a quorum of them', and the chamber of the town clerk. [5]

The steeple contains a bell 0.54m in diameter, cast by Mears, London, in 1802, and another, 0.65m in diameter, cast by John Warner and Sons in 1906. The gable to Church Street incorporates a re-used panel inscribed '1730', and a small iron yett has been built into the wall beside the main entrance. [6] In front of the building stands the mercat cross, probably of 17th-century date, which consists of a chamfered stone shaft with a simple finial, decorated with incised geometric patterns.

HISTORY

Although some previous accounts suggest that the town-house may contain a 17th-century core, it was recorded in 1692 that Dingwall had no tolbooth. [7] In 1729 the town council agreed that the burgh was at 'a considerable loss for want of a town house and prison', and a site was obtained from Alexander Dingwall, burgess, who exchanged his tenement at the junction of the Kirk Street and the High Street for a 'sufficient house of common mason work consisting of three highland cupples and two standing gavels'. [8] A detailed description of the proposed building was presented to the Council in 1732, and plans were subsequently prepared by 'Mr Dowie, architect'. [9] Construction began in 1735 and was finally completed in 1745, the contractor being William MacNeill, a mason and member of the council. [10] In 1772 Major-General Scott gave £100 for the purchase of a town clock, and a clock-tower was added to the steeple in the following year, when John Boog, architect, Donald Morrison, wright, and Donald McNeil, mason, were sent to Forres 'to view the stiple, clock and bells there'. John Boog was paid one guinea to 'make a modell thence as a plan for the proposed operations'. [11]

In 1830 the jail was condemned as unfit to receive prisoners, who were to be sent to Tain, and some repairs were subsequently made. It was re-opened for criminal prisoners in 1835, but no application was made to legalise it for debtors, since the burgh had previously suffered heavy losses through their escape. In 1836 it was described as containing three 'rather large rooms', two of which were on the ground floor, and a small one for violent lunatics. [12] A small new prison was built outside the town in 1843-4. [13]

A. Dingwall Town-house (No.21) from SE, c.1880   (R M Bremner)

B. view from SE   (B 57178)

70

22 DUMBARTON COURT-HOUSE
Dumbarton and Clydebank
NS 3981 7535

The court-house, which is now occupied by Dumbarton Sheriff Court, is situated on the E side of Church Street, about 300m ENE of the site of the old tolbooth in High Street. When first built in 1824-5, to a design by James Gillespie Graham, it occupied a spacious enclosure at the NE edge of the burgh, and a prison by the same architect stood 55m to the E. The court-house was extended in 1862 with flanking wings designed by William Spence, and was further extended to the rear in 1895 and 1898. The prison was enlarged in 1840, but went out of use in 1883 and was demolished, except for the round-arched entrance-doorway, in 1973.[1]

21A

The original building is two-storeyed and rectangular, measuring 19.5m across the main (W) front by 11.4m, while the lower wings of 1862 extended the frontage to 42m. The main front is of three bays, with a pedimented and advanced centrepiece and projecting end-plinths which support paired Ionic pilasters at the upper level. Similar pilasters frame the centrepiece, and they carry a bold entablature and blocking-course within which is set the hipped roof. The ground storey is faced with channelled ashlar, and the round-arched central doorway is enclosed by a pedimented Doric portico. The rectangular ground-floor windows are plain, but those at the upper level have recessed aprons below moulded sill-courses. The flanking ones have tall consoles supporting entablatures, and the central window is set in a round-headed recess, with a blind roundel in the tympanum.

In the original arrangement of the ground floor, the vestibule opened into a stair to the S and an office used by the county in the NW angle. To the NE was the office of the sheriff-clerk, and to the SE that of the town clerk, separated by two document-stores.[2] These offices have been encroached on by a modern corridor, but they retain decorated cornices and tripartite windows with panelled architraves, and a barrel-vaulted store with a six-panelled iron door is entered from the NE room. The scale-and-plat stair, with its cast-iron balustrade, gives access to the first-floor court-room, which was originally shared by the burgh and county. This preserves its panel-fronted jury-box and a round-ended enclosure below the bench, whose front is flanked by timber Corinthian columns. At the S end, entered from the upper flight of the main stair, there is a gallery supported on Doric cast-iron pillars and with a decorative iron balustrade. Until 1862 the town council met in the room adjoining the court-room to the SE, but this has been much altered.

The added wings of 1862 have symmetrical three-bay W fronts in character with the original work. Their central round-arched doorways have pilastered surrounds, and the wall-heads are balustraded. The N wing was reserved for county and sheriff-court use, while the town council was allocated meeting- and committee-rooms and a town clerk's office in the S wing.[3] This area was extensively altered in the 1890s, when a large staircase was inserted.

HISTORY

The old tolbooth of 1642-5, which was demolished in 1832, stood on the N side of High Street on the site of an earlier building. It was three-storeyed, with a forestair to a round-arched doorway at the E end of the S front and an open belfry on the crow-stepped E gable.[4] Until 1794 there were separate rooms for council meetings and the sheriff court, but the demands of space for prisoners led the council to transfer their meetings to the court-room.[5]

By 1819 the tolbooth was insecure and beyond repair, and the town council requested financial assistance from the county for a new jail. After much negotiation it was agreed that the burgh would contribute £700 of an estimated cost of £3,500, and the value of the site and materials of the old building. In 1822 the Jail Committee considered alternative plans from Gillespie Graham, who strongly recommended the separation of the public buildings from the prison, and two years later his plans were adopted, with unspecified alterations by Robert Scott. The contractor was a local mason and councillor, Robert Campbell. The foundation-stone was laid with great ceremony in July 1824, and both buildings were completed in the following year.[6]

In 1861 the county authorities and government decided to enlarge the court-house, and sketch-plans by the Glasgow architect William Spence were found so acceptable that a proposed competition was cancelled. The town council agreed to vacate the original building, in return for equivalent accommodation in the new S wing.[7]

A. **Dumbarton** *(No.22), court-house from SW*   *(DB/179)*

B. prison from NE, 1969   *(DB/183)*

C. old tolbooth from SE   *(C 47325)*

71

23 DUMFRIES TOWN-HOUSE
Dumfries and Galloway
NX 9723 7611

11C
74A,C

The town-house or 'Midsteeple', which was built in 1705-8, occupies a prominent island site in the High Street, to the SW of Queensberry Square. Its S end-wall, which has a straight forestair to the first-floor main entrance, overlooks the former market-area. The N wall is abutted by two-storeyed properties which in the 19th century replaced a lower block of shops supporting on its flat roof the 16th-century mercat cross.[1]

The three-storeyed main block is rectangular on plan, measuring 11.8m from N to S by 7.5m, and a square steeple, 28m in height, extends the E front a further 4.2m to the N. The masonry is of red sandstone ashlar which was originally obtained from the town's quarry at Castledykes, but was extensively refaced in 1909. The roof is hipped and slated, and the spire is lead-covered.

The forestair of the S front, which incorporates a small ground-floor shop, has an elaborate wrought-iron balustrade or 'ravel' made by Patrick Sibbald, an Edinburgh smith, in 1709.[2] It comprises a series of panels, divided by thistle-shaped balusters and each containing two scrolled and floriated tendrils which have been much restored. The first-floor doorway, which has Ionic pilasters and a segmental pediment, bears the date 1707 on its lintel, but in its present form it dates from 1909. An earlier doorcase with thin pilasters and a plain
74A entablature appears in a drawing of 1828, shortly before the construction of the Doric portico that is a familiar feature of early views of the building.[3] The fenestration of the S and side walls is regular, with the windows of the upper storeys having projecting aprons and those at first-floor level also having moulded and lugged surrounds with cornices.[4] The ground storey, and the stepped quoins of the main block and steeple, are of channelled ashlar, and the upper storeys and parapet, as well as the stages of the steeple, are defined by moulded string-courses. Both the main block and the steeple

have stone parapets containing square openings which enclose pierced roundels set within crosses, and the wall-head parapet is continued as a decorative frieze round the steeple. The next three stages of the steeple contain respectively a round-headed window to the E, a series of oculi, and circular clock-faces within square moulded frames. The parapet encloses a square timber belfry with an ogee-capped lead-covered spire whose angles were originally crocketed.

The building has undergone several changes of use (*infra*), and for many years after 1866 it was occupied by shops and warehouses. The interior now contains one large room at each level, divided by modern partitions and preserving no early features. The ground storey of the steeple is entered by a doorway in the E wall, and the upper storeys by a forestair against the W wall which leads to a newel-stair in the SW angle. Direct access to the steeple from the main block was created in 1909 by inserted doorways at first- and second-floor levels.[5]

Set at the centre of the S front, at first- and second-floor levels, there are two carved panels.[6] The upper one contains a full armorial achievement bearing the royal arms of Scotland, with unicorn supporters. The lower panel shows the winged figure of St Michael, patron of the burgh, wearing a mitre-like head-dress and long robe and standing on a dragon, into whose mouth he thrusts the point of a crozier. These carvings are probably of mid 17th-century date, and two others built into the W wall in 1909 came from the nearby old prison of about 1579 (*infra*). One bears the initials H R and R MK, with a pair of shackles and a bow and arrow and the word BAILLIES, for Herbert Raining and Robert MacKinnell who held that office in the 1570s.[7] The other shows a shield bearing a chevron between three fleurs-de-lys, with the town's motto A LOR/ BURNE.[8] Also built into the S front there are the metal 'bed'

Dumfries Town-house (No.23) from S, c.1890

(DF/1780)

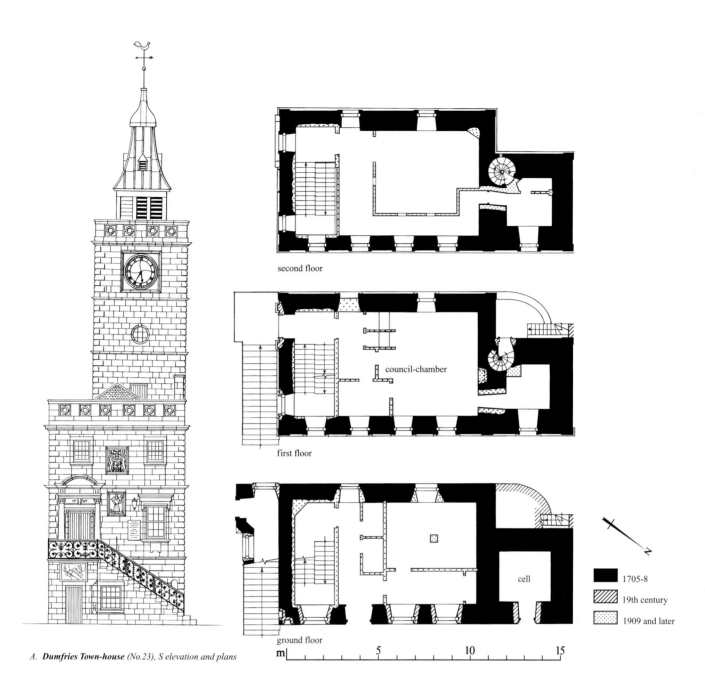

A. *Dumfries Town-house (No.23), S elevation and plans*

second floor

council-chamber

first floor

cell

ground floor

■ 1705-8

▨ 19th century

⊡ 1909 and later

m | 5 10 15

B. *royal armorial* (A 44452)

C. *panel showing* (A 44451)
St Michael

of a yard-measure, probably of about 1830,[9] and a cast-iron distance-plate of 1827.

The three bells in the belfry, of eight, five and three hundredweights, were cast by George Barclay of Edinburgh in 1708. The larger ones were recast in 1903 and 1901, but the original small bell, whose 'small and short' tone was the subject of initial complaints, survives in good condition.[10] It measures 0.62m in diameter and is inscribed: FOR THE TOWN OF DRUMFRIES 300 LIB WT ED(INBU)R(GH) 1708. When the bells were set up, there was insufficient room for the two smaller ones to be rung together, and the timberwork of the belfry was altered.[11] A projection in its N wall still accommodates the wheel of one of the bells. The original clock of 1708, which had four dials, was made by John Bancroft of Stockport, and some fragments of the mechanism remain in Dumfries Museum.[12]

HISTORY

The 'Old Tolbooth', situated on the E side of the High Street close to the site of the Midsteeple, was probably built in the last quarter of the 15th century. At the time of its rebuilding about 1719 it contained vaulted cellars in the basement, shops on the ground floor and a council-chamber and 'open prison' on the upper floors. In 1578-9 the Privy Council ordered the town to build 'ane sufficient prisoun-hous of three hous hicht' adjoining the tolbooth to the N. This 'pledge house', which was vaulted at two levels and incorporated the carved stones described above, remained in use until a new jail was built in 1807.[13]

In 1697 the burgh was granted a share of Scottish customs

A. *Dumfries Town-house* (No.23) from S by Johnson, 1828 (Dumfries Museum)

B. view from SE   (C 16724)

and foreign excise duties, and after pressure from the community over the council's conduct of the affair a sum of 20,000 merks (£1,111 sterling) was secured.[14] In 1703 a joint committee of the council and community was appointed to apply this sum in building the midsteeple, and its minute-book preserves a uniquely detailed account of the execution of a major civic building-project.[15]

After an unsuccesful attempt to secure the services of 'Mr James Smith, James Smith his nevoy[16] or any other Architect' in Edinburgh, a Liverpool 'masterbuilder' named John Moffat was employed 'to draw a scheme and modall of the designed fabrick'. Moffat produced his plans in April 1704, after viewing the steeple of Glasgow College as a possible model, but declined to undertake the contract. An offer from Bailie Kennan to erect the building on a reduced scale was refused, and in February 1705 a contract was made with Tobias Bachup of Alloa 'to construct the samen conform to the scheme drawn and the alterations of the dimensions which the committee had made'. In May 1705 it was agreed to lengthen the council-house from 9.75m to 11m and to adjust the windows, and the foundation-stone was laid at the present site, which had finally been chosen in preference to that of the old tolbooth. It is probable that the building as executed owes its main elements to Moffat's 'scheme', but that the details were amended by Bachup. The latter in 1708 claimed expenses given to the deacon of the wrights 'for going to see other steeples that he might know how to make the spire of the Steeple', which closely resembles those of Glasgow College and Stirling town-house.[17]

Since 1703 the committee had been acquiring building-materials, and contracts were negotiated for the re-opening of

the town's quarry and for the supply of lime from Annandale. Efforts to secure a ship for bringing timber from the Baltic failed, and suitable material was finally located at Garlieswood near the River Cree. These materials were made available to Bachup, who agreed to furnish the remainder as part of his contract price of 19,000 merks. Thereafter the minute-book records the payment of regular instalments until the completion of the contract in 1708, and the subsequent negotiations for the bells, clock and iron 'ravel'.

In 1703 the town council had agreed that 'the town is not at present provided with sufficient prisons ... as also that there is not ane steeple in the whole town, nor a suitable council-house and clerk's chamber for keeping the charter-chest and records of the burgh, nor a magazine house nor room for the safe-keeping of the town's arms and ammunition'.[18] However, most of these functions were retained in the old prison and in the adjacent building which replaced the old tolbooth in 1725.[19] The first floor of the Midsteeple was used as a court-room and town hall rather than its intended function of a council-house until 1830, when the new portico was added to mark its additional dignity. In the 18th century the ground storey contained a weigh-house and guard-house, and there was also prison-accommodation which may have been in the steeple. Later the ground storey was given over to shops and a lock-up, probably in the base of the steeple, and the second floor became the police superintendent's residence. After 1866, when a new town hall was built, the whole building was used for shops and warehouses, and it remained in commercial use even after the extensive renovation of 1909, which was superintended by the local architect James Barbour. In the early 1970s the interior was adapted for local authority use.[20]

24 DUNBAR TOWN-HOUSE
East Lothian
NT 6793 7895

The town-house[1] is situated on the N side of High Street, diagonally opposite the opening of West Port, the main road to Edinburgh. It is almost rectangular on plan, measuring 12.9m along the main (W) front by 7m, and is of three storeys, the upper one rising into the roof-space and having two dormers to the W. At the centre of the W front there projects a semi-hexagonal stair-tower or steeple which carries a small timber-framed spire. The building is constructed of random red-sandstone rubble, now badly weathered, and was previously harled.[2] In origin it may be ascribed to the late 16th or early 17th century, but it has undergone considerable later alteration. The N gable-wall is abutted by council offices which replaced an earlier house in 1927,[3] while the S wall adjoins a lane, but some projecting tuskers in its lower part may indicate that an adjacent building, perhaps over a pend, stood here.

The windows of the W front are disposed irregularly, and represent various periods of work. The two ground-floor windows were enlarged in 1913, after the removal of a lean-to structure which contained a shop and the police office and enclosed the entrance.[4] The two-light mullioned N window at first-floor level is of about the same date, but early views show that it replaced a slight projection containing a narrow slit. At least part of the opening S of the stair-tower is early, and it retains iron bars from the period when the room inside was used as a prison. The area S of this window has been much disturbed, and another early opening may have been blocked. The two dormer-windows, which have oval recesses in their pediments and quirked edge-rolls on the jambs and lintels, may be ascribed to the late 17th or early 18th century. The gables have crowsteps, and those facing the main front have gabled fronts, with bevelled sides and miniature ridge-mouldings. The chimneystacks have bevelled copings, but that on the S gable has been much renewed.

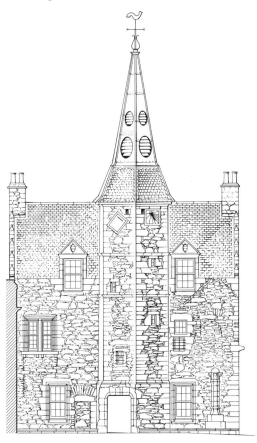

Dunbar Town-house (No.24), W elevation and plans

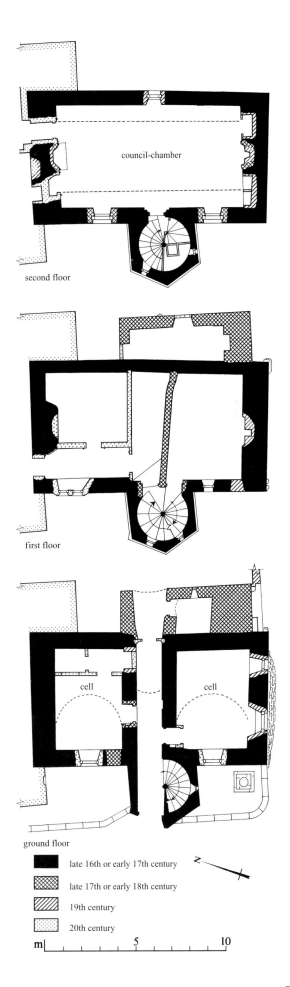

second floor

council-chamber

first floor

ground floor

cell   cell

■ late 16th or early 17th century

▨ late 17th or early 18th century

▨ 19th century

▨ 20th century

m   5   10

A. **Dunbar Town-house** (No.24) from W   (B 39177)

B. sundials in steeple   (B 39186)

C. second-floor room from N   (C 50184)

The stair-tower has a bevelled plinth at a height of 2.6m. Its NW face contains the entrance-doorway, a flat-arched opening with a broad shallow-moulded surround, and this and the SW face contain small plain windows in the upper stages. The lower quoins are of weathered white sandstone, and differ from those of the two top stages, which rise above eaves-level and are defined by moulded string-courses; it is possible that these stages represent a slightly later addition. The top stage has clock-faces to N and S and square sundials, one with a stilted rectangular gnomon, in the NW and SW faces. [5] The lower part of the spire is slated and its steep upper part is lead-covered, each face having oval louvred sound-holes. [6]

The entrance-doorway leads past a stone newel-stair on the S side into a vaulted passage which continues to the rear of the building. Flanking this pend there are two barrel-vaulted rooms, which have been subject to alterations and blockings at various periods. It is probable that they were originally used as cells, and the windows in the S wall of the S room are later insertions, as are the front windows in both rooms (*supra*). There is also a blocked doorway in the W wall of the N room. To the rear of the S part of the building there is a small square chamber which may have been the 'thieves' hole' noted in 1802. [7] In 1818 it was reported that the first storey contained the jailer's house, [8] but in the late 19th century the S room housed the cell for the police office in the adjacent lean-to.

At first-floor level the stair-landing gives onto two rooms which are divided by an obliquely-set cross-wall. They are entered by substantial cross-lined and studded wooden doors. In 1838 the N room was being used to house criminals and the S one for non-burgess debtors. [9] The N room has a massive fireplace in the centre of the N wall. The council-chamber, which occupies the whole of the second floor, has a deeply-coombed ceiling, and fireplaces in each gable-wall. The original doorway from the stair has a cross-lined wooden door. A doorway in the E part of the N wall was slapped through when the adjoining block was built in 1927. The walls are lined with fielded panelling, probably of early 18th-century date as are the two fireplaces which have quadrant-curves at the ends of their lintels. Above the N fireplace there are the royal arms of James VII and II, painted on a wooden 'broad' (board) by Alexander Mackbyth in 1686, and over the S fireplace there are the Hanoverian royal arms on canvas. [10] From this level of the stair-tower access is by ladder to the clock-stage. The bell, which hangs in the upper part of the spire, was cast by Thomas Mears 'in the first year of burgh reform, 1834'.

HISTORY

An earlier tolbooth was probably undergoing repairs in 1545-6, when the bailies held courts in the churchyard, and it was claimed during a lawsuit that 'quhair ever the Bailies holdis the Court, that is thair Towbuth'. In 1593 the inhabitants were ordered to cart stones from the quarry at Innerwick 'for the bigging of the Tolbuth', and two years later an agreement was made with William Nicholson, 'mender of the tounis knok'.[11] It is possible that part of the surviving structure may date from this period, with the upper part of the stair-tower as a later addition. The only recorded work during the 17th century is the painting of the sundial, council-room and armorial panels undertaken by Alexander Mackbyth in 1686 (*supra*).

Repairs were undertaken to the masonry and window-fittings of the prison in 1705, and to the steeple in 1707, but in 1714 a Parliamentary duty on ale was obtained 'whereas the Town House and school are very old and of age decayed and must go to ruin unless speedily repaired'.[12] The subsequent repairs may have included the large dormer-windows and the panelling of the council-chamber, and in 1723 timber was obtained to make three sash-windows for it.[13] In 1816 the spire was repaired at an estimated cost of £80, but two years later it was proposed to build a new town-house, on the same site, to include 'a Council Room, Assembly Room, an Academy, and a Farmers' Hall'.[14] Nothing came of this, although new Assembly Rooms were built in 1822, and the building was little altered until the renovations of 1911-13.

B. painted armorial of King James VII and II, 1686   (C 50142)

A. **Dunbar Town-house** *(No.24)*   (C 50146)
   fireplace and painted Hanoverian royal armorial

25 DYSART TOLBOOTH
Fife
NT 3041 9316

The tolbooth[1] is situated in the SE angle of High Street and Victoria Street, at the central crossroads of the burgh. It comprises a five-storeyed steeple with a two-storeyed hall adjoining to the S. The steeple was probably built in 1576, the date that appears on a panel reset in the main (N) front and is confirmed by local records.[2] Its upper stages, and the octagonal belfry, date from 1743-4. The hall was rebuilt and enlarged, to designs by the Glasgow architects Campbell Douglas and Sellars, in 1885.

The steeple is rectangular on plan, measuring 8.3m by at least 6.5m. With the exception of the ashlar-built belfry, it is harled and has dressed margins, with stepped quoin-stones and moulded string-courses up to third-floor level. An early photograph showing some harling removed at first-floor level indicates that the masonry is of coursed rubble.[3] A forestair gives access to the first-floor entrance-doorway in the W wall while an extruded stair-turret at the NE angle rises to the third floor. The forestair and doorway appear to have been rebuilt in the early 17th century. A panel carved with the date 1617 and a shield bearing a stylised tree[4] is set into the W wall of the forestair.

The upper stages of the tower, as rebuilt in 1743-4, have plain ashlar margins and string-courses, and terminate in a heavy wall-head cornice. The clock-faces are set in square surrounds with segmental heads which rise into the cornice, and the octagonal belfry has round-headed louvred openings with slightly projecting keystones. It terminates in a cavetto cornice which carries an ogival stone roof with concave facets.

Up to third-floor level the rooms are rectangular on plan,

although the ground-floor one has been curtailed by extensive blocking at the S end. This room is entered by a doorway in the N wall and has no communication with the upper floors, which are barrel-vaulted. From the first floor upwards, each room has access to the stair-turret, and in the NW angle there is a rectangular shaft for the clock-weights. The walls and vaults of these rooms were covered with coarse render, much of which has disintegrated. Few original fittings survive, but there are iron yetts to the doorways of the second- and third-floor rooms, the latter still retaining its inner wooden door.

The provision of a new clock was discussed in 1825, but the existing one was made in 1876 by H and R Miller of Edinburgh, at a cost of £110.[5] The belfry contains two bells, one of which is of late medieval date. In 1808 it was proposed to replace the old church bell, which was broken, and the town-house one which was too small, with a single large bell to be hung in the tolbooth steeple 'as the most central situation'.[6] The new bell, which measures 0.9m in diameter, was cast by Thomas Mears and Son of London, and bears the names of the burgh magistrates and officials for 1808. The medieval bell, 0.64m in diameter, was evidently intended for ecclesiastical use. It bears a black-letter inscription, with the words divided by symbols including an initial cross and a crown: PRECURSOR D(OMI)NI DEI NOBIS GAUDIA [...] ('the forerunner of the Lord God [...] joys to us').[7] Kirkcaldy Museum houses some items believed to have come from the tolbooth, including a marquetry panel of a ship dated 1613, a large key and various weights and measures.

23B

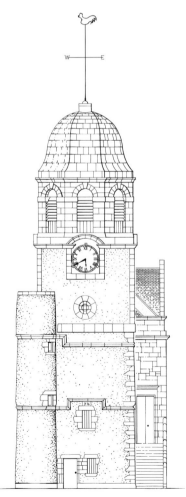

A. **Dysart Tolbooth** (No.25), N elevation   B. view from NW, c.1880   (MacGibbon and Ross)

A. **Dysart Tolbooth** (No.25) from NW   (B 39196)

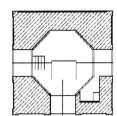

clock stage

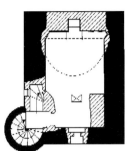

third floor

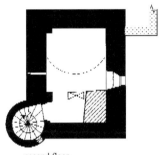

second floor

C. plans

■	1576
▨	early 17th century
▧	18th century
░	19th century and later

m |_____|_____|_____|_____| 5

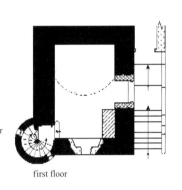

first floor

B. second floor, yett   (B 39471)

D. second floor from S, showing pendulum-box   (B 39472)

79

Dysart Tolbooth (No.25), inscription on bell (scale, 1:7.5)

HISTORY

A previous tolbooth, 'devysed on the hie gate where the mercat croce stude', was built in 1567 but appears to have been demolished in 1575, when a new site was found 'on the south side of the hie gate', where the present building stands.[8] Repairs were undertaken in the early 17th century, when the forestair was built. Major repairs were also required after an accident in 1656, when Cromwellian troops used the steeple as a magazine and inadvertently caused a gunpowder explosion which blew off the roof.[9] The building appears to have been in a damaged state for a long period, while further repairs were required in 1707-19.[10]

In 1743 Lord Sinclair, owner of Dysart House, 'influenced Mr Douglas architeck to come and look at the Tolbooth, and who has drawen ane draught or scheme how it should be repaired'. This was presumably the Edinburgh architect John Douglas.[11] The upper portion of the steeple and the belfry were rebuilt in 1743-4 at a cost of £499, the mason-contractor being Alexander Mawer, one of the council.[12]

The building fulfilled a variety of functions, including a hall for the magistrates and council, a prison, a public weigh-house, guard-house and 'black hole'. A room adjoining the council-room was leased as a coffee-room in 1811, and a library was housed in the same room in 1815.[13] The council-house had been enlarged in 1765 by 'extending the partition as far as the arch of the pend', to make it more suitable for business and for public entertainments.[14] The physical evidence of this, and of the main block as a whole, does not survive, having been replaced in 1885 by the present town hall to the designs of Campbell Douglas and Sellars.[15] Some time after 1934 a large round-headed first-floor window in the N wall of the steeple, which was probably an early 19th-century insertion, was replaced with a smaller lintelled window of traditional character.[16]

26 EARLSFERRY TOWN-HOUSE
Fife
NT 4834 9991

The steeple tower of an earlier town-house is incorporated within the SW end of the present town hall, which stands on the SE side of High Street. The town-house occupied part of the site of its single-storeyed successor, which measures 17.4m along the NW front by 9.5m, but it was two-storeyed and probably narrower.[1] It was rebuilt to a simple baronial design by an Elie architect, John Currie, and bears the date 1872 above the door.

The tower, whose SW wall is incorporated in the gable of the later building, measures about 2.6m square over all, with walls 0.66m thick at ground level. It is preserved to a height of about 10m, and where it rises clear of the roof it is built of red sandstone rubble, in contrast to the grey sandstone ashlar of the Victorian belfry, which carries a slated spire. There is a narrow ground-floor doorway in the NW wall, and another at first-floor level in the SE wall. At the next level in the same wall there is a small four-pane window, still glazed but now opening into the roof-space of the hall. At the highest stage in the NW and SW walls there are blocked two-light windows with pairs of round arch-heads cut out of single slab-lintels. That in the NW wall bears on the lintel the inscription EMD / EF 1772, in which EF presumably represents 'Earlsferry'. A continuous corbel-course of red sandstone, which is probably original, supports the Victorian belfry.

The interior of the tower contains a series of timber floors and short ladders giving access to the clock stage, where the mechanism has been renewed, and to the belfry. The bell, which is 0.63m in diameter, was cast by John C Wilson, Glasgow, in 1864.

HISTORY
Earlsferry was an ancient burgh, which in 1589 was erected into a royal burgh with liberty to hold markets and have a market cross, although the charter makes no mention of a tolbooth.[2] The town-house was described in 1840 as 'an old building', which contained 'the town-hall, and a very wretched cell'. The cell was about 4.6m square and partly-sunk, but on the rare occasions when debtors were imprisoned, they had the use of the town hall on the first floor.[3] The outside stair was demolished in 1849, to improve the street.[4] The decision to rebuild the hall was one of the first acts of the new town council elected in 1871, after the burgh had been controlled by managers for twenty years. Currie's first scheme was rejected because of its 'great expence', and the fenestration of his revised design was simplified, but work began in September 1872 and was completed about six months later.[5]

A. Earlsferry Town-house (No.26) from N   (C 48158)

B. detail of steeple   (C 48160)

The Old Tolbooth of Edinburgh, the most celebrated of
Scottish tolbooths, stood on an island site in the High Street,
immediately NW of St Giles's Church, from the 14th century
until its demolition in 1817. Originally the meeting-place of
parliaments and royal as well as burgh courts and councils, it
became exclusively a prison when these functions were
transferred after 1562 to new rooms fitted up in the W end of
St Giles's Church, and to a 'new tolbooth' or council-house
built a few metres to the S.

The new tolbooth, which latterly was used for burgh
business only, was demolished in 1811 to make way for the
Signet Library, and the town council then occupied rooms in
the Royal Exchange, on the N side of the High Street. This
imposing classical building had been erected by the town in
1753-61 as an exchange for merchants, to a design by John
Adam as amended by the contractor, John Fergus. During the
19th century the council systematically bought up the property
rights to the whole of these 'City Chambers', and they were
altered and extended by successive city architects.

THE OLD TOLBOOTH[1] (NT 2562 7358)

In 1365 David II granted to the burgh a strip of ground
measuring 30.5m by 9.75m on the W side of their old
tholoneum, to build a new one.[2] This building may have been
the *pretorium* mentioned in a rental of 1369 which, it has been
suggested, lay in a venell SE of St Giles's Church, and it was
probably burnt in the English invasion of 1385. In the
following year Robert II granted an area of 18.3m by 9.15m on
the N side of the market-place, by a charter endorsed 'the
charter of the Belhous'.[3] The original building was probably
the 'towre of the auld tolbuith' which was repaired in 1575.[4]
The E block that survived until 1817 appears from its style to
have been an addition of the 15th century. In 1501 a contract
was made with John Marser, mason, for 'completing of the
towre' with ashlar.[5]

Extensive repairs were carried out in 1555-6, especially in
the area of the 'gre(a)t yet'. By 1562, however, the building
was so ruinous that Queen Mary ordered it to be demolished
and the Lords of Session threatened to remove their court to St
Andrews.[6] The council provided accommodation nearby
(*infra*), and temporarily repaired the tolbooth for used as a
prison, but the older W part was evidently demolished in or
before 1610. In that year, following instructions from the
privy council 'to big ane wairdhous', a contract was made with
Andrew Symsoun, mason, for building 'the new Prysoun Hous
in the awld Tolbuith bewest the present Tolbuith quhair the
grund is presentlie red (cleared)'.[7] A series of booths outside
the W gable of this new block was rebuilt in 1678 as a two-
storeyed extension, whose flat roof was used from 1785 for
public executions. The tolbooth was demolished in 1817
despite protests led by Walter Scott, who was to immortalise it
as the 'Heart of Midlothian' in his novel published the
following year.[8]

The outline of the building is marked by brass studs in the
paving, and the position of its main entrance by a heart-shaped
setting of cobblestones. The 15th-century E block measured
about 10.5m from N to S by 7.5m and that of 1610 was 11.5m
from E to W by 10.5m, the overall dimensions being close to
those specified in the charter of 1386. Both blocks were four-
storeyed, with dormer windows in the building of 1610 whose
upper storey was an addition to the original contract.[9] The
older building was ashlar-built and decorated on the N and S
gable-walls with ornate niches,[10] and the ogee-headed
entrance-doorway was in a circular stair-tower at the SE
angle.[11] There was also a projecting tower for an internal stair
at the centre of the S wall of the addition of 1610, flanked at
each side by a window-bay. The upper stages of the N wall of
this block, which were defined by string-courses, were also of
two bays, but the round-headed windows of the ground storey
may have occupied an infilled arcade.[12]

The ground storeys of both blocks were vaulted and
contained shops as well as accommodation for the jailer and,
from about 1787, the guard-house. The principal hall, lit
originally by large windows in the end-walls and E wall,[13]
occupied the first floor of the E block, with a felons' room
containing the stocks and an iron cage on the floor above.
Latterly the hall was used as a day-room for debtors, and a
pulpit was kept there for the use of the minister who acted as
chaplain.[14] Most of the rooms on the upper floors of the 1610
block were allocated to debtors, but the first-floor one nearest
the hall was used as a tap-room.

5B
5A, 84A

84B

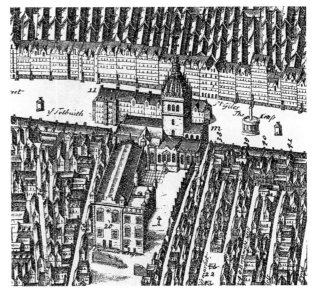

A. *Edinburgh (No.27), detail of plan by Gordon, 1647*   (C 48619)

B. *Old Tolbooth, view from SW by Nasmyth, 1817*   (EDD/579/2)

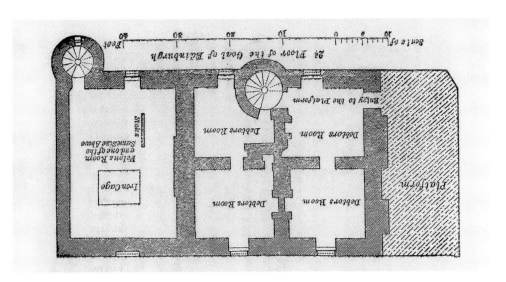

Scale of Feet

2d Floor of the Goal of Edinburgh

Felons Room and one of the Same Size Above

Iron Cage

Stairs

Debtors Room

Debtors Room

Debtors Room

Debtors Room

Entry to the Platform

Platform

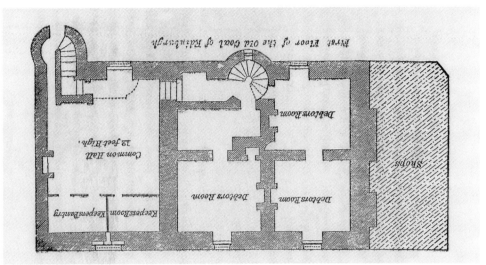

First Floor of the Old Goal of Edinburgh

Common Hall 12 feet High.

Keepers Room Keepers Pantry

Debtors Room

Debtors Room

Debtors Room

Shops

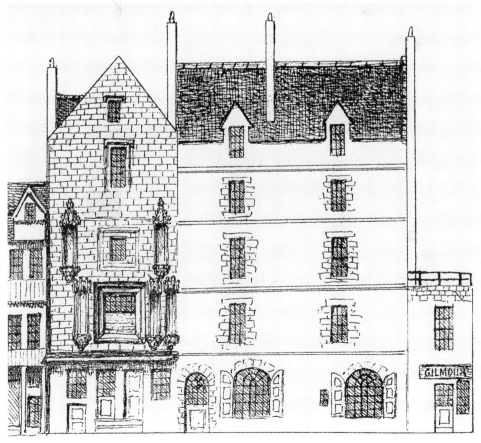

GILMOUR

Edinburgh Old Tolbooth *(No.27)*
plans after Chambers and
N elevation after Sime
(scale, 1:200)

A. **Edinburgh Old Tolbooth** (No.27), hall from W (Miller)

B. tap-room, drawing by Archer, 1817 (National Museums of Scotland)

C. **Edinburgh City Chambers** (No.27), engraving of Adam's proposed design, 1753 (EDD/372/1)

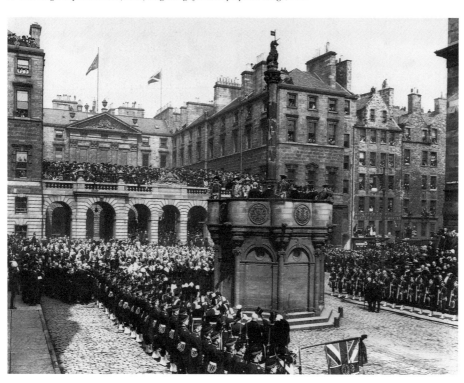

D. view from S, showing proclamation of
King George V at Mercat Cross, 1910
(ED/9296)

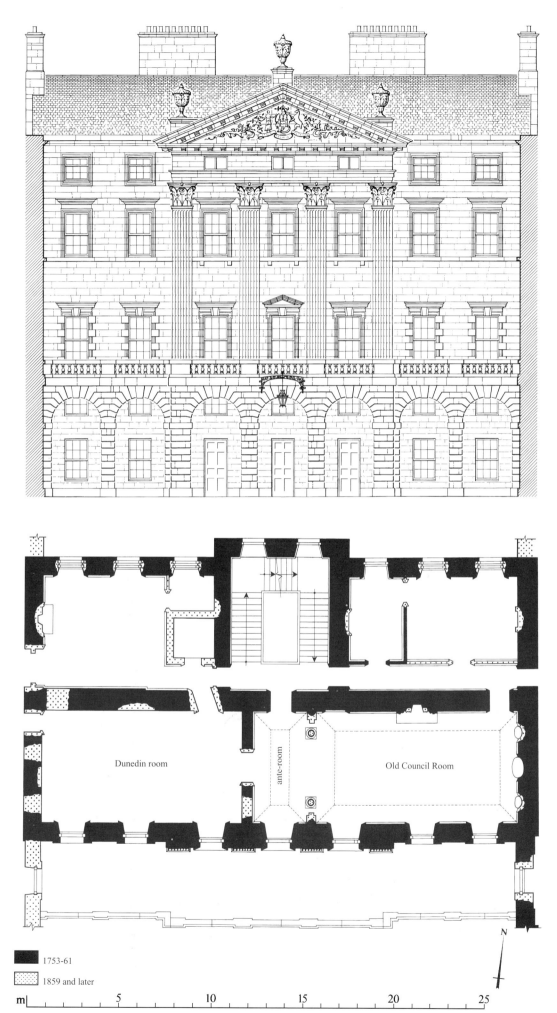

**Edinburgh
City Chambers**
*(No.27)
S elevation and
first-floor plan*

■ 1753-61

⠂ 1859 and later

m | 5   10   15   20   25

Dunedin room

ante-room

Old Council Room

N

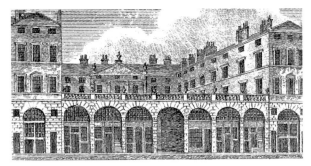

A. *Edinburgh City Chambers (No.27)* (C 48601)
view from S showing arcade, c.1810

C. *view from S by Shepherd, 1829* (C 47328)

B. *Old Council Room from W* (C 4185)

D. *Old Council Room, fireplace* (C 4187)

THE NEW TOLBOOTH (NT 2559 7356)

Immediately after the Reformation the town council gave
orders in 1560 for the W end of St Giles's Church to be
divided for use as a school and an additional prison.
Following the threatened removal of the Court of Session in
1562 (*supra*) this area was quickly fitted up for court and
council business. The church continued in use by the royal
courts until the building of Parliament House in the 1630s, and
the town clerk's ofices remained there until the early 19th
century.[15]

The burgh records of the late 16th and 17th centuries
frequently refer to the old or new, high or low, and inner or
outer tolbooths and council-houses. While many of these
references are presumably to the rooms in the church, the
payment in 1562 of ground-rent for 'the landis quhair the new
tolbuth is bigand (being built)' indicates that the council-house
that survived until 1811 was built at this time.[16] It stood about
18m S of the old tolbooth, at the SW angle of the church and
abutting it at first-floor level with a narrow public passage
below.[17] It was of L-plan, measuring about 16m by 11m, and
was three-storeyed, the access to the upper floors being by a
semi-octagonal stair-turret at the N end which was later
enclosed by the goldsmith's booth occupied by George Heriot.
The principal rooms on both the ground and first floors were
used for courts and council meetings until the transfer to the
Royal Exchange in 1811. The second floor was used as a
meeting-room for various bodies including the Society of
Writers to the Signet and the Merchant Company of
Edinburgh, and latterly as a masonic lodge.

EDINBURGH CITY CHAMBERS (NT 2576 7367).

The former Royal Exchange[18] is ranged around three sides of a
screened forecourt on the N side of the High Street, opposite
the restored mercat cross at the E end of St Giles's Church and
Parliament Square. The general form of the original building
is still clearly recognisable, and closely follows the conditions
of the 1754 building-contract. It was to comprise a hollow
square, with the main block to the N and a wing running S
from each end to meet a low range which faced the street and

84C,

completed the enclosure. Through the centre of this range was to run the entry to a courtyard measuring 25.3m from N to S by 27.1m, which on the N was to open into a piazza 4m deep, within the ground storey of the main block. This block was to measure some 34m by 17.5m, and each of the wings was to extend 39.9m towards the street. The proposed layout remained incomplete, however, for an older building used by the Writers to the Signet was incorporated at the N end of the W range, eventually being remodelled and refaced in 1898-9.[19]

Facing the High Street, a flat-roofed and balustraded seven-bay arcade links the S ends of the E and W wings to form a frontage almost 45m in width. Although dated 1903 (beneath the armorial pediment), this screen replaces an original arcade in which a central opening was flanked on each side by three arches containing shops.[20] In the centre of the courtyard is a bronze statue of Alexander taming Bucephalus by Sir John Steell, erected in St Andrew Square in 1884 and moved to this site in 1916.

The S elevations of the main block and wings are of four main storeys, but at the rear the building rises impressively through twelve storeys to a height of over 36m. The masonry is of Craigleith stone throughout. On the main front the lowest storey is of polished ashlar, channel-jointed in part, while the upper wall-surfaces are generally scabbled, with polished and moulded dressings. The sides and rear are of rubble masonry, but some ashlar has been used in later alterations.

The main block measures 28.3m from E to W by 16.3m, exclusive of the adjacent portions of the wings. At ground-floor level a seven-bay arcaded and balustraded piazza of channel-jointed ashlar projects into the court, its slightly advanced central bays respecting the advanced centrepiece of the main block. In the upper storeys the three-bay centrepiece is articulated by giant fluted Corinthian pilasters which were one of Fergus's additions to Adam's design. They rise to an entablature at third-floor level and a triangular pediment, surmounted by urn-finials, which encloses the City arms in relief between elegant floral scrolls. Small horizontal windows, reduced in size from Adam's design, are sandwiched within the frieze. The first-floor windows have key-blocked moulded architraves, lugged in the central bays and with Gibbs surrounds in the flanking bays, the central opening also being pedimented. The second-floor windows have moulded architraves with simple entablatures, the sills of those in the end-bays being joined by a plain string-course and the central bays having consoled sills. The treatment of the fenestration and arcaded ground-floor in the wings is generally similar to that of the main block, the Writers' Court section at the N end of the W wing having been rebuilt in 1898-9 to harmonise with the remainder.

The principal entry, in the centre of the ground floor of the N block, was originally flanked by coffee-houses. It leads to the great staircase through a lobby and stair-hall which were largely re-fitted in 1936-8. The stair itself, which is of scale-and-platt type with turned balusters and moulded handrail, originally started at ground level but from 1875 was extended downwards.

On the first floor, the committee-room that occupies the front E half of the main block served originally as the board-room of the custom-house and then, from 1811 to 1903, as the council-room for Edinburgh City Council. The E wall of an original ante-room, entered from the landing, was in 1859 converted into a columned screen opening into the room itself, which has a modillion cornice and coved ceiling. Room and screens area are uniformly lined with pine panelling and the doorways in each division have carved friezes and broken pediments. The surround and overmantel of a black marble fireplace in the N wall are of similar and slightly more elaborate treatment, a painting of Edinburgh Castle dated 1886 being inset in the overmantel. The central of three niches in the E wall contains a bronze figure in Roman military costume, probably of 17th- or early 18th-century French or Italian workmanship.[21]

A few early features survive elsewhere in the building, notably a chimneypiece with scrolled overmantel and painted City arms in the SE room on the first floor of the W wing. The Dunedin Room, adjoining the Old Council Room to the W, is substantially of 1870 and later, but most of the principal interiors date from the turn of the century. The most sumptuous of these were created in neo-Baroque style in the re-designed W wing, a court-room of 1898-9 on the ground floor and a new council-chamber of 1901-4 at the N end of the first floor.[22]

The site of the Royal Exchange included four closes, Mary King's, Stewart's, Pearson's and Allan's, which extended N from the High Street to the Nor' Loch. Later extensions led to the acquisition of Craig's Close to the E and Writer's Court and Warriston's Close to the W. The various properties were purchased and with the exception of the building in Writers' Court were largely demolished, the debris going to make up the Castle Esplanade. Mary King's Close was partly overlaid by the Exchange in 1753-61, and further enclosed by the NW extension of the City Chambers in 1901, but some 60m of the 2.1m-wide close still survives beneath the building, incorporating domestic architectural remains of the 17th and early 18th centuries.[23]

HISTORY

The Royal Exchange was designed and built between 1753 and 1761, replacing a building in Parliament Square which had been designed for this purpose in the late 17th century and destroyed by fire in 1700. It was the first of a series of civic improvements initiated by Lord Provost George Drummond, who laid the foundation-stone with great ceremony in September 1753.

In 1753 competitive plans and estimates for the new exchange were obtained from John Adam and from 'the Gentlemen of Mary's Chapel', a group comprising a mason and three wrights directed by John Fergus, architect. Adam's design was adopted, but in 1754 the contract was awarded to 'the Gentlemen', under the supervision of the Deacons of the Crafts. The elevation drawn by Fergus as a frontispiece to the contract of agreement was a slightly amended version of Adam's scheme.[24] The piazza was intended to be used by the merchants as a place of exchange, but in practice they continued to transact business in the open street. The remainder of the building was to include a custom-house, thirty-five shops (fourteen of which were to have rooms above them), ten dwelling-houses (four of them below courtyard-level), two printing-houses and three coffee-houses.

Having sold off most of the properties within the exchange, the town council reserved ownership of twenty rooms intended for the custom-house, leasing them to the government through the Court of Exchequer.[25] In place of one of the shops an office in the W range of the new building was occupied by the town chamberlain. In 1810-11, after the New Tolbooth had been condemned and the lease of the custom-house had expired, the council decided to occupy as City Chambers that part of the building which they owned, installing various municipal offices and meeting-rooms in the main N block. The remaining properties that had previously been sold off were re-acquired in stages between 1849 and 1893, the council eventually regaining possession of the entire complex and extending it. Significant work was carried out by David Cousin in the 1850s and 1870-1, by Robert Morham after 1875 and again in 1898-9 and 1901-4, and by E J MacRae in the 1930s.[26]

84C

28 FALKIRK TOWN STEEPLE
Falkirk
NS 8882 7991

xiiC

This imposing structure [1] stands at the E end of the wide central section of High Street, which was used as a market-place. It was built in 1813-14 to the designs of the Glasgow architect, David Hamilton. [2] It replaced a steeple of 1697, which was demolished in 1803 after subsidence caused by the removal of the adjacent tolbooth, on whose site a four-storeyed block was built. [3]

Hamilton employed a range of neo-classical motifs in the upward transition from a square base to an octagonal spire, and in 1815-16 he used a modified form of the design for the steeple of Port Glasgow Town Buildings (No.73). Both steeples bear strong points of similarity to that of St Enoch's Church, Glasgow, with which Hamilton was no doubt already familiar and which he preserved in his own rebuilding of that church in 1827-8. [4]

The steeple measures 6.15m square on plan and 42.7m in height, and is free-standing except on the E, where the large building of about 1800 has been replaced by lower structures. It is built of yellow sandstone ashlar, with channelled masonry in the lowest stages. At ground-floor level there are a round-arched entrance-doorway to the S and a large window in the W front, both having fanlights, and above these at third-floor level there are large fictive square-headed windows. At the next stage each face is treated as a Doric portico, having a pediment supported by angle-columns and enclosing a deep-set round-headed window. The stage above this is an unequal-sided octagon, with panelled pilasters framing clock-faces on the four longer sides. The belfry is a regular octagon with square-headed louvred openings between attached Ionic columns which carry an elaborate double cornice. This is in turn surmounted by a short octagonal stage from which the spire tapers to a ball-finial and weather-cock bearing the date 1814. [5]

While the ground floor was originally leased as a shop, the first floor served as a jailer's room and the second and third floors as cells, which about 1834 were fitted with iron-cased doors. [6] Access up to third-floor level is by a spiral stair in the NE angle, but above that it is provided by wooden stairs. The fifth floor is at the level of the clock, which has a modern mechanism. [7] In the belfry above there hang two bells, the larger of which was cast by Thomas Mears of London and installed in 1816. [8] It is 1.13m in diameter and is inscribed: MAY FALKIRK FLOURISH 1815. The other bell was cast in 1897 by John C Wilson, Glasgow, to replace one from the late 17th-century steeple, which is now in Falkirk Museum. [9] This measures 0.66m in diameter and is inscribed: IAMES EARLE OF LINLITHGOW AND CALLANDER IOHN MEIKLE FECIT EDINBURGI / 1697 FOR FALKIRK.

HISTORY
The building occupies the site of two earlier steeples, the first of which was built in the 16th century. This was replaced in 1697 by a steeple with a forestair and a steeply-pitched double-ogival roof, built by a local mason, William Stevenson, at a cost of 700 merks. [10] This steeple was itself demolished in 1803 after subsidence caused by the removal of the adjacent tolbooth to the E, and the construction on its site of a four-storeyed building. [11] A consequent legal action between the Falkirk stentmasters, owners of the steeple, and the owner of the new block, caused a delay of some ten years before the present building was begun. [12] It was erected by a local mason, Henry Taylor, at a contract price of £1,660, [13] and has remained virtually intact, although the spire required repair after lightning-damage in 1927. [14]

Falkirk Town Steeple (No.28)
W elevation by Hamilton, 1812 (scale, 1:200)   *(C 34104)*

A. **Falkirk Town Steeple** (No.28)
W elevation of old steeple
by J Shaw, 1803 (scale, 1:200)
(Falkirk Museum)

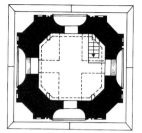

clock stage

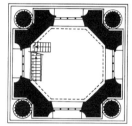

fourth floor

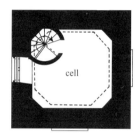

cell

third floor

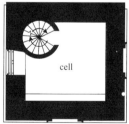

cell

first floor

| | 1813-14 |

m |_____| 5

B. plans

C. view from W   (B 39214)

D. cell door   (B 58201)

29 FALKLAND TOWN-HOUSE
Fife
NO 2529 0739

Falkland Town-house, sometimes referred to as the Town Hall, occupies the SW angle at the junction where Back Wynd enters the broadest part of High Street. Its principal (N) front faces High Street, but the E front has a central steeple which was probably more conspicuous before the enlargement of the corner building to the E of Back Wynd, and whose position may follow that of its 17th-century predecessor.

The building, which is constructed of light-brown sandstone ashlar, measures 12.2m across the N front by 11.9m, and is of two storeys surmounted by a hipped and slated roof. Its N elevation is a regular three-bay composition with stepped quoins and a projecting central bay. The ground-floor windows, and the arch enclosing the central doorway, are round-headed and the upper ones are lintelled, with balustraded aprons below a continuous moulded sill-course.

C. pediment of N front (B 39225)

A. Falkland Town-house (No.29), N elevation and plans

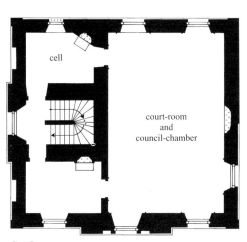

first floor

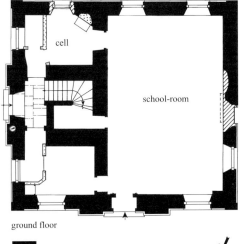

ground floor

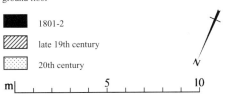

B. burgh armorial (B 58192)

90

A. **Falkland Town-house** (No.29), first-floor room from S   (F/1040)

HISTORY
Little is known of the 17th-century tolbooth that stood on this site. A proposal was made in 1800 to erect a new school, and since the tolbooth itself was 'in indifferent repair' the town council agreed that a single building should 'answer the purposes of the Town House, Tolbooth and School'. A design was provided by Thomas Barclay, mason at Balbirnie, and in 1801 a tender by Barclay and another mason, David Gardner, was accepted as 'by far the cheapest'.[2] That date is carved on the armorial in the N pediment, but work on the steeple may have continued into 1802.[3]

B. ornament of bell (scale, 1:7.5)

Above the tripartite central window there is a pediment surmounted by three urns and enclosing the burgh arms encircled by its motto. The E elevation is of similar design to the N one, but the first-floor windows in the side-bays are blind. Above the central pediment a three-stage steeple rises to an overall height of 24m. It is square to the level of the clock-stage, which carries an octagonal belfry and a short spire decorated with blind oculi.

The main room on the ground floor was originally occupied by the school and that on the first floor, which has a decorated plaster ceiling, was used as the court-room and council-chamber. In its W wall there is a pine-and-gesso chimneypiece whose central plaque shows a trophy of arms. The infrequent need to house prisoners was served by the SE room at each level, and that on the first floor, which retains its window-grille, formerly had a strengthened door.[1]

20B   Displayed in the building there are two stone panels carved with the burgh arms and dated 1618 and 1715, the former being set above the W doorway in the NE first-floor room. In the steeple there is a Dutch bell, 0.55m in diameter, bearing a
22B frieze of plant-scrolls punctuated by classicising heads, and the inscription: SOLI DEO GLORIA MICHAEL BVRGERHVYS ME FECIT 1630 ('Glory to God alone, Michael Burgerhuys made me, 1630'). The clock was made by James Ritchie, Edinburgh, in 1858.

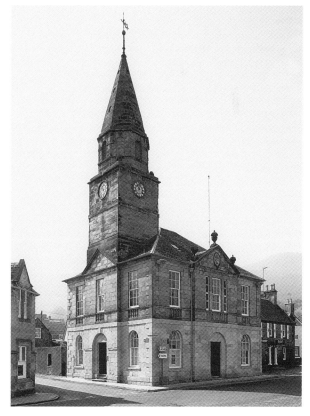

C. view from NE   (B 39219)

30 FOCHABERS TOWN-HOUSE
Moray

NJ 3453 5873

The town-house of 1790-2 (number 7 the Square) is situated on the SW side of the central square of Fochabers. It stands SE of Bellie Parish Church (1795-7) and is matched by a corresponding house, now the manse but originally built for the baron-bailie, to the NW. This group, and the rest of the planned town, were designed for the 4th Duke of Gordon by the Edinburgh architect John Baxter (d.1798), to replace the old town which stood 0.6km to the NE in the policies of Gordon Castle.

The two-storeyed town-house measures 12.2m by 10m, and a rear wing extends SW from its SE angle. The main (NE) front is of yellow-brown sandstone rubble with dressed margins, and the rear and gable walls are of roughly-coursed red sandstone. The five-bay main front, which corresponds to an elevation-drawing by Baxter,[1] has a round-arched ground-floor arcade enclosing a central round-headed doorway and square-headed windows. The arches and openings of this front are all chamfered and it has narrow off-set quoins and a broad first-floor string-course. The roof is covered with blue-grey slates[2] and there are ashlar skews and original chimneystacks with off-set margins. There is a small round-headed window high in the SE gable, and two blocked square-headed windows in the NW gable.

The harled rear wing was originally single-storeyed, containing a prison and meal-store, but it was subsequently lengthened, and a second storey was added in 1982. In the NE portion of its NW wall there is a blocked prison window with iron bars. The linking walls between the town-house, church and manse are later additions, but the SW wall of the yard to the rear of the town-house may be original.

Internally the building has undergone extensive modern alterations, although a staircase with turned wooden balusters retains its original position in the E angle.[3] The former school-room in the NW part of the ground storey has been subdivided, but the first-floor rooms retain six-panelled doors and fielded shutters. The court-room to the front of the NW end of this floor has a coombed ceiling with a deep cornice[4] and a wooden chimneypiece with simple moulded capitals. In the SE wall there is a large round-headed press with reeded pilasters which has evidently been inserted, probably in the 19th century. The rear NW room also has a coombed ceiling, but this has been curtailed by a modern partition.

HISTORY

A tolbooth in the old burgh of Fochabers was built or extensively repaired in 1735-6, and a plan of about 1766 shows a rectangular building, 14.5m by 6.7m and with a double forestair, situated in the middle of the market-place. A Tuscan column, formerly used as the mercat cross and retaining the chain of the jougs, is believed to mark the site (NJ 3477 5923), and some grass-covered building-footings are visible.[5] In 1766 Abraham Roumieu produced designs for a new tolbooth with a seven-bay pedimented façade and central spire. This elaborate building, which was to house a girnel, weigh-house, and small prison on the ground storey, and a large court-room above, was never erected.[6]

In 1774 John Baxter produced a first sketch for the new town of Fochabers, on a site removed from Gordon Castle which had been under construction to his designs since 1769.[7] Although the location of the church and flanking houses were decided at an early stage, work on the town-house did not begin until 1790. The builder was William Logie, a local mason who also worked on the church, houses and estate lodges, and the cost was £114 16s 10d.[8] Two undated sets of drawings by Baxter survive, one of which is very similar to the building as erected. This shows living-accommodation in the SE part of the first floor, and a meal-store below it, but in

1791 the 'small granary and prison' were being built in the rear wing, which had originally been designed for the prison alone and may have been extended beyond the 7.2m length shown by Baxter.[9] The adjacent church, whose steeple was to house the town clock,[10] was begun in 1795.

A. *Fochabers Town-house (No.30)*   (C 4334)
view from NE, showing Bellie Parish Church

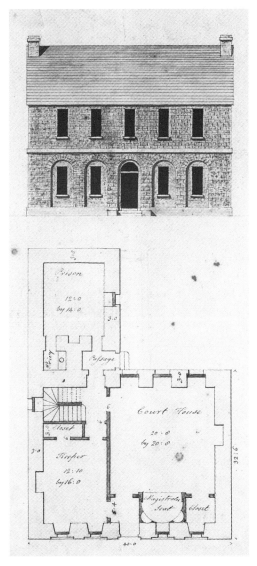

B. *ground-plan and NE elevation by Baxter (scale, 1:200) (C 44911)*

31 FORFAR TOWN AND COUNTY HALL
Angus

NO 4561 5064

The Town and County Hall occupies a central site at 'the Cross', the junction of Castle Street and High Street, on the S side of the former market-area. It was built in 1786-8 to designs by the Angus-born but London-based architect James Playfair. In 1824 a neo-classical sheriff court-house was erected at right angles to the N of the building and separated from it only by a narrow lane, still known as Buttermarket.

94A   The hall is rectangular, measuring 18.5m across the main (S) front by 14m. Its main front is of two storeys and four bays, the central two being advanced and pedimented. The ground-floor openings are round-arched, with windows in the centre bays and doors in the outer ones. The large first-floor windows have advanced aprons and originally had entablatures, which were removed in the late 19th century. [1] This front is built of sandstone ashlar from the 'Tolbooth Quarry' at Craignathro (NO 4545 4865), while the remaining elevations are of dressed rubble with raised dressings and were originally harled. [2] The E and W walls are of three bays and two storeys, the upper having blind windows, whereas the five-bay N elevation is three-storeyed, with an arcaded ground storey. The roof is piended and slated, with a central leaded platform which in 1804 replaced an original cupola. [3]

The original layout of the ground floor is uncertain, since Playfair's final design-drawings do not survive and there have been many subsequent alterations. It contained the weigh-house and a market-area, entered through the rear arcade, as well as prison-accommodation which even when new was considered 'dark, damp, and dismal'. [4] After the jail was removed in 1843 it housed a coffee-room, shops and a library. [5] In the 1970s a meeting-room was created along the S front, with public offices and shops occupying the remaining space.

The principal access to the first floor was always by the W door in the S front, but the simple original stair and landing were enlarged in 1846-7. The County Hall, originally lit by the cupola, occupied the two central bays of the S front, with a sheriff court-room to the E and a council-chamber at the W end. [6] In the N front there were two storeys of smaller rooms,

served by a secondary staircase at the W end, which have survived largely unaltered. The council-room, however, made way for the enlarged stair and landing in 1846, when the former sheriff court-room was absorbed into the County Hall. This now measures 12.8m in length and about 7.3m in height, and has a compartment ceiling of 1846, but the musicians' gallery at the W end, with a panelled front carried on Corinthian pillars and consoles, may be original.

Four stained-glass war-memorial windows, designed by A L Russell, were installed in the principal first-floor windows in 1952. [7] The County Hall retains two of a set of three crystal chandeliers donated by David Scott of Dunninald, MP, on its completion in 1788. There is also an important collection of portraits of county and other notables, including works by Hoppner, Romney and Raeburn, and a marble bust of Dr John Wyllie which was carved by the Danish sculptor, Bertel Thorwaldsen, in 1831. [8]

HISTORY

In 1590 the Privy Council required the magistrates of Forfar to build and maintain in all time coming 'ane sufficient wardhous for prisonaris and keiping of thame'. [9] During the early 18th century numerous modest repairs were made to the tolbooth. William Seton, writing in 1743, stated that 'the tolbooth ... consists of a close [close] prison and some shops off the street. In the second story are another prison on the East, in the middle, The town house in which the Sheriff and head courts sit. a council house upon the W. end of the building.' [10]

The provision of a new town-house was under discussion by the late 1770s, and additional land was acquired to the W of the old building. In December 1785, after various schemes had been examined, James Playfair was awarded a contract to execute his own designs at a price of £1,100. [11] The contract specified that the building was to contain 'five prisons for felons, three prisons for debtors, a Guard House, Sheriff Court, a Sheriff Clerks Office, a Town Clerks office, a record

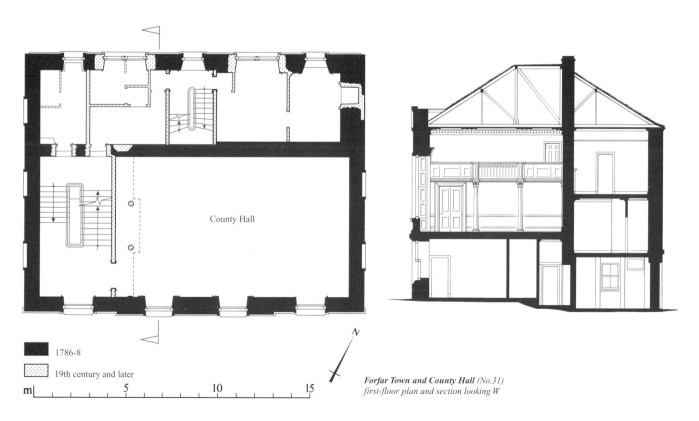

Forfar Town and County Hall (No.31)
first-floor plan and section looking W

County Hall

■ 1786-8

▨ 19th century and later

m | 5   10   15

N

A. Forfar Town and County Hall (No.31) from SE   (B 58088)

office, two staircases, a County Hall and a cupola with a proper way up to it'. Playfair had already prepared two related designs, in 1784 and in 1785,[12] which provided for the building to be erected in two parts as money and ground became available. In June 1786 he suggested a further revision, to produce 'a more compact, uniform and warm building', and although his proposal to add a 27m steeple was not accepted, it is likely that this revision formed the basis of the present building. Playfair's suggestion in the following year to add flanking wings, with a Doric colonnade at the W end, was also rejected, and the building was completed early in 1788. In 1804 the cupola, which it appears had always leaked, was removed and replaced with a flat roof, and a clock was installed in the pediment.[13]

In 1824 the sheriff court was removed to the new court-house designed by David Neave,[14] and in 1843 a new prison was built at the edge of the town, allowing alterations to the older building. The work of 1846-7, which included the enlargement of the County Hall (*supra*), was carried out by William Scott, a Dundee architect, at a cost of £400 shared equally between the town and county.[15]

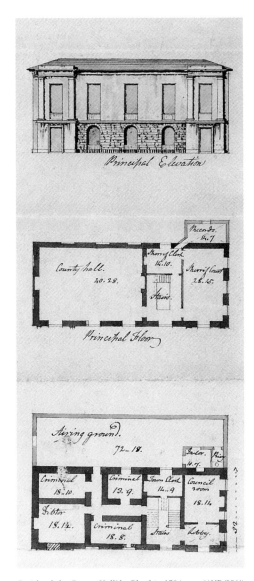

B. 'sketch for County Hall' by Playfair, 1784   (AND/99/4)
(scale, 1:400)

94

32 FORTROSE CATHEDRAL CHAPTER-HOUSE
Highland
NH 7273 5653

The medieval N range attached to the demolished choir of Fortrose Cathedral is understood to have been used for burgh purposes from a period soon after the Reformation. The vaulted chapter-house on the ground floor served as the prison, while courts and council meetings were held in the remodelled first-floor room until 1939.[1]

The range is rectangular, measuring 16.1m from E to W by 5.8m, and its roof is gabled as shown in Slezer's late 17th-century engraving. The masonry is of red sandstone and is mainly random rubble, although the S wall, which was the internal N wall of the medieval choir, is of coursed rubble. It incorporates a broad-chamfered lancet doorway and appears to be of medieval construction to full height, but the upper parts of the other walls have been extensively rebuilt. The daylight-opening of the medieval E window has been enlarged and a large rectangular window has been formed at first-floor level, while in both the N and S walls there are three windows, of varying sizes, at that level. Most of these openings have chamfered jambs, evidently medieval material in re-use, and there are no dateable features, but a panel above the rectangular first-floor doorway in the W wall records that the building was 'Decorated in the year 1780, General Sir Hector Munro K.B. & M.P.' This doorway is reached by a dog-leg stone forestair, but the only feature of this wall shown in Slezer's view is a rectangular window in the gable. The S part of this wall is corbelled out to contain an original mural stair.

The ground-floor room preserves a six-bay quadripartite ribbed vault with bosses of 13th-century character.[2] In the E part, which was presumably used as the chapter-room, the E bay has an aumbry in the N wall, and the next two bays have mural seats in the N and S walls. The freestone of the mural recesses, aumbry and E window-jambs bears many graffiti, including several elaborate examples of 1655 and 1659 with decorated frames and the MacKenzie stag's-head crest. The W part of the ground floor, lit only by small lancet-windows in the N and W walls, has access to the upper floor by the mural stair in the W wall.

The first floor now forms a single room, measuring 14m by 4m, which preserves no early features. There is a plain fireplace towards the E end of the N wall, and a cupboard has been formed in a blocked window-recess in the S wall, while the central window in that wall remains in use. At least part of this room was used for the detention of debtors until the 1830s,[3] and it may have been subdivided, but it now has a uniform high panelled dado of 19th-century type.

HISTORY
In 1661, when Fortrose was chosen in preference to Rosemarkie as the centre of the joint burgh, it was claimed that it had 'a most sure and strong firmance, waird-house, and tolbuith for keeping of prissoners'.[4] Slezer's view of the last quarter of the 17th century, however, shows the chapter-house as roofless, and repeated attempts were made by the impoverished burgh at this period to obtain grants or impose labour-services on the local community for its repair.[5] The repairs carried out in 1700 were evidently of simple character, and a heather roof was replaced by slates in 1721.[6] Until 1716 the burgh school was held in the council-house, which in 1723 was fitted up as a temporary place of worship.[7] The repairs recorded on the inscribed panel of 1780 were financed by Sir Hector Munro of Novar, then member of parliament for the Inverness burghs, of which Fortrose was one.[8] The vaulted undercroft continued to be used as a prison until the middle of the 19th century.[9] Since that period the cathedral ruins have been maintained by the state, and the chapter-house is now a guardianship monument in the care of Historic Scotland.[10]

*A. **Fortrose Cathedral Chapter-house** (No.32) from SW*   *(C 45828)*

B. interior of chapter-house from W   *(Historic Scotland)*

33 GIRVAN STEEPLE
South Ayrshire
NX 1853 9806

Known locally as 'Auld Stumpy', this steeple is situated on the S side of Knockcushan Street, overlooking the Water of Girvan and the harbour. It was erected in 1825-7 to serve as a jail, and although now freestanding it originally adjoined the E side of a town hall of about 1822, while the ground-floor pend gave access to a courtyard on the S.[1] Following the demolition of the town hall in 1909 the steeple was incorporated into the side-elevation of the new McMaster Hall, but this was destroyed by fire in 1939. This fire also destroyed the spire of the steeple, which was subsequently renewed.[2]

The steeple is built of sandstone ashlar and is almost square on plan, measuring 7.5m across the main (N) front by 6.6m. Its overall height is 29m and the walls of the lower half, which is divided by string-courses into four stages, rise with a slight batter to a corbelled parapet. At the next stage the clock-faces

are enclosed by open pediments carried on Tuscan angle-pilasters. The belfry stage above this is octagonal, having a louvred round-headed opening in each principal face and blind arches in the oblique ones, and it terminates in a crenellated parapet enclosing the rebuilt octagonal lead-covered spire.[3]

Segmental-headed archways in the N and S walls are framed by battered pilaster-buttresses terminating in cornices, and there are small recessed thermal windows in these walls at the next three stages. Access as far as third-floor level is provided by a newel-stair in the SE angle, and all of the storeys up to the clock-stage are barrel-vaulted. The first, second and third floors each comprise a single cell having a latrine in the SW angle.[4] The intended arrangement of two cells at each level was altered at the suggestion of the contractors, 'thereby giving additional strength to the outer Walls'.[5] The belfry

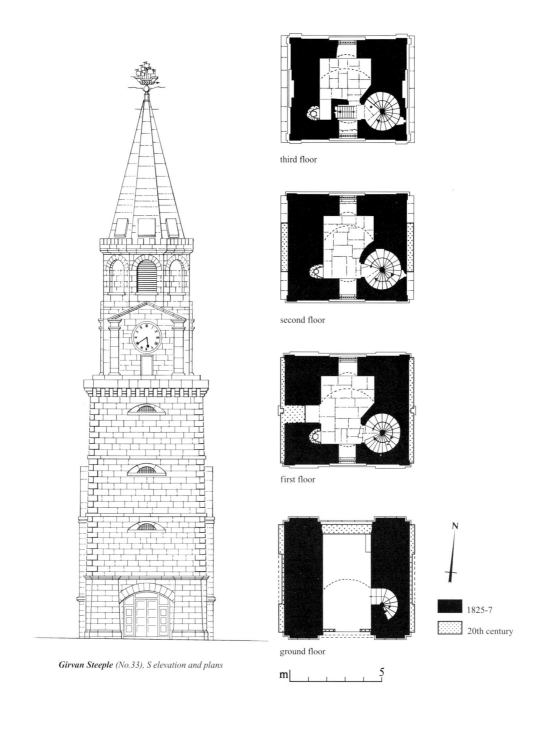

third floor

second floor

first floor

ground floor

N

■ 1825-7
⬚ 20th century

m ⌊_____⌋ 5

Girvan Steeple (No.33), S elevation and plans

96

contains a bell, 0.84m in diameter, which was cast by Stephen Miller, Glasgow, in 1826 and installed in the following year.[6]

HISTORY

A plot of ground bounded on the N by Knockcushan Street and on the E by Dalrymple Street was acquired by Girvan town council in 1787 for market and other use.[7] A tolbooth was built on part of the site, but by about 1820 it was ruinous. A market-house having a town hall on the upper floor was built on the W part of the site about 1822,[8] and the steeple in 1825-7. The architect is unknown but the steeple and three houses on the E part of the burgh's property were built by local contractors, Denham, Davidson and McWhinnie, at a total cost of £1,633.[9] Ten years after the completion of the steeple the prisons inspector noted that 'a marked improvement in the peace of the town is said to have followed the building of this prison'.[10]

Girvan Steeple (No.33) from NE   (B 39231)

From the 15th century the tolbooth of Glasgow was located in the NW angle of High Street and St Thenew's Gate (Trongate), at the junction that was later known as Glasgow Cross. As rebuilt on the same site in 1626-7, it attracted the admiring notice of English visitors as 'a very fair and high built house ... said to be the fairest in this kingdom', and 'their western prodigy, infinitely excelling the model and usual build of town halls'.[1] This great civic building, however, was rebuilt in 1814 and demolished in 1915 except for the steeple with its prominent crown spire, which now stands isolated on a traffic island.

In 1814 the functions of the tolbooth were transferred to a new building on the W side of Glasgow Green. Designed by William Stark in 1810, this was the first major monument of the Greek Revival in Scotland, but it was much altered for court use in 1910-13. It still houses the justiciary courts, and included the municipal offices until 1845 when they were moved to new City and County Buildings in Wilson Street, a neo-classical design by Clarke and Bell.[2] The monumental Municipal Buildings on the E side of George Square were built to William Young's eclectic design in 1883-8.[3]

3B

GLASGOW TOLBOOTH STEEPLE (NS 5960 6490). The steeple measures 4.7m square and is seven storeys in height, measuring 37m to the apex of its crown spire. The original NE and SE angles have buckle quoins, but the five lower storeys of the W elevation, with the adjacent angles,

*A. **Glasgow Tolbooth Steeple** (No.34) from SE*   (B 58268)

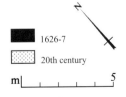

B. *S elevation and plans*

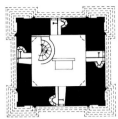

clock stage

sixth floor

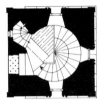

fifth floor

fourth floor

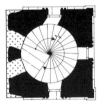

third floor

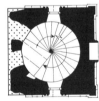

second floor

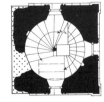

first floor

ground floor

were largely rebuilt in 1921 when the tolbooth was demolished. At the ground storey there are simple moulded doorways in the N and S elevations, the E one being plain. Each of the upper storeys of the original elevations is defined by a moulded string-course and contains a window surmounted by a strapwork pediment. The only other adornments are an inserted carving with a crowned head in place of the pediment of the first-floor S window and a larger triangular pedimented aedicule on the second floor of the E wall, which presumably held an armorial panel. The highest storey contains a large clock-face in each wall. The corbelled parapet has square angle-turrets surmounted by obelisk finials, and smaller finials are carried on the diagonal buttresses of the crown, which support a miniature balustrade and spire.

The ground floor contains a stone-flagged passage running N-S between the two doors, and a tight winding stair on the E leads to the first floor. From this level a spacious newel-stair, which served the tolbooth itself, rises to the fifth floor, and at each storey there is a blocked doorway in the E wall. That at *101B* fourth-floor level is marked by a simple carved crown, and evidently led to the 'King's Room' (*infra*). From the next level a small newel-stair in the NW angle rises to the clock-

chamber, which contains a clock-mechanism of 1993 and a disused clock of 1963 which replaced one installed in 1816. A cast-iron spiral stair now gives access to the upper two storeys and the parapet, although traces of the original stone turnpike can be seen. The seventh floor contains the keyboard of the carillon that was installed in 1881 by John C Wilson, Glasgow, replacing an earlier set of 'tuneable bells'. Its sixteen bells are suspended from the crown spire.[4]

10

HISTORY

In 1454 a deed was witnessed in the *pretorium* of Glasgow, and about 1530 there is reference to an adjoining property on the N side of St Thenew's Gate.[5] In the 16th century there were booths below the tolbooth. Repairs were made in 1574, and four years later payment was made for 'the biggin of the foir work of the tolbuithe and settin up of the bell', and for the purchase and 'upsettin' of a clock.[6]

In 1625 it was agreed to build a new tolbooth on the existing site, and the town council discussed the quantity of stones required from a local quarry. In March 1626, 'the grund stane of the tolbuithe of Glasgow was laid', and in April 1627 it was sufficiently complete to receive the town's books and charters.

Glasgow (No.34), tolbooth and town hall from SE by Paul, c.1760

(GWD/19/3)

The design may be attributed to John Boyd, who was the master of works. At its completion the town council voted him for his 'bountethe and diligens in building the Tolbuithe, the soume of ane hundrethe pundis money'. The English painter Valentine Jenkin was paid for gilding the weather-cock, clock-dials, and parts of the royal and burgh arms.[7]

xiiB, 99

The tolbooth occupied a site 20m from E-W by 7.5m and consisted of five storeys with a five-bayed S front to the Trongate.[8] This 'very sumptuous, regulated, uniform fabrick'[9] had buckle quoins and string-courses similar to those of the steeple, which stood at the centre of its E end-wall. The windows had alternate triangular and round pediments, with rose and thistle finials. Tall square angle-turrets with ogival roofs were corbelled out at fourth-floor level to rise above the crenellated wall-head. The round-arched and pedimented doorway at the W end of the first floor was reached by a forestair which incorporated an entrance to the ground storey. To the E of the central second-floor window there was a panel bearing the Scottish royal arms, and below it a sundial and, above the foot of the forestair, a Latin inscription.[10]

McUre, writing in 1736,[11] described the ground floor as containing six vaulted rooms, including the Dean of Guild's court and a room for the collector of the town's excise. The first floor contained the 'Justice Court Hall', from which the turnpike in the steeple rose to the council-chamber. This housed an oval council-table, at which the town clerk was murdered in 1694,[12] and a series of large portraits of Stuart and Hanoverian monarchs.[13] The third floor had contained the Dean of Guild's hall, 'but now is turned into two prison houses for prisoners of note and distinction'. The King's Hall, on the fourth floor, was described as the finest room of all, measuring 13.3m in length. The building also contained

five large rooms for 'common prisoners'. Brereton in 1634 was shown an iron-lined closet for the city records.

About 1730 a new council-room and town clerk's chamber were built on the site of a house behind the tolbooth.[14] In 1736-40 a five-bayed three-storeyed clasical block was added to the W, comprising a new town hall with pilastered upper storeys over an open arcaded piazza which served as an exchange for merchants. The tradesmen employed included the mason James Cross, the wrights Robert Dreghorn and his son Allan (who was burgh treasurer in 1739), and the stone-carver David Cation.[15] Between 1758 and 1760 a further five bays to contain an assembly-room were added in matching style, the work again being undertaken by Cross and Allan Dreghorn, with the stone-carver Mungo Naismith.[16] The assembly-room was later sold to the Tontine Society and reconstructed as a coffee-room and hotel.[17] Plans by James Adam 'for altering and enlarging the council-room and town clerk's chamber, and for making a court house in the house in High Street, adjoining to the tolbooth', were approved and executed in 1793-5.[18] In 1814 David Hamilton rebuilt the main block, to the same height but with a six-bay S front and with Gothic ornaments.[19] The building was sold at this time, except for the steeple and the town hall, and the new court-house and offices on Glasgow Green were occupied.

In 1874 the tolbooth and the Tontine building were acquired by the City Improvement Trustees, the whole the becoming the Tontine Drapery Warehouse. In 1911 the original Tontine building was damaged by fire and replaced by a range of red sandstone buildings. In 1921 the remaining tolbooth buildings were demolished, leaving the steeple on its present isolated site.[20]

Glasgow (No.34), town hall and rebuilt tolbooth from SW, c.1890 (GW/3614)

GLASGOW GREEN COURT-HOUSE (NS 5950 6455).

This building, now known as the High Courts, was erected to a Greek Revival design by William Stark in 1810-14, and extensively reconstructed by J H Craigie in 1910-13. It was built at the W side of Saltmarket, which at that time was being extended S to the River Clyde, and its main front looked E over the Laigh Green, now known as Glasgow Green. The building included the municipal offices until 1844 when they were moved to Wilson Street. In 1995 major alterations were in progress to accommodate four new court-rooms on an adjacent site to the W.

Stark's E front included a massive central hexastyle Doric portico with sculptured pediment. This was flanked by two-storeyed five-bayed wings terminating in single-bay end-blocks having paired pilasters and high blocking-courses. Craigie's remodelling retained the main structure of the frontage, but stripped it of many of its ornamental features, including much of the distinctive horizontal channelling of the sandstone ashlar, and introduced new window-architraves. The original court-room had a colonnaded apse, and some of the columns from this were re-used in the two court-rooms of 1913.

HISTORY

In 1807 the inadequacies of the jail within the tolbooth led the council to select a site on the Laigh Green for 'a new jail, County Hall, Council Chambers, Clerks' Chambers and other conveniences'.[21] Stark's design was chosen in 1810 after a limited competition with David Hamilton and Robert Reid, and it was agreed to finance the building by the sale of the tolbooth and by revenues from the Broomielaw quay.[22] It was completed in 1814 at a total cost of £34,811 which was met by the Corporation.

The prison-accommodation, which was situated round a courtyard to the W, soon became insufficient. The building was remodelled for use exclusively as law-courts by Clarke and Bell in 1845 after the municipal offices moved to Wilson Street. It was completely reconstructed as the Justiciary Courts by J H Craigie for Clarke and Bell in 1910-13.[23]

*A. **Glasgow Tolbooth Steeple** (No.34), bells*   (B 58291)

B. crown on door-lintel (B 58300)

*C. **Glasgow Green Court-house** (No.34) from SE, c.1900 (GW/4915)*

35 GREENLAW TOLBOOTH STEEPLE
Scottish Borders

NT 7125 4620

The late 17th-century parish church of Greenlaw with its tall W tower is situated in a large churchyard on the N side of the Green. The tower, which served as a prison, a clock-tower and a belfry for the church, is all that remains of the tolbooth, built about 1700 and demolished in 1830. A two-storeyed court-house abutted the tower to the W, and an early view shows its seven-bay S front which matched the scale and form of the church.[1] The relationship between the three buildings led one visitor to say:

'Here stands the gospel and the law
Wi' Hell's hole atween the twa'.[2]

The six-storeyed tower, which is built of red sandstone rubble, rises to a corbelled parapet enclosing a low octagonal belfry and slated spire.[3] A medieval date has been suggested for all or part of it, but there are no visible features of that period and the masonry appears similar to that of the church.[4] It is about 5.2m square, and a square stair-tower projects from the centre of its E wall, rising through the roof of the church. The vaulted ground storey was the 'Thieves Hole', and originally had no internal access to the rest of the tower. After the demolition of the court-house, which had provided access to the first floor, a stair was cut through the S part of the vault. The present doorway in the S wall is probably of the same period, and replaced a blocked opening immediately to the E which retains an iron yett. It is recorded that an iron cage stood in front of the door to allow prisoners the opportunity of fresh air.[5]

The first-floor doorway in the W wall was converted into a window in 1830, and there is an original window in the S wall which, like those on the upper floors, is protected by an iron grille. All of the internal woodwork at this level is modern, having been replaced after a land-mine exploded nearby during the Second World War.[6] A door in the E wall leads to the newel-stair that serves the upper floors. It is lit by narrow slits in its E wall, the lower of which (since blocked) opened into the church, enabling the prisoners to hear services.

The upper floors are of timber, supported on sandstone corbels. The second-floor cell has a heavily studded door and the inner sill of its S window has been raised, as have those of the windows above. This was done in the late 18th century, at the insistence of the parish minister, to stop prisoners fraternising with his congregation.[7] A number of graffiti are incised on the E wall, including the date '1791' and several names, with the statement '3 gardnars from [Gree]nlaw put in hear for du[c]king a woman but wrong informed on, devil curs them'. The third floor also has a studded door, and in the N wall there is a dressed sandstone embrasure, rebated for a door and containing in the sill a blocked circular opening, probably a slop-sink or urinal. The fifth floor is now open to the belfry, whose floor has been removed although its supporting corbels survive. The stair continues to belfry-level but the door has been blocked, and the parapet and belfry are now reached by ladder from the fifth floor.

The present clock by Robert Bryson and Sons of Edinburgh, which is housed at fifth-floor level, was installed in 1887, and its dials, to N, S and W, are set a little lower than those of its predecessors.[8] The dial-plate of an earlier clock has been retained, and is inscribed: HUGH EARL OF MARCHMONT / MDCCLXIX / JOHN KIRKWOOD MELROSE.

The belfry contains two bells. The 'Town Bell' measures 0.51m in diameter and is inscribed: PATRICK EARL OF MARCHMOVNT LORD HIGH CHANCEL/OUR OF SCOTLAND. IO(HN) MEIKLE FECIT ED(INBU)R(GH) 1702. The 'Kirk Bell' measures 0.56m in diameter and is inscribed: THOMAS BROVNFIELD HIS GIFT TO THE KIRK OF / GREENLAW ANNO 1696 AND REFOUNDED 1726 R(OBERT) M(AXWELL) / FECIT ED(INBU)R(GH).[9]

HISTORY

Greenlaw was created head town of Berwickshire in 1596, but lost this status to Duns in 1661. Through the influence of Patrick Hume, subsequently 1st Earl of Marchmont, an Act of Parliament in 1696 restored Greenlaw as the head burgh of the shire.[10] The court-house and tower were built by the earl soon after this, and the former is said to have borne the date 1712, although the donation of the Town Bell in 1702 may indicate that the steeple was completed earlier. The court-house was a two-storeyed structure with a court-room and record-room on the upper floor and a debtors' room and jailer's house below.[11] The church had been virtually rebuilt in 1675, but is said to have been extended to the W in 1712 to abut the steeple.[12]

The steeple was replaced as a jail in 1824 by a new County Prison, which was itself demolished in 1956.[13] The court-house was demolished in 1830 during the construction of the County Buildings on the Green to the S. This noble neo-classical edifice, with its pillared and domed Ionic portico, was designed by the Berwickshire architect John Cunningham in 1829. It was completed in 1831 at a cost of £6,500, which was borne by Sir William Hume Campbell of Marchmont.[14] In 1960 it was converted into a community centre, and for some years after 1973 it was used as a swimming pool.

The original mercat cross, a Corinthian column erected by Earl Patrick, now rests against the W wall of the tower. A replica of this pillar, with a lion as finial, was erected in front of the County Buildings in 1832.[15]

A

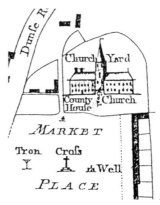

B

Greenlaw (No.35)
A. church and steeple from SW (BW2169)
B. detail of Armstrong's map, 1771

36 HADDINGTON TOWN-HOUSE
East Lothian
NT 5146 7389

The spire of the town-house, 46m in height, dominates the W approach to Haddington, and the centre of the burgh. Its show-front looks W along Court Street and its E front, with the steeple, opens on to an alley, Jail Wynd, which divides it from the narrow block of property between High Street and Market Street.

104   The town-house is T-shaped on plan, with a two-storeyed W block of 1788 which measures 17.5m from E to W by 11m and includes an assembly-room on the first floor. The E block, 18.2m from N to S by 12.2m, replaced a town-house of similar scale which was designed by William Adam in 1742.[1] Its S and N divisions were rebuilt, to contain respectively three and two storeys, in 1823-5 and 1855-6,[2] and the central steeple was replaced in 1830-1 by one designed by Gillespie Graham. The various parts are constructed of sandstone ashlar and coursed rubble, with random rubble in the E face of the SE block.

The W block has three-bay elevations in the N and S walls. The ground-floor openings occupy infilled segmental-headed arches, and at first-floor level there are tall windows with moulded surrounds. The pedimented W front is framed by paired Tuscan pilasters which rise from slightly projecting plinths banded by a string-course. At ground-floor level there is a segmental-headed three-light window, and at first-floor level a large Venetian window above a balustraded apron. The pediment and its flanking plinth-walls are surmounted by urns.

The three-storeyed SE block of 1823-5, which was designed by William Burn, is of three bays to the S and two to the E, and has a double-hipped roof. Its angles are marked by panelled pilasters and the ground-floor windows have segmental heads. The first-floor windows resemble those of the W block, and those of the low second floor are square.

The NE block of 1855-6 is of two low storeys and is also three bays in width, with simple windows and a hipped roof.

The six-stage steeple, which projects slightly at the centre of the E front, has round-headed windows in the three lower stages of its E face, above a modern doorway. The dials of the clock-stage, which is set above a bold cornice, are framed by paired Tuscan pilasters carrying moulded pediments. The belfry-stage is octagonal, with round-headed louvred openings set between attached Tuscan columns and surmounted by a heavy cornice. The spire is also octagonal and is slightly concave above a stepped base.

It was originally intended that the ground floor of the W block of 1788 should be reserved for a grain-market, but when work was far advanced it was decided to infill the two W bays to provide a sheriff court-room in the W end and two record-

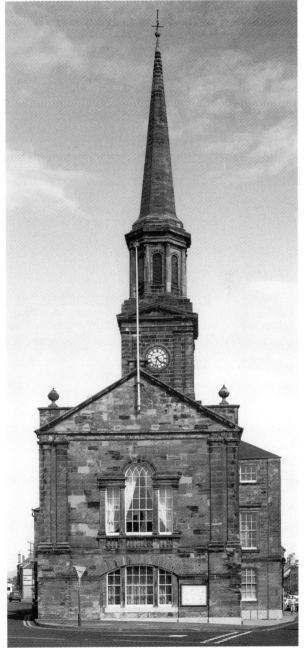

A. Haddington Town-house (No.36) from W, 1853   (C 62955)

B. view from W   (B 39491)

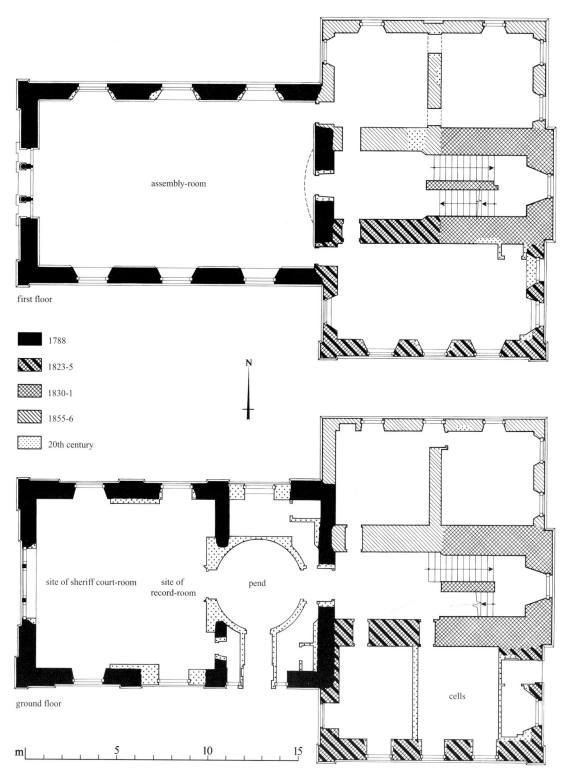

first floor

assembly-room

■ 1788

▨ 1823-5

▩ 1830-1

▨ 1855-6

░ 20th century

N

ground floor

site of sheriff court-room

site of record-room

pend

cells

m | 5 | 10 | 15

Haddington Town-house (No.36), plans

rooms, for burgh and county use, to the E.[3] A blank wall separated these rooms from the W bay, which remained an open pend, used by sedan-chairs and carriages,[4] and opened to a central vestibule and stair in the town-house. This lay-out is shown on plans of 1941,[5] and may have survived until the alterations of 1953-6 by the architect Peter Whiston. At this time the arches of the pend were infilled and a circular neo-Georgian vestibule installed in it, and the rooms to the W were combined to form a council-chamber.[6] The assembly-room occupies the whole of the first floor, as it probably did from the beginning. Its plaster frieze, with fan-vaulted arches enclosing swags, was renewed in 1956 from original sections, but the arcaded plasterwork in the arch-head of the Venetian window has been removed. The cantilevered musicians' gallery or 'fiddle box' above the doorway was also renovated in 1956.[7]

William Adam's town-house included a central vestibule leading to a stair in the steeple, and was 'vaulted in the south end of the ground story for criminals', while the N end included a guard-house, and subsequently also a jailer's house. On the first floor there was a council-chamber and a sheriff-court.[8] These arrangements were retained in the successive rebuildings described above, except for the removal of the sheriff-court in 1788. The heightening of the SE block in 1823-5 provided additional prison-space, and three ground-floor cells were retained there until the 1940s. The central vestibule, whose massive walls may survive from Adam's building, gives access from the W block to a scale-and-platt stair in Graham's steeple, but otherwise the whole building has been much altered in 1953-6 and again in the 1970s.

On the lower stair-landing there stands an iron-bound wooden document-chest, 0.93m in length and 0.5m high.[9] The town clock was repaired in 1531,[10] but the present one was made by James Clark, Edinburgh, in 1832. The steeple also contains four bells, of which the oldest, 0.48m in diameter, has an ornamented frieze and is inscribed: JAN BURGERHUYS ME FECIT 1604. The 'Great Bell', 0.8m in diameter, was cast by John Meikle, Edinburgh, in 1700 to replace an earlier bell,[11] and was again recast by John C Wilson, Glasgow, in 1879. The two others, of 0.6m and 0.72m in diameter, were cast by Thomas Mears, London, in 1831. A converted hand-bell in North Berwick Museum, 0.21m in diameter, bears the inscription: HADINOTOVN A(NN)O 1669 P OSTENS. Below the name of the burgh there is a plaque bearing its emblem, a goat, and this is presumably 'the hand bell of this burgh' which was recast at Rotterdam in that year, at a cost of £18 11s 8d Scots.[12]

HISTORY
The first surviving reference to a tolbooth at Haddington is in 1426.[13] It is believed to have been situated in Market Street facing Newton Port, about 120m E of the present site.[14] In 1572, and again in 1658, the 'drawbrig' of the tolbooth was said to be in need of repair, and in 1683 there was mention of 'the turnpike to the Bartizane', where the bells and clocks were kept.[15] In 1692 the common good of the burgh was reported as being exhausted 'by reason of the many publict works ... such as the repairing the roof of the tolbooth, building a new roof to the steeple, and covering the samen with lead'.[16]

By 1732 the tolbooth was so ruinous that council meetings were held in the library, and in 1740 it was described as 'in danger of falling'. It was resolved that it should be partially demolished, and the clock and bells were removed from the steeple and stored in the 'wester vault'.[17] With the help of the gentlemen of the county a subscription was raised, and in 1742 a contract was made with two local tradesmen to 'build and erect in good and sufficient work a town house and tolbooth', to a design by William Adam. The contract price was to be £500, and masonry from the previous tolbooth was to be re-used in its construction.[18] Several loans had to be obtained to pay the contractors, but the new building was in use by 1744,

and was completed in the following year.[19] It was decided to add 'a battlement with Balisters' round the steeple, which was later described as being 'in the old Dutch round style'.[20] The prison-accommodation proved inadequate, and at various times attempts were made to make it more secure by adding partitions and dividing walls.[21]

In 1774 a request was made to the town council by the 'gentlemen of the county' to build an assembly-room, and it was decided to build on 'waste ground' belonging to the burgh immediately W of the town-house.[22] When work began in 1788 the town contributed the site and gave twenty-five guineas on condition that 'a good prison room' was built 'over the present Burgher room'. The proposal to reserve the arcaded ground floor for the market was abandoned 'owing to the great increase of the barley and oat market', and this allowed the creation of two record-rooms which had long been required.[23] The architect of the assembly-block is not recorded, but it has been ascribed to the local builder-architect James Burn.[24]

In 1823 the county complained of the inadequacy of the jail, and it was agreed to heighten the side walls of the S block to provide four or five aditional rooms, to a plan by William Burn. Local contractors were employed, and it was decided to extend the block 0.9m to the E 'to lengthen the council room'.[25] In 1830 the council considered 'the great disrepair of the town clock and the delapidated appearance of the steeple'. Various plans for a new spire or steeple were submitted, and they concluded 'that a spire according to a drawing by Mr Gillespie Graham would be highly ornamental and suitable for the situation'.[26] Graham quickly produced a revised plan and specification and the contract was awarded to James McWatt. It proved necessary to dismantle the old steeple to its foundations 'in consequence of the insufficient state of the building', and an extra £40 was added to the original contract price of 'above £1,000' for making the front of 'hewn work' or ashlar.[27]

In 1837 there were eleven rooms 'connected with the town-house' and used as prison-cells, but a new prison was opened ten years later, although some lock-up space was retained.[28] The sheriff-court also moved to a new building, in 1832, and the room below the assembly-room was later used as a reading-room. By 1854 the surviving N block of William Adam's building was ruinous, and although its enlargement to the same height as the S block was discussed, it was rebuilt in a modest style in 1855-6.[29]

Haddington Town-house (No.36), document-chest   (C 4115)

105

7 INVERARAY TOWN-HOUSE
Argyll and Bute

NN 0962 0855

The former town-house stands facing Loch Fyne on the S side of Front Street, the main show-front of the Georgian town.[1] Like the two symmetrical private houses that flank it, and the Great Inn (intended for the use of visiting judges) which is separated from it by the entrance to the Avenue, it was designed by John Adam in 1750, and was built in 1754-7.

The original design incorporated a ground-floor prison with vaulted cells at the rear and an arcaded piazza with iron gratings at the front; a first-floor court-room, used for the twice-yearly crown courts and also as a council-chamber; and an upper flat which was adapted for use as a grammar-school even before the building was completed.

The town-house, which measures 18.4m by 6.5m, is three-storeyed and has a five-bay N front with a slightly advanced three-bay pedimented centrepiece. The ground floor of the centrepiece is faced with channelled ashlar of grey-green schist, which was also used for the polished dressings. These include a broad band at first-floor level, linked to corresponding features of the flanking houses. The remaining masonry is harled and whitewashed rubble, and the roof is of Easdale slate.

The ground floor of the centrepiece forms a triple arcade with impost-bands and advanced keystones. The damaged sockets of the original iron gratings are visible in the openings, which contain a central door and windows set in rubble infill in the early 19th century. A door in the W side-bay and a window in the E bay have round-arched frames with plain impost-blocks. The tall first-floor windows of the centrepiece, and the lower ones of the second floor, have moulded architraves, the central first-floor one having an entablature and cornice, while those in the flanking bays have plain surrounds. The moulded surround of the pediment encloses a circular recess.

The interior has been much altered, except for the stone scale-and-platt stair in the W bay which conforms closely to Adam's plan of 1750.[2] His original proposal was for the rear half of the central area of the ground storey to be groin-vaulted and divided into three cells and a lobby. The only surviving cell is a barrel-vaulted chamber measuring 3.1m by 1.8m, and 2.7m high, in the SW angle. The main room in this area has plasterwork of mid-19th-century type, and there is a stair of the same period at the S end of the E cross-wall.

At the first-floor landing of the main stair an irregular patch in the W wall marks a blocked doorway, probably that which Archibald Campbell of Danna, sheriff-clerk, was given permission in 1773 to 'strike out ... between his house and the County House'.[3] The original court-room was subdivided in the 19th century, while the E bay is occupied by the open-well 19th-century stair and landing, but retains an early simply-moulded cornice. The top floor preserves no early features, but alterations in 1988 showed that a fireplace in its S wall occupies an original embrasure. This was presumably one of the three windows that the town council ordered to be made in that wall in 1759 to light the grammar-school.[4]

HISTORY
The town-house replaced a tolbooth of about 1650 which occupied a two-storeyed S wing attached to the parish church in the old burgh adjoining Inveraray Castle.[5] John Adam's first design of 1750 was built in modified form between 1754 and 1757, the contractor being George Hunter. The contract price of £631, which was increased by extra works, was paid by the county authorities, most of it being provided by the sheriff-depute, Archibald Campbell of Stonefield, as compensation for excess county taxes collected many years earlier.[6]

Despite the building's elegance, judges and other visitors to

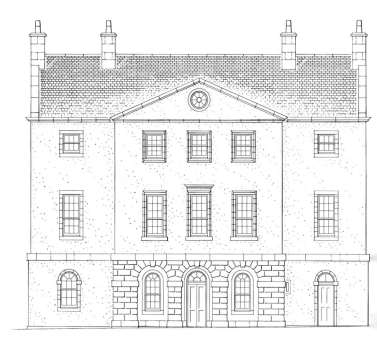

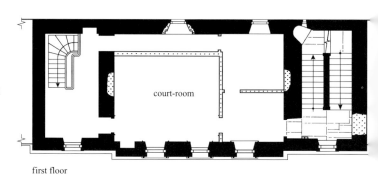

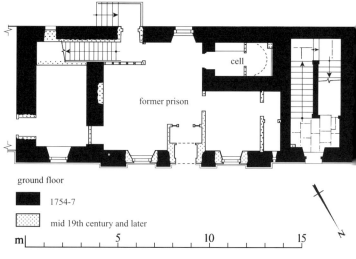

ground floor

- ■ 1754-7
- ▨ mid 19th century and later

Inveraray Town-house (No.37), N elevation and plans

Inveraray criticised the cramped accommodation, as well as the easy communication afforded to prisoners by the iron gratings, and the consequent ease of escape.[7] Plans for a new court-house and jail, obtained from Robert Reid in 1807, were considered by the county to be too expensive, and Richard Crichton was consulted before designs were commissioned from James Gillespie Graham in 1813. The buildings were erected on the E side of Church Square, adjoining the shore of Loch Fyne, in 1816-20, and rooms were made available there for the use of the town council.[8] Thereafter the town-house was used as an estate-office by the Argyll Estate until the 1950s, when the town council resumed occupation.[9]

38 INVERBERVIE TOWN-HOUSE
Aberdeenshire
NO 8300 7265

This two-storeyed rectangular building stands on the S side of Church Street. Measuring 17.4m across the five-bayed main (N) front by 6.6m, it is built of coursed rubble and the hipped roof is slated. The projecting central bay of the N front contains a round-headed arch enclosing a lintelled entrance-doorway, and a round-headed first-floor window rises into the wall-head pediment. This carried a round-arched bellcot which was removed in 1965. Built into the E wall at the wall-head there is a re-used lintel inscribed '1569', possibly from an earlier tolbooth in the market-place at the NW end of the High Street.[1]

Although the appearance of the building indicates that it was extensively rebuilt in the middle of the 19th century, its fabric may incorporate work of 1720, a date which was formerly inscribed above the doorway.[2] In 1837 the upper floor was used as a meeting-hall and council-chamber, while the ground floor contained a market-area and vaulted cell.[3] Modern conversion of the building has obscured any early features of the interior.

On the open platform above the central pediment there is a bell, dated 1792 and believed to have come from the old parish church, which was exchanged with one cast by Thomas Mears and inscribed: GIVEN BY PROVOST BARCLAY TO THE BURGH OF BERVIE 1791. This now hangs in the parish church, and the exchange probably took place when that building was opened in 1837.[4]

A. *Inverbervie Town-house (No.38) from NE*   (C 45942)

B. *re-used date-stone in E wall*   (B 39689)

Inveraray Town-house (No.37) from N   (B 425)

39 INVERKEITHING TOWN-HOUSE
Fife

NT 1304 8292

The town-house stands on the N side of Townhall Street, at the S edge of the medieval parish churchyard and overlooking the former market-area at the N end of High Street, which is now occupied by an island block. [1] It comprises a three-storeyed main block of 1770 abutting a steeple of 1754-5 at the SW angle. The steeple is constructed of local sandstone ashlar laid in courses of varying height, while the main block is of caulked ashlar. Both the gabled roof of the main block and the cupola of the steeple are slated.

The main block measures 13.4m from E to W by 7.8m. Whereas its upper storeys comprise four regular bays, the ground storey has a principal doorway, bearing the incised date 1770, to the W of centre, and a round-headed doorway, originally leading to a pend, in the E bay.

The steeple is almost square on plan and is of four storeys, access to the upper stages being by a simple forestair on the W. In the S front, framed by rusticated quoins, there is a round-headed doorway surmounted by a window of similar form, both openings having bold architraves and projecting keystones. The imposts of the window continue as a convex band which is linked in the W wall to a similar doorway at the head of the forestair. Above this level the S face has a pediment which encloses a burgh armorial and is surmounted by a simply-moulded surround for a lost panel. The octagonal belfry has a round-headed opening in each face and is surmounted by an ogee roof.

The council-chamber was situated on the first floor, to the E of a centrally-placed staircase. A doorway at the S end of the W wall led into a document-store, with a cupboard built to contain council minute-books. Provision was made for prison-accommodation at ground-floor level, with cells in the room immediately E of the staircase and in the steeple. The second floor was altered in 1777 to provide rooms for debtors.

Inverkeithing Museum houses a number of artefacts from the town-house, including a bell, 0.44m in diameter and inscribed: SOLI DEO GLORIA IOHANNES BURGERHUYS ME FECIT / GIFTED BE CAP(TAIN) IAMES BENNET & IOHAN DICKSOONE BALZIES FOR THEWUS / OF THE TOUNE OF INTERKEITHINGE 1667.

HISTORY
Inverkeithing had a tolbooth as early as 1550, when rents were received from the booths on the ground floor, but in 1687 it was considered to be insufficiently secure to prevent the escape of prisoners. [2] The present building may be ascribed to two main building campaigns in the 18th century. The steeple was built in 1754-5, under the supervision of John Monroe, to replace one which was in danger of collapse. [3] In 1769 the town council, after considering the ruinous state of the remainder of the tolbooth, agreed that it should be 'taken down, widened and repaired'. This work was completed in the following year, and payment was made to George Monroe, mason, for 'his trouble in drawing plans'. [4] In 1777 the second floor was altered to provide secure accommodation for debtors, [5] but there is no evidence to suggest that it was an addition.

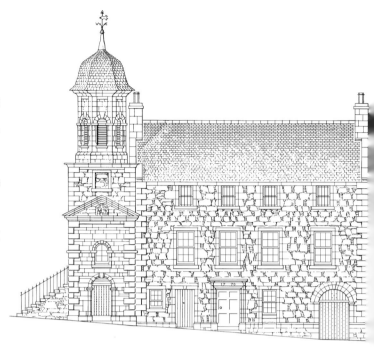

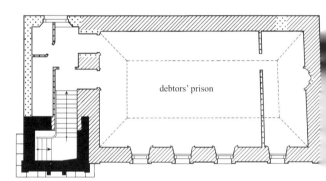

second floor

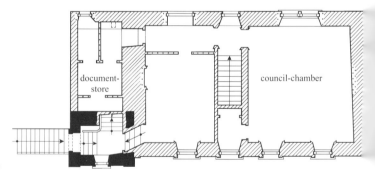

first floor

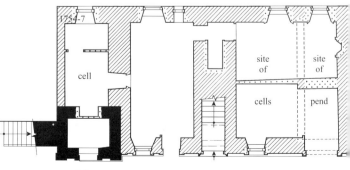

ground floor

Inverkeithing Town-house (No.39), S elevation and plans

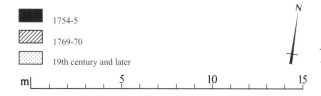

■	1754-5
▨	1769-70
▨	19th century and later

40 INVERNESS TOWN STEEPLE
Highland

NH 6665 4535

This impressive steeple, 43m in height, is situated on the N
side of Bridge Street, at its junction with High Street and
Church Street and about 100m E of the bridge over the River
Ness. It was built in 1789-91 on the site of a steeple of about
1690, and adjoined on the W a court-house and jail which
were begun in 1788 on the site of the tolbooth and were
replaced in 1853 by a three-storeyed block containing shops.
From the first decade of the 18th century the burgh had a
separate town-house on the S side of High Street, 30m SE of
the steeple, and this was rebuilt in Gothic style in 1878-82.

The ashlar-built steeple comprises seven highly-modelled
stages, the lowest forming a plinth with a round-arched
doorway flanked by matching windows in the S wall. The next
stage rises through two floors; there are elongated Venetian
windows with blind centres in the S and E elevations, and
round-arched windows break through triangular pediments
above. The third stage, which rises above the adjoining
building, has paired angle-pilasters enclosing round-arched
louvred openings and supporting a heavy cornice. A
prominent moulded course, on which the pilasters are
superimposed, encircles this stage at the impost-level of the
openings. A clock-face with a carved label dated MDCCXCI
(1791) breaks through the pediment on each façade at the next
stage, whose angles are recessed and panelled. The fifth stage
is cut back to form an octagon with swag-decorated vases at
the angles of the plinth. The main faces of the octagon are
flanked by Ionic pilasters and have round-arched louvred
openings linked by a string-course as at the third stage. The
next stage, again octagonal, forms the plinth to the spire, each

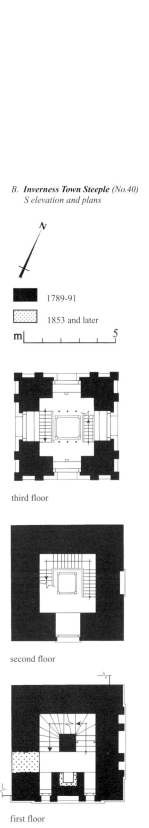

B. ***Inverness Town Steeple*** *(No.40)*
S elevation and plans

N

■ 1789-91

▦ 1853 and later

m |_____| 5

third floor

second floor

first floor

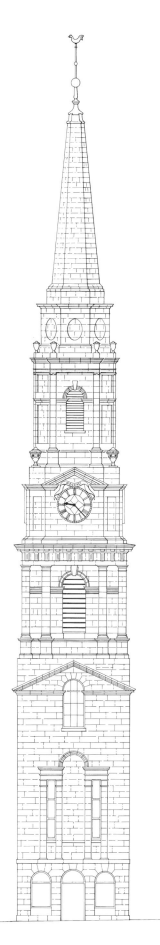

A. ***Inverkeithing Town-house*** *(No.39) from SW*   *(B 39386)*

Inverness Town Steeple (No.40) from SW   (C 45825)

face being adorned with a recessed oval. Its S base-course is inscribed 'finished in 1791', with the names of the burgh magistrates and other officials. There was originally a small urn at each angle and one of these is preserved in the belfry. The octagonal spire is topped by a weather-cock above two ball-finials, one of which is said to contain a pint of whisky. [1]

The ground floor is occupied by a shop from which a stone dog-leg stair rises to the second floor. On the first-floor landing an archway, now blocked, led originally to the court-house. From the second floor a series of wooden ladders affords access to the clock-chamber. The clock's chassis was made in Inverness in 1931, and the mechanism by James H Bridger of Glasgow. The bell-chamber contains three bells known locally as the 'Skellats' or tin-pans. The oldest bears the date 1658 and is 0.38m high by 0.52m in diameter. The second is inscribed: I HOSSACK, LEICESTER, INVERNESS 1759, and the third is inscribed: LONDON. [2]

HISTORY
In 1436 Christine Makferry sold to the burgh of Inverness a piece of land in the NW angle of Bridge Street and Church Street, by a charter which was endorsed 'the charter of the tolbuth'. [3] A substantial steeple existed by 1593, when it was described as 'the house and fortalice called the steeple of Inverness'. [4] In 1663 instructions were given to 'thattche' the tolbooth steeple, and about 1690 it was rebuilt by James Dick at a cost of 3,000 merks, using stones from the demolished 'blew bridge'. [5] This work was completed by 1692 when Thomas Kilgour, watchmaker, repaired the town clock and set it up 'in the new steeple of the tolbuith'. [6]

Meanwhile, some of the functions of the tolbooth were being housed elsewhere. A prison-cell was incorporated in one of the spandrels of a new bridge built over the Ness in 1683-5, [7] and in 1688 the council resolved 'that the Bridge

house should be reserved for the townes use ... to be a Counsell House and Chamber for the common clerk of the towne and for other uses necessary for the towne'. [8] This building, which was probably part of the gateway at the E end of the bridge, itself became unsatisfactory. In the first decade of the next century the council acquired a property fronting the High Street at the foot of Castle Wynd, where a three-storeyed town-house with a seven-bay arcaded N front was built. This contained the council-chamber on the first floor and the guildry room above it, and in the 19th century there was a reading-room on the ground floor. [9] Two armorial panels of 1686 from the old bridge, formerly set at second-floor level in the N front of the town-house, are built into the gables of the present town hall, which was erected in 1878-82 to designs by the local architects Matthews and Lawrie. Two painted wooden armorial panels of 17th-century date from the old tolbooth are also preserved in the town hall. [10]

In 1732 repairs were carried out to the steeple, which included a charter-room and a prison-room. The steeple, as well as the adjacent tolbooth and the new town-house, had shops on the ground floor. [11] In 1786 the court-house in the tolbuth was described as 'very antient', and its jail as comprising 'only two small cells for criminals, and one miserable room for civil debtors', and a year later they were 'very old and incapable of repair'. Since they served not only the burgh and county of Inverness, but the other counties of the Northern Circuit, an appeal was made to these counties and to government for assistance to rebuild them, and the burgh bought adjacent ground to enlarge the site. [12] By April 1789 the new court-house and jail were 'now building' and by May 1791 they were 'now completely finished'. The contractors were John Symens, mason, and William MacDonald, wright, at a price of £1,497. [13] The accommodation in 1818 included four cells, a 'black hole' and four rooms for debtors, a guard-room, a jury-room and a witness-room. The court-room, which measured 10.2m by 5.5m, was used for 'the sittings of the Sheriff Court, the Burgh Courts, the Justiciary and Jury Courts and the County Meetings'. [14]

In 1789 the adjacent steeple was described as 'dangerous ... very old and judged by many to be insufficient', and it was proposed 'that nothing can be so proper for pulling down and rebuilding it as the present, because it might be properly connected with the new court house and jail now building'. The foundation-stone was laid in August 1789 and it was completed two years later. [15] The steeple is said to have been designed by the Edinburgh architect Alexander Laing and the upper part was built by Alexander Stevens, an expert in the construction of spires. [16] The cost of £1,598 was raised through subscriptions, loans and the sale of the old materials, as well as from burgh funds, and Sir Hector Munro MP subscribed an additional £105 for the clock. [17] The upper part of the spire was displaced by an earth tremor in 1816 and it was restored in 1828, as Hugh Miller thought, 'to its state of original insignificance'. [18] Despite minor repairs, it remains little altered except for the removal of the upper series of vases.

By 1818 the jail was considered overcrowded, but although it was condemned in 1836 as cramped and ill-ventilated, a new prison was not completed until 1848. [19] Prominently situated on the site of Inverness Castle, this castellated building by Thomas Brown adjoined William Burn's County Buildings of 1833-5, which housed new court-rooms. The old jail and court-house were replaced in 1853, despite local criticisms of 'the absurdity of attaching a steeple to a row of drapers' or grocers' shops', and the eight-bay Victorian frontage was retained when the N side of Bridge Street was redeveloped in 1967. [20]

41 JEDBURGH
Scottish Borders
NT 6505 2045

The Newgate, which served as the town and county jail between 1756 and 1823, is situated on the S side of Abbey Place, about 75m N of the medieval abbey church and on the probable site of the main entrance into the monastic precinct.[1] The County Buildings of 1812 (now the Sheriff Court), occupy the site of the old council-house immediately to the W, at the S end of the Market Place but with their main (W) front to Castle Street.

THE NEWGATE

112C This comprises an oblong structure, 14.9m from E to W by 6.2m and pierced by a central pend above which there rises a tower surmounted by a spire 36m high. The main block and the lower stages of the tower are of harled rubble, but the upper part of the tower and the spire have been rendered and lined to imitate ashlar, over decayed ashlar which was exposed until the 1960s.[2] The pend, which is entered by recessed segmental arches and has a joisted ceiling, was originally closed at each end by folding gates. In its side-walls there are doorways giving access to vaulted cells in the flanking blocks, which were originally three-storeyed. The E block retains its hipped roof, but the W end was heightened, probably when it was annexed to the County Buildings in the early 19th century. The fenestration is irregular, but some small original openings are preserved in the N front.

The lower stages of the tower are slightly recessed between the flanking blocks, like the pend-arches below. Its E angles have stepped quoins in the stage that rises above the slated roof of the E block, but the W elevation is concealed by the heightened adjacent block. Above a plain band, which probably marks the limit of the work completed in 1755-6, there is a tall plain stage with round-headed belfry-openings and a moulded cornice. The clock-stage has a simple pedimented projection on each face, and a similar cornice. The broached base and the octagonal spire are ashlar-built.

The N arch of the pend bears the painted inscription, 'Entrance to Bridewell Jail', and above it there is a simple date-stone inscribed 'Newgate 1755'. Set in the blocked first-floor window above this there is a panel which was formerly incorporated in a public well in the market-place. It bears a shield with the burgh arms, a mounted warrior armed with a spear, with the motto 'Strenue et Prospere' ('With vigour and success') and the painted date '1720'.[3] A stone inscribed '1761', marking the completion of the tower and spire, is built into the lower part of the S face of the belfry-stage.

A forestair against the E wall gives access, through a door with a simple architrave, to the rooms in the E block and thence to the tower. The first-floor room was in use as a museum in 1859,[4] but it was subsequently fitted up as a kitchen with a large range. It opens into the lowest level of the tower, from which a series of metal stairs and platforms gives

access to the upper stages, and also to the much-altered second-floor room. There was also access at both levels from the tower to the W wing, but the original openings have been blocked and the rooms there, which have been altered, are now entered from the County Buildings.[5]

The lowest level of the belfry contains three early bells. The oldest, which is of pre-Reformation date and probably belonged to the abbey, measures 0.37m in height by 0.43m in diameter and bears a black-letter inscription: CAMPANA BEATE MARGARETE VIRGINIS ('the bell of the blessed virgin Margaret'). The second bell, which came from the old parish church in the nave of the abbey, is 0.58m in height and 0.76m in diameter. It is inscribed: ROBERT LORD IEDBURG HIS GIFT TO THE KIRK OF IEDBWRG 1692 / IOHN MEIKLL ME FECIT EDINBURGI, and bears two medallions with the donor's arms.[6] The third bell is uninscribed, but it is probably the one supplied by the Mines Royal Company of London in 1780, after a bell made by them in the previous year 'had entirely lost its sound'.[7] The upper levels of the belfry contain four quarter-bells, cast by J Warner, London, in 1880 to serve the clock of 1881 on the level above.

THE COUNTY BUILDINGS

These were erected in 1812 at the sole expense of the heritors *112C* of the County, but the burgh contributed 'the old hall or stance, in consideration of which the heritors granted the community rights to an apartment in the upper flat for an office to the clerk of the burgesses and record-room; two apartments on the ground-floor for the public weights; the privilege of the Hall for the magistrates holding their courts and other public meetings of the burgesses'.[8] The original W and N fronts are respectively of nine and three bays, and each has an advanced centre and a pilastered upper storey. The main court-room occupied the upper floor of the N front,[9] but it was subdivided in 1861-2 and the interior arrangements were considerably altered then and at later times. Also in 1861-2, a new principal court-room was provided in a new S wing designed in matching style by David Rhind.[10]

HISTORY

The existence of a tolbooth in Jedburgh is recorded in the early 16th century but its location is not known.[11] In 1664 the magistrates declared that their council-house was ruinous, and ordered that the ruinous part of the church should be taken down and its stones re-used in erecting the new council-house.[12] This appears to have been on the site of the County Buildings, and in 1779 it was described as containing a court-room, new council-room and closet.[13] A separate prison, built above a vault which was latterly allocated to the town drummer, formed part of a row of houses called 'the Tongue', which was demolished in 1756 after the erection of the Newgate.[14]

The 'new prison' adjoining the council-house was ready to receive its window-gratings in 1755, but a plan and estimate for the steeple by the contractor, Bailie James Winter, exceeded the available funds. In 1756 it was built to a height of only 3.7m above roof-level, to house the 'watch bell', and the work was completed in 1761 through the munificence of the parliamentary candidate, Sir Hew Dalrymple.[15] In 1779 the council declared that the magistrates were empowered, as formerly, to imprison debtors in the council-house rather than in Newgate, and in 1789 the first improved bridewell in Scotland was opened by the county authorities. The old prison finally became redundant, save for its bell and clock, when a model jail designed in castellated style by Archibald Elliot was built on the site of Jedburgh Castle in 1820-3.[16]

Jedburgh (No.41)
N archway of Newgate
(B 39496)

42 KELSO TOWN HALL
Scottish Borders
NT 7277 3395

Built in 1816 at the expense of the 5th Duke of Roxburghe and local subscribers, the town hall is set in a conspicuous position projecting into the Square from the NE.[1] The present hall stands on the site of the tolbooth, which was described as 'old and ruinous' in the late 18th century. A painting of that period shows a three-storeyed hip-roofed building with an arcaded ground floor and a tall steeple projecting from the SW front.[2] It is probable that some of the masonry of the tolbooth was re-used in the construction of the present building.

The town hall is built of finely-wrought ashlar and is of rectangular plan, measuring 17.4m by 9m and having two storeys with twin hipped and slated roofs. The main (SW) front has a three-bay pedimented centrepiece surmounted by an octagonal clock-tower. The fenestration is regular and the round-headed ground-floor windows and doorway are recessed within the arches of an original open arcade.

The building's present ornamental character, with Gibbs surrounds around the first-floor windows and an elaborate pedimented entrance-doorway, is largely the result of work carried out by J D Swanston of Kirkcaldy in 1904-6.[3] Before these alterations, the ground-floor arcade was open on three sides to form a market-area.[4] At first-floor level the detached Ionic columns of the centrepiece were replaced by attached columns raised on pedestals linked by a balustrade. The wall-head balustrade was removed, and Gibbs surrounds were added to the round-headed openings of the clock-tower. The interior was also extensively remodelled and most of the original fittings were replaced. The first floor, reached by a staircase to the rear, incorporated the council-chamber.

*B. **Kelso Town Hall** (No.42) from W, c.1880*   *(RX/1644)*

C. view from W   *(B 47502)*

*A. **Jedburgh Newgate and County Buildings** (No.41) from NW   (B 39495)*

43 KILBARCHAN STEEPLE
Renfrewshire

NS 4030 6326

114A

Situated on an elevated island site at the E end of Steeple Street, this building dominates the centre of the village. It is two-storeyed and rectangular on plan, measuring 13.8m from NW to SE by 11.8m, and an elaborate steeple, 3.7m square and 21m in overall height, is set against the NW front. The main SW block, 7m in width, is hipped to the NW and gabled to the SE, with two hipped wings projecting to the NE and linked by modern infill. Both parts are built of roughly-coursed sandstone rubble with dressed margins, but the steeple has an ashlar belfry and spire.

The building originated about 1751 in a proposal to build a small parish school, to which the principal heritor, James Milliken of Milliken, suggested the addition of a steeple for the village bell and a room for a meal-market. It was built in this form in 1755, probably by the local mason David Kerr, and Milliken at first retained the upper room in the NE wing, above the meal-market, but later resigned it to the kirk-session for the use of the local ladies, between church services and during hunt meetings. In 1782, however, the school was demolished at the insistence of the presbytery of Paisley, and enlarged to form the present main block, and then or soon afterwards the E wing was built as a strong-room serving the market, with a schoolroom or dwelling above. [1]

The steeple, which measures 3.7m square and is 21m high, is of six storeys. In its NW front there is a doorway with a Gibbs surround and an exaggerated keystone. At the third stage there is a Venetian window with a central arched niche

14B

containing a statue of Habbie Simpson (*c*.1550-1620), a celebrated local piper. The present bronze figure, erected in 1932, is a replica of a wooden one installed in 1822, the date that is carved on the pedestal. [2] At clock-level in each wall there is a painted clock-face in a square moulded surround. [3] The balustrade of the parapet, which projects on a prominent moulded cornice, combines shaped stone balusters of flat section with plain angle-pillars and copings. The belfry, which is stepped in from the lower stages, has a louvred lancet-opening in each face and houses a bell cast by Thomas Mears of London in 1811. It is surmounted by an octagonal stone spire with ribbed angles, which has obelisks at the bases of the oblique faces.

The original school of 1755, described as measuring 9.1m by 6.1m over all, [4] probably occupied the site of the enlarged one and, with the NE wing, would have formed a symmetrical NW front having the steeple at the centre. The masonry of the existing main block suggests that its outer walls, including the irregular NW front, were entirely rebuilt in 1782, and its internal dimensions of 12.2m by 5.5m correspond with those specified at that date. [5] Its SW front is of three bays of windows at both levels, with a doorway NW of the central ground-floor window. A segmental-headed archway in the NE wall of the square NE wing of 1755 gave access to the meal-market on the ground floor, where a fire-engine acquired in 1765 was housed for many years. [6] The rectangular E wing is probably also of late 18th-century date, although its masonry

A. Kilbarchan Steeple (No.43), NW elevation

B. view from W   *(B 47509)*

113

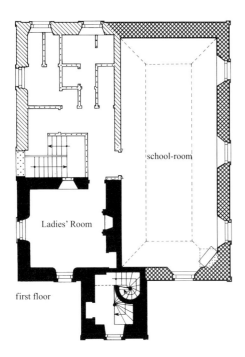

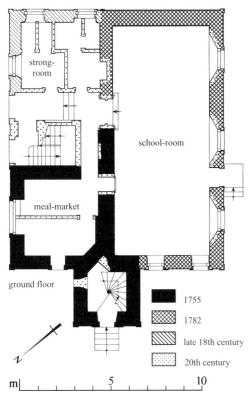

A. **Kilbarchan Steeple** (No.43), plans

1755
1782
late 18th century
20th century

m | 5 10

B. *window in NW front of steeple* (B 47516)

C. **Kilmaurs Town-house** (No.44) from SW (B 39246)

differs from that of the 1782 block.

The interior has been extensively altered, most recently in a major restoration of about 1955-8, and only the former 'Ladies' Room' on the first floor of the NE wing retains its original character. The interior walls of the steeple, which has a newel-less spiral stair housing the bell-rope, have also been altered, and it is not certain whether it provided access to the other parts of the building, although there is a blocked archway at first-floor level. A modern stair now occupies the area between the two wings, and the access to the 'Ladies' Room' was probably always in this position.

44 KILMAURS TOWN-HOUSE
East Ayrshire
NS 4104 4120

This small building formerly occupied a conspicuous island site in the centre of Main Street, but in recent years the E pavement has been extended to encroach upon it. [1] The two-storeyed main block, which measures 7.9m by 6.1m, may date from 1709 and was certainly in existence by 1743 when the town council agreed to carry out repairs. [2] A four-storeyed steeple only 2.8m square and slightly indented into the S gable was built by the masons Hugh and David Barclay in 1799-1800. [3] While the gabled main block is of coursed rubble, which was harled some time after 1964, the steeple is built of lightly-droved ashlar. The roof of the main block is slated, with slab skews which may date from repairs undertaken in 1800-1. [4]

The base of the steeple is solid to the first floor, where the S doorway is round-arched with slight impost-blocks and keystone and a mock fanlight. At the next stage its S face has a lunette above a low projecting panel supported at each end by guttae. The clock stage is intaken slightly and the clock-faces in the N and S walls, which bear the date 1866, are framed in roll-moulded surrounds. The belfry is also intaken, above a moulded cornice, and has a broad louvred lancet in each face. The pyramidal spire has a blind quatrefoil in each face and is surmounted by an ovoid finial. The belfry and spire were rebuilt in 1874 following lightning damage, and the different stone used for this work is still visible. The clock-mechanism and bell were renewed in 1896, [5] and the bell replaced one cast in 1794, whose weight was found to be too great for the old bell-house. Since this could not be easily strengthened 'because of the weakness of the gavel [gable]', funds to build the steeple were raised by public subscription and a levy on leases of burgh property. [6]

At ground-floor level the main block contains two barrel-vaulted chambers, the S one entered by a doorway in the W wall and the other by a rebuilt doorway in the E wall, which were evidently used as cells. [7] A projecting forestair on the S gives access through the steeple to the council-chamber on the first floor, which has a blocked fireplace in the N wall.

Locally the building has been known as 'the jougs', from the instrument of punishment which is attached to the S wall 1.8m above present ground-level. [7] The butter-market was formerly held in a D-plan enclosure outside the N wall of the main block, and the mercat cross stands at the N end of this enclosure.

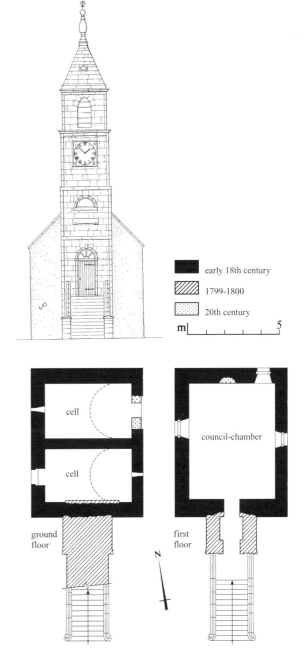

early 18th century

1799-1800

20th century

m |_____| 5

A. *Kilmaurs Town-house (No.44)* *(B 39446)* jougs

B. *S elevation and plans*

115

45 KINGHORN TOWN-HOUSE
Fife

NT 2702 8710

Before 1822 Kinghorn town council met in St Leonard's Tower, which was badly damaged by lightning in that year.[1] The present town-house, on the same site at the junction of Bruce Street and Overgate, was designed by the Edinburgh architect Thomas Hamilton in a castellated neo-Tudor style and built in 1829-30.[2] The two-storeyed main block is of rectangular plan, measuring 12.2m by 9.7m, with a recessed single-storeyed wing to the NE. To the rear there is an obliquely-set rectangular courtyard enclosed by a high perimeter-wall. The building is constructed of coursed sandstone, with ashlar facing of Cullaloe sandstone in the main (SE) front.

The three-bay main block has a projecting central bay framed by faceted buttresses which rise as octagonal turreted pinnacles above a low central tower. This has a crenellated parapet supported by triple-stepped corbels. The clock-face in the centre of its main face is enclosed within a round-headed moulding set on a corbelled cornice. The main parapet, also supported by stepped corbels, has a plain coping but its angles are marked by projecting turrets. The turret at the N angle functions as a chimney, while the main chimneys, each having three hexagonal stone stacks, are set on the side-walls. The centrally-placed doorway and the windows are all square-headed with hood-moulds and the tall first-floor windows are of two and three lights with rectilinear tracery. Original cast-iron railings and a light archway flank the steps and entrance-path. The perimeter-wall of the rear courtyard, which has an ogee-headed entrance-doorway near the SE angle, is decorated with blind crosslet-loops.

The ground-floor vestibule gives access to a barrel-vaulted chamber at each side, and there is a third in the NE wing. All have fireplaces with simple moulded surrounds and two of them were used as cells,[3] while the central one was probably a guard-room. It communicates by a newel-stair with a first-floor office adjoining the court-room, while the main staircase is situated in the W angle at the rear of the central hall. The guard-room also gives access to the courtyard to the rear which was used as an exercise-yard for prisoners.

The court-room and council-chamber, a rectangular room running the full width of the main block, has an ogee-headed fireplace with faceted jambs in each end-wall and a cornice incorporating foliate lozenges.

B. *St Leonard's Tower*   *(MacGibbon and Ross)*

A. **Kinghorn Town-house** *(No.45) from S*   *(B 47518)*

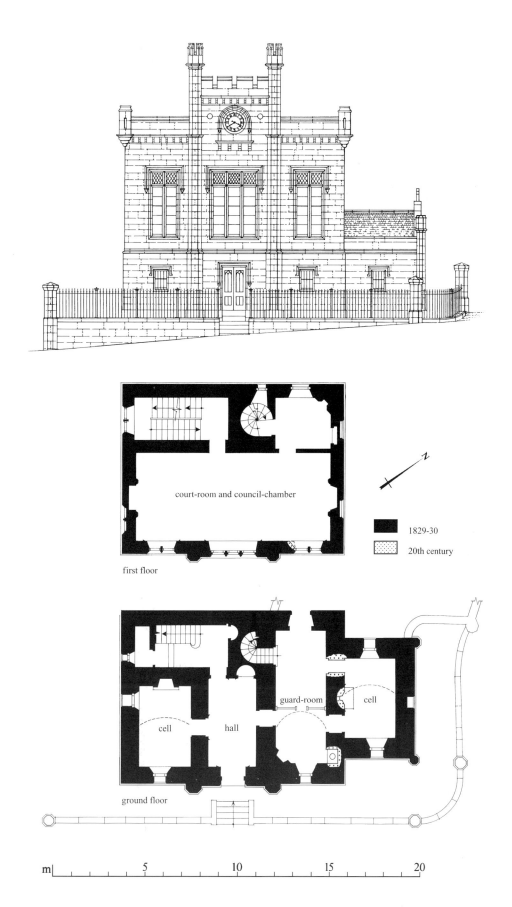

court-room and council-chamber

1829-30

20th century

first floor

guard-room

cell

cell

hall

ground floor

m   5   10   15   20

Kinghorn Town-house (No.45), SE elevation and plans

Although never a royal burgh, Kinross served as the head town of its shire and its 'towbeoth' was mentioned by an English visitor in 1629. A commission was granted in 1690 by Sir William Bruce to the jailer of the tolbooth.[1] This probably already occupied the site, on the E side of the elongated market-place which forms part of Main Street, where the Town and County House was 'repaired' in 1771, partly to the design and at the expense of Robert Adam. In 1742 a new parish church was begun on the W side of the market-place, diagonally opposite this site, and a steeple to house the town clock and bell was built against its N wall by a committee which came to function as a town council.[2] In 1826 new County Buildings, including a jail, were built to the N of the town, to a simple classical design by Thomas Brown of Uphall.[3]

Kinross (No.46), steeple from NE   *(B 47520)*

THE STEEPLE (NT 1195 0215)
The church to which the steeple was originally attached was demolished in 1831, and it is now abutted to the S and W by the Town Hall, built by a private company in 1841.[4] It measures 3.95m square, and comprises a four-storeyed tower with corbelled balustrade enclosing a slated spire, 23m in overall height. It is built of coursed rubble with raised margins and dressings of tooled ashlar, and the ornament is concentrated on the principal (N) front, where each stage is marked by a string-course.

The surround of the round-headed doorway has alternate projecting blocks, and a large keystone bearing the oak-branch symbol of the town. Below the bracketed sill of the round-arched first-floor window there is a relief panel with moulded frame which bears a lion rampant holding a shield and standing on a wreath.[5] The voussoirs of this window are more emphasised than those of the doorway below, and over the keystone there is a blank panel, perhaps intended for a date or inscription, which rises into the string-course above. Construction halted in 1751 at a height of 11m, at the top of the plain third stage, and the fourth stage was completed four years later,[6] but its masonry shows no discernible difference from that below. In each face there is a circular clock-face, and above it a round-arched louvred belfry-opening. The 'raill of stones' or balustrade resting on the simple corbel-course, which comprises alternate rectangular and shaped balusters, was added in 1778.[7] The octagonal broached spire rises from a low square rubble base and is surmounted by a weather-cock.

Inside the steeple a straight flight of stairs leads from the doorway to the Town Hall of 1841, and a series of ladders rises to the fourth stage where the clock is housed.[8] Robert Millar, clockmaker in Alloa, was contracted in 1759 to make a clock, for which Sir John Bruce of Kinross donated £20. It was to be 'of the same dimensions and upon the same plan with the steeple clock of South Queensferry, which was made by Mr Dunlop watchmaker at London'. After Millar's death it was completed in 1761 by Mr Dickie, clockmaker in Dunfermline.[9] The present clock dates from 1875 and was restored in 1964.

The present bell, whose cost of £112 was the subject of 'some altercation' with the heritors, is inscribed: INVITO AD VERBUM AD CHRISTUM ('I summon to the Word (and) to Christ') KINROSS 1814. The earlier bell was cracked 'on some day of public rejoicing'.[10]

HISTORY
In March 1742 it was reported to a public meeting that the heritors were willing for the inhabitants 'to build a steeple upon the side of the (new) church', and a committee was appointed to raise funds and supervise the work. The foundation-stone was laid in June 1742, a month after that of the church, and the same group of local contractors was employed, but work proceeded with many delays due to shortage of funds until the completion of the mason-work in 1755 and of the spire three years later.[11] The steeple committee continued to organise the municipal affairs of the town until it became a police burgh in 1864.

THE TOWN AND COUNTY HOUSE (NT 1190 0215).[12]
The bowed S end of this building, which occupies a triangular site, is prominent in the view N up Main Street. It rises through three storeys over a basement and presents to the W a five-bayed elevation, whose S bay is the flank of the bow end and whose central three bays are advanced. This front is built of coursed rubble with plain ashlar dressings, whereas the ornate S bow is entirely of ashlar, now painted. Its stages are divided by string-courses, overlain in the upper storeys by pilasters which define three bays, with a central architraved first-floor window flanked by round-headed niches. In the centre bay of the low top stage there is a marble tablet inscribed: THIS COUNTY HOUSE WAS / REPAIRED BY

8

THE CROWN / 1771 / ROBERT ADAM KNIGHT / OF THIS SHIRE DECORATED / THIS FRONT AT HIS OWN / EXPENSE. Above a high entablature there is a prominent cornice which is echoed by that of the W front. The rear elevations have undergone numerous alterations, but one window with iron bars survives.

The interior has been drastically altered but originally contained a prison in the basement, which has now been refloored and converted into a cellar. The ground storey has probably always been occupied by shops, which have been completely remodelled; the S one formerly contained a fine set of curved drawers. On the first floor there was a meeting-room at the S end with ancillary rooms to the N, and the court-room and a small debtors' room[13] were housed on the top floor. The two upper floors have been converted into flats, but the stair linking them appears to be original.[14]

The 'repairs' of 1771 appear to have been extensive, and although some older internal walls may survive, the W front is of a single build with Adam's S front, while the SE rear wall appears to be of the same period. It is not known whether Adam made any contribution to the design beyond the S front, and the ostentatious character of the inscription, along with the modest scale of the building, aroused contemporary comment.[15]

The steeple committee met in this building from 1814, and it was used as a jail and for county business until the 1820s, when the lack of a record-room led to proposals for new County Buildings.[16] Thereafter the building was probably adapted for private use, and it was not described as a public building by the Ordnance Survey in 1854.

A. *Kinross (No.46), Town and County House, S front*   (C 48023)

B. *view from SW*   (C 48021)

47 KINTORE TOWN-HOUSE
Aberdeenshire

NJ 7929 1629

This two-storeyed town-house stands on an island site in the central square of the burgh. Constructed of coursed pink granite, it is of L-plan, having an original S block measuring 16.7m by 6.8m which is said to have been begun in 1737 and completed ten years later.[1] A square NW wing, of the same width and aligned with the original W end-wall, was added in the late 18th or early 19th century. Although the designer of the building is not known, its unpretentious form suggests that he was a local mason.

The principal (S) front is of five bays, with ground-floor doorways in the end- and centre bays. A semicircular double forestair encases the central doorway and rises to the main first-floor entrance. This forestair, which obstructs a blocked doorway in the bay W of the central one, probably replaced a previous stair of less elaborate form. The hipped roof of the main block carries a square ogee-roofed clock-tower. The clock-face has a circular moulded surround, while the other faces of the tower have small windows.

The central doorway at ground-floor level leads to a barrel-vaulted pend-like cell running the full depth of the main block. The whole of the ground floor and the W part of the upper floor have been extensively altered for domestic or commercial use, and preserve few early features. At first-floor level the central area of the vestibule has round-headed arches supporting the clock-tower, those to W and E enclosing square-headed doorways. The W doorway has been blocked, allowing the W portion of the building to be self-contained. The E room, used as the council-chamber, has architraves and doors of mid-19th-century character.

The clock-machinery bears inscriptions recording that it was made by Hugh Gordon, Aberdeen, and was donated by the 10th and last Earl Marischal in 1774. The bell, which was used for both church and burgh purposes, measures 0.58m in diameter and is inscribed: FVNDOR SVMPTIBVS ET IN VSVM ECCLESIAE PAROCHIALIS DE KINTOR / MEMORES ESTOTE SUPREMI IVDICII ALBERTUS GELY FECIT AN D MDCCII ('I am cast at the expense of and for the use of the parish church of Kintore. Remember the Last Judgement. Albert Gely made me in the year 1702').[2]

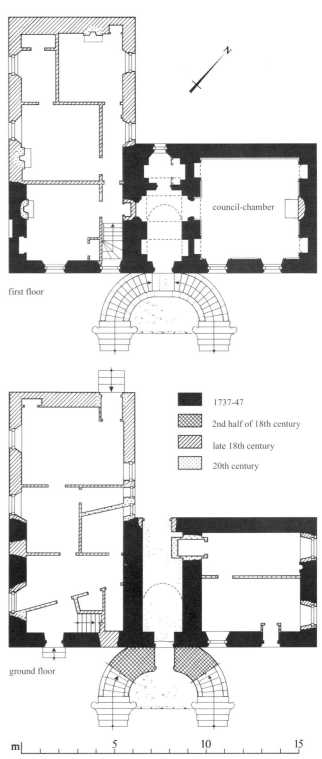

first floor

council-chamber

■ (black)	1737-47
▨ (crosshatch)	2nd half of 18th century
▨ (diagonal)	late 18th century
▨ (dotted)	20th century

ground floor

m | 5 | 10 | 15

Kintore Town-house (No.47), S elevation and plans

A. **Kintore Town-house** (No.47) from S   (B39690)

B. first-floor vestibule   (B 39729)

C. interior of council-chamber   (B 39728)

D. town council, 1894   (B 39732)

121

48 KIRKCUDBRIGHT TOLBOOTH
Dumfries and Galloway
NX 6807 5089

The tolbooth with its impressive steeple occupies a prominent position at the SW angle of the right-angled High Street, adjoined by houses of early 17th-century date to the E. Its main (N) front faces up the NW limb of High Street. The mercat cross of 1610, which originally stood at the centre of the High Street in front of the tolbooth, was set on the platform of the forestair in 1760.[1]

124C

124A The greater part of the three-storeyed main block, which measures 22.1m by 6.6m, dates from 1627-9, but some 6.6m of this length resulted from its extension to the W in 1754.[2] The lower part of the steeple, which extends the N front to the E for 4m and is 4.8m in depth, was built in 1642-4, but the upper part was extensively rebuilt, probably after a severe fire in 1723. A straight forestair rises against the N wall to a first-floor doorway in the steeple, and the adjacent platform was rebuilt in 1763 to incorporate a water-supply. The building is of sandstone rubble with dressed margins, except for the N front of the steeple above wall-head level, and the forestair and platform, which are of ashlar.

The irregular disposition of the openings in the N front reflects various periods of alteration. The remains of a segmental-arched opening towards the centre of the main block, and evidence of blockings in the rear wall, indicate that originally a pend gave access to the rear of the building.[3] Its *124D* archway had a roll-and-hollow moulding, and the W jamb was later incorporated in an inserted square-headed doorway which also re-used other moulded stones. There are an early doorway and a small window, both with roll-moulded surrounds, near the foot of the forestair. The first floor is lit from the N by four large windows with quirked-roll-and-

hollow surrounds. Disturbed masonry between the two E windows at first-floor level may mark the site of an original doorway approached by a forestair.

However, the main entrance in the period before 1754 was at the W end of the original building, close to the present entrance, and it evidently gave access to a stair marked at first-floor level by a blocked slit-window and a reduction in the internal wall-thickness. This was presumably the 'turnpike' whose top rose above the wall-head until 1732 when it was 'thrown doun' and made level with the main roof.[4] A recess above the pend, which held an armorial panel within a moulded surround,[5] was replaced in 1955 by a panel commemorating the quincentenary of the burgh. At second-floor level, three slit-windows for prison use have been created within earlier embrasures, but two circular pistol-loops with *124B* curved internal recesses remain. The rear wall of the main block appears to retain no unaltered early windows, but a chimney-breast is corbelled out at first-floor level.

The W extension of 1754 comprised a single bay, of the same height as the main block, with barrel-vaulted cells at ground- and first-floor levels. The junction with the old work is marked by a rough vertical break at the upper level, 6.6m E of the present W gable. Below this joint, a doorway which was inserted at this time, and probably re-uses masonry from the original main entrance (*supra*), gives access to the main staircase. Another plain doorway provides the only access to the dark ground-floor cell. The lower part of the NW angle of this block is bevelled, and set into the stonework at a height of about 1.5m there is a set of jougs.[6]

A second set of jougs hangs beside the first-floor doorway to the steeple. This has a roll-moulded surround and like the blocked window above, which may have been remodelled in 1724, it has a relieving-arch.[7] The ashlar-faced N front of the steeple, which rises from a chamfered intake at wall-head level, was probably rebuilt in 1724 along with the upperworks. There are clock-faces to N and E, and pointed belfry-openings[8] in each wall below the parapet, which projects on an arched corbel-course. Each face of the parapet has two stone water-spouts at the base and three semi-circular apertures below the coping, and its angles are surmounted by ashlar pyramids with ball-finials. The conical spire is also of ashlar, and has at least one blocked square vent at about mid-height. 'Ane ship maid of bras for putting upone the top of the steipill' was obtained from the Netherlands in 1646, but the present

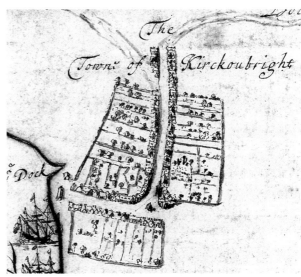

A. Kirkcudbright Tolbooth (No.48) from NE (B 47531)

B. 17th-century view of Kirkcudbright (Public Record Office)

c.1630

c.1650

Kirkcudbright Tolbooth (No.48), conjectural reconstructions and plans

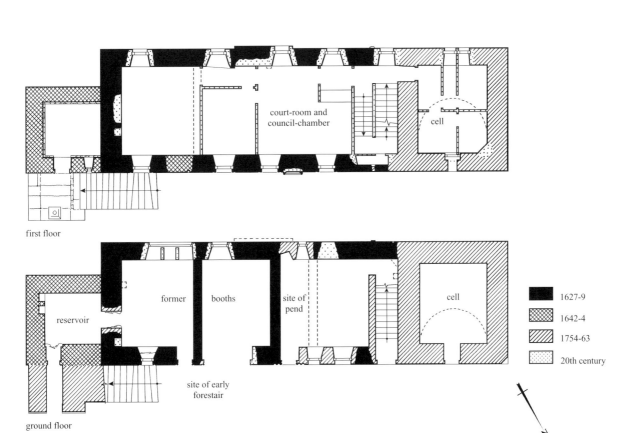

second floor

court-room and
council-chamber

cell

first floor

former   booths   site of   cell
                    pend

reservoir

site of early
forestair

ground floor

■	1627-9
▨	1642-4
▧	1754-63
⠿	20th century

m   5   10   15   20   25

123

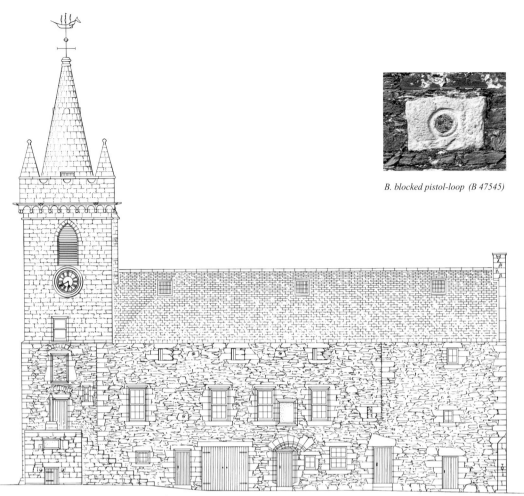

*A. **Kirkcudbright Tolbooth** (No.48), N elevation*

B. blocked pistol-loop (B 47545)

C. forestair, mercat cross and entrance to steeple (B 47540)

D. doorway in blocked arch of pend   (B 47536)

weather-vane, in the form of a three-masted sailing-ship, is believed to have been erected after 1805 to commemorate the Battle of Trafalgar.[9]

In 1763 a lead water-cistern was installed below the platform of the forestair, restricting the original ground-floor access to the steeple. In its ashlar-faced N front there is a panel (renewed in 1840 and 1985) with the inscription:
THIS FOUNT - NOT RICHES - LIFE SUPPLIES,
ART GIVES WHAT NATURE HERE DENIES;
POSTERITY MUST SURELY BLESS
SAINT CUTHBERT'S SONS WHO PURCHAS'D THIS.
WATER INTRODUCED 23D MARCH 1763.
To the E of this panel there is a slot for a pump-handle, and two water-spouts of 'sun-face' type flank a small doorway below.

The interior of the tolbooth has been much altered, and even before its recent adaptation as an Arts Centre the existing partitions were modern, except in the ground storey. This originally contained three booths, which were sold in 1629 to finance the new building,[10] and it is likely that two of these were in the E part, which until recently was divided from the former pend by a solid wall. The first floor contained a large room which served as court-room and council-chamber and there is a blocked fireplace in the S wall. Until modern alterations there was a cross-wall some 3.9m from the E gable-wall,[11] originally forming an ante-chamber which would have been entered from the presumed forestair, and subsequently an inner room. The present staircase, in the W extension of 1754 but close to the site of the earlier 'turnpike', is of stone to the first floor, but of modern timber construction above. The vaulted first-floor cell in the W extension, formerly guarded by double doors in the SE angle, had a slop-sink in the sill of its S window,[12] now altered. The second-floor rooms, which rise into the roof-space, were used at various times for social functions or as debtors' accommodation, but retain no early features.

The interior of the steeple contains at ground-floor level a cell, known as the 'laich seller', with two aumbries in the SE corner. It is now entered by a doorway slapped through the E wall of the main block, presumably in 1763 when the room became the main reservoir for the new piped water-supply. At

A. *Kirkcudbright Tolbooth (No.48), 1646 bell and wheel*   (B 70841)

B. *detail of 1646 bell*   (B 70838)

C. *ornament and inscription of 1646 bell (scale, 1:7.5)*

D. *inscription of 1724 bell (scale, 1:7.5)*

the same time, the original vault was removed, and until recently a large block of inserted masonry supported the floor above.[13] The upper floors originally had no communication with the main block and access was by timber stairs. The spire is supported by arches spanning the angles of the top storey.

The principal bell in the steeple measures 0.52m in height and 0.61m in diameter, and below a dragonesque strapwork frieze it is inscribed: SOLI DEO GLORIA. MICHAEL

BVRGERHVYS ME FECIT ANNO 1646. This was evidently the bell cast, 'in ane mold of ffour hundreth wecht', from three bells sent to Veere in the Netherlands in that year.[14] The second bell was cast by Thomas Mears, London, in 1841. Also displayed in the building is 'the toun's litle bell', 0.34m in height and 0.44m in diameter, which was cast in Rotterdam to replace one damaged in the fire of 1723 and is inscribed: QUIRIN DE VISSER ME FECIT 1724 / KIRKUDBRIGHT.[15]

Stewartry Museum houses a single-hand clock set within a wrought-iron frame, which remained in use until 1897. This is believed to be of Dutch manufacture and may have been in existence by 1580 when a 'knock-keeper' is referred to.[16]

HISTORY

The present tolbooth had at least two precursors, its immediate predecessor being situated a short distance to the E, on the site of the County Buildings on the N side of High Street. This was the former church of St Andrew, which was acquired by the burgh in 1570 and converted into a tolbooth. The 'auld tolbuith', which it replaced, may have stood further W, and in 1577 its site and building-materials were sold.[17] Although contracts were made for the maintenance of the former church, and other repairs were carried out, in 1625 the town council complained that their tolbooth was 'ane ald decayit kirk ... now altogidder decayit and fallin doun'.[18] Declaring their resolve 'to big ane Tolbuith and strong prisone-hous within the hairt and bodie of thair toun', the council was granted a share of the fines imposed by local justices for two years. Funds were also raised from landowners, including a loan of £2000 from Sir John Gordon of Lochinvar which was repaid from rents owed to the council and the sale of the booths in the new tolbooth. For temporary accommodation the council leased from one of the bailies 'the meikill hall of his tenement to be ane tolbuithe and the northe chalmer to be ane jevill (jail)'. The new building was not begun until 1627, and it appears to have been completed two years later.[19]

The old tolbooth, although ruinous, continued to house the clock and bell, but in 1642 the council considered 'the necessitie of ane steiple and bel hous ... quhilk is ane speciall ornament belanging to every burgh'. The inhabitants 'cheirfullie' agreed to a local tax for this purpose, and by 1644 the steeple was ready to receive the bell from the old church. It was probably built by John Dunbar and Herbert Anderson, two masons who entered the town's service in 1642, and it is said to incorporate re-used masonry from Dundrennan Abbey.[20]

Various alterations and repairs were made to the building in the 17th and 18th centuries. The fire of 1723 broke out in the steeple, in straw illegally stored there by the clock-keeper, and although it was contained when 'men of a venturous spirit got up to that west window above the tolbooth and got water carried to them', the internal timberwork was destroyed. Extensive repairs were carried out in the following year, and it was probably at this time that the upper storeys were rebuilt. At about the same time repairs were required to 'the Councell Chamber which wes brought doun to the ground by an unlucky accident'.[21] In 1732 the tolbooth was described as 'ruinous' and its roof was repaired, with alterations to the stair-head.[22]

19A Between 1744 and 1747 Thomas Kerr, mason, repaired the steeple at a cost of £3 17s 2d. In 1751 he produced a plan for 'making a sufficient prison on the West end of the Tolbooth', and in 1754, when he was burgh treasurer, he was employed to build this extension.[23] Bailie Kerr also supervised the bringing in of 'fresh soft water' in 1763-4, and altered the steeple and forestair to house the reservoir and cistern. The upper storey of the town-house was also repaired in 1763, and was made available for dancing-classes.[24]

The burgh had no convenient place to keep its records, and for many years these were stored in the houses of the magistrates, or in a rented house.[25] The council-room was also found 'too confined' for county meetings and elections, and in 1774 it was agreed that the county should 'contribute largely' to the cost of its enlargement. It was not until 1788 that a new Town and County House was completed on the N side of the

Kirkcudbright Tolbooth (No.48), clock-mechanism   *(B 70322)*

High Street, with a council-chamber in the front half of the lower storey and the County Hall, also used as the burgh court-room, on the upper floor.[26]

The tolbooth was the model for the 'old-fashioned dungeon' of Freeport in Scott's *Guy Mannering*,[27] and it remained in use as a jail until the early 19th century. At that period it contained two rooms for debtors and two for criminals.[28] In 1815-16 a new jail was built adjoining the court-house to the N, the estimated cost of £3,978 being shared between the burgh and the county. The massive castellated tower, containing seventeen cells and with a higher SE angle-tower, was designed by Richard Crichton, the Edinburgh architect, who also undertook the contract. The court-house was rebuilt in baronial style, as the County Buildings, about 1870.[29] The tolbooth was used for a variety of purposes including storage, a glove factory, government offices and coastguard station, and in 1993 it was converted and opened as an Arts Centre.

49   KIRKINTILLOCH STEEPLE
East Dunbartonshire
NS 6528 7399

The steeple, also known as the Town-house and the 'Barony Chambers', was built in 1814-15. It replaced a tolbooth which probably stood on the same site at 'The Cross', the junction of High Street and Cowgate.[1] It is situated at the S side of the Auld Kirk churchyard, and the fall of the ground allows for two storeys to the S and three to the N, fronting West High Street. The main block measures 12.3m from E-W by 6.8m, and a six-stage steeple projects some 3.75m at the centre of the N front. The main block is constructed of coursed rubble, with more regularly-wrought masonry to the N front, and the steeple is of ashlar.

The main block is a plain gabled structure of four bays with symmetrically-disposed windows, those of the N front having slightly-projecting surrounds. Access is by a doorway set to the W of centre in the S front, and by another in the W face of the steeple which is reached from street level by a forestair. The steeple has a plain basement surmounted by a tall second stage with round-headed windows within broad angle-pilasters which rise to a bold cornice at eaves-level. The third stage has segmental-headed windows between panelled angle-pilasters, and its cornice supports the plain clock-stage, above which there is a square belfry with chamfered angles and rectangular louvred openings. The ashlar-built spire is of plain octagonal form.

Originally the ground floor contained a court-hall and two small prison-cells, while the first floor was occupied by the council-room and the upper floor by the 'steeple school'.[2] The interior, which has been extensively altered in the 20th century, preserves few early features, but the staircase of the steeple retains its original balustrade and newel-post. The clock-mechanism is modern, and the clock-faces were replaced in 1950.[3] The bell, which was hanging in the steeple by 1829, cracked and was recast in 1835 and again in 1849. It bears the latter date and the founder's name, David Burges, Glasgow, and is now displayed in the Auld Kirk Museum.[4]

HISTORY
A tolbooth was in existence at Kirkintilloch in 1659, when a meeting of the burgh court was held there.[5] In 1749 the town council agreed with the heritors to insert a loft, build an outside stair, and form a new door and windows so that the upper floor could be used as the parish school.[6] The old building was demolished in 1813 and the present steeple built at a cost of almost £850, the money being raised through public subscriptions, loans and 'assessments' on local landowners.[7] Furniture for the council-room included a table, two elbow chairs and twelve other chairs, with a bench 'erected in proper and economical manner' as a slightly later addition.[8] By 1860 the building was in need of extensive repairs and the possibility of building a new Town Hall was discussed, although this was not achieved until 1905-6.[9] The steeple now houses a local museum.

Kirkintilloch Steeple (No.49) from NE   (B 47548)

50 LANARK TOWN-HOUSE
South Lanarkshire

NS 8817 4365

The former town-house is situated on the S side of High Street at its junction with Wellgate, and separated from the parish church to the W by an open space in which the mercat cross formerly stood.[1] It comprises a two-storeyed rectangular block, built in 1778 on the site of the previous council-house and originally attached on the W to the jail portion of the old tolbooth, which was replaced about 1837 by a bow-ended extension.[2]

The main block measures 20.2m from E to W by 8.5m, and the later block extends a further 4.3m to the W. Both parts are built of stuccoed rubble with dressed margins and the roofs are slated, that of the extension being hipped. The main block has stepped and channelled quoins and moulded eaves-cornices, and the ground storey of the N front, which was converted in the 19th century into two shop-fronts, has paired end-pilasters. At first-floor level in this front there are five round-headed windows with impost-blocks and keystones, and the two-bay E front has similar first-floor windows, and a blind lugged oculus in the gable. In the early 19th century an enclosed stair was built against the E end of the S wall. Its pilastered E doorway, originally reached by a flight of steps, was itself enclosed in a porch early in the 20th century. The W block has straight side-bays linked by recessed quadrants to a W front which has a tripartite first-floor window and a central chimneystack above the blocking-course.

Internally, the building retains no early features at ground-floor level, although two cast-iron columns with decorated capitals are believed to have been removed about 1980.[3] The first floor of the main block contained a single large room, later subdivided, whose dimensions of 13.2m by 7.2m correspond closely to those agreed for the County Hall in 1779.[4] In each gable-wall there is a fireplace with a quadrant-moulded stone surround. The doors, which include a blocked one at the centre of the S wall, are six-panelled and fielded, and there is plain wainscotting and a simple cornice. The interior of the W block preserves no early features.

From at least the 17th century the burgh bells and clock were housed in the steeple of the nearby parish church. The 'large bell of Lanark' was recast by Thomas Mears in 1835, and a long inscription records that it was 'originally founded in 1110, recast in 1659 and again in 1740'.[5]

HISTORY

A tolbooth, which included rented booths and a 'belhous' or steeple, existed at Lanark in 1488.[6] A rebuilding, funded from the common good and from a tax on the inhabitants, was executed in 1572-3 by Thomas Tuodall. The ground storey was to contain eight vaults, and the new N wall was to have four ashlar doorways, and another on the 'fore entry'. Fitting up of the building was still in progress in 1576, when a smith and two other craftsmen were warded until they should complete 'the werk of the tolbuith and cunsall hous'.[7]

Further alterations, including the construction of an internal wall and a vault 1.8m wide, were carried out in 1657 when a fleshmarket was established against the S wall. In 1711 the town council agreed to borrow 1,000 merks to prevent the 'utter ruin' of the church and tolbooth, and in 1714 they discussed 'the ruinous conditione of the high tolbooth', which was used as a debtors' prison.[7]

In 1777 the council decided to rebuild the council-house, now so ruinous that it 'would not admitt of any repair or alteration on account of its insufficiency'.[8] The gentlemen of the county had for some years been seeking a site to build a meeting-room, and they agreed to contribute £100 to the new building in return for the use of a suitable room. A plan and estimate were prepared by John Purdie, 'mason and wright in Lanark', who undertook the contract along with Thomas McGhie, mason, and James Lockhart, wright, for £215. The building was to comprise a lower storey (probably at basement-level) containing a guard-house and weigh-house, a 'middle storrie consisting of a Council Room, Sheriff Court Room, and the third storie to consist of one large room'. While work was in progress it was noted that 'the tolbooth gavell stands higher than the Townhouse', with a risk of water-penetration, and the tolbooth roof was lowered so that both buildings could be slated at the same level. The contract was agreed in January 1778, and work seems to have been completed by the end of that year.[9]

The jail in the old tolbooth became so insecure that in 1834 it was remarked that 'for many years ... none have staid in it but such as were prisoners *de bonne volonté*'.[10] Following the completion in 1836 of new County Buildings and a jail in Hope Street, the upper room of the town-house was subdivided, the ground floor was leased as shops, and the remaining part of the tolbooth was demolished.[11]

A. *Lanark Town-house (No.50) from NE*   (B 47557)   B. *view from NW*   (B 47555)

51 LANGHOLM TOWN HALL
Dumfries and Galloway
NY 3647 8449

The town hall is situated in the centre of Langholm on the SE side of the Market Square. It was built in 1811 on the site of the old tolbooth, which was in existence by 1726. The building is two-storeyed and measures 12.6m by 9.15m, with a three-stage tower above the projecting centre of the three-bayed NW front. It is built of stugged ashlar from the Whita Quarry,[1] and has a hipped and slated roof. The exterior is little altered, but it is now over-shadowed by the Jacobethan-style library that was built against the SE wall in 1875-8, replacing an earlier building.[2]

The regular NW front has stepped quoins and a first-floor band and eaves-cornice which return along the side-walls. The advanced central bay contains a plain rectangular doorcase, and the round-headed first-floor window, which has a projecting keystone and impost-blocks, is framed by paired angle-pilasters. The lowest stage of the tower has smaller windows of similar form, and the intaken upper stages, which contain clock-dials in plain square frames, and then a belfry with round-headed louvred openings, are topped by a concave stone roof with a weather-vane. The belfry no longer contains a bell, and the clock of 1886, which replaced the original one of 1813, was in turn rebuilt in 1962.

The interior of the building was radically altered for local government use in 1973 and there is little information about the previous arrangement. The ground floor originally contained three prison-cells,[3] with the town hall above.

HISTORY
In 1726 it was noted that the village of Langholm 'is now very much improven and beautified with a townhouse and prison for the Regality of Eskdale, [and] a cross', and that it was the meeting-place of the regality and Justice of Peace courts.[4] Thomas Telford recalled that the tolbooth was 'partly a prison and partly a justice hall ... with an outside stair for ascent: a sort of bell tower ... occupied the middle of the edifice, and its narrow iron-grated windows and the vault-like entrances gave it a gloomy gaol-like appearance'. He contrasted this with the new building which was 'in some places, decorated from Greek and Roman examples'.[5] The new town hall, whose foundation-stone was laid in 1811, was built to 'Mr Elliot's plan', probably the work of the Kelso architect William Elliot who was employed by the Duke of Buccleuch at this time.[6] When the adjacent library was built in 1875-8 it was initially proposed to replace the town hall also, but this scheme was abandoned.[7] The interiors of both buildings were altered in the 1970s.

Langholm Town Hall (No.51) from NW   (B 47559)

52 LAUDER TOWN-HOUSE
Scottish Borders
NT 5309 4757

The 18th-century town-house is situated N of the parish church, at the NW end of an island block known as the Mid Row, and facing NW up Market Place. It is a three-storeyed rectangular structure of harled rubble measuring 6.7m across the main (NW) front by 12.9m along the side-walls. A straight forestair rises to the main doorway at first-floor level in the NW end-wall, and the gable above carries a rectangular clock-tower capped by a pyramidal slated roof. The doorway has a heavily-moulded Gibbs surround and above it there are two blind oculi. These features have evidently been renewed, but early views show that they follow the original forms.[1] Both NE and SW fronts have simple openings placed asymmetrically, with a ground-floor doorway at the centre of the SW wall.

The ground floor now consists of two barrel-vaulted cells, but appears originally to have been divided into three by a cross-wall to the centre of the present NW cell. The construction of a small vestibule inside the SW doorway, and the rebuilding of the fireplace in the SE wall of the SE cell, may be ascribed to the early 19th century. The space below the forestair, which was originally entered from the NW cell, contains a small window-less cell known as the 'black hole'.[2]

A. **Lauder Town-house** (No.52) and church, aerial view from W   (B 49013)

B. view from W   (B 47562)

The first floor, which was used as the court-room and council-chamber, has a blocked fireplace in its SE wall and inserted storage-cupboards at the NW end. Access to the second floor, which rises into the roof-space, is provided by a wooden staircase entered from the first-floor vestibule. This vestibule area is enclosed within masonry piers rising from ground-floor level to support the clock-tower, which contains a bell said to have been renewed in 1790.[3]

HISTORY
In 1543, in a period of English raids and invasions, the town council of Lauder ordained that there should be a watchman 'on the tolbuith heid'.[4] An English agent reported in 1598 that 'Lord Home yesterday came to Lauder and burnt the tolbooth and took out and killed one William Lawther that with his brethren had lately hurt one John Cranston, who before had killed their father'.[5]

In 1729 the 6th Earl of Lauderdale gave the burgh £100 for the repair of the school and the tolbooth, and a new clock was made for the steeple in 1735.[6] In 1770 the thatched roof was replaced with slates, but very extensive work was required in 1773 when the building was reported as being ruinous and dangerous, and plans and estimates were obtained by the town council. While council minutes refer to the 'repairing' of the tolbooth, £160 was borrowed for the work, and contracts were made with two wrights and two masons.[7] The appearance of the building suggests that it was largely rebuilt at this time, perhaps re-using earlier masonry and following the original plan. It continued to be used as the town jail until 1843.[8]

■ 1773 (probably incorporating earlier work)

▦ early 19th century and later

m |__|__|__|__|__| 5

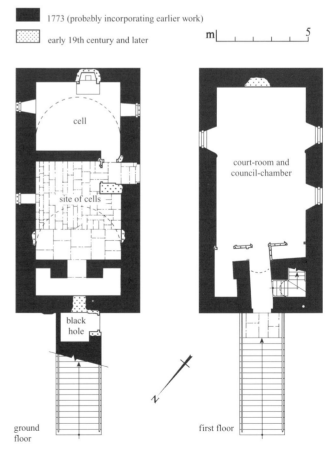

C. plans

53 LEITH
City of Edinburgh

From an early period South Leith formed part of the barony of Restalrig, but a *pretorium* (court-house) in the port itself was burnt in the English invasion of 1544. To replace this, and to provide a 'strength' or fortification against the English ships then active in the Forth, the Regent Mary of Guise granted to the inhabitants the small tower at the E end of the King's Wark, with a 'house' above the vault adjacent to the W.[1]

A new tolbooth on the S side of Tolbooth Wynd was built by the inhabitants of Leith, with the support of Queen Mary, in 1564-5. However, the superiority of the port was acquired in the latter year by the burgh of Edinburgh, which appointed bailies to hold courts in the tolbooth. It was demolished in 1824 on the orders of the city magistrates, and replaced by a jail, never used for that purpose, which was itself demolished in the 1960s.

A police act of 1827 gave powers to the 'Magistrates and Masters', a body with local representation, and in 1828-9 they built a neo-classical town hall in the NE angle of Queen Charlotte Street and Constitution Street. This was used as the headquarters of Leith town council from 1848 to 1920.

LEITH TOLBOOTH (NT 2699 7633)
Queen Mary in 1564 directed the burgesses of Edinburgh to cease obstructing the efforts of the inhabitants of Leith 'to big and edifie oure hous of justice', and the new tolbooth prominently displayed her arms, with the date 1565.[2] In the same year, however, the burgh of Edinburgh acquired the superiority of the port, and during the siege of Edinburgh Castle in 1571-3 the courts and councils of the Regents and of the burgh were held in Leith Tolbooth. The port became a burgh of barony in 1636 and continued to be governed by bailies appointed by the city magistrates.[3] In 1715 a force led by Mackintosh of Borlum briefly occupied the town and liberated a number of Jacobite prisoners held in the tolbooth.[4]

The building was demolished in 1824, despite the protests of Sir Walter Scott and C K Sharpe, but its appearance is well known from early views.[5] Its three storeys were divided by stepped string-courses, and it had a central pend leading to the fleshmarket that was installed at the rear in 1569.[6] A forestair rose to a square-headed moulded doorway at the W end, which was separated by two large windows from a three-bay oriel window with animal finials above its cornice. The royal armorial of 1565 was set at the centre of the second floor, which had small heavily-barred windows, and the parapet was crenellated.

The ground-floor vault was used for a guard-house from 1725, its entrance being in the forestair.[7] The court-room occupied most of the first floor, and in 1817 there were also a small room and closet for the clerks, while the main prison-accommodation was evidently on the second floor, from which prisoners escaped in that year to the roof.[8] In 1665 South Leith kirk-session complained of 'the naughtinesse of the bell that we have in the Tolbuith Steeple, that cannot be hearde be the halfe of the toun', and in 1678 it was reported that 'the top of the Tolbuith steeple of Leith the horolodge [clock] and cock are all rowinous and defective'.[9] One view shows a gablet with a weather-cock at the wall-head above the oriel.[10]

The tolbooth was replaced in 1824 by a castellated jail, court-house and council-chambers designed by Thomas Brown, at a contract price of £2,000. The jail was never legalised, but the building was occupied by the town clerk, and by the new Leith town council from 1833 to 1849. It was then leased, and in 1868 sold, for commercial use, and was demolished in the 1960s.[11]

*A. **Leith Tolbooth** (No.53) from NE by Storer, 1820*   *(C 47332)*

B. armorial of Queen Mary, 1565   *(C 65068)*

LEITH TOWN HALL (NT 2722 7624)

The town hall was designed by the Edinburgh architects R and R Dickson and built in 1828-9 at a cost of £3,260.[12] The adjoining, and slightly earlier, three-storeyed terrace in Queen Charlotte Street was converted to police and burgh offices by the local architect James Simpson in 1868 and refurbished by him, along with the original council-chamber, in 1891-2.[13] Simpson also designed, in 1878, the two-storeyed classical prison-block that adjoins the N end of the original building and faces Constitution Street.[14] Further alterations were made in 1903 (including another extension to the E), in 1938 and in 1983, when inserted partitions in the former court-room were removed.[15]

The original block is three-storeyed and of slightly-splayed rectangular plan, the entrance (S) front measuring 13.5m and the W front 17.7m in length. The main façades are constructed of sandstone ashlar of excellent quality, specified as from 'the best Rock' of Craigleith Quarry.[16] The masonry of the ground storeys is channelled, and the whole centrepiece of the S front is treated similarly, giving it a somewhat baroque character. This front has a three-bay portico with Tuscan columns *in antis*, flanked by segmental-headed windows, and at first-floor level there is a large tripartite window, with consoles set in the rebate of the central round-headed light.[17] Flanking its arch-head, and above the side-lights, there are small square windows.

The ground storey of the five-bay W front also has segmental-headed openings, the central one being a doorway giving access to the stair, while the central and the two outer windows at first-floor level are pedimented. The recessed central three bays of the two upper floors are divided by giant Ionic columns and framed by plain pilasters, which are repeated at the angles of the building. They carry a high entablature and a massive dentillated cornice. Both wall-heads have long pedimented tablets framed by giant scrolls. The W one is inscribed: ERECTED BY THE MAGISTRATES AND MASTERS / MDCCCXXVIII, and that to the S: TOWN HALL / R & R DICKSON ARCHITECTS.

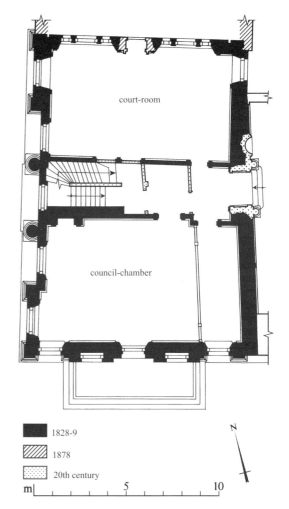

court-room

council-chamber

■ 1828-9

▨ 1878

▦ 20th century

m   5   10

N

B. first-floor plan

A. **Leith Town Hall** *(No.53) from SW*   (B 58118)

A. **Leith Town Hall** *(No.53), council-chamber from E*   *(B 58126)*   *B. ceiling of council-chamber*   *(B 58124)*

C. view from SW by Shepherd, 1829   *(C 65569)*

The interior has been much altered, particularly at ground-floor level, in connection with its present use as a police station, but the principal first-floor rooms are well preserved. Set to either side of a central staircase, which was rebuilt in 1983 but occupies its original position, there are the sheriff-court room, to the N, and the council-chamber to the S. The former has an anthemion frieze with a dentillated cornice, and its panelled plaster ceiling has a central rose within a fret pattern. The windows are framed by tapered architraves surmounted by shallow pediments, and in the S wall there are blocked double doors which formerly provided separate access from the stair-landing and from an ante-room. The magistrates' bench was set against the E wall, and in the N wall there is a doorway with a round-headed architrave, inserted in 1878 to give access to the adjacent prison-block.

The council-chamber was enlarged in 1891-2 by the removal of inserted offices, and it is now entered from a richly-decorated marble staircase of 1903 in the adjacent Regency block. The principal decorative feature of the chamber itself is the ornate and brightly-painted plaster ceiling, decorated by Thomas Bonnar.[18] On the walls there hang portraits of local provosts and a large painting by Robert Carse of George IV's landing at Leith in 1822.

HISTORY
The town hall was built for the Magistrates (appointed by Edinburgh) and Masters (of the four local incorporations), a body which under the Leith Police Act of 1827 was given administrative powers and the duty to provide a sheriff-court and offices. The foundation-stone was laid in March 1828 and the completion of the town hall a year later was marked by the removal from the jail of the painting of George IV's landing. The main hall, which was to become the council-chamber, was used from the first for public meetings and ceremonies, and the Police Commissioners and the Magistrates and Masters themselves met there. A town council was established when Leith became a parliamentary burgh in 1833, and it used the building from 1849 until 1920 when the burgh was amalgamated with Edinburgh.[19]

After many years in commercial occupation, the town hall was converted in 1983 for use as a police station.[20]

54 LERWICK TOLBOOTH
Shetland Islands

HU 4783 4127

This plain rectangular building, which was begun in 1767, stands on the N side of Commercial Street, on ground which originally sloped down to the shore and now adjoins the harbour esplanade. It is two-storeyed above a basement and measures 16.35m from E to W by 7.4m, excluding a two-storeyed outshot to the N. It is built of rubble quarried on Bressay and cement-rendered, but has stepped quoins and scrolled skewputts of sandstone imported from the Scottish mainland,[1] and its gabled roof is covered with grey-green slates.

The five-bay S front has regular fenestration, and the central doorway, which has been heightened, formerly had a lugged and roll-moulded surround with a cornice. It was reached by a low forestair, now replaced by a ramp, which had slightly-splayed enclosing-walls terminating in ball-finials.[2] The upper storeys of the end-walls were of two bays, above basement doorways, but one window in the E wall has been altered to a door reached by a forestair. A lean-to shed was built against the N wall in 1790, for the use of a local builder, but the present outshot dates from the early 20th century, and replaced a small yard and stable.[3]

Early views show a small square clock-tower set centrally on the roof-ridge.[4] This steeple, which was added in 1772, was stone-built and terminated in a simple slated spire above louvred belfry-openings. It was repaired and altered in 1780 to house a larger bell for church and public use, and a clock was installed a few years later, but the entire steeple was removed in 1927.[5]

The interior has undergone many alterations and now possesses few early features. The court-room was in the W half of the main floor, and the room to the E was used in the first quarter of the 19th century as a school-room, and thereafter as the sheriff-clerk's office. Originally a stone stair gave access to a room 5.5m square in the E half of the top

B. reconstruction from SW

floor, which was used for masonic meetings and as a ball-room. On the same floor there were two prison-rooms, which were notoriously insecure. The E end of the basement contained two vaulted criminal cells, entered through a lobby from an area doorway in the S wall, and to the W there was a store-room, entered by a door in the W end-wall. At various times the building also housed a custom-house and weigh-house, but their locations are uncertain.[6]

HISTORY

The tolbooth stands on the site of a previous one, which was presumably built in the 17th century.[7] In 1755 the local Commissioners of Supply, who were responsible for the administration of justice in the islands, decided that it should either be enlarged or replaced by a new building.[8] In 1760 Lord Morton, feudal superior of the islands, approved the latter proposal. After failure to obtain a new site it was decided to retain the existing one, re-using or selling the materials of the old building, and an adjacent house was demolished to enlarge the area.[9] In addition to donations and loans from individuals and increased taxes imposed by the Commissioners, funds were obtained from the proceeds of local wrecks and from a subvention by the Morton Masonic Lodge, who were granted the use of a room for their meetings.[10]

A plan of the proposed building was submitted in January 1767, and the foundation-stone was laid in June of that year. The principal builders were Robert and James Forbes, masons in Lerwick, who were appointed 'to furnish and work all the Free Stone necessary in the foresaid intended Tolbooth', and a considerable work-force was employed. The final account, which was settled in 1770, amounted to £798 3s 5d.[11]

In 1774 the Rev George Low noted that 'the most remarkable building [in Lerwick] is a new Town-House, a neat fabrick with a small spire, but no clock', and that deficiency was remedied in the following decade.[12] In 1784 a new door was installed at the base of the stair and in 1789 various alterations were made to the prison, roof and steeple. A new clock was installed by public subscription in 1825, and the steeple was again repaired in 1844 at the insistence of the parish heritors.[13] The prison inspector in 1836 was appalled by the laxity of conditions in the jail, and the dampness of the basement cells, and it was declared unfit. In 1838 the prisoners were moved to Fort Charlotte, although the tolbooth continued in occasional use as a lock-up.[14]

In 1878 the main floor was converted for use as a post office, which came to occupy the whole building, and after 1912 it was used for a Fishermen's Institute.[15] A new town hall in Gothic style was built to the designs of Alexander Ross in 1882-3.[16]

*A. **Lerwick Tolbooth** (No.54) from SW by Dryden, 1855*   ***(C 47165)***

55 LINLITHGOW
Lothian

NT 0023 7720

The Burgh Halls of Linlithgow occupy a dominating position on the N side of the Cross, the original market square of the burgh, overlooking the ornate restored well that marks the site of the mercat cross. The building is set at the E side of Kirkgate, the approach to St Michael's Church and the Royal Palace, and adjoins the churchyard. It comprises the town-house, which was designed and built by John Smith in 1668-70 and, on higher ground to the N, the County Buildings, a two-storeyed range built to William Burn's designs in 1819-21.

THE TOWN-HOUSE

xiiA
36A, 137A

This is a three-storeyed rectangular block measuring 19.1m by 9.3m and having a square six-storeyed stair-tower at the centre of the rear (N) elevation. Its seven-bay S front was refaced with ashlar, and the upper part rebuilt, after a severe fire in 1847.[1] The ground floor is entered by a central doorway enclosed by a double flight of balustraded steps, constructed in 1905, which rise to a principal entrance at first-floor level and mask the lower part of the elevation.[2]

Throughout the building the windows of the upper floors are surmounted by triangular pediments containing thistles and other symbols of the Union. A slightly larger pediment over the first-floor doorway, which shows the 'black bitch and tree', the emblem of Linlithgow, was installed during the repairs of 1848 to replace an armorial panel above a somewhat lower doorway.[3] The cornice and blocking-course, both renewed in 1848, enclose a hipped roof of the same date, whose predecessor was built in 1790 to replace an original flat leaded roof with balustrade. This was reached from the stair-tower through a surviving doorway above which there is a roll-moulded frame for an armorial panel.

The two-bay W wall facing Kirkgate is built of weathered yellow ashlar, which was not renewed in 1848,[4] whereas the N and E walls are of rubble, also much weathered, and most of their sculptured window-pediments appear to be unrestored. The two moulded string-courses, cornice and truncated chimneystacks were renewed in 1848 using a darker stone.

The tower is built of similar rubble, and its six stages are defined by string-courses. In the second stage of its W face there is a blocked doorway with a lintel inscribed 'Doorway to debtor's prison struck out in 1792 built up in 1812'.[5] The two upper stages of the tower contain narrow round-arched windows, and clock-faces to E,S and W.[6] Its balustrade was rebuilt in 1848, and originally enclosed a lead-covered timber spire.

In the original arrangement,[7] the central area of the ground floor was used as a weigh-house and also contained, to the W, a timber-built girnel. This was separated by a masonry wall from the 'wester tolbooth', which occupied the W end and was entered by an external door in the S wall, as was the corresponding but smaller 'easter tolbooth'. In the NE angle behind the latter prison there was a 'black hole', entered from the weigh-house as was a vaulted 'dark prison' in the base of the stair-tower.[8] In 1827 the E wall of the W prison was moved some distance to the E, and two parallel E-W vaulted cells were formed.[9] Until 1845 the ground floor was independent of those above, but following the removal of the prison to a new building it became one of the main entrances to the court-room and County Buildings. The former 'black hole' in the NE corner became a lobby, with a doorway in the N wall opening into a new staircase which communicated with the court-room above and with the County Buildings. This door was blocked in 1962-3, and the vaulted cell in the tower was replaced by a new stair, while the dividing-wall between the two W vaults was removed, and the two E rooms were combined for the first time.

The first floor was entered from the forestair through a central lobby at whose N end there was a newel-stair in the tower. In the 18th century the council-chamber was to the W, where its original fireplace survives, and the court-room was to the E. These positions were reversed in 1962-3, and the new court-room was enlarged to include the former lobby. The entrance to the tower is through a lugged stone doorcase which appears contemporary with the building and may be the

Linlithgow (No.55), detail of view from S by Slezer, c.1690

(WLD/37/4)

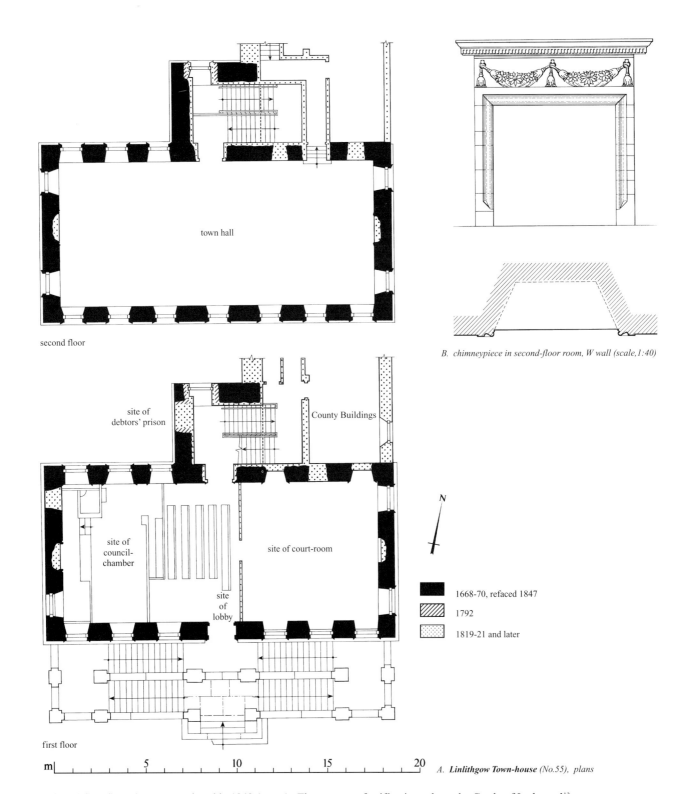

second floor

first floor

site of debtors' prison

County Buildings

site of council-chamber

site of court-room

site of lobby

town hall

N

■ 1668-70, refaced 1847

▨ 1792

▦ 1819-21 and later

m | 5   10   15   20

B. *chimneypiece in second-floor room, W wall (scale,1:40)*

A. *Linlithgow Town-house (No.55), plans*

original first-floor doorway, replaced in 1848 (*supra*). The whole of the second floor is occupied by the town hall, a magnificent chamber which was formed in 1848[10] but retains in the end-walls two original stone chimneypieces complete with overmantels. Their friezes are decorated with thistles, roses and fleurs-de-lis, reflecting the symbolic programme in the external pediments.

HISTORY

'The ancient council-chamber of the burgh' was one of the endowments of the altar of St Mary in St Michael's Church, founded before 1374.[11] It is not known when the tolbooth was built on the present site, but it is mentioned in a charter of 1507-8.[12] This building was 'razed to the ground be the Inglish at thair incoming to this kingdome in anno 1650', and the stones and timber were 'applied towardis the workis and

fortifications about the Castle of Lythgow.'[13]

In 1661 the town council set about raising funds to rebuild the tolbooth and a royal grant of a levy on malt and ale, obtained in 1666, was supplemented by voluntary subscriptions.[14] In November 1667 John Mylne, the King's Master Mason, prepared a design for the new building for which he received immediate payment of £88 12s Scots. He died in the following month, and in January 1668 the Council approved 'the concording with John Smith maister measson for edifieing our tolbuith in all respects conforme to the draught thereof drawn up be him'.[15] A contract was made in the same year for the supply of stone from Kingscavil quarry, and the inhabitants were called on to transport stone and other building-materials.[16] Smith completed the masonwork in 1670, although work on the roof and steeple, using Dutch lead, continued until 1673.[17]

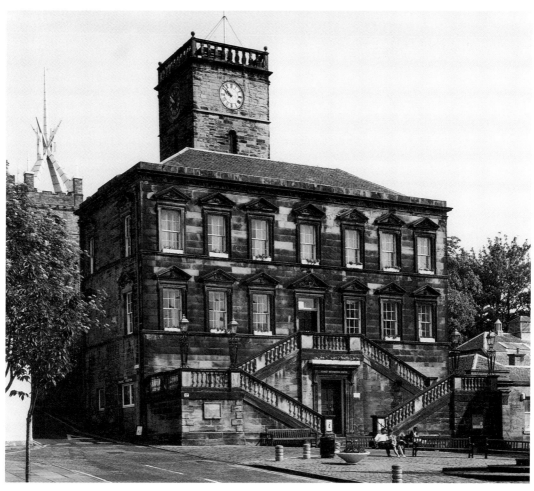

A. *Linlithgow Town-house* (No.55) *from SW*   (B 58095)

A series of drawings for the tolbooth, now lost but published in 1893,[18] includes three different schemes. The first, whose ground-plan bears the initials of John Mylne and the date 7 November 1667, shows a three-storeyed L-plan building with vaulted rooms, presumably cells, in the NE wing. The seven-bay main front, 23m in length, has a central entrance-tower rising above a high roof with pedimented dormers, and there is a faceted stair-tower at the rear. Elements of this plan reappear in a set of floor-plans, presumably by John Smith, for a seven-bay rectangle, 28m long, having a central door below a double forestair, and a square stair-tower at the centre rear. A single ground-plan shows a less elongated version of the same plan, and corresponds closely to the town-house as built.[19]

In 1710 certain windows on the ground floor were blocked to improve the security of the jail. In 1722 the steeple and 'bartesan' were repaired and in 1752 it was proposed to install sash-and-case windows and to refurnish the court-house. The court-room was repaired in 1786 at the expense of the county, for use by the Sheriff Court.[20] The major alteration during this century was the replacement in 1790 of the balustraded flat roof with a hipped one of 'skailie' (blue slate) by James Buncle, deacon of the wrights.[21]

The original forestairs to the first floor were described in 1810 as 'much decayed', and Richard Crichton was employed to erect a cast-iron verandah in Regency taste, which may have been the work of the Carron Iron Company.[22] This provided market-space and carried a first-floor balcony, but removed the access to the former principal entrance. It is possible that a substitute stair to the court-room was built against the E part of the N wall,[23] but the erection of the County Rooms to the N of the town-house in 1819-21 provided access via a spacious hall and staircase to both buildings. Improvements made to

B. *ground-plan and S elevation by Mylne, 1667 (scale, 1:400)*   (B 41762)

138

the jail in 1827 by Thomas Brown, an Uphall builder-architect, included the creation of two vaulted cells, one of them for debtors.[24] Following the building of a new jail in 1845, the ground floor was transferred by the prison board to the county authorities, who opened a doorway from the NE ground-floor room to the main staircase.

The fire of 1847 caused extensive damage to the upper floors of the building, and the whole roof was lost, as well as the spire. Following a dispute between the burgh and the county authorities over their respective rights in the building, it was agreed that it should be restored to its pre-fire state. William Nixon was appointed to report on the damage but withdrew due to ill health, and was replaced by another Edinburgh architect, Thomas Brown. The work was completed during 1848, at its estimated cost of about £800.[25] The exterior required extensive repair, including new roofs for the main block and tower, but the most expensive element was the treatment of the S front, which was refaced and partly rebuilt 'in the same style and exactly in the form of the present building'.[26] The façade was completed with an inscribed frieze below the cornice, commemorating the fire and rebuilding. The iron verandah at the ground level was retained. The only major internal work undertaken was the formation of the large top-floor hall, and the alterations to its floor and roof described above.

A bell by John C Wilson and a clock by Mr Mackenzie, both of Glasgow, were installed through public subscription in 1857.[27] During the late 19th century a fire-station was created in the SW vault of the ground storey, where the lintel of double doors opening into Kirkgate is still visible. Alterations proposed in 1886 by J Russell Walker were not executed, but in 1905 the cast-iron verandah was replaced by a double flight of return stairs, restoring the principal door to its original importance.[28]

The most extensive alterations made to the building since its erection were carried out by Rowand Anderson, Kininmonth and Paul in 1962-3, to create a suite of burgh halls.[29] On the ground floor the wall dividing the two vaulted rooms to the W was removed, and the two rooms E of the entrance-hall were also combined. The vault of the cell in the base of the tower was destroyed and a staircase inserted to the first floor. On the first floor the W room became the court-room and was extended to incorporate the original entrance-hall, and the newel-stair in the tower was replaced by a concrete scale-and-platt stair.

THE COUNTY BUILDINGS

A site for new County Rooms designed by William Burn, 'immediately behind the Town House, and connected with the Sheriff Court Room', was granted to the county by the town council in 1819 at a low feu-duty.[30] The W front, which faces Kirkgate, is of six bays, the end ones being slightly advanced. These end-bays contain segmental archways, the S one enclosing the entrance-doorway and the other opening to a pend. The ground-floor windows are round-arched within recesses of similar form whereas the upper storey has large rectangular windows. The entrance-hall, whose ceiling was supported on four timber columns, and the elaborate staircase to the S, were removed in 1962-3, when the first-floor committee-room and county hall were combined.

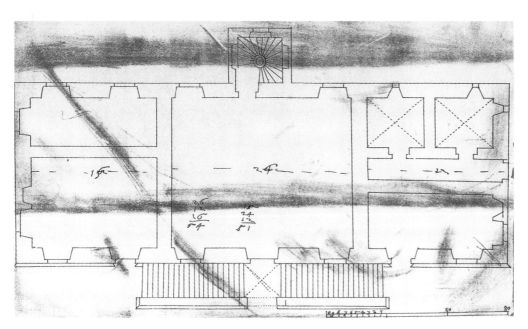

Linlithgow Town-house (No.55), ground-plan attributed to Smith, 1668 (scale, 1:200)   (B 41765)

56 LOCHMABEN TOWN HALL
Dumfries and Galloway
NY 0818 8257

Situated on an island site at the N end of High Street, which forms a broad market-place, the town hall is a two-storeyed T-plan building with a steeple at the centre of the S front. This steeple was added in 1743 to a hip-roofed main block of 1723, comparable in scale to the existing one but with a central projection to the N, and part of the S wall of this block survives, including a 1723 date-stone.[1] Except for the steeple, however, the building owes its present appearance to an extensive rebuilding in 1877, to the designs of David and John Bryce.

Before 1877 the steeple was flanked by two single-storeyed lean-to bays having open round-headed arches with projecting keystones and impost-bands, and known as the 'bows of the town hall'.[2] In that year they were heightened to two storeys, surmounted by balustraded parapets, and their ground stages, with that of the steeple, were refaced with rusticated sandstone ashlar, the arches being infilled with windows. The round-arched entrance-doorway in the steeple was also renewed, as was the first-floor Venetian window whose central opening was altered to a niche which contains a statue of the Rev William Graham (d. 1887), a local benefactor. The square ashlar-built steeple rises to a heavy cornice below which there are four circular clock-faces. Above it there is an octagonal belfry rising from a plinth with concave sides. The belfry has louvred round-arched openings with keystones and impost-bands, and below the cornice there is a raised band which on the S face bears the inscription 'Built by Ja(me)s Forrest 1743'. Above this a convex plinth carries a short octagonal spire, rising to a height of 22m.

The N block of 1877, which measures 16.5m from E-W by 7.6m, has a gabled roof and there are large Venetian windows

A. Lochmaben Town Hall (No.56) from S   (B 47567)

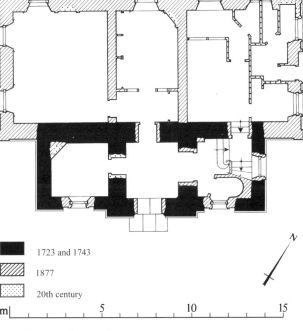

1723 and 1743

1877

20th century

B. S elevation and ground-plan

A. *Lochmaben Town Hall* *(No.56) from S by Aitken, c.1850* (DFD/133/2)

B. *burgh arms in stained glass of first floor, W window* (B 47594)

C. *detail of steeple* (C 2598)

D. *date-stone* (B 47576)

in the E and W walls. Even where the early structure has been preserved the interior was heavily remodelled, and a staircase was formed in the bay E of the steeple in place of a forestair against the E wall of the original main block. Built into the N wall of the second-floor room in the steeple there is a panel bearing the date 1723. This is above the probable wallhead-level of the building of that date, but it may have been incorporated in a central pediment or a bellcot (*infra*). The belfry contains a bell 0.5m in diameter at the mouth, which bears the inscription: EX DONO NOBILISSIMI CAROLI DUCIS QUEENSBERRY / ET DOVER 1757 W(ILLIA)M EVANS FECIT.

HISTORY

While there are references to a tolbooth at Lochmaben in 1563,[3] it was stated in 1625 that the courts of the warden of the West March and the steward of Annandale had hitherto been held in the church. In that year James VI gave orders for his Master of Works to choose a site and build a tolbooth at Lochmaben, that 'the lower roumes may serve for prisons to malefactoures and the upper for keeping of courtes and administration of justice'. The work was to be financed by fines imposed on inhabitants of the neighbouring sheriffdoms for illegal carrying of 'hagbuttes or pistolettes'.[4] The 'toune court' was 'haldin in the tolbuith' in 1627.[5]

In 1705 the Convention of Royal Burghs paid £100 Scots to the burgh 'for building and repairing the(i)r tolbuith'.[6] Despite this, a new building was required by 1720, when minutes record 'the great loss the community of the Burgh is at through the want of a Tolbooth'. Subscriptions were raised from the inhabitants and from local landowners, and the date-stone of 1723 presumably records the completion of the building in that year.[7]

In 1741 the 3rd Marquis of Annandale presented £150 'for building a meall house and steeple' in accordance with a plan which had been in the possession of the town-council 'for somtyme past'. They decided to proceed with this, but to create a new doorway in the west gable of the town-house, giving access by 'a straight scaile stair' to the council-chamber, and to remove the 'cupala' on its roof. The contract was awarded to Mr Henderson of Broadholm, for £150 and the value of the materials of the old staircase, cupola and town cross, and the James Forrest whose name appears on the belfry may have been a sub-contractor.[8] The Edinburgh architect John Douglas may have had some involvement in the design, for an elevation-drawing attributed to him shows a tolbooth steeple whose lower stages and belfry are almost identical with those of the existing one.[9]

The two open bays flanking the steeple were probably used for market purposes, and one of them served at some periods as a weigh-house, while the meal-market was probably on the ground floor of the main block, along with a shop which is first recorded in 1765. As well as the council-chamber, the building contained a town clerk's office, and two ground-floor rooms were used as a prison until 1844.[10] Minor repairs were carried out in 1826 and 1839, but in 1870 it was decided to replace the main block.[11] The designs by David and John Bryce were probably produced before the death of David Bryce in May 1876, but work began in February 1877 and the building was opened on the last day of that year.[12]

57 MAYBOLE TOLBOOTH
South Ayrshire

NS 3001 0986

A late 17th-century account describes how the High Street of Maybole was 'beautifyed with the situation of two castles'. At the (N)E end was that of the Earl of Cassillis, while 'on the (south-)west end is a castle, which belonged sometime to the *Laird of Blairquhan*, which is now *the Tolbuith*'.[1] Both buildings survive, the tolbooth being situated on the SE side of High Street and about 230m SW of the earl's castle.

The tolbooth was extended to the NE in baronial style in 1887 to form the town hall, but little attempt was made to harmonize this work with its predecessor. The original main block is rectangular on plan, measuring 10.5m from NE to SW by 6m, and a stair-tower/steeple 3.4m square projects to the NE. The main block is now two-storeyed, and gabled to the SW, but early views[2] show an additional storey covered by a lean-to roof, which has left scars on the steeple and terminated in crow-stepped half-gables with cavetto skewputts.[3] The masonry throughout is of coursed rubble with dressed margins. The early openings are rectangular, and most retain broad-chamfered surrounds, but some have been blocked and others enlarged.

The surviving original entrance is in the NE wall of the stair-tower at ground-floor level, adjoining the NW wall of the main block. This doorway has a roll-moulded surround of late 16th-century type, rising into two round-headed arches which meet in a central cusp on the straight lintel.[4] At a higher level there is a small moulded panel-surround. The stair-tower rises to a continuous moulded corbel-course at wall-head level. Its next stage has to the NE a recessed panel which formerly contained a clock-face, and to the NW there are windows at two levels. At the SE junction with the main block at this level

142A

B. view from N by Billings, c.1845   (C 47329)

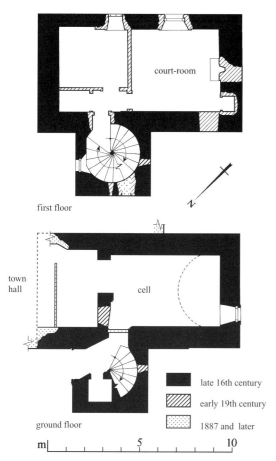

court-room

first floor

town hall

cell

ground floor

■ late 16th century

▨ early 19th century

░ 1887 and later

m |___5___|___10___|

*A. **Maybole Tolbooth** (No.57), plans*

C. doorway in tower
(B 58116)

A. *Maybole Tolbooth* (No.57) from W (B 70320)

HISTORY

A contract of 8 May 1673, between the Earl of Cassilis and the bailies of Maybole with the heritors of Carrick, stated the need for 'ane sufficient tolbooth consisting of twa leigh voults Ane courthaall, Tua heigh chalmers above the same with ane priket of ane Stiple, with ane bell and Knock and ane Orlage'. The burgh was to provide 500 merks and the heritors £1,000, by assessment, and the earl undertook to 'build or procure and perfect' a suitable building upon the High Street. The burgh also committed itself to the future maintenance of the building.[7] The following October, William Kennedy, formerly of Blairquhan, sold to the earl 'that toure house in Mayboill ... commonlie called Blairquhanes Place', with its contents 'within the toure yeat (tower doorway) thairofe except bedds and chimneys', and with the adjacent 'close'.[8] Despite difficulties in collecting the promised assessment, it is likely that the adaptation described by Abercrummie was carried out soon afterwards. The clock- and belfry-stages above the original stair-tower, and possibly the lean-to top storey, may be ascribed to this period.

Repairs were carried out in 1798, with assistance from the 11th Earl of Cassillis,[9] and it appears from the date carved on the existing parapet that it was rebuilt in 1812. During the early 19th century the court-room was used as a 'dancing-room' and for dramatic performances.[10] In 1837 there was a single cell, described as 'a miserable place', and the court-room and the room above were also used as occasional places of confinement.[11] The new town-hall of 1887 was built to designs by R S Ingram of Kilmarnock, at a cost of £2,000.[12]

B. *detail of inscription on 1696 bell* (B 70319)

there are remains of a corbelled stair-turret, with a pistol-hole in its base, which probably gave access to an original 16th-century cap-house. The belfry-stage, which is defined by a moulded string-course, has pointed openings with cusped Y-tracery. At the end of the 17th century Abercrummie reported that the tolbooth 'is adorned with a pyramide, and a row of ballesters round it, raised upon the top of the staircase, into which they have mounted a fyne clock'.[5] The balustrade was replaced by a corbelled and crenellated parapet, which bears the date 1812, and the present iron-crowned spire, incorporating four clock-faces, is of late 19th-century date.

Internally the building has few features of special note, but the main ground-floor room is barrel-vaulted and the tower retains a stone newel-stair. The large bell in the belfry was cast by J Murphy, Dublin, and 'presented by a few friends' in 1895. The original tolbooth bell, which is preserved in the council-chamber of the town hall, measures 0.48m in diameter. It is inscribed: THIS BEL IS FOVNDED AT MAIBOLL BI ALBERT DANEL / GELI AFRENCHMAN THE 6 NO(VEMBE)R 1696 BI APPOINTMENT OF / THE HERITORS OF THE PARIOCH OF MAIBOLL AND WILLIAM / MONTGOMERI AND TOMAS KENNEDI MAG(IST)RATS OF THE BURGH.[6]

C. *inscription on 1696 bell (scale, 1:7.5)*

58 MOFFAT TOWN-HOUSE
Dumfries and Galloway

NT 0952 0527

The former town-house, known locally as the 'Green Steeple', is situated with its principal (W) gable facing High Street, which forms a broad market-place. It is advanced beyond the adjacent street-front to the N, and on the S it extends a four-bay frontage along Well Street. It was built in 1772 to designs by Alexander Stevens, 'mason in Prestonhall',[1] and replaced an earlier building on an island site in the High Street, possibly the 'tollbooth in Moffet' for which plans were drawn in 1695.[2]

The building, which is of coursed rubble with painted sandstone dressings, is two-storeyed and of rectangular plan, measuring 13.7m along the S front by 6.2m. At ground-floor level the S front has two shop-fronts flanking the doorway to a central stair, with four regularly-spaced rectangular windows on the upper level. The W front has central windows at both levels, the lower one converted from a doorway and the upper one blind, and a simply-moulded surround defines a gable pediment enclosing a bull's-eye window. Above this there rises the plinth of a square steeple whose main stage displays four clock-faces. The belfry stage above, which carries a pyramidal slated roof, was truncated when the bell was removed in the early 1960s.

The interior contained a prison and a first-floor court-room, and was also used for a period in the late 18th century as a grammar-school.[3] It has since been converted for a shop on the ground floor and for domestic use above, and retains no original features, except for the thick W wall of the central staircase.[4] The bell, whose present location is unknown, is said to bear the date 1660 and the Annandale family arms and coronet, and was evidently the 'Mofitt bell' for which William Langshaw, 'plummer', submitted an account in that year.[5]

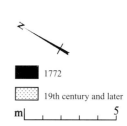

1772

19th century and later

m | 5

A. *Moffat Town-house* (No.58) from SW   (C 50223)

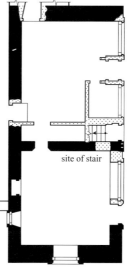

ground floor

site of court-room

site of stair

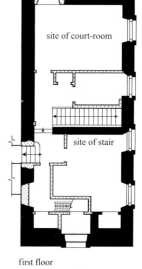

first floor

B. W elevation (partially reconstructed) and plans

143

59 MONTROSE TOWN-HOUSE
Angus
NO 7166 5749

The town-house adjoins the parish churchyard on the E side of High Street, projecting from the street-frontage to form an imposing termination at the S end of a wide market-area. When first built in 1762-4 it was two-storeyed and rectangular, with the main (N) front facing the market-place. The building obstructed the entry to the churchyard and an opening, known locally as the 'deid arch', was formed in the rear wall to allow continuing access through the ground-floor piazza. The present L-plan dates from 1819 when a new SW wing was built, extending the W front by two bays, and an extra storey was added. This wing encroached on the churchyard itself, and a burial-vault was created on the ground storey.

The original building measured 21.5m across its N front by 12.3m, and the addition of 1819 extended its W front to a length of 20.4m. The principal elevations are each of five bays with arcaded ground storeys and symmetrically-disposed windows. They are faced with ashlar, much of which dates from an extensive refacing in 1908, whereas the S and E frontages are of coursed rubble.[1] The piers and round-headed arches of the arcades are faced with channelled masonry, and the upper storeys have channelled quoins and horizontal ashlar bands. The date 1763 is inscribed over the central arch of the N front. As remodelled in 1819, both fronts have modillioned cornices and central pediments, that to the W with a roundel bearing the burgh arms and that to the N enclosing a circular clock-face.[2] The W parapet is fluted while the N one has an open-work balustrade, and both have urns set at intervals and surmounting the pediments. The roof is of irregular double-hipped form.

The N part of the ground storey is an open arcaded area with a flagstone pavement, two bays in depth and flat-ceiled. A segmental transverse arch, two bays from the W end, carries a major internal wall above. Against the E wall there is an open stair with cast-iron balustrade, which rises to a lobby at entresol level. Adjoining the stair, in the E part of the S wall, there is the broad lintelled 'deid arch' that afforded continuing access to the churchyard.[3] The range of small rooms in the SW part of the original block was occupied at various times by a guard-house, a coffee-room and shops, while a town clerk's office, later used as a post-office, was included in the S block of 1819. These rooms are much altered, but in the W half of the S block, on ground which had formed part of the churchyard, there remains a burial-vault entered by a round-headed arch in the W wall.[4]

The 18th-century layout of the first floor allowed for two principal rooms in the N front, the 'town hall' occupying the three-bay E division and a 'tea-room' being included to the W. The 'town hall' retains in the W wall an 18th-century stone chimneypiece with moulded inner and outer edges, framed by tall Corinthian pilasters. In 1819 a partition-wall was inserted in the S part of this room to enclose the main scale-and-platt stair and a lobby. The room in the W end of the original block was described in 1819 as a 'coffee room', and was subsequently used as a reading-room, while the W room in the new S block was originally a library but became the council-room.[5] All of these rooms have been extensively altered and partitioned to form offices, but in the E end of the S block the court-room of 1819 retains its door- and window-architraves and a panelled ceiling. Entered from the main stair, and constructed within the adjacent building to the E, there is a barrel-vaulted document-store with inner and outer cast-iron doors. A secondary stair, rebuilt in its original position, is set in the centre of the S block.

The second floor contains two principal rooms, in the N and W fronts, with the main stair and lobby in the same position as on the first floor. The 'assembly-room' now occupies the whole length of the W front, but originally terminated at a cross-wall some 4.2m from the N wall, the division still being

Montrose Town-house (No.59) and tolbooth from NW by Milne, 1826

(B 58171)

A. **Montrose Town-house** (No.59) from N   (B 47596)

B. view from SW   (C 4001)

C. ground-floor piazza from E   (C 4002)

D. first floor, former court-room   (C 4013)

marked by the N end of the coombed ceiling. The former NW
room was described in 1819 as the 'card room', and the large
room in the N front was the 'supper room', but was
subsequently used as the council-chamber.[6] Some original
panelled architraves survive, but all the fireplaces on this floor
have been blocked or removed.

A set of thirty-five chairs and seven tables was made for the
town-house by William Strachan in 1765-6,[7] but the earliest
surviving furniture appears to be of early 19th-century date.
On the second floor there hangs a set of painted panels with
emblems of the various trades, presented to the Guildry in
1818 by the radical Joseph Hume, a native of Montrose and
newly elected member of parliament for the burgh.

The burgh clock and bells were kept in the old steeple
adjoining the parish church, which also served as an
occasional prison and was replaced by Gillespie Graham's tall
spire in 1832-4. The present clock was made for the new
steeple in 1835 by James Clark, Edinburgh, and was repaired
in 1887 by James Ritchie and Son. The principal bell, 'Big
Peter', is rung for the curfew two-hundred times, 'at ten
o'clock nichtlie, except ye Sabbathe nyt', as ordained by the
council in 1674. It measures 0.96m in diameter and bears the
inscriptions: SOLI DEO GLORIA: PETRUS OSTENS

8A, B

E. burial-vault   (C 4005)

ROTERODAMI ME FECIT 1676 ('Glory to God alone; Peter
Ostens, Rotterdam, made me, 1676'), and at the rim, between
medallions: THE ARMES OF MONTROS. The three other
bells were cast by Thomas Mears and two of them bear the
dates 1801 and 1836.[8]

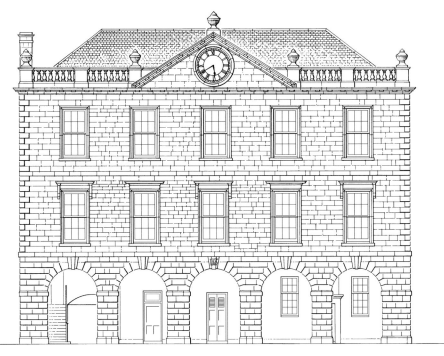

A. **Montrose Town-house** *(No.59), N elevation*

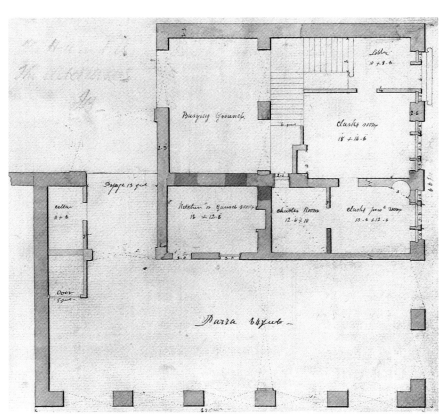

B. ground-plan by Smith, 1819 (scale, 1:200)

(B 67884)

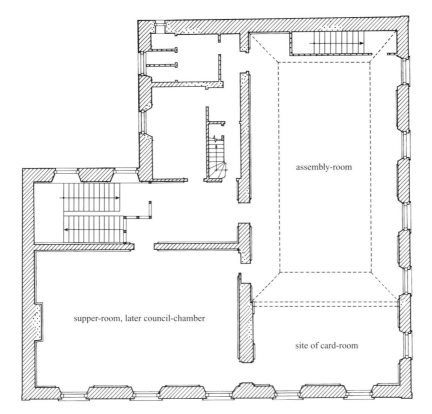

assembly-room

supper-room, later council-chamber

site of card-room

second floor

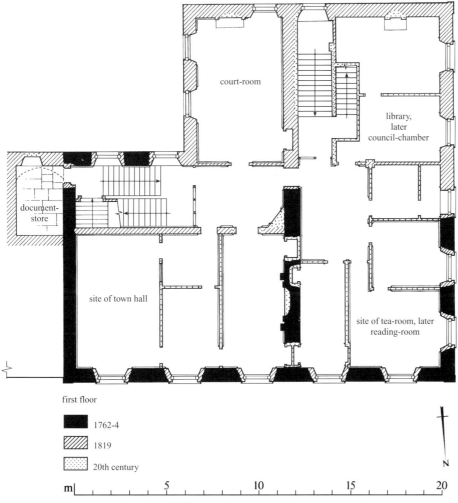

court-room

library,
later
council-chamber

document-
store

site of town hall

site of tea-room, later
reading-room

first floor

■ 1762-4

▨ 1819

▦ 20th century

N

m | 5 | 10 | 15 | 20

Montrose Town-house *(No.59), plans*

HISTORY

In 1375 Robert II granted to the burgh of Montrose a piece of ground measuring 80 by 40 feet (24.4m by 12.2m), lying in the common street between the mercat cross and the church (?chapel) of the Holy Cross, on the S side of the parish church. It was to be used 'for rebuilding a house for the public court-house or toll-house, commonly called a tolbooth' (*ad edificandum de novo unum domum pro communi pretorio sive tholoneo vulgariter dicto tolboth*).[9] This may have been the island site about 120m S of the present town-house on which the town council decided in 1467 to 'byg thair tolbuthe'. An upper storey and two stone forestairs were added in 1550, while the slated roof was repaired in 1626.[10] The upper rooms remained in use for various social and educational purposes after the new town-house was completed in 1764, while the tolbooth continued as a prison until its demolition in 1837. The bad conditions in which innocent lunatics were detained there led to the foundation of the Montrose Lunatic Asylum in 1781.[11]

10A The collections of Montrose Museum and Art Gallery include manacles, a key and two branks' bridles, all probably from the tolbooth, and paintings of the High Street by
144 Alexander Milne (1826) and Alexander Madoland (1832-7), which show both the tolbooth and the town-house.[12]

In 1759 a committee of local 'noblemen, gentlemen and others' offered to raise subscriptions for a new assembly-room, and two years later the town council decided to build 'a new Town Hall with other conveniencies'. This was to contain 'a handsome publick room with proper waiting and retiring rooms adjacent, (erected) upon pillars to the front having a handsome piazza below to serve for the merchants and inhabitants to meet and transact business together after the manner of an exchange'.[13] Work began in 1762 and the building was completed in 1764.[14] In 1766 a 'timpany' (pediment) and clock were added to the N front, since the new building obscured the view of the N dial of the burgh clock in the church steeple.[15] When Johnson and Boswell visited Montrose in 1773, they 'saw the town hall, where is a good dancing-room and other rooms for tea-drinking', and Johnson described it as 'a handsome fabrick with a portico'.[16]

The major alterations of 1819 were carried out, at an estimated cost of £1,700, to designs by the local architect William Smith. The added second floor was largely intended for the social functions of the Guildry Incorporation, who helped to fund the additions but lost use of the building in 1838 in a dispute with the town council.[17]

As early as 1839, the floor of the 'assembly room' required strengthening, and the musicians' gallery was removed. In 1846 a report by the architect William Middleton noted the poor condition of masonry laid on the wrong bed. Internal alterations reached a cost of £232 by 1849, but refacing was not carried out until 1908.[17] Extensive internal alterations were made in the third quarter of the 20th century.

A. **Montrose Town-house** (No.59), panel bearing weavers' arms (C 4015)

B. painted panel bearing bakers' arms (C 4019)

C. manacles from tolbooth (B 58149)

D. document-store (C 4010)

MUSSELBURGH TOLBOOTH
East Lothian
NT 3459 7272

The tolbooth occupies a prominent position on the N side of the narrowest part of High Street, to the W of a broad area containing the reconstructed mercat cross. The distinctive tower with its octagonal spire rises within the SW angle of a rectangular castellated block of late 16th-century date. At right angles, to the NE, there is a two-storeyed Palladian court-room wing of 1731-3, and in the re-entrant there is a large 19th-century hall.

50-1 The original rectangular block measures 19.2m from E to W by 7.4m and is three-storeyed. It is built with squared rubble in courses of varying heights, much renewed in 1827, 1885 and later,[1] and the window-surrounds of the lower storeys are chamfered. A corbelled parapet-walk, with a SE angle-round, runs along the S and E walls and encloses the third storey. Although its windows have been renewed in the 19th century, this level is probably contemporary with the lower floors. Its E gable includes a chimney-breast which is corbelled to allow access from the cap-house to the parapet-walk, and the skews show evidence of the heightening of the wall-head that was ordered in 1758.[2] The copings of the two mid-wall chimneys and that of the E gable bear dog-tooth and billet ornament which, although renewed, is of 16th-century character.

It has been assumed that the rubble-built tower is a survival of the tolbooth that was destroyed in 1544, but the comparative slightness of its walls does not support this analysis. The slight projection of the wall-front below, which contains the arched entrance to a former pend, and the stepped moulding above the first-floor window, are consistent with a late 16th-century date. Above parapet-level the tower is 3.1m square as far as the clock-stage, where its angles are bevelled to support an octagonal modillioned timber platform, perhaps dating from repairs in 1744.[3] This carries the octagonal slate-hung belfry and an ogival slated spire which is divided by string-courses into three stages.

The ground floor E of the tower is divided into four transverse vaults, which from an early date were used for shops, but one was opened in the 19th century to form a pend. The first-floor entrance to the upper floors was probably always at the N end of the E end-wall, and a newel-stair rises immediately inside it to the N, while at the W end of the second floor there is a fireplace of possible 17th-century date. The doorway was enclosed in a porch in 1762, and in 1773 the council ordered a marble slab to be set 'above the doorhead of the entry to the prison'.[4] This bears the burgh arms flanked by the inscriptions: 'Magistrates do justice / in the fear of God, Ju(ne) 16 / 1773', and 'He that God doth fear / will not to falsehood lend an ear'.

In the first half of the 19th century the interior was

B. view from SE (B 58047)

*A. **Musselburgh Tolbooth** (No.60) from SE, c.1900* (C 47334)

149

extensively altered. Pairs of vaulted cells were installed on the first and second floors, served by axial vaulted corridors. The vaults are constructed in ashlar and the complex system of air-vents appears to be contemporary. The cell doors survive intact, as does a stove-recess in the first-floor corridor. Rooms at both the E and W ends of the building were left unvaulted, presumably serving as jailers' rooms and a debtors' prison.

The wing that was added to the NE angle of the tolbooth in 1731-3 is two-storeyed and measures about 11.5m by 7m, with a narrower extension to the N. The N end of its E front is overlapped by an adjacent building, and the exposed part is treated as a symmetrical three-bay frontage 8.5m in width, with the roof hipped to the S. The ashlar of the E and S fronts was refaced early in the 20th century. The ground floor, which is of channelled ashlar, was originally the arcaded entrance to a market-area, and the infilled arches have bold imposts and keystones, while the first-floor windows have Gibbs surrounds with pediments, triangular in the centre and segmental in the flanking openings. The doorway in the S wall had a head of the latter form, but in 1762 the forestair was rebuilt, with a moulded stone coping, and the doorways of both wings were enclosed in a two-storeyed porch which retains a date-stone above the S door and a moulded window-surround to the E.

The upper floor of the wing originally contained a single room, which was used both for courts and council meetings, but in the 19th century it was subdivided, with the S half becoming a lobby to the public hall, and the W-facing windows were blocked or altered. To the N it opened into two rooms in later extensions.

In 1811 instructions were given for the 'long room to be widened for a ball room', and this may refer to the present hall, built in the angle of the tolbooth and the court-room, which measures 15.5m by 11.8m and has a brick-built N wall above a stone-built ground-floor arcade. It was further altered in 1875-6, and the blind but glazed Venetian windows of the W gable probably date from William Constable's alterations of about 1901.[5]

In the lobby of the NE wing there is displayed a clock-mechanism which was reputedly gifted to the town by the States of Holland in 1496.[6] A new clock was made and installed by James Ritchie, Edinburgh, in 1901.[7] In 1822 a Dutch bell dated 1619 was given in part exchange for a new bell cast in London, whose present location is not known.[8]

HISTORY

In 1544 the tolbooth of Musselburgh was 'more or less destroyed' in Hertford's invasion.[9] The ancient burgh was re-erected into a burgh of regality for the commendator of Dunfermline Abbey in 1562. Ten years later the bailies and council began to build adjacent to their tolbooth 'ane hous to have for thair counsalhous, a warding place and a place of pressoun for keping of malefactouris'. Servants of two local landowners destroyed the building-materials and forcibly resisted the watchmen.[10] The outcome of this dispute is not recorded, but the existing building may well belong to the 1570s rather than to the traditional date of 1590. Later tradition held that stone for the new tolbooth came from the ruined chapel of Loretto, situated about 0.6km to the E. It was also recorded that, according to masons still living in 1792, the old steps to the tolbooth were the bases of pillars from the chapel, but no such re-used masonry is identifiable.[11]

There is little record of building work in the 17th century, but the steeple was repaired in 1700 and 1744, and in 1758 the tolbooth roof was raised and reslated with 'blew' slates in place of 'gray' ones.[12] One of the omissions in the design appears to have been a fireplace in the council-room, and in 1716 a 'brace' or fireplace was requested by the councillors for use during cold weather.[13] In 1731 ground was enclosed 'at the back of the tolbooth for a new Mercat place and for building a new Court place above the entry theirto to enter off the present stair of the Tolbooth'. The new wing was built by James Crighton and completed in 1733.[14]

The widening of the 'long room' for a ball-room in 1811 was carried out to the designs of James Hay.[15] During the 19th century the ground floor of the tolbooth was used as a police-station, and a pend was formed through one of the original vaults when access to the courtyard behind was blocked by the construction of a shop in the arcade under the court-room.

In 1885 the walls of the town-hall stair were rebuilt and polished pillars of Dalmeny stone installed at the bottom of the stair. The work carried out to designs by the local architect William Constable in 1901 included general improvements to the building as well as the enlargement of the public hall.[16]

A. **Musselburgh Tolbooth** (No.60) from SW by Storer, 1820   (C 47331)

B. view from SW   (B 58050)

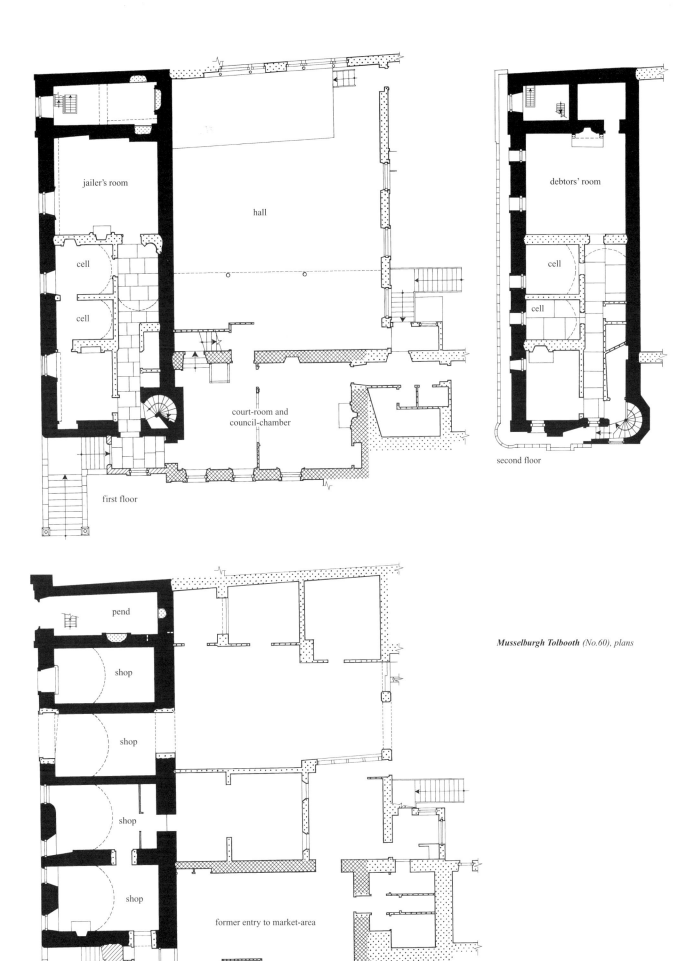

jailer's room

hall

cell

cell

court-room and
council-chamber

first floor

debtors' room

cell

cell

second floor

Musselburgh Tolbooth (No.60), plans

pend

shop

shop

shop

shop

former entry to market-area

ground floor

m   5   10   15

N

late 16th century

1731-3

1762

19th century and later

151

61 NAIRN TOWN AND COUNTY BUILDINGS
Highland
NH 8836 5651

This building, which occupies the site of an earlier tolbooth, is situated on the NW side of the High Street, slightly recessed from the adjacent street-front. It comprises a two-storeyed L-plan block of 1818-19, which was considerably altered in 1868-70, and a rear prison-wing of 1844 flanking an elongated courtyard.

The main block measures 20.2m across its principal (SE) front by 7.2m, with the original SW wing projecting a further 4.7m to the NW. The main front is of sandstone ashlar, with rusticated quoins at the angles and at the steeple, while the other elevations are of coursed or random rubble, harled in some parts. The SE front is of five bays, having tall rectangular first-floor windows above a moulded string-course, and terminates in flat-topped parapets enclosing hipped roofs. The advanced central bay forms the lower part of a three-stage steeple which carries a pyramidal lead-covered spire 27.4m in overall height. Its ground-floor doorway has a round-arched tympanum in a rectangular frame, and the first-floor window is of two tall round-headed lights within a label-mould, while at the third stage there is a round-arched niche flanked by narrow windows. The elaborate parapet and spire of 1868-70 replaced a simple crenellated parapet enclosing an octagonal belfry and spire, with clock-dials on the principal faces of the belfry and round-arched openings in the oblique ones.[1]

The interior of the building has been extensively altered, and most of the fittings date from the renovations of 1868-70, or a restoration for local authority use in the 1980s. The court-room at first-floor level, which runs through the depth of the main block and SW wing, has a coved ceiling enriched with a guilloche frame and central rose. The scale-and-platt stair retains its position in the NW half of the steeple, and rises to the second floor where there is a vaulted document-store. In the belfry there is a bell 0.59m in diameter and cast by Thomas Mears in 1843, which replaced two smaller bells dated 1699 and 1769.[2]

Although the building was commonly referred to at the time of its construction as 'the jail', only two cells were provided and it was reported in 1837 that one of the court-rooms had been converted for the use of prisoners, as well as a smaller room.[3] Plans were produced by Thomas Brown in 1842 for a two-storeyed prison-wing having cells entered from stone-flagged corridors, and construction was in progress in 1844; the wing was extended to the NW, with additional cells and a new stair, after 1868.[4]

HISTORY
Nairn had a tolbooth whose poor state of repair was the subject of complaint by a prisoner in 1670. In 1716 the town-house and tolbooth were burnt 'by His Majesty's Forces when they kept guard therein', but funds for rebuilding were not available until about 1740.[5] An engraving of the tolbooth that was demolished in 1818 shows a massive tower carrying a tall polygonal belfry and short spire, but a reference to 'the steeple of the prison' in connection with an election riot of 1754 may imply that there was also a lower block.[6]

The need for a new jail, whose cost would be shared equally with the county, was first discussed in 1816, and additional ground was obtained in the following year. Its construction was carried out in 1818-19, the mason-contractor being John Wilson, under the superintendence of 'Mr Smith, architect', at a total cost of £1,391 15s 9d.[7] In 1868 tenders were invited for 'considerable additions', to plans by the Inverness architects A and W Reid, and the work was completed in 1870.[8]

A. **Nairn Town and County Buildings** *(No.61) from E* (B 57177)

B. old tolbooth, c.1818 (Highland Council)

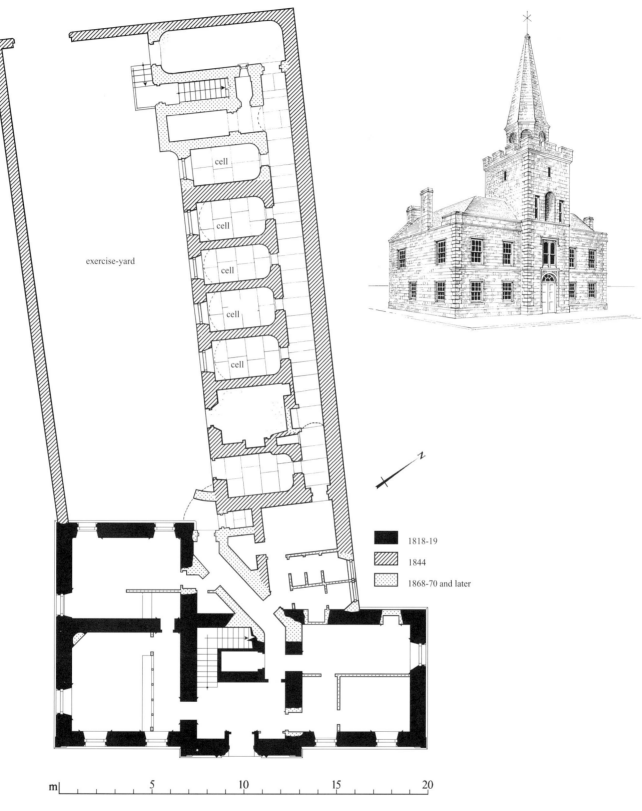

exercise-yard

cell

cell

cell

cell

cell

N

■ 1818-19

▨ 1844

▨ 1868-70 and later

m| 5   10   15   20

Nairn Town and County Buildings (No.61), ground-plan and conjectural reconstruction

62 NEWBURGH TOWN-HOUSE
Fife

NO 2353 1828

The early 19th-century town-house is situated on the S side of the High Street in a central position in the burgh. It is a two-storeyed building about 11.5m square with a projecting steeple at the centre of the three-bay main (N) front. This front is faced with ashlar, while the sides and rear are of coursed rubble and the roof is hipped and slated.

The main floor, set 1.2m above street-level, is reached by a balustraded flight of steps which in its present form dates from 1887-8. The entrance-doorway in the steeple is framed by a round-headed arch. Above this at first-floor level there is a Venetian window and at the next stage a round-headed window, and between these openings there is a date-stone inscribed '1808'. Above the clock-stage the steeple is broached to the octagonal belfry, which has alternate open and blind round-headed arches and a crenellated parapet. Its spire is octagonal and is enlivened by oculi which on each face are alternately open and blind.

The ground storey has been converted for domestic use, but the first floor, which has a large council-chamber to the rear, remains largely unaltered. This room, which occupies the full breadth of the building, has a small gallery in the N wall and a coombed ceiling. Built against the W wall, but probably occupying the position of an original fireplace, there is a box-pew of early 19th-century date.

The acquisition of a bell was proposed in 1815, but the large bell hanging in the steeple was cast by Mears and Stainbank, London, in 1859, and recast ten years later.[1] In the Laing Library and Museum, Newburgh, there is a painted chest inscribed 'Newburgh Friendly Society', probably of mid-19th-century date, with a naive view of the town-house on the inside of its lid.

*A. **Newburgh Town-house** (No.62), chest with view of town-house* (B 64968)

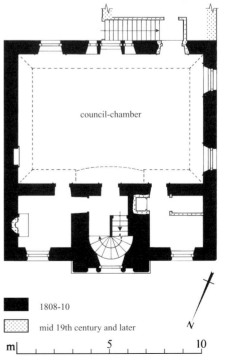

1808-10

mid 19th century and later

B. N elevation and first-floor plan

A. *Newburgh Town-house (No.62) from NE*   (B 39432)

B. *first-floor room from SW*   (B 64971)

HISTORY

Although Newburgh had a tolbooth as early as the middle of
the 16th century,[2] in 1796 the town council considered that
they required 'a new Tolbooth and Council House' and
resolved to obtain government assistance by petitioning the
Secretary of State for War, Henry Dundas.[3] A 'Tenement of
Houses and Croft of Land' was acquired for the purpose in
1800, but work did not begin until 1808, when a loan of £500
was raised to finance the building.[4] Plans were prepared by
John Speed, 'mason in Newburgh', who received a payment of
£5 'as the same (plan) had been approved of and another
tradesman appointed to execute it'.[5] Materials from the old
town-house were to be re-used in the new building or sold by
roup.[6] The building was ready for glazing in 1810, but the
'large room' or 'Town Hall' was not completely fitted up until
1815.[7]

About 1830 two debtors' cells to the rear of the ground
floor, which were seldom used, were converted into a small
corn-market, but one of the front rooms, which for a few years
had housed a library, became a second criminal cell.[8] Further
alterations took place in 1887-8, but little work of this period
is evident except for the balustraded steps and landing of the N
front.[9]

63 NEW GALLOWAY TOWN HALL
Dumfries and Galloway

NX 6341 7750

The town hall stands at the centre of the burgh, on the E side of High Street at its junction with East Port. Its present appearance, as a two-storeyed rectangular block measuring 16.2m from N to S by 10.6m, dates from 1875-6 when it was 'rebuilt and enlarged'.[1] A considerable widening was proposed at this period,[2] and the wall-heads were heightened. The least-altered part of the building is the 4.2m-square tower at the NW angle, and its slated spire of 1872 encases the timbers of an older spire, about 16.5m in overall height.

The main (W) elevation is of five bays, with low rectangular ground-floor windows and tall round-arched ones in the upper part, which in 1875-6 was rebuilt from the level of the first-floor joists.[3] The ornate round-arched doorway in the W face of the tower probably dates from 1895, when a new entrance and stair were formed,[4] but above it there is a small panel bearing the burgh arms, which may be of early 18th-century date.[5] At second-floor level in the W wall there is a window having a yett-like grille, while in the S wall, blocked by the heightened roof, there is an opening which preserves a roll-moulded jamb and a possible glazing-groove.

The clock-faces in the highest stage of the tower, and the small paired corbels at the base of the dormered spire, date from 1872, but the ball-finials on panelled pedestals at the angles of the spire were retained from the earlier arrangement, which had a parapet. Within the spire there are preserved the rafters of its predecessor, which rise from the inner wall-head and retain some of their broad sarking-boards, originally covered with lead.[6] An engraving of about 1798[7] shows a thin spire rising within a crenellated parapet, but the surviving timbers, which are nailed rather than pegged, may date from alterations when a recast bell was installed in 1812.

In 1878 the building was cement-rendered, with raised cement margins and quoins,[8] and this render makes detailed analysis impossible, but it is likely that the lower part of the W wall, as well as the tower, are of 18th-century date, and the latter may be as early as 1711. The axial wall at ground-floor level may perpetuate the E wall of an original block about 6.5m in width, but the two-bay E half of the N front was probably added in 1875-6.[9] In 1837 there was one room for criminals and a larger one for debtors, both on the first floor.[10]

The existing clock-mechanism was made in 1872 by Gillett and Bland of Croydon to replace an early clock, now in the Stewartry Museum at Kirkcudbright, which by then was considered 'utterly worthless ... as a Time Keeper'.[11] In the spire there are two bells, both recast but reproducing inscriptions and ornament from the originals that were cast by Robert Maxwell at Edinburgh in 1711. The larger, 0.57m in diameter and recast in 1872, bears the burgh arms and those of William, 6th Viscount Kenmure, who was executed for his leading part in the Jacobite rebellion of 1715. The second bell, which is 0.46m in diameter and was recast by Stephen Miller, Glasgow, in 1812, was gifted by Mr William Cochran of Kilmaronock, younger brother of the 2nd Earl of Dundonald and another Jacobite supporter.[12]

A. *New Galloway Town Hall (No.63) from NW* (B 47602)

B. *view of New Galloway and Kenmure Castle by Nattes, c.1798* (C 62914)

156

New Galloway Town Hall (No.63)
A. armorial panel and jougs
   (B 47605)

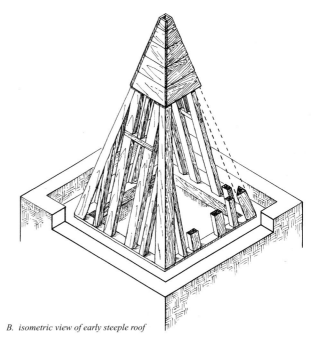

B. isometric view of early steeple roof

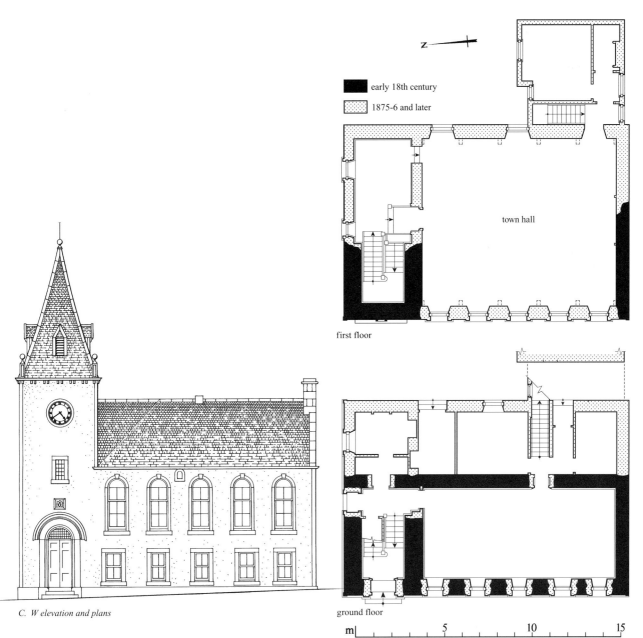

■ early 18th century

░ 1875-6 and later

town hall

first floor

ground floor

m   5   10   15

C. W elevation and plans

64 NEWMILNS TOWN-HOUSE
East Ayrshire

NS 5362 3730

This diminutive town-house stands on a prominent site on the S side of Main Street, the adjacent houses to the E being set back to reveal its main (E) gable-wall. It is a two-storeyed rubble-built structure with dressed margins and crowsteps, measuring 6.1m across the E front by 6m to its junction with a later building which encloses its W wall. A double forestair on the E rises to a central doorway flanked by heavily-moulded round-headed windows. Surmounting the crowstepped E gable there is a stone bellcot with plain columns, carrying a heavily-corniced ogival cupola whose vane bears the date 1739. The N front has at ground-floor level a central doorway and a small window immediately E of it, and at first-floor level there are two windows with chamfered surrounds.

The ground floor is barrel-vaulted and presumably functioned as a prison, while the first-floor room was the council-chamber. This has been modernised, but retains an original fireplace and grate in the W wall.

It is possible that the N wall, whose masonry is less regular than that of the E wall, may preserve part of an earlier building, although this may reflect the greater level of refinement appropriate to the main front. The survival of an earlier window-jamb E of the W first-floor window in the N wall also suggests the re-working of an older structure.

The main fabric may be ascribed to about the middle of the 18th century, and perhaps to 1739, with alterations to the embrasures of the N and E fronts later in the same century. The heavily-moulded E windows may indeed have been renewed at a later date. The forestair is probably also of late 18th-century date, but may replace one of similar form. It has been extensively renewed in recent restoration, along with the pedimented timber door-surround.

An early wayside-marker set against the W end of the N wall gives distances to Kilmarnock, Galston, Darvel and Edinburgh.

A. *Newmilns Town-house* (No.64) from NE   (B 47612)

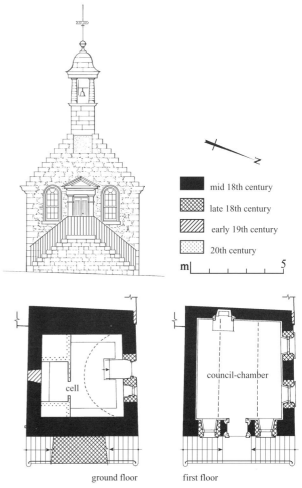

B. *E elevation and plans*

mid 18th century
late 18th century
early 19th century
20th century

m |___|___|___|___|___| 5

cell

council-chamber

ground floor   first floor

65 NEWTON ON AYR STEEPLE
South Ayrshire

NS 3383 2236

This steeple was built in 1792-5 as the central feature of a town-house, most of which, along with the adjacent parish church to the E, was demolished in 1967 for road-widening. The church had been built in 1777, partly on the yard attached to an earlier town-house,[1] and the steeple rises over a pend which formed the main entrance to the churchyard. It now stands on a traffic-island, facing W to Main Street.

The steeple comprises a five-stage tower, 5m square at ground level, which carries an octagonal stone spire, and it is 21.7m in overall height. The masonry is harled rubble, with painted sandstone dressings which include narrow quoins and plain horizontal bands dividing the three lower stages, and moulded cornices below the upper stages and at the wall-head. There are wide elliptical arches in the E and W faces of the ground-floor pend, while each of the next three stages has one window in the W face, respectively rectangular, round-headed and octagonal. At the fifth stage there are four clock-faces, each bearing the date 1795, and the angles at the base of the spire are marked by ball-finials. The bell-chamber is in the spire, which has a narrow louvred opening in each of the principal faces.

The steeple was originally incorporated in a two-storeyed rectangular block measuring about 22.5m from N to S by 6.3m, from which its W face projected slightly.[2] Both wings had shops on the ground floor and two first-floor windows in the W front, with two lengths of balustrade in the wall-head parapet. Access to the first floor was by an enclosed stair against the rear wall to a small vestibule E of the first-floor room in the steeple. This room itself served as a lobby to the upper floors of the wings, and two blocked doorways are identifiable which in the 19th century gave access to a parish school on the N and assembly-rooms on the S.[3]

The belfry in the spire contains two bells cast by Thomas Mears, London, in 1795, which measure 0.51m and 0.6m in respective diameters.[4]

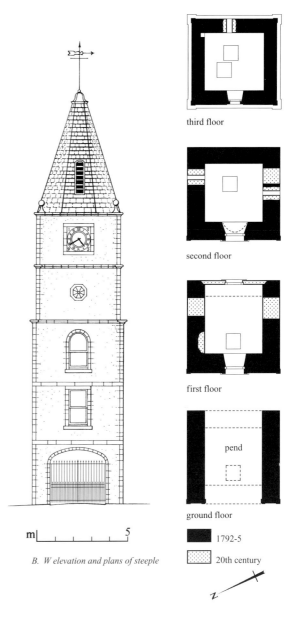

third floor

second floor

first floor

pend

ground floor

m |_____| 5

B. W elevation and plans of steeple

■ 1792-5

▨ 20th century

*A. **Newton on Ayr** (No.65), town-house from SW, 1967*   (AY/772)

HISTORY

The burgh of Newton on Ayr was permitted to erect a tolbooth by royal charters of 1595 and 1600, but courts were regularly held in private houses until 1650, when the 'new tolbooth' is mentioned.[5] By 1792 the existing town-house was in a ruinous state, and a contract was made with John Neill, 'mason in Wallacetown', to erect a town-house and steeple, according to a plan supplied by himself, for £425.[6] The contract was entered into and payments made by the town council, but they acted on the instructions of a separate body known as 'the Community'. The council agreed 'to drink the King's health in the New Council House' in June 1793, but the height of the steeple was still under discussion later that year when Neill offered to raise it by another storey for an extra £20, and the final inspection took place in 1795.[7] In March of the same year the council and a local merchant were instructed to obtain the bells, which were delivered in August, and a clock which was installed by James Allan.[8]

159

66 NEWTON STEWART TOWN-HOUSE
Dumfries and Galloway

NX 4111 6557

Situated on the E side of Victoria Street, at the junction with a lane leading to the W bank of the River Cree, the town-house is a conspicuous building of two storeys. It is rectangular on plan, measuring 13.5m from N to S by 6.9m, and is constructed of whitewashed rubble with dressed and raised margins. Set at its SW corner and rising a stage above the main wall-head there is a simple steeple. The building may be ascribed to about 1800, but it has undergone some minor alterations in the early and mid 20th century, including the addition of a two-storeyed outshot to the E.

The main block, which is gabled to the N and hipped to the S, faces W and is of three bays. At ground-floor level there are three large round-headed openings with projecting impost- and key-blocks, the central one being the principal access-doorway and the others windows with modern frames. Their sills have been inserted, suggesting that all three openings originally gave access to an arcaded market-area.[1] Internally, the ground floor has been partitioned for use as an office. The first floor has three tall Venetian windows to the W front, all with impost- and key-blocks, which light a large meeting-room with fireplaces at each end, presumably the court-room. Access to the first floor is through the base of the steeple, by a staircase which rises to the SE angle of the main room. A cell roofed by a half-barrel vault was contrived below the staircase, and this lock-up was the only prison-accommodation provided.[2]

Externally the steeple has round-headed windows, that in the S face of the second stage being blind, and those at the third stage enclosing clock-faces. It terminates in a lead-covered bell-cast roof with a prominent weather-cock. The clock was made by W F Evans of the Soho Clock Factory, Birmingham, and the uninscribed bell measures 0.3m in diameter.

HISTORY
Despite its rather irregular layout, Newton Stewart was a planned village which developed from a burgh of barony founded in 1677 by William Stewart of Castle Stewart. During the second half of the 18th century it grew at a pace described in 1792 as 'amazing',[3] and the town-house may be ascribed to this period of rapid expansion. In 1846 it was described as being the property of the Earl of Galloway, and the ground floor was occupied by shops, with 'a session house [used] by the Magistrates of the District' above.[4]

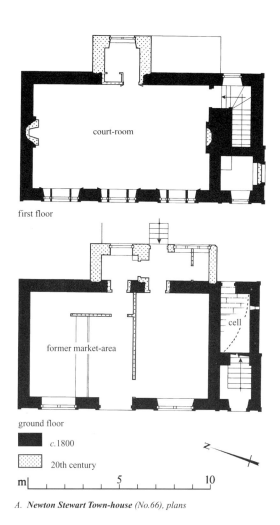

court-room

first floor

cell

former market-area

ground floor

■ c.1800

▨ 20th century

m |___|___|___|___|___|___|___|___|___|___| 5 |___|___|___|___| 10

A. **Newton Stewart Town-house** *(No.66), plans*

B. view from SW

(B 47614)

67 NORTH BERWICK TOWN-HOUSE
East Lothian
NT 5543 8532

This two-storeyed building of 1723-4 stands at the SW angle of Quality Street and High Street, abutted by an adjoining property to the W. It is rectangular on plan, measuring 14m from E-W by 8.1m, and the upper floor is reached by a forestair against the S wall. It is constructed of roughly-coursed rubble[1] covered with harling, and the original roof-slates were replaced in 1825 by pantiles.[2] The principal (N) elevation, to High Street, has two ground-floor doorways which give access to shops, and symmetrically-disposed windows. These appear to have been enlarged, except for the central one at first-floor level. Set on the roof-ridge there is a diminutive timber-built clock-tower, whose apron and ogival roof are slated.

The present divisions of the ground storey date from about 1985. In 1770 the W part of this storey formed a single prison-room, 5.5m by 3.4m, lit by a slit in the N wall, but it was subsequently divided into two cells.[3] The corresponding area of the first floor was occupied by the debtors' room, and the E part by the council-chamber. This preserves a plaster cornice of guilloche pattern, but the interior of the upper storey was renovated in 1970-1 and the original gable-fireplaces in both rooms have been removed.

A clock by an English maker, Roger Parkinson, was installed in 1735, and was replaced in 1809-10 at the expense of Sir Hew Dalrymple-Hamilton, but the present clock is modern.[4] The clock-tower houses a bell 0.54m in both diameter and height, and inscribed: EX DONO DOMINI JACOBI DALRYMPLE DE HAILLS EQUITI BARONETTI R M FECIT EDR 1724 ('By the gift of Sir James Dalrymple of Hailes, knight baronet. R(obert) M(axwell) made, Edinburgh 1724'). Despite this `gift', the burgh paid £196 Scots `for the toun's bell' in 1726.[5]

HISTORY
A tolbooth situated at the E end of the High Street, and probably on the present site, was in existence in North Berwick by the middle of the 16th century.[6] In 1723 a contract for erecting a new tolbooth was entered into with local tradesmen, and the provision of the bell in 1724 suggests that the building was substantially complete.[7] The forestair was rebuilt in 1751, probably using material from the mercat cross.[8] 'Storm windows' (dormers) were removed in 1778, and the weather-cock on the clock-tower was repaired in 1782.[9] The council-room was made available in the 1770s for performances by 'strolling companys of show and playactors',[10] and was subsequently used as a reading-room, while the former debtors' room was also used in the 19th century as a library.

The roof-structure and clock-tower were reconstructed by T E Inglis in 1967. In the early 20th century a single-bay outshot was added to the W wall of the forestair.

North Berwick Town-house (No.67)
view from NE   *(B 47620)*

68 OLD ABERDEEN TOWN-HOUSE
City of Aberdeen

NJ 9405 0636

The town-house of 1788-9 forms a distinguished termination at the N end of the High Street of Old Aberdeen. Its predecessor, which occupied the same site, had been built in 1702 on the S side of an earlier council-house and song-school. The present island site was formed in the 1920s by the demolition of adjacent properties to the N to allow the construction of St Machar's Drive.

The town-house is three-storeyed and rectangular on plan, measuring 12.4m across the main (S) front by 9.7m. The front and side walls are built of coursed granite blocks, with raised and stepped quoins at the angles of the S front and of its projecting central bay. The rear wall is of granite and sandstone rubble which may have been re-used from the previous building.

The S front has regular fenestration in three bays, the central bay being pedimented and surmounted by a small clock-tower with stone urns at the upper angles. Above this there is an octagonal domed belfry with round-headed louvred openings. The lintelled doorway in the central bay is surmounted by a stone panel carved with the burgh arms. In 1789 the town council ordained 'the old date of the Coat of Arms to be chiseled out and the date of the building of the new house put upon it and painted and gilded',[1] but the panel retains its 1721 date. Built into the S end of the E wall is another survival of the previous building, a dormer-pediment carved with the Scottish royal arms and two thistles.

While some of the character of the interior has been lost in later changes of use, it preserves notable features such as the flagstone floor of the entrance-corridor and the timber

balustrade of the staircase to the upper two floors. The E portion of the ground storey retains two prison-cells, extensively altered in the late 19th century. Both upper storeys have large rooms to the front, with smaller offices and stores to the rear. The council-chamber appears to have been on the second floor, with the main room on the first floor used for other meetings, and there were also school-rooms on both floors,[2] The second-floor room, which now houses a Masonic Lodge, has a coombed ceiling and original cornices.

In 1713 the French bell-founder Albert Gely, who was then resident in Old Aberdeen, recast the old tolbooth bell, adding the motto: AD SACRA ET CONCILIA VOCAMUS ('We

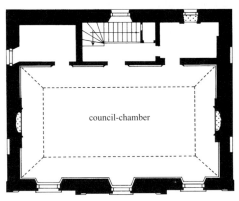

second floor

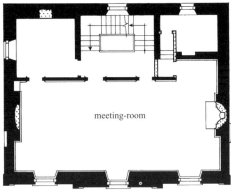

first floor

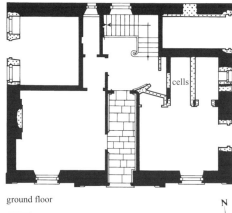

ground floor

■ 1788-9

▨ 20th century

N

m | 5 | 10

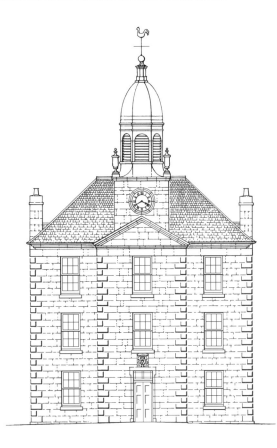

Old Aberdeen Town-house (No.68), S elevation and plans

C. pediment   (B 10828)

A. **Old Aberdeen Town-house** (No.68), second-floor room from E   (B 10832)   D. armorial panel   (B 10827)

B. view from S   (B 10820)

summon to sacred rites and to councils').[3] The present bell, which was cast in 1754 by Gely's successor, John Mowat, is 0.52m in diameter and bears a variant of the same motto.[4] Mowat also made a clock for the tolbooth in 1719-20, and a 'globe for the moon's age' was set up at the same time.[5]

HISTORY

For some time previous to 1642 the town council of Old Aberdeen met in the session-house above the S porch of St Machar's Cathedral. A new building erected in that year, using material re-used from the bishop's dovecot, incorporated a song-school and weigh-house as well as a first-floor room 'called the Council-House'.[6] A new tolbooth, 'ane prison house with ane bell and a clock', was built to the S in 1702.[7] In 1769 it was decided to install the cistern for a new water-supply in the ground-floor room of the prison, but the 'decayed state' of the building soon led to its complete replacement.[8]

In 1787 the council instructed a local builder, Convener George Jaffray, to prepare plans for rebuilding their town-house, and after receiving tenders for executing two plans of differing scale they accepted that submitted by Jaffray himself.[9] His estimates were 'as reasonable as any given in and much below several of them'.[10] The cost of a new building was a particular concern of the council, whose members were partly responsible for funding it, and they had already determined that materials from its predecessor should be re-used.[11] Work began in 1788, and was completed in the following year.

The local merchants' society, incorporated trades and masonic lodge had all contributed to the cost of the new building and they were permitted to use it for meetings, subject to the requirement to share a single key.[12] Revenue was also raised by renting out the meeting-rooms for a variety of purposes including dancing-lessons and dramatic performances.[13]

163

69 PEEBLES TOWN-HOUSE
Scottish Borders
NT 2522 4042

The town-house[1] occupies a position on the S side of the High Street which, when chosen in 1752, was considered 'the best situation for such a building as was in the burgh'.[2] It was begun in that year and occupied by the town council in 1756. Although the architect is unknown, the N front is an accomplished Palladian design.

The building-stance forms an irregular quadrilateral measuring 11m across its main (N) front by 8m. It projects beyond the later buildings to E and W, and the W half of the rear wall is abutted by the Corn Exchange, an addition of 1860.[3] This communicates with the ground storey of the town-house, which housed the fire-brigade before being converted to commercial use. A pend running through the E part of the building forms the entrance to a lane which gives access to Tweed Green.

The town-house is two-storeyed, with a hipped and slated roof. Its main front has to the E the pend, whose segmental arch is symmetrical with that of the entrance to the ground storey and linked to it by a broad impost-band. Up to the arch-springing ashlar masonry was used; above this level the building is harled, and this now extends to the central part of the ground storey. An ashlar band at first-floor level forms the sill for three windows with lugged architraves. At the centre of the wall-head there is a small pediment set on consoles and surmounted by a foliated urn with flanking ball-finials. Within the pediment there is the incised date '1753' above a carved shield bearing the burgh arms, three salmon contra-naiant.

The ground storey now comprises one large room but appears originally to have been divided as there are traces of two blocked doorways in the E wall of the pend, and associated internal partitions. It is likely that one of these rooms functioned as a prison, while provision may also have been made for a school-room.

The first floor contains a single room reached by a staircase in the rear addition; the original means of access is not known. This room, which served as the council-chamber, has a high coombed ceiling and a stone chimneypiece with bead-moulded surround in its W wall. In the SW angle there is the entrance to a small barrel-vaulted strong-room in the 19th-century S wing.

HISTORY

As early as the 15th century Peebles possessed a tolbooth, which stood at the foot of the 'Briggait' (Bridgegate). The stone wall-footings of part of a substantial building, standing within an enclosed yard with an associated well, were excavated there in 1985-7. In 1555 the burgh schoolmaster was allowed the use of the tolbooth.[4] At an uncertain period its functions were transferred to 'the steeple', a fortified tower of late 15th-century origin which adjoined St Mary's Chapel at the W end of the High Street.[5] In 1722 a new clock was placed in the steeple and the 'thieves' hole' was repaired, and the building remained in use as a jail until 1775.[6]

In 1749 the burgh council noted that other royal burghs 'have of late built new Houses, commonly called Town Houses', and resolved to do the same.[7] Work began in 1752, when the treasurer was ordered to 'employ the masons and wrights in the burgh to build the said Town and Schoolhouses'. The incised date in the pediment shows that work was well advanced in 1753, but it was not until 1756 that the council met in the new town-house.[8] The bells remained in the old steeple until its demolition in 1776, and they were transferred to a new parish church, begun in 1778, whose steeple was built at the expense of the town council.[9]

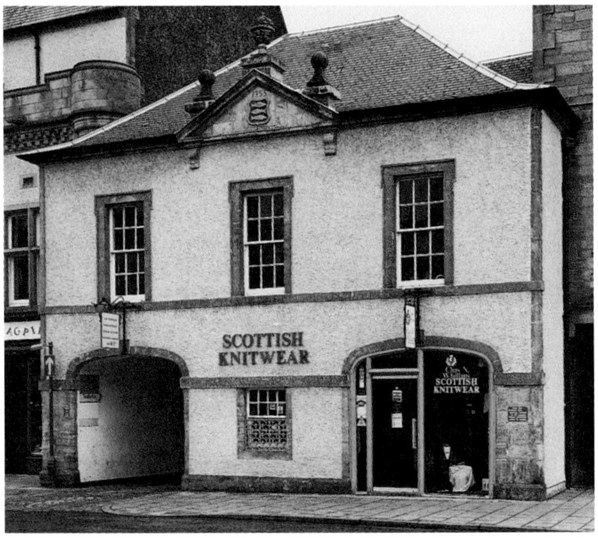

A. ***Peebles Town-house*** *(No.69) from N* *(C 4111)*

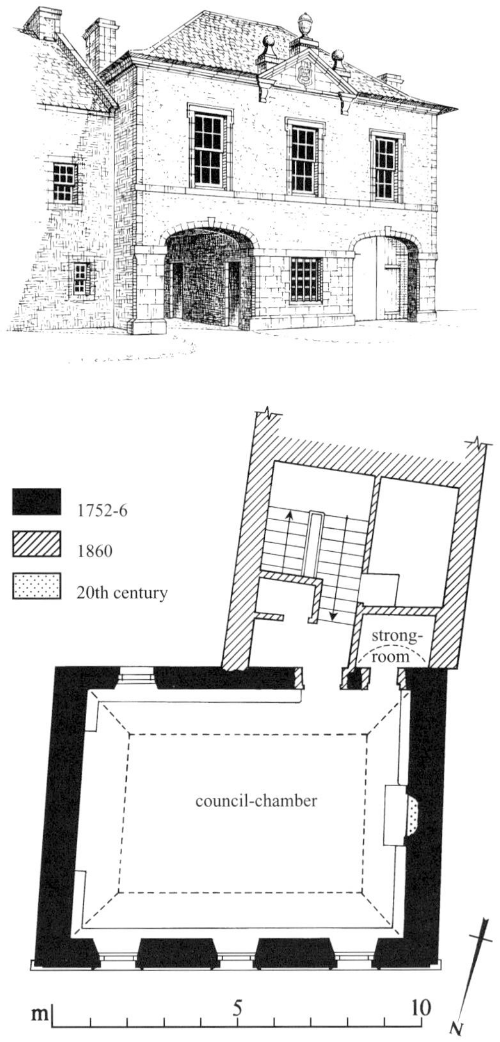

B. conjectural reconstruction and first-floor plan

70 PETERHEAD TOWN-HOUSE
Aberdeenshire

NK 1342 4610

166-7

This town-house was built to John Baxter's designs in 1788 and its 38m-high spire remains one of the most impressive architectural landmarks in Peterhead. It is situated at the highest point of the town, on a corner-site between Marischal Street and Tolbooth Wynd, and faces E down Broad Street, the former market-area. It was originally rectangular on plan, measuring 20m by 17.1m, but a projecting porch and enclosed stair were added in 1881 to its main (E) front.[1] It is constructed of dressed local grey-brown granite, and the roof is hipped and slated.

The main front is of five bays, with an advanced and pedimented three-bay centrepiece to which the pedimented staircase-porch is attached. The ground-floor windows in the main and S fronts are round-headed and occupy an original open arcade, while the first-floor openings of the main and N fronts have entablatures. The end-walls are of two bays, but the former arcade to the N has been replaced by a shop-front. Above it, however, there is a central round-headed niche, and at second-floor level an unattached pediment. Surmounting the moulded main pediment, which bears the date 1788, there is a three-stage steeple rising from a square base. Its clock-stage has pedimented faces stepped in at the angles, and carries an octagonal belfry with a round-headed louvred opening in each face. The spire is also octagonal, and is decorated with three bands of oval vents.

In the original arrangement the ground storey was used as a market, subsequently divided into shops, while the first floor housed two school-rooms, and the second floor contained 'two elegant halls, and an anti-room, which are used on public occasions'.[2] Two large rooms now occupy the side-bays of the ground storey, divided by a square vaulted cell in the base of the steeple and a room of similar size to the rear. Except for the cell or 'black hole', which was in disuse some time before 1836,[3] this floor has undergone extensive modern alterations. At first-floor level the central block houses a semi-circular stair and flagged landing, and a square room to the rear. This room originally had access to both principal rooms, but this uninterrupted circulation is restricted by later partitions. The second floor was of similar layout, and the N room retains a coombed ceiling, but the S room has been subdivided.

The steeple houses a bell 1m in diameter, which was recast by G Mears of London in 1858. A bell from the previous tolbooth, cast in 1725 by Robert Maxwell, Edinburgh, for the exiled Earl Marischal, is in the collection of Arbuthnott Museum.[4]

HISTORY
A tolbooth was probably built some time after 1593, when the local feuars gave an undertaking to their landlord, the Earl Marischal, to erect one as soon as their numbers and funds permitted.[5] This building is believed to have stood near the harbour, and to have been abandoned after use as a plague hospital in the 1640s. It was replaced, perhaps in the 1660s, by a building on the present site which comprised a two-storeyed rectangular block with a circular tower abutting one angle. It was altered in 1759 to improve its prison-

A. Peterhead Town-house (No.70) from E   *(B 39699)*   *B. view from N*   *(B 39717)*

165

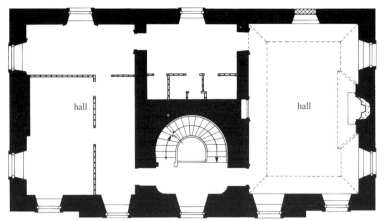

second floor

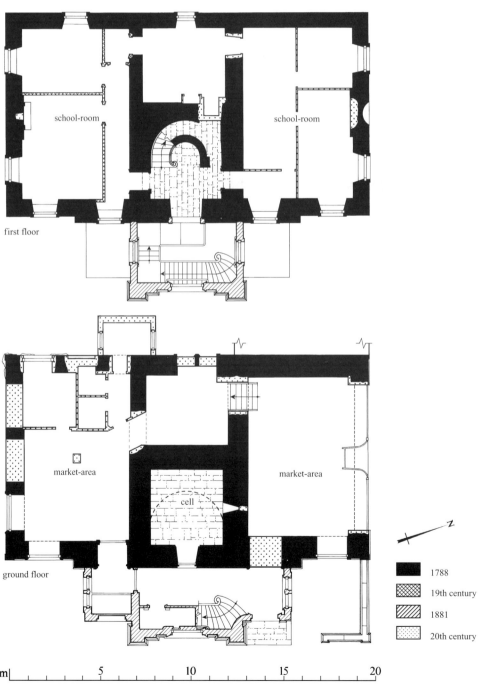

first floor

ground floor

	1788
	19th century
	1881
	20th century

m [scale: 5 10 15 20]

Peterhead Town-house (No.70), plans

Peterhead Town-house (No.70), conjectural reconstruction

accommodation, and was demolished *c*.1786 to make way for the present building.[6]

The new town-house was 'built from a plan of Mr. (John) Baxter, architect',[7] for the Community of Feuars of Peterhead, who still own it. They donated the site and contributed to the public subscription for its cost, which amounted to £2,000.[8] Although the dated pediment shows that work was well advanced by 1788, the interior was not completed until 1812-13, when doors and fireplaces and the hand-rails of the staircase were fitted.[9] A two-storeyed building erected in 1832 in Marischal Street, adjoining the NW angle of the town-house, provided market-space, a temporary holding-cell, and a witness-room. In 1841 the S first-floor room in the town-house was partitioned to provide rooms for the sheriff-substitute and his clerk.[10] The original straight forestair was in disrepair by 1843, and was rebuilt with a double flight in 1859. In 1881 the contractor William Stuart built the present enclosed staircase at the centre of the main front and carried out alterations to the ground floor, at a cost of £572.[11]

In 1588 the burgh of Pittenweem received from William Scott a grant of the 'Great House', the SW range of the medieval priory, [1] for use as 'a decent, honest and comely kirk'. The charter confirmed by Parliament and Crown in 1592-3, however, specified uses including a grammar school, tolbooth and prison, and the church was built a short distance to the NW, incorporating parts of the medieval church. [2] Prolonged litigation with the commendator delayed the burgh's access to the priory for many years, and the massive tower built at the SW end of the new church was used as a prison, and perhaps for other civic purposes.

The SE part of the 'Great House' had presumably been converted for council use by 1661, when the 3rd Earl of Kellie requested to have the tolbooth for a residence, on condition that he built another one in a convenient place. [3] It is unlikely that this proposal was carried out, and in 1693 the bailies were instructed 'to visit the tolbooth, and think on a convenient way for making ane partition for a council house within and place for the court to sit without'. [4] By 1821 the town-house was in a dangerous state, and its rebuilding was completed in the following year.

THE TOLBOOTH STEEPLE (NO 5491 0260).

10B The steeple [5] is situated opposite the NE end of High Street, at its junction with Kirkgate and Cove Wynd. It is 5.2m

square on plan, with a circular stair-tower projecting from the NE wall, and its main (SW) front is continuous with the SW gable of the parish church. [6] It is of five principal stages, the four lower ones being of harled rubble with sandstone dressings. The fifth stage, which is corbelled out from the main wall-line, and the spire that it carries, are of coursed ashlar, and were probably added in the early 17th century.

The smaller windows have chamfered surrounds, while the first-floor window in the SW front has a roll-and-hollow moulding, and the NW one a plain surround. The latter opening appears to have been rebuilt, probably in the 18th century. Below some of the windows in the NW front and the stair-tower there are small round vents which may have been inserted in the sills as gun-loops.

The added fifth stage, which houses the clock and bells, is surmounted by an elaborate corbelled parapet with groups of three balusters set between panelled central and angle-pillars. [7] The central pillar of the SW front bears three stylised thistles in relief, and the pillars are surmounted by obelisks decorated with a fish-scale or tree motif. The waterspouts of the parapet are treated as fictive gun-barrels, presumably intended to give the building a military aspect. Each face of the hexagonal spire has a lucarne, set alternately high or low, and the three lower ones have balustered surrounds surmounted by small obelisks like those of the parapet. The weather-cock may be the new one that was ordered in 1739. [8]

The rounded stair-projection that provides access to the upper floors is entered by a NW doorway reached by a short flight of steps. Its cap-house is corbelled out to a rectangle at the same level as the added fifth stage of the tower and is of similar ashlar-construction. Its gabled roof, which abuts the spire, is covered with stone slabs and has a crown finial set on the ridge. Access from the stair to the SE parapet is by a square-headed and pedimented doorway with chamfered jambs.

The ground storey, which is barrel-vaulted and earth-floored, is entered by a doorway in the SW front and has no access to the upper floors, although there are openings, presumably for bell-ropes, in the vault. Internally the building has few features of particular note, but there are square

*A. **Pittenweem** (No.71), church and tolbooth steeple from W*   (B 39397)   *B. town hall, painted burgh armorial*   (C 44385)

aumbries in the first- and second-floor rooms set close to their access-doorways. The first-floor room is partly divided by modern wooden partitions. A blocked doorway at this level gave access to a gallery in the church. In the NE angle at third-floor level there is a small closet hacked into the wall, which may have served as a privy. The clock-openings have splayed internal jambs and are segmental-headed. The junction of the tower and the spire is marked internally by corbelled set-offs at each angle.

The belfry houses a clock made in 1858, which was repaired in 1966. It replaced a clock made in 1773 by a celebrated local clockmaker, John Smith, at a cost of £25.[9] The older of the two bells, which measures 0.65m in diameter, is inscribed in Swedish: HAFVER SIORAN PVTENS EFTER LATNA ENKA LATITGIVTA AR 1663 ('Cast by the late Joran Putensen's widow and successor in the year 1663'). It is decorated with scroll-work, fillets, a medallion of a half-length figure, and what appears to be a fish. Putensen was a Danish-born bell-founder who worked in Stockholm.[10] The curfew bell measures 0.54m in diameter and is inscribed: FOR THE BURGH OF PITTENWEEM 1742.

On stylistic grounds a late 16th-century date is probable for the lower stages of the tower. The top stage and the spire probably belong to the second quarter of the 17th century, and 'the bertisene of the steeple' was decorated with flags in honour of Charles II in 1651.[11] The steeple was used for the detention of alleged witches in 1704, and there are references to the 'thieve's hole', perhaps the ground floor of the tower, and a 'dark dungeon'.[12]

THE TOWN HALL (NO 5495 0257)

The town hall of 1821-2 is two-storeyed and rectangular on plan, measuring some 13.7m across its main (SW) front by 7.9m in width. It incorporates elements of its predecessor and of the priory buildings. The rear (NE) wall, which is a survival of the refectory and continuous with the 'Great House' to the NW, includes an oriel-window with moulded surround. The other two larger windows in this wall appear to have been inserted, but a small low-level opening at the NW end may be original. The SE gable may also incorporate masonry from the earlier tolbooth, which rose to the same height as the 'Great House' and had a crow-stepped SE gable.[13]

The SW front, which is set forward from the line of its predecessor, is constructed of roughly-coursed ashlar, with polished and raised quoins and margins. Access to the ground floor is by a round-headed doorway set NW of centre, and the first floor is reached by an original forestair, with late 19th-century iron balusters and porch,[14] at the NW end of the front. The windows are round-headed and, with the exception of a small ground-floor window, have intersecting curved glazing-

bars. Built upside-down into the top of the SE gable there is a re-used armorial panel bearing the arms of James Kennedy, Bishop of St Andrews (d.1465).[15]

Internally, the ground floor has been extensively modernised in the 1960s and 1970s and it possesses few notable features. About half of its area, probably to the NW, was occupied by a criminal cell and two debtors' rooms until 1847 when it was converted to police accommodation.[16] The first floor appears to be largely unaltered from its construction in the 1820s. At the NW gable there is a landing which retains a remarkable Regency chimneypiece, whose stone surround encloses a cast-iron inset having Egyptian 'mummy' figures to each side, surmounted by lion-heads set in roundels within projecting squares; along the lintel of this inset there is a design incorporating *fasces* and twin-headed axes.

The former council-room, which was also used for courts,[17] is lit by two large windows in the SW front. It has a coombed ceiling and at the NW end there is a small 'orchestra or music gallery'[18] with turned wooden balusters, set above a curved recess and below a slightly-pointed barrel-vault. A large timber chimneyiece in the SE wall has been painted with nautical motifs including a figure of Neptune in the central panel. Painted in grisaille above this chimneypiece there is a very elaborate version of the burgh arms, incorporating thistles and the royal arms of Scotland. A small version of the burgh arms above a thistle-and-rose border is painted in colour in the central panel of the gallery. The ceiling has a central rose comprising long radiating acanthus-leaves framed with crossed sprigs. There are doors in each corner of the end-walls of the room, and these and the shutters have fielded panels of Regency type. The roof-structure, which has been partly renewed, is of collar-rafter form, but with an A-frame employed every sixth beam, marked by raised tie-beams.

HISTORY

A petition by local residents in June 1821 protested that the condition of the town-house rendered it dangerous to neighbouring property and to passers-by. One of the petitioners, James Horsburgh, was asked to prepare a plan and elevation for a new building, observing 'the utmost economy', and an estimate of £205 by David Brown, mason in Pittenweem, was accepted. The specification required as much as possible of the old materials to be re-used, and the two large windows in the new council-room were to be similar in size and shape to the old ones, so that the existing frames could be used. Other timberwork and a fireplace-surround from the old council-room were to be used in the debtors' rooms. The work was completed in March 1822.[19]

Pittenweem (No.71)
town hall and 'Great House' from W
(C 48402)

72 POLLOKSHAWS CLOCK-TOWER
City of Glasgow
NS 5638 6152

This steeple, with its two narrow flanking bays, formerly marked the NE end-frontage of the town hall erected in 1803, most of which was demolished in 1935.[1] The building originally occupied an island site, bounded to the NE by Pleasance Street and to SE and NW by streets which in the 1960s were absorbed into a pedestrian precinct.

The steeple is 5m square and 19m high, and its two-storeyed flanking bays extend the width of the NE front to 8.4m. Early views show a slightly narrower main block to the SW, the ends of its SE and NW side-walls being marked by two-bay advanced sections with crenellated wallheads.[2] The side-walls of the projections that abut the steeple were rebuilt in 1935, retaining their original crenellations, and a new SW wall was constructed 1.2m from the SW wall of the steeple. This work, like the steeple itself, was faced with ashlar, but the masonry of the demolished main block appears to have been rendered.

The NE front of the steeple has a rusticated ground storey with a round-arched doorway (now blocked, like the other openings in the façade) whose keystone bears the incised date 1803. The second stage has a rectangular window within a large round-arched recess, and rises to a triangular pediment whose cornice returns along the other walls of the steeple. Above this there are two very low intaken stages containing respectively rectangular and round-headed windows and terminating in an ashlar band embellished with sunken oblong panels. At the next stage, where cones at the angles cover the transition from square to octagon, there is evidence of original narrow openings in the cardinal faces, but these have been enlarged to house four clock-faces, probably in the second half of the 19th century. The low belfry with its oversailing cornice, and the squat pyramidal spire, probably belong to the same period.

Each of the flanking bays had a ground-floor doorway and a first-floor window with a cusped round-arched head and bracketed arch-decorated sill. Their parapets have single round-bottomed crenelles, and this type of crenellation continues in the re-used parapets of the side-walls.

The interior has been much altered and the position of stairs is uncertain, but the ground storey of the steeple had tall openings to SW and SE and presumably served as a vestibule. Its internal walls converge, like those of a pyramidal spire, from a height of about 7m, although this is not reflected on the exterior.

HISTORY
The 'Community or Common Council of the Town of Pollokshaws' was a body of subscribers who established themselves in 1793 to fulfil many of the duties of a town council, and who bought the site for the town hall as one of their first activities. In 1813 the Community, by now bankrupt, transferred the building to the council of a burgh of barony established in that year by Sir John Maxwell of Pollok.[3] The ground floor was used until 1872 as a burgh school, and the upper floor contained a court-room and a police cell, while from 1818 the building also housed a library.[4] The decision to retain the steeple when the main block was demolished in 1935 followed a public campaign to preserve this local landmark.

Pollokshaws (No.72), town hall from E, c.1935

(C 39496)

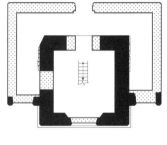

1803

1935

m |___|___|___|___|___| 5

N

A. **Pollokshaws Clock-tower** (No.72)
NE elevation and ground-plan

B. *view from E*   (C 4416)

73 PORT GLASGOW TOWN BUILDINGS
Inverclyde
NS 3221 7456

This distinguished building, whose steeple dominates the harbour area of the port, was designed by the Glasgow architect David Hamilton and built in 1813-16. It is situated on the E side of Fore Street, at the core of the remaining portion of the town's original grid-plan. This position on the quayside of the principal harbour, which was infilled in 1961-2, reflected its importance in the mercantile life of the port. When built, it housed a 'Council Chamber, Justices' Court House, Prison, Bridewell & other public accommodations'.[1] From at least the middle of the 19th century, part of the ground floor contained shops and the first floor a reading-room and merchants' counting-offices. The building has undergone considerable later alteration and partial changes of use. The ground storey was refurbished in 1995-6 for library use.

11A, 175A,B

The building is irregular on plan, reflecting the availability of ground for its lay-out. The main (N) front, which incorporates a massive portico, measures 21m in length, while the S front is divided into separate E and W blocks measuring 29m over all. There are two principal storeys and the steeple, which rises from the centre of the building to a height of 47.6m, is of four main stages. With the exception of the S front, which is harled, the building is constructed of finely-wrought ashlar which it was proposed to obtain from the Garscube quarry.[2]

174B

The fenestration is largely regular with the exception of the S front. The main focus is the N front, whose Doric tetrastyle portico encloses the principal entrance and is surmounted by a massive entablature. This supports a central roundel, flanked by bold volutes and carved with the burgh arms, a ship in full sail. At each angle of this front there are pilasters, and at the wall-head there is a parapet with an open-work balustrade. The round-headed ground-floor windows of the E front, linked by impost-bands, were probably converted from open arcading. The roof is of irregular hipped form.

174C

The steeple, which is very similar to that designed by Hamilton in 1812 for Falkirk (No.28), employs a range of classicising motifs. Above a plain base-course there is a pedimented stage framed by Ionic angle-columns which enclose recessed round-headed windows over blind balustrading. Above this the octagonal clock-stage displays circular clock-faces in the principal fronts and recessed panels in the subordinate faces, with anthemions at the angles. The belfry has rectangular louvred openings in the principal fronts flanked by Tuscan columns, with the associated entablature stepped in at the angles. The low stage above is octagonal, with alternating louvred vents and recessed panels, and the octagonal spire has recessed faces. It carries a weather-vane in the form of a three-masted ship.

The interior of the ground floor has been extensively altered, with much of the NW wing recast as offices and the main stair, which occupies the steeple, rebuilt in the 20th century. It is reached by a vestibule passage which has a segmental barrel-vault. The E block, as remodelled in 1891 (*infra*), houses a range of prison-cells entered from a corridor. The cells were originally on the first floor, with jailer's accommodation below.[3] The first floor has also undergone 20th-century alterations, most extensively in the SE block. The principal room, in the NE angle, has a coffered segmental vault and reeded door- and window-architraves, but its fireplaces have been removed. An unaltered groin-vaulted document-store with an inner door of cast iron is set in the N front above the entrance-vestibule.

The second floor, which contains a series of small offices, retains few early features except for the cupola over the main staircase, which is a massive cross-ribbed structure lit by four round-headed openings and having a foliated centrepiece. The second stage of the access-stair to the steeple comprises a

174D

Port Glasgow Town Buildings (No.73) from N   *(B 47632)*

timber spiral stair enclosed in a slatted wooden cylindrical cage. The clock-mechanism is undated and the existing bell, 1.12m in diameter, was cast by James Duff and Sons, Greenock, in 1879.

HISTORY

As early as 1668 the magistrates of Glasgow were granted a free port at Newark, with power 'to erect and build bulwarks, As also ane tolbuith or wardeing place upon any parte of the saids lands'.[4] In 1803 the old town hall was found to be inadequate and an Act of Parliament was obtained to allow for new public buildings.[5] A Mr Wood was requested to 'prepare a plan of the proposed Prison, Council Chamber and other publick buildings to be set down on the Breast',[6] but it was to be ten years before work began in earnest.

New plans were obtained in 1813 from William Burn and David Hamilton, those by Hamilton being chosen while Burn, after insistent demands, was paid £100.[7] Local contractors were employed, John Robb of Johnstone being responsible for mason-work and Roderick Young of Port Glasgow for wright-work.[8] When completed, at the end of 1816,[9] the total cost of the new building was £12,000, funded mainly by bonds and public subscription.[10]

The building underwent alterations in 1860-2, but required further repairs under the supervision of J T Rochead in 1862, after damage by lightning.[11] Further alterations to the police

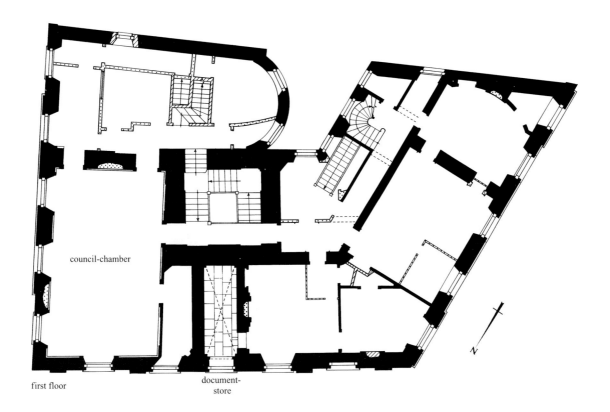

council-chamber

first floor

document-
store

N

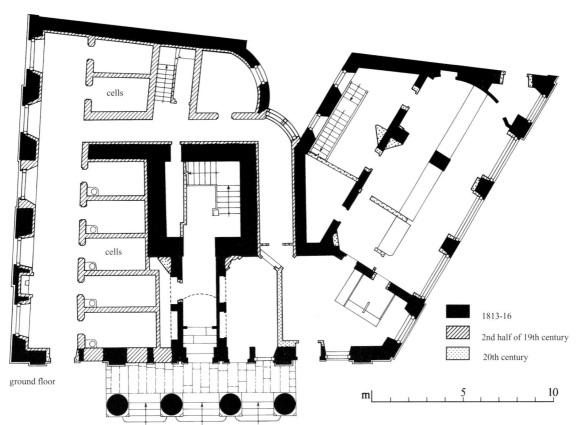

cells

cells

ground floor

■ 1813-16

▨ 2nd half of 19th century

⬚ 20th century

m ⊦————————————⊦————————————⊦ 5 10

Port Glasgow Town Buildings (No.73), plans

cells were carried out in 1883-4,[12] and the prison-accommodation was remodelled in 1891, to designs by J B Stewart of Greenock, after a government committee had condemned it as 'insufficient'.[13] Although a new town hall was built in 1868-70, the building remained in use for local government purposes.

173

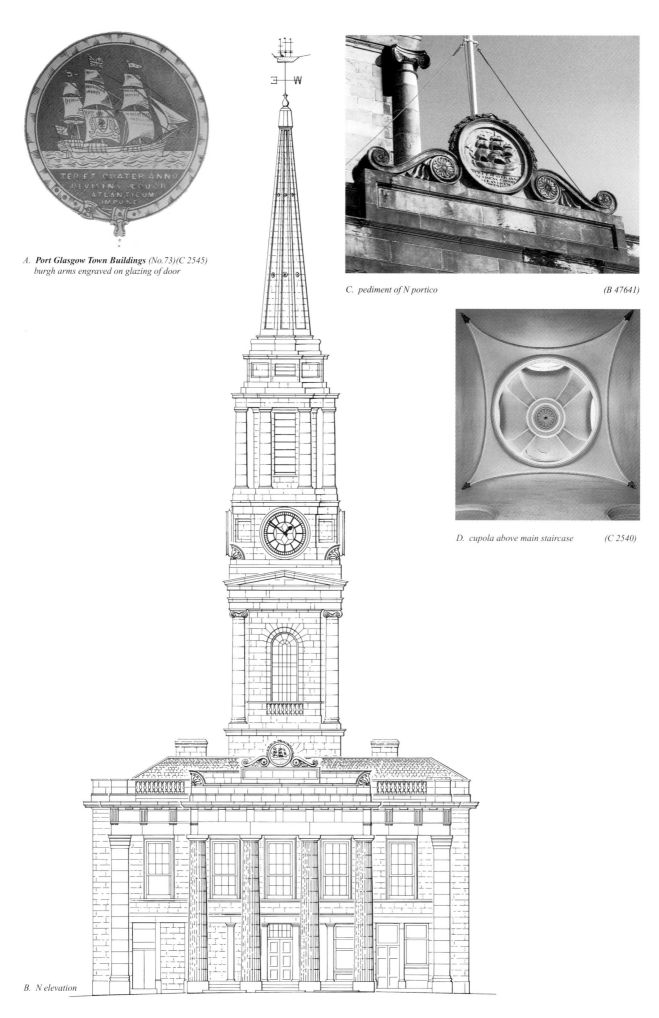

A. **Port Glasgow Town Buildings** (No.73)(C 2545)
   burgh arms engraved on glazing of door

C. pediment of N portico   (B 47641)

D. cupola above main staircase   (C 2540)

B. N elevation

174

A. *Port Glasgow Town Buildings* (No.73) from N, c.1890   (C 54992)

east harbour

mid quay

west harbour

B. *aerial view from NE showing site of harbour*

NS 0885 6458

This building occupies an extensive site in the NE angle of High Street and Castle Street, bounded to the E by Watergate. It contains two principal storeys and is of inverted E-plan, with a 32.5m S front to Castle Street, shorter return wings to High Street and Watergate, and a central wing to the rear. It was built in 1833-5 in a castellated Gothic style, appropriate to its function as a jail and its location overlooking Rothesay Castle. This style was retained in alterations of 1865-7 and of the late 1880s, both of which included extensive additions to the rear.[1] Its masonry is of brown ashlar with orange-yellow sandstone dressings.

The main front has slightly-projecting angle-towers and groups of triple-lancet transomed windows recessed between pilaster-buttresses which rise to a crenellated parapet. A five-stage central clock-tower with corbelled parapet contains the ogee-headed entrance-doorway. This is now at ground-floor level, but originally a double forestair rose to a first-floor entrance which in the 1880s was replaced by an oriel-window within a corbelled and crenellated balcony.

16

In the original arrangement the whole of the ground floor was devoted to prison-accommodation, with the jailer's house and further cells in the rear wing. The first floor housed 'a spacious court room in which the Sheriff, Burgh and Justice of the Peace courts are held, with the Town and Sheriff Clerks' offices, and other requisite apartments'.[2] Extensive alterations were made following the closure of the jail in 1883,[3] and the oval staircase to the rear of the entrance-tower is probably of that period. The building has undergone further alterations for use as local-government offices, but the Sheriff court-room retains its original position in the E part of the first floor, and

to the W there is an imposing council-chamber with portraits of local notables.

The tower houses the original clock-mechanism, which was donated by the 2nd Marquis of Bute and made by Arnold, Dent and Co. of London in 1834. The bell was cast in the same year by Stephen Miller and Co. of Glasgow,[4] and stands in its original position on the roof of the tower.

B. 19th-century model (C 48080)

A. Rothesay Town Hall and County Buildings (No.74) from S (C 48057)

HISTORY

At least two previous tolbooths stood on the site of the present building, the first of them supposedly on the W side of Watergate. This was replaced in 1614 by a tolbooth in Castle Street, at the SW angle of the present site.[5] A 'belhous' was added to this building in 1688, and an engraving of about this period shows a bird-cage bellcot surmounting the W gable above a first-floor doorway reached by a forestair.[6] It underwent frequent alterations during the late 17th and 18th centuries, and was demolished in 1834.[7]

In 1831 an Act of Parliament was obtained for improving Rothesay harbour and 'for building a Gaol, Court House, and Offices for the said Burgh and County'.[8] Even before the act was passed, the Duke of Hamilton, proprietor of Arran, protested that the proposed buildings were 'much too expensive', and forwarded plans of the County Buildings at Kinross as a more suitable model.[9] The present building was designed by James Dempster, a Greenock architect, and the foundation stone was laid in 1833, when a contract was made with a group of local tradesmen. Work began in the E half of the site, allowing the retention of the old town-house until part of the building was completed. The contract price was almost £2,800, but the final cost was about £4,000.[10]

B. *prison-wing from W* (C 48067)

A. **Rothesay Town Hall and County Buildings** (No.74) (C 48063)
   council-chamber

C. *staircase* (C 48069)

75   SALTCOATS TOWN-HOUSE
North Ayrshire
NS 2475 4113

The town-house, which was built in 1825-6, is situated on the W side of Countess Street, and is distinguished by an elaborate steeple at the centre of the main (E) front. Adjoining it to the S, and communicating with it at first-floor level, there is the town hall, which was built in 1891-2 on the site of the parish school. The building is constructed of sandstone ashlar from Ardrossan quarry. [1]

The two-storeyed main block is three bays in width and about 10m square on plan. A curved projection at the rear encloses an oval spiral staircase. The ground storey of the steeple incorporates an arch-headed doorway framed by Tuscan pilasters and surmounted by a cornice decorated with acroteria. At the next stage, a diminutive oculus framed by swags is set below a moulded pediment at the level of the main wall-head. The third and fourth stages have blind segmental-headed windows, and the clock-stage is framed by Ionic angle-pilasters capped by urns. At the next level there is an octagonal belfry, with round-headed openings in the principal faces, which carries a stone spire. This was reduced in height in the 20th century, but originally had conical finials at the bases of the oblique facets, and a miniature balustraded parapet at mid-height. [2]

When erected, the town-house was intended 'to contain certain shops below, and a large room with two retiring rooms above, alongst with a place of confinement for disorderly persons and a steeple to contain a bell and clock'. [3] Internally it has been much altered, but the main first-floor room, which was used as a reading-room and a court-room for the local justices, [4] retains two original chimneypieces in the N wall. In the steeple at this level there is a cell, lit by the oculus in the main front, which retains a stone bench built against the N wall. [5]

An uninscribed bell, 0.71m in diameter, was installed in 1829 and removed to the High Kirk at Stevenston in 1988. The clock-mechanism was removed at the same time to North Ayrshire Museum. [6]

HISTORY
Saltcoats was erected into a burgh of barony in 1576, and had an early tolbooth in Girnal Close, which contained a vaulted prison. The town's burghal status appears to have lapsed, and the tolbooth was in disuse by 1714. [7] The present building was erected by a group of inhabitants, who 'felt great inconvenience for the want of a Public Clock, and a temporary place of confinement for disorderly persons, and considering that few towns of its size are destitute of some ornamental spire, resolved to erect this building by subscription, according to a plan furnished by Peter King, mason'. The subscription was opened in 1823 and the foundation-stone was laid two years later. [8]

The cost exceeded the sum subscribed, and the debt was extinguished only after further appeals in 1856 and 1868. Saltcoats became a police burgh in 1885, but the building remained the property of the Town-house Society until 1891, when the adjacent town hall was begun to designs by the Glasgow architects, Howie and Walton. [9]

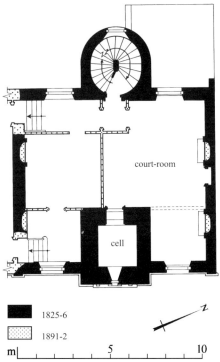

Saltcoats Town-house (No.75)
E elevation (partially reconstructed)
and first-floor plan

court-room

cell

■ 1825-6

▨ 1891-2

m   5   10

Saltcoats Town-house (No.75) from NE   (B 47652)

76 SANQUHAR TOWN-HOUSE
Dumfries and Galloway
NS 7809 0990

Designed by William Adam and built in 1735-9, the town-house stands on an island site in the market-place to the S of High Street, 'fronting down the street toward the cross'.[1] It is two-storeyed and rectangular on plan, measuring 15.8m from N-S by 11.1m, and has a prominent hipped roof. Its main (E) front is of five bays, the central three forming a slightly-advanced pedimented elevation above which there is a three-staged steeple. The principal rooms on the first floor are reached by a double forestair which encloses a ground-floor doorway.

The E front and steeple are built of ashlar, and the other walls are of coursed rubble which has been painted over a thin layer of render. The angles are marked by stepped channelled quoins, and the openings throughout have freestone surrounds. In the front and rear walls they are disposed symmetrically, and all have lugged surrounds and projecting keystones, except for two small original windows behind the forestair and an inserted one in the S wall. The windows in the E and N walls have consoles supporting their sills. In the S end-wall an original window has been contracted in size, and another slapped through at the centre. The lowest stage of the steeple was lit by an oculus in the pediment, set in an irregular raised surround on which the date 1735 was incised early in the 20th century.[2]

The steeple has a square base terminating in a roll-moulding, below a plain clock-stage with a circular clock-face in its E front. Above this there is an octagonal belfry with narrow round-headed louvred openings, surmounted by a heavy roll-moulding and a cornice which carries an ogival lead-covered cupola.

The ground storey has a central corridor reached by a shouldered doorway enclosed by the forestair. In the end bays of the E front there are doorways, the N one giving access to a rectangular barrel-vaulted cell which has been divided by a later cross-wall. The S doorway enters a rectangular room in the S part of the ground floor, formerly used as a school-room, which has been partially divided by modern partitions. In the NW angle of the building there is a rectangular barrel-vaulted cell reached by a doorway from the central passage. The vaulted inner part of this passage was itself formerly a cell, while the square lobby below the steeple was used as an exercise-area.[3] The E doorway appears to have been heightened by re-cutting, and two small vents flanking the doorway in the W wall of the passage have been blocked in recent years.

The first floor is regular on plan, containing two rectangular rooms to N and S, and a central vestibule to the E with a barrel-vaulted chamber to the rear. The vestibule is roughly square on plan, but has half-round recesses with stone seats and scalloped heads in each angle, and doorways to N and S leading to the main rooms. The S room, which was the council-chamber, has two windows in the S wall at slightly different heights, both of them now blocked. The equivalent windows in the former court-room to the N appear always to have been blind. The central rear chamber has a fireplace with a plain surround in its N wall, and in the NE and SE angles there are document-cupboards, probably inserted in 1781 when it was being used as the town clerk's room.[4] Recent

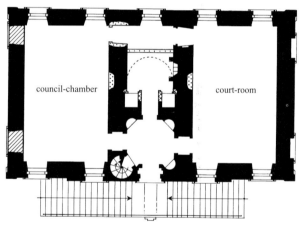

first floor

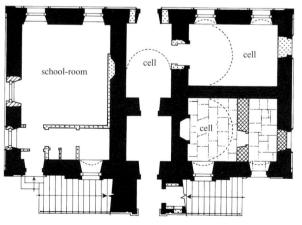

ground floor

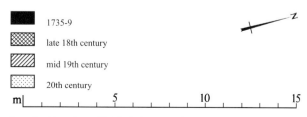

	1735-9
	late 18th century
	mid 19th century
	20th century

Sanquhar Town-house (No.76), E elevation and plans

Sanquhar Town-house (No.76) from E   (B 47661)

alterations include the slapping through of a doorway to the NW angle of the S room, and the removal or blocking of fireplaces. The N room formerly had a large 16th-century fireplace which was presumably brought from Sanquhar Castle.[5] Within the wall-thickness at the SE angle of the vestibule there is a spiral stair rising to the attic, which preserves much of the original collar-rafter roof-structure.

Built into the outer wall N of the main doorway there is an armorial panel bearing a dragon's head spouting fire, the crest of the Crichton family, and inscribed: GOD SEND GRACE / 1751. This was presumably associated with John Crichton, provost of Sanquhar from 1744 to 1765,[6] but the panel was placed in its present position some time after 1957, and its original location is not known. At the N side of the N ground-floor doorway there is a vertical bar with a sliding ring to which the jougs were formerly attached.[7]

HISTORY
The present building replaced an earlier tolbooth on the same site, described as a two-storied building thatched with heather, which by 1731 was 'very insufficient and almost ruinous'.[8]

The new town-house was built at the expense of the 3rd Duke of Queensberry, and materials were procured in 1735 to 'shew the people that the Duke is in earnest to make that building'.[9] Construction began in 1736 and was completed in 1739. As with many of his commissions, William Adam acted both as architect and supplier of materials, especially timber, which was brought from Leith. A letter of 1735 mentions 'the

Draft made by Mr Adams for the Town and School House of Sanquhar', and states that 'Mr Adams is to order six cart loads (of timber) to be sent immediately'. In 1738 he received immediate settlement of an account of £119 9s for timber supplied, 'because he has had a good deal of trouble since drawing the Plan of the within Tounhouse in sending advice & Direction to the Undertaker for carrying on the building'.[10] The mason-contractors were George Laurie, deacon of the squaremen of Sanquhar, with Thomas Laurie and James McCall.[11] Stone was obtained not only from a newly-opened quarry at Cleughfoot but also from the ruins of Sanquhar Castle, and material from the latter is said to have been employed in the construction of the vaulted rooms on the ground floor.[12]

Only minor alterations were undertaken before 1857, when the old bell of 1694 was recast and a new clock installed, and the forestair and railing were renewed.[13] At about the same period a doorway was slapped through the S wall when the S room was used as a contractor's office for the building of the local railway.[14] In 1987-9 the town-house was converted into a museum.

181

77 SELKIRK COURT-HOUSE
Scottish Borders
NT 4702 2847

The court-house[1] is situated on the upper side of the triangular Market Place in the centre of Selkirk, at the NE angle of its junction with Fleshmarket Street. It was built in 1803-5 to replace an earlier jail and council-room on an island site a few metres to the W.[2]

The building is two-storeyed and was originally almost square on plan,[3] measuring 12.2m across the main (W) front, with a projecting central steeple about 4.3m square and some 30.5m in height. It was subsequently extended by two annexes at the rear to a length of 17m. The upper two stages of the steeple are ashlar-built, while the rest of the building is of dark coursed rubble with stepped sandstone margins, covered with render at the first and third stages of the steeple. The roof of the main block is hipped and slated.

The central entrance-doorway is round-headed, and until about 1870 the side-bays and the side-walls of the steeple at ground-floor level contained openings of similar form, which have been replaced by shop-fronts filling the re-entrant angles.[4] The first-floor windows are rectangular, but that in the steeple is set in a round-headed surround.

A heavy wall-head cornice continues round the steeple, and is repeated at the next three stages. The first of these has slightly-sunk horizontal panels in moulded surrounds, and the clock-stage has recessed angles which define square panels carrying circular dials. The octagonal belfry has alternate louvred and blind round-headed embrasures, and its cornice carries the spire, also octagonal, which rises from a splayed base-course and roll-moulding. Its facets have oval sound-holes, alternately blind and open, and it terminates in two ball-finials surmounted by a weather-cock.

The entrance-doorway gives access to a stone staircase which rises through the steeple to the first-floor court-room and two small rooms at the rear. The court-house has a coved ceiling, and all three rooms retain some original fittings including wooden panelling and benches, but they were extensively renovated in the third quarter of the 20th century.[5]

In the belfry there is a bell, 0.63m in diameter and cast by Lester and Pack, London, in 1757, which is rung every evening as a curfew-bell. The existing clock dates from about 1870.

HISTORY

A tolbooth is known to have existed at Selkirk by 1517, and in 1536 it was quoted as a landmark in alloting stances in the market-place.[6] In 1722 there was 'ane strong prison, fine Councell house and markit cross',[7] and in 1742 the 5th Duke of Hamilton gave £100 to improve or rebuild the tolbooth to provide separate accommodation for debtors.[8] A steeple to replace that of the demolished church was built in 1746 'above the high pend at the east end of the tolbooth', and in 1760 a debtor absconded after working 'as a day labourer at the building of the council-house'.[9] A plan drawn shortly before its demolition in 1803 shows a rectangular building containing the council-room at the W and a square prison-room and a stair to the E, with a square steeple projecting from the E wall and the fleshmarket adjoining the N wall.[10] It was demolished following a complaint in 1801 by the local sheriff-depute, Walter Scott, that 'the Town Jail was totally insufficient', and Scott acquired for his own collection a lock and key which are now displayed in the court-house.[11]

The new 'jail and Town House' was funded partly by the burgh, which offered £500 and the materials of the old building, and by the county, and partly by subscription.[12] Various sites were considered, and an early request for advice was addressed to 'Mr William Elliot, architect in Kelso'.[13] In March 1803, however, 'three different plans of a Town house and Steeple, one by Mr Boyd Architect, one by Mr Easton and

Selkirk Court-house (No.77) from W　　　　　　(B 47672)

one by Mr Lees Architect', were laid before the council. That chosen was evidently by Lees, who proposed a similar design for a town hall at Duns.[14] The building was completed by 1805, when Robert Southey contrasted 'a new town-house with a spire' with the general simplicity of the town.[15] The ground storey presumably included prison-accommodation, but a separate prison in castellated style was built a few years later, at the NW edge of the town.[16]

The building has particular associations with Sir Walter Scott, who was sheriff-depute of Selkirkshire from 1799 until his death in 1832. The court-room is often known as 'Sir Walter Scott's court-room', and a bench and chair preserved there are believed to have been used by Scott.[17]

B. *view from SW, c.1870* *(SE/680)*

C. *court-room from N, c.1900* *(SE/656)*

A. **Selkirk Court-house** *(No.77), W elevation (partially reconstructed)*

m | 5 | 10

78   SOUTH QUEENSFERRY TOLBOOTH
City of Edinburgh
NT 1295 7833

The tolbooth stands on a raised terrace on the S side of High Street, its prominence enhanced by later lowering of the street-level. It comprises a main block of 17th-century origin, and a five-storeyed steeple of 1720 projecting at the N front. A forestair rising along the N and E walls of the steeple gives access from street level to the terrace and to the first-floor entrance of the main block. The building is constructed of a combination of harled rubble and dressed sandstone, and the roof of the main block is tiled to the front like that of the adjacent Rosebery Memorial Hall of 1893.

The main block has been rectangular on plan, measuring 5.5m in depth, but because of rebuilding to the E in 1893 only about 10m of its length is preserved. The entrance-area, dormer-windows and chimneys were altered at the same time. The central and W portions of the ground storey, including two doorways with chamfered surrounds in the N wall, may be ascribed to the 17th century. The W part of this storey was in use as a weigh-house by 1641, housing a beam and weights imported from Holland, while the remainder probably served as a prison.[1] The first floor was extensively altered in the 18th century, and in 1770 it was fitted up as a new court-room and a council-chamber. Despite its limited size the first floor of the steeple was also used as a court-room, its fittings surviving as late as the 1890s, and in 1813 the ringing-chamber was converted to a writing-office for the town clerk.[2]

The lower part of the N front of the steeple at ground-floor level is built of sandstone ashlar, as are the rusticated quoins, the window-margins and the moulded string-courses dividing the stages, while the remainder is harled. A small oval panel in the N wall below the first-floor string-course bears the burgh arms[3] within mantling of 18th-century character. The existing octagonal slate-hung belfry and slated spire date from 1807, but the belfry was altered in 1888 to house a new clock and large clock-faces commemorating the jubilee of Queen Victoria.[4]

The walls enclosing the passage through the steeple at the level of the terrace were constructed in 1832, and the arches in its E and W walls may have been altered at the same time, but a reference of that date to the 'Steeple Pillars' suggests that there was always public access through its base.[5] A cast-iron plaque attached to the forestair records that in 1817 the 4th Earl of Rosebery, then provost of the burgh, provided a water supply and a bleaching green for its inhabitants.[6] The cistern for one of the wells was placed beneath the forestair, which was evidently rebuilt at this time. The channelled quoins of the steeple begin at the level of the terrace, suggesting that the street-level was also lowered at this time.

The steeple houses a bell 0.54m in diameter, inscribed: EX DONO HENRJCJ CVNJNGHAME DE BOQUHAN 1723. In 1927 it also contained another bell, 0.37m in diameter and bearing the incised inscription: THE SEAMEN OF QVEENSFERRIE DID GIFT THIS BELL TO THE TOWNE ANNO 1694 ADRIAEN DOP FECIT. This bell was removed from Bailie John Syme's house in 1750 to be hung in the tolbooth, but it is now in the tower of the nearby Episcopal church.[7]

HISTORY
A tolbooth was in existence at South Queensferry by 1635, and in 1649 its repair was the subject of an application to the Convention of Royal Burghs.[8] A new door 'at the foot of the tolbooth stair', to give access from the street to the 'thieves' hole', was added in 1703,[9] but its exact position cannot be determined.

Substantial rebuilding took place in 1720 when the present steeple was erected. Its construction was financed by Henry Cunningham of Boquhan, MP for Stirling Burghs, who also

provided a new clock and bell, and in 1732 the floors of the steeple were strengthened to support the weight of the clock.[10] Further repairs were carried out in 1740 to prevent the building 'going entirely to ruin'.[11] In 1770 the first floor of the main block was fitted out as a new court-room and council-chamber, divided by a wall which in 1784 was replaced by a moveable partition.[12]

In 1893 the 5th Earl of Rosebery gifted the adjacent hall, set at a slight angle to the E of the main block, as a memorial to his wife Hannah (d.1890). It was designed in an Arts and Crafts style by the Edinburgh architects Sydney Mitchell and Wilson, to provide rooms for reading, games and smoking in addition to a small auditorium.[13]

*A. **South Queensferry Tolbooth** (No.78) from NE*   (B 58238)

B. burgh armorial in steeple (B 58250)

A. **South Queensferry Tolbooth** *(No.78), burgh from E, c.1860*   *(B 19802)*

BY THE MAGISTRATES & TOWN
COUNCIL IN GRATITUDE FOR THE
LIBERALITY AND KINDNESS OF
ARCHIBALD JOHN EARL OF ROSEBERY
PROVOST OF THIS BURGH TO WHOM
THE INHABITANTS ARE INDEBTED
FOR A BLEACHING GREEN & THIS
SUPPLY OF WATER

1817

C. cast-iron panel on forestair   *(B 58240)*

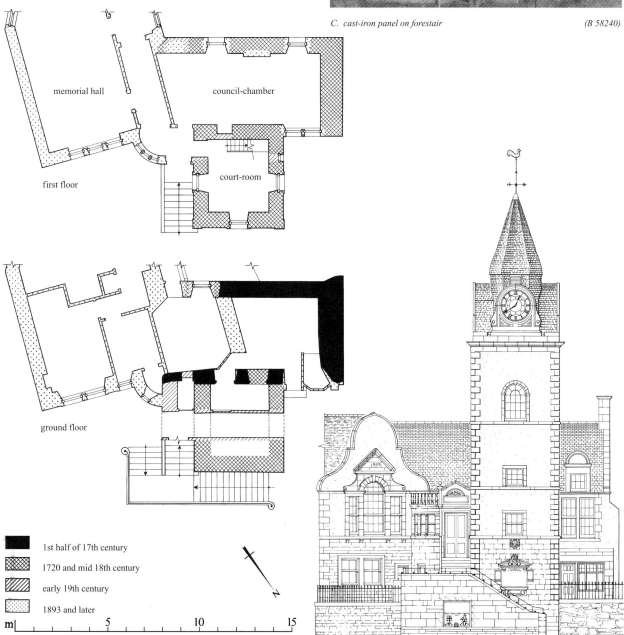

memorial hall

council-chamber

first floor

court-room

ground floor

■ 1st half of 17th century

▨ 1720 and mid 18th century

▨ early 19th century

▨ 1893 and later

m   5   10   15

B. plans and N elevation

79 STIRLING TOWN-HOUSE
Stirling

NS 7931 9369

This building[1] stands on the SW side of Broad Street at its
junction with Jail Wynd, on a site which had been acquired in
1473 for use as a tolbooth. It was built in 1703-5 to a design
by Sir William Bruce, who may have done no more than
provide sketch-plans and an outline specification.[2] In 1785
the N front was extended eastwards by three bays to include an
older property which was already in use as an annexe to the
town-house, but the architect, Gideon Gray, copied Bruce's
elevation so faithfully that the junction with the original work
is hardly apparent. A court-house and jail, designed and built
by Richard Crichton, were added to the S, fronting Jail Wynd
and St John Street, between 1806 and 1811.

As enlarged in 1785, the town-house is an oblong building
aligned nearly E and W, with a NW tower which projects 1.8m
beyond the main (N) front. It is of three storeys and an attic,
with six window-bays to the N and three to the W, all
symmetrically disposed. The original portion measures 11.5m
in length and, excluding the tower, 8.9m in breadth, but the
extension of 1785 increased the overall length to 18.8m. The
Broad Street frontage and the upper part of the tower above
eaves-level are ashlar-faced, while the rest of the main
building is of rubble masonry. On the Broad Street front the
windows have lugged and moulded architraves with pulvinated
friezes and their sills continue on the first and second floors as
string-courses. On Jail Wynd the windows have plain offset
margins, and on both elevations their upper halves retain
sockets for iron grilles. Two ground-floor entrances
correspond in style with the windows, one being in the N wall
immediately E of the tower and the other, converted into a
window, in the W wall immediately S of it. In the upper part
of the tower, above a string-course at eaves-level, the voids and
quoins are channelled; elsewhere, both in the tower and the
main block, the quoins are simply offset.

The tower, which is 4.6m square, contains six storeys and
finishes in a moulded cornice and an iron-railed parapet
enclosing a timber belfry with crested ogival roof. A richly-
ornamented round-headed arch in the N wall gives access to a
wide straight stair rising to the first floor. Immediately above
the arch there is an empty round-headed niche set within a
rectangular frame carved with egg-and-dart ornament. The
tower is lit by square-headed windows in the N wall, while the
belfry has a louvred opening, formerly pedimented, in each
side, and its roof, which is topped by a weather-cock, has four
corresponding lucarnes. In each face of the tower, just below
the parapet, there is a timber clock-face set in a square
moulded stone frame.

Parts of the early 18th-century block may incorporate the
remains of a two-storeyed tenement-building which stood
immediately E of the old tolbooth,[3] and it may even include
part of the S wall of the old tolbooth itself. The main
structural partitions, which rise to the attic and may in part
have derived from the older building,[4] divided each floor into
two large equal rooms with a small one S of the tower, which
itself contained a still smaller room.

On the ground floor an additional transverse wall in the E
half forms a narrow vaulted strong-room, each side-wall
containing two cupboards with iron doors. A blocked
fireplace in the S wall of the W room may survive from the
building that existed before 1703. From the adjacent room
behind the tower a flight of steps leads down to a tiny vaulted
cell, lit by a small window on the W, no doubt 'the holl
beneath the steeple' in which a prisoner was confined in
1707.[5]

*A. **Stirling Town-house** (No.79), N elevation*

xiiD
15A

B. prison-block from SW

(ST/1941)

186

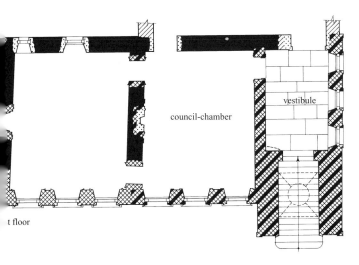

vestibule

council-chamber

t floor

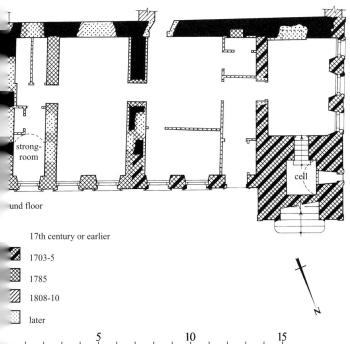

strong-
room

cell

und floor

17th century or earlier

1703-5

1785

1808-10

later

5   10   15

N

Stirling Town-house (No.79), plans

B. view from NW   *(ST/709)*

The approach-stair in the tower is ceiled with a quadripartite plaster vault, whose central bell-hole is now closed with a painted panel showing the burgh's later seal, a wolf couchant on a rock, with the motto STIRLINI OPPIDVM.[6] The semicircular-headed doorway at the head of the stair has a roll-and-hollow-moulded surround, and the door itself is constructed of vertical nail-studded boards, cross-lined at the rear. From the first-floor vestibule a doorway with lugged architrave in the E wall gives access to the two main rooms and in the S wall an early 19th-century arched doorway, itself subsequently altered, serves the SW range of that period. The westernmost of the main rooms retains much of its early 18th-century interior. It is panelled, and a moulded stone fireplace in the E wall has a painted landscape overmantel and is framed by fluted pilasters with Ionic capitals. The original doorway S of the fireplace has a lugged architrave, but that to the N is an insertion.[7] The E room, which is plastered above a panelled wooden dado, has a ceiling, chimney-piece and doorways of late 18th-century character.

188

Now subdivided, the second floor retains few early features. It is reached by an early 19th-century staircase in the SW extension, probably replacing a forestair or turret stair which rose to a doorway, now blocked, in the S wall of the room S of the tower. The original door to the adjacent room has also been built up and in the inserted S passage there is a blocked original fireplace. A small room in the tower retains its original door, a roll-and-hollow-moulded fireplace in the E wall and a rebated locker opposite.

The attic, which contains three intercommunicating rooms, is reached by a newel-stair in the SE angle of the tower. Two corbels in the E wall of the room behind the tower suggest that this room may originally have been covered by a lean-to roof. The early 18th-century block has a collar-rafter roof,[8] that over the extension of 1785 being of king-post type. The upper stages of the tower are reached by wooden loft-stairs.[2]

The early 19th-century addition, largely ashlar-faced to the street, comprises a first-floor court-room which rises through two storeys facing Jail Wynd, and a higher prison-block whose main (S) front is aligned to St John Street. The three tall window-bays of the court-room are contained in recesses which also enclose round-headed clerestory openings. The doorway to a stair serving the court-room and prison-block, in the W wall of the latter, has a round-headed Gibbs surround, probably of the 1860s.[9] The three-storeyed, four-bay S block is of plain neo-classical design; its ground-floor windows and central doorway are set within arched recesses and at the wall-head there is a long blank panel carried on guttae.

186B

The ground storey of the court-house contains seven vaulted rooms which probably included a guard-house and cells, and a passage from Jail Wynd to a courtyard on the E. The first-floor justiciary court-room, which was entered through the town-house and had its bench to the S, has a high coved ceiling. The prison was described in 1836 as containing sixteen cells, but six in the lower part had been abandoned because of damp, leaving seven for criminals and three for debtors.[10] There are five vaulted rooms on the ground floor of the S block, and two more in the W half of both the first and second floors, as well as two unvaulted cells in the attic. The E half of the upper floors is occupied by a single high chamber, probably formed as a county court-room after the removal of the jail to a new site in 1848.[11]

BELLS
The bell that hangs in the fifth storey of the tower is 0.41m in diameter and is inscribed: THE COVNSEL BELL OF STERLINE OVDEROGGE FECIT 1656, being the work of Cornelis Ouderogge of Rotterdam.[12] Below appears the single letter S. In the belfry another bell, recast in 1864, bears a copy of the original inscription: PETRUS HEMONY ME FECIT AMSTELODAMI AD 1669 SIT NOMEN DOMINI BENEDICTUM ('Peter Hemony made me at Amsterdam, 1669. Blessed be the Name of the Lord'). The bell of 1669 was itself a recasting of an earlier one.[13] At the same level there is a chime of sixteen bells, two of which are dated 1729, one also being inscribed with the initials IW. A set of 'musick bells for the towns clock' was bought in London in that year.[14]

HISTORY
The site of the tolbooth was acquired by the burgh in 1473.[15] Repairs to the building were recorded at intervals throughout the 16th and 17th centuries, and the construction of a wardhouse was authorised and funded by a general stent on the inhabitants in 1616.[16]

The decision to demolish and rebuild 'the tolbooth steeple and tenement upon the east syde thereof' was agreed by the town council in 1698, and funds were set aside from the malt tax. In March 1702 Harry Livingstone, a Stirling mason, was sent to Kinross to consult with Sir William Bruce, taking 'ane exact account of the breadth and lenth of the ground alongs with him' and having instructions to bring back Bruce's 'draught or sceme of the work'.[17] The council received Bruce's 'draught of the new hous and steiple' by August 1702, and demolition of the old steeple began immediately. The new town-house was built in 1703-5 by Livingstone and John Christie, a local wright.[18] 'Hyeland oak trees' were used for the spire and 'to hing the great bell', and in 1707 'Fyne French glass' was ordered for the windows.[19] In 1710 Alexander McGill was paid three guineas for 'drawing a scheme for reforming the court place and benches therein'.[20]

Instructions were given in 1724 for the prison walls and partitions in the cellar to be thickened, to prevent the escape of prisoners.[21] Thereafter little significant work is recorded, other than repeated repairs to the roof, until the main front was extended by the local architect Gideon Gray in 1785.[22]

The available space was found inadequate to house a prison,

Stirling Town-house (No.79), *chimneypiece in first-floor W room* (ST/710)

and Justiciary and Sheriff as well as Burgh courts. In 1805 the Edinburgh architect Richard Crichton prepared plans for a major extension to the S, and work began, to a somewhat altered design, in 1808. The court-house was completed in 1810 and the prison a year later.[23] The new prison itself proved unsatisfactory, and by 1836 six cells in the lower part had been abandoned because of damp, leaving only ten in use, while the masonry was 'so bad, that holes can be easily made through the walls'.[24] It was replaced in 1848 by a large new county prison of castellated design by Thomas Brown, situated on the opposite side of St John Street.

Thereafter the old prison, which had come into the possession of the County Prison Board, was sold to the County authorities for use as a County court and police office. The Justiciary court remained the property of the burgh, and the police station was housed on its ground floor, while the original town-house included the town clerk's rooms on the ground storey and the council chamber and police court on the first floor, with store-rooms above.[25]

The Edinburgh architects, Brown and Wardrop, prepared plans in 1862 for modest alterations which were not fully executed and, in the same year, a scheme for a baronial-style Sheriff Court-house adjoining the prison on the S side of St John Street. The court-house which was finally erected to a similar design by the same firm in the 1870s, however, stands in Viewfield Place.[26]

80 STONEHAVEN
Aberdeenshire

Although Stonehaven was never a royal burgh, its Old
Tolbooth at the quayside housed the head courts of
Kincardineshire and the county prison from 1600 to 1767. In
the latter year these functions were removed to new County
Buildings in Dunottar Avenue, which were altered in 1822 and
largely rebuilt in 1863.[1] In 1789-90 a steeple to house a new
bell and clock was built at the E end of the market-area in
High Street, in the heart of the old town.[2] Meanwhile a
'Newtown of Stonehaven' was being laid out N of the Carron
Water, and in 1826 its arcaded market-house (also used at
some periods for county offices) was built by the proprietor in
Market Square. This had a central spire built at public
expense, which in 1856 was heightened to 40m, again at the
expense of the feuars of the new town. A new town hall was
built in Allardice Street, opposite the market-house, in 1878.[3]

THE OLD TOLBOOTH (NO 8781 8552).
Situated on the old N quay of Stonehaven harbour and facing
S, this gabled two-storeyed building is L-shaped on plan. It
comprises a rectangular principal block, which was probably
built as a storehouse in the late 16th century, and a 17th-
century wing, also rectangular, extending to the N. In the NE
re-entrant there is a paved courtyard with an E annexe whose
curved E wall abuts the SE angle of the main block.

The main block measures 18.8m from E to W by 6.5m,
while the N wing, whose W side-wall is slightly out of
alignment with the original W gable, measures 10.5m by 6m.
A straight forestair rising against the W gable-wall of the main
block provides the only access to the first floor. The walls of
the tolbooth and the courtyard are constructed of local
sandstone and conglomerate rubble, now very weathered. The
chimneystacks, on the W gable of the main block and the N

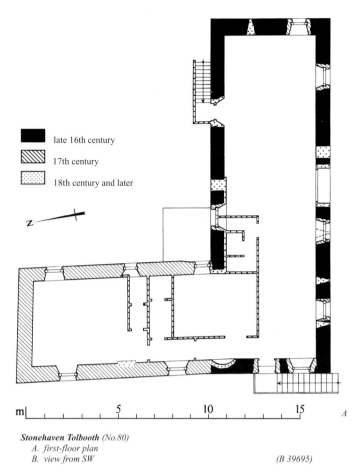

■	late 16th century
▨	17th century
⬚	18th century and later

Stonehaven Tolbooth (No.80)
A. first-floor plan
B. view from SW

(B 39695)

B

gable and W wall-head of the N block, are of ashlar and have high bevelled copings with drip-courses. The gables are crow-stepped, with cavetto skewputts, one of which, at the W gable, is said to have borne the arms of the Earls Marischal. [4]

The openings of the main front have undergone extensive alterations, some early slit windows being blocked and larger chamfered ones inserted, possibly when the N block was added. The three blocked slits at an intermediate level in the W half of the S wall suggest that the internal floor-level has also been altered. The doorway in the W part of this wall may be original, but a larger loading-door has been slapped through its E part, and a similar central opening at first-floor level has been converted into a picture-window. While there have been minor alterations to the windows of the N block, their present appearance may be regarded as fairly original. A large modern opening has been slapped though its W wall, [5] and there is evidence of a former opening at the centre of the E wall.

Internally there are few early features, but the ground floor of the N block retains both rubble and flagstone flooring. The ground floor of the main block contains two rooms divided towards the W end by a stone partition-wall. At first-floor level much of the interior has been obscured by modern partitions. A curved recess in the W wall of the main block near its junction with the wing probably housed a free-standing stove. A large fireplace midway along the W wall of the rear wing, indicated by an external relieving-arch and the chimneystack above, has been blocked.

HISTORY

It is probable that the building was erected towards the end of the 16th century by the superior of the burgh, the 5th Earl Marischal, as a storehouse. [6] It is believed to have become a tolbooth in 1600 when an Act of Parliament provided that 'the Schireff of the schiref-dome of Kincardin in all tyme to cum sall sit and hald their courtis at the Stanehyve'. [7] In 1645 the Marquis of Montrose, following the Earl Marischal's refusal to support him, 'syne fyris the tolbuith of Stanehevin, quhairin thair wes stoir of beir (barley) and cornis, and [the] haill toun also'. [8] The building presumably required considerable repairs, and an account written before 1685 described 'the seat of justice for the shire, a spatious and large Tolbooth of two or three stories'. [9] In addition to the sheriff court, it housed a prison and a meeting place for county gentlemen, and burgh business was conducted there after the Earl Marischal in 1624 authorised the election of a town council. [10] It is probable that the ground storey of the main block was used as the prison, and through one of its windows worship was conducted by three local Episcopalian clergymen imprisoned in 1748-9 for holding illegal services. [11] The building reverted to use for storage after the erection of the new County Buildings in 1767 (supra). It was restored in 1963 for use as a museum and, on the upper floor, a restaurant.

THE STEEPLE (NO 8766 8551).

The steeple stands in the SE angle of High Street and John Street, on the site of a house which belonged to the burgh, [12] and it is abutted by other houses to S and E. It comprises a four-storeyed tower about 4.8m square and 11m high to the coping below the open-work timber parapet. This encloses an octagonal timber belfry with elliptical-headed louvred openings, which carries a lead-covered bell-cast spire. The N and W walls are built of red granite ashlar with channelled quoins, and the visible parts of the other walls, which contain no openings, are of random rubble. The doorway, in the W wall and reached by two steps, bears the date 1790 on the lintel. All but two of the windows are blind, and the one above the doorway houses a large barometer-dial. Early views show a large wooden clock-dial at the W wall-head, which in 1896 was replaced by a pedimented dial-surround of masonry.

Immediately N of the doorway there are the handle-socket and spout for a pump, and its stone-slabbed cistern occupies the N and E sides of the ground storey. The upper floors are

A. *Stonehaven Steeple (No.80) from W*   (B 76985)

reached by a timber stair, and a central box for the stone clock-weights runs the entire height of the tower although the clock now has an electric mechanism. The main timbers of the belfry and spire are probably original, although the cladding has been renewed. The belfry contains a bell 0.56m in diameter, bearing the date 1793 and a band of neo-classical ornament, which is connected to the clock, and a smaller bell of late 19th-century date. [13]

HISTORY

In 1788 the feuars of Stonehaven asked the town managers to purchase a bell and 'to build a proper place for ... hanging her on'. In March 1789, after the bell had been purchased, a plan for a spire was approved, and in May a contract was awarded to James Rhind, mason in Aberdeen. The purchase of a clock 'to be put up in the Town's Steeple' was recommended in 1790, and the clock which is now displayed in the Tolbooth Museum was made by James Duncan, clockmaker in Old Meldrum. Two years later a great number of the feuars requested the purchase of a larger bell for the clock, which is presumably the 1793 bell still hanging in the belfry. [14]

B. *Stranraer Town-house (No.81)*
armorial panel in steeple
(B 47683)

81 STRANRAER
Dumfries and Galloway

The town-house of 1776-7 stands on the S side of George Street at its widest point, at the junction with Church Street and close to the site of an earlier tolbooth. It was extended to the S by a market-house in 1802 and this, with later ranges surrounding a triangular courtyard, was replaced in 1855 by a large corn-exchange with a court-room on the upper floor. Except for a shop in the E part of the ground floor, the whole building was adapted in 1988 for the use of Stranraer Museum. Some 150m to the E there stands the early 16th-century 'Castle of St John', which was adapted in 1820-2 for use as a Town and County Prison and is now also a museum.

THE TOWN-HOUSE (NX 0594 6083)

192A The original town-house comprises a two-storeyed rectangular block measuring 11.8m across the three-bay N front by 8.75m, with a steeple 15m high rising above the slightly advanced central bay. Its masonry is of rubble, rendered in the N and E fronts and with freestone dressings, all heavily painted, and the hipped roof is slated, while the timber-framed spire is covered with lead.

In the central bay there is a doorway, now altered to a window, with a round-headed glazed tympanum below a moulded pediment which is linked to a freestone band in the side-bays. At first-floor level there is a carved panel bearing the burgh arms, installed in 1886,[1] and the steeple rises above the moulded eaves-cornice in two low stages, the upper one incorporating a short length of balustrade. The square clock-stage bears a plaque of 1936 commemorating the donor of the present clock, and above its four segmental wall-head pediments there is a low octagonal belfry with five circular openings,[2] which carries the short octagonal spire. The ground-floor doors and windows in the side-bays date from their later use as shops, and there is some evidence that the N front may have been arcaded.[3] The fenestration of the side-walls is irregular, but a blocked high-level window in the W wall of the ground floor may relate to the use of this area as a prison. A blocked door in the E wall was exposed in 1996.

The interior preserves few early features, but two round-headed arches in the massive side-walls of the steeple gave access to the entrance-lobby at the foot of the central stair from the front areas of the side-bays, which may originally have been open. Until the opening of the castle prison in 1822 the ground storey included a guard-house and jail, and the first floor a debtors' prison whose removal allowed the enlargement of the council-chamber.[4] The ground storey was divided into two shops in 1837, and the court-room appears to have been housed in the E part of the upper floor.[5]

The E front of the added block of 1855, fronting Church Street, has a four-bay ground-floor arcade, formerly open, while the first floor displays three pilastered bays containing large round-headed windows and carrying a gabled pediment. There are three windows of similar type in the upper part of the S wall. The interior of the block has been altered, but in 1988 traces of the N gable of the much lower market-house of 1802 were identified against the exterior of the S wall of the original town-house.[6]

HISTORY
The old tolbooth, which contained a jail on the ground floor,[7] was ruinous by 1775, as was the church which lay immediately to the S, and the council accepted plans for rebuilding both, given in by Edward Wallace, mason, and Thomas Hall. A contract was made with Archibald Paterson, mason, and John McBride, wright, but it was soon decided that 'the Town's funds will not answer to build both at one time'. A revised price of £270 was agreed for the town-house only, 'adding to the height of the steeple four or five foots more', and the work

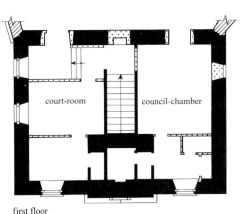

first floor

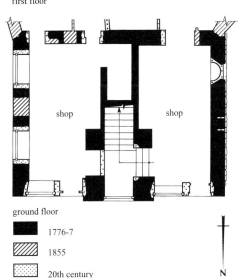

ground floor

	1776-7
	1855
	20th century

m |_____| 5 |_____| 10

N

Stranraer Town-house (No.81), N elevation and plans

*A. **Stranraer Town-house** (No.81) from NE*   (B 47680)   *B. **Stranraer Castle** (No.81) from SW, c.1910*   (WG/91)

was completed in June 1776.[8] The adjacent market-house was built in 1802 by John Hornsby, mason, at a cost of £146, while the corn-exchange and court-room that replaced it in 1855 cost £842.[9] Following the opening of a new town hall in Lewis Street in 1874, the old building was used by various organisations, including the fire brigade and the Athenaeum Club, before becoming the home of Stranraer Museum.[10]

STRANRAER CASTLE (NX 0609 6083)

The castle is a four-storeyed L-plan tower of early 16th-century date which measures 10.8m by 10.1m over walls 1.6m thick.[11] In 1815 it was bought by the town council for £340, and in 1820 the Commissioners of Supply accepted plans by Kenneth Mathieson, a Glasgow architect, to convert it into a 'secure and salutary jail', with cells on the two upper storeys, at an estimated cost of £600. The town council undertook to fit up the first floor as a court-room at a cost of £185, but it is not certain whether this work was carried out.[12] A new prison was built in Lewis Street in 1847, but occasional use was made of the cells in the castle until 1907.[13]

The main external alterations were in the upper storeys, where Mathieson inserted a series of segmental-arched windows in heavy sandstone frames.[14] He also heightened the S wall to replace the original gabled roof with a flat roof, which may have been used as an exercise-area, within a crenellated wall-head.[15] In 1837 the W vault of the ground storey was in use as a lock-up, while there were three criminals' cells on the second floor and two larger debtors' rooms above.[16] All are barrel-vaulted and all but one have fireplaces whose sandstone jambs bear many graffiti. They have heavy iron-plated doors, and their walls were similarly strengthened where they adjoined chimney-flues. Except for the women's cell, which is entered from the main newel-stair, access at each level is from a vaulted N corridor provided with an iron grilled gate.

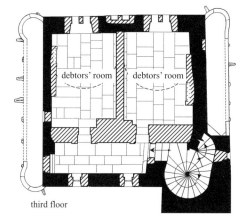

third floor

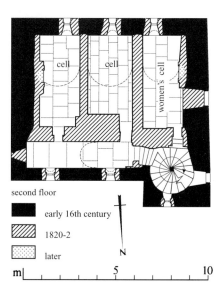

second floor

■ early 16th century

▨ 1820-2

▨ later

m | 5   10

C. plans

82   STRATHMIGLO TOWN-HOUSE
Fife

NO 2150 1024

This steeple is situated on the N side of the High Street, in the centre of the village and about 80m W of the supposed site of a tolbooth of 16th-century origin. It was built in 1734 as an addition to the S gable of a building which had been acquired some years earlier for use as a town-house.[1] This hall was rebuilt in the 19th century and has since been converted into a private dwelling. Incorporated in the SE quoins of its crow-stepped S gable there is a head from a skewputt of 17th-century type.

The steeple, which is 5.05m square on plan, is constructed of sandstone rubble with dressed margins and string-courses which define its five stages. Its walls are slightly battered in profile and the spire rises to an overall height of 21.7m. In the main (S) front there is a round-headed doorway giving access to a ground-floor cell which is lit by a slit-window in the W wall. A forestair which rises E of the doorway returns to a first-floor entrance in the E wall. Access to the hall was provided at this level by an internal doorway, now blocked, in the N wall of the steeple.

There are windows in the S wall at first- and second-floor levels, the former now partly blocked. Above it there is an armorial panel, apparently integral with the building, which bears the date 1734 and the name and arms of the Honourable Margaret Balfour of Burleigh, the superior of the burgh.[2] At third-floor level on each front there are original moulded surrounds enclosing square clock-faces which were renewed in 1921.[3] The fourth stage has paired belfry-openings of lancet form and is surmounted by a corbelled balustrade with panelled angle-pillars, which encloses an ashlar-built broach-spire of slightly bell-shaped profile.

The interior retains few early features. The wooden stairs to the upper floors have been largely renewed and the floor-levels somewhat altered, most noticeably at second-floor level where the original joist-holes are still visible. The belfry houses a bell 0.76m in diameter, bearing the motto TEMPUS FUGIT ('Time flies'), which was cast for the burgh in 1766 by Lester and Pack of London.[4]

Built into the sill of the first-floor S window there is a quadrangular pyramid-capped sundial which surmounts a foliate capital supported by a short length of semi-circular shaft. This is said to be a remnant of the burgh's mercat cross.[5]

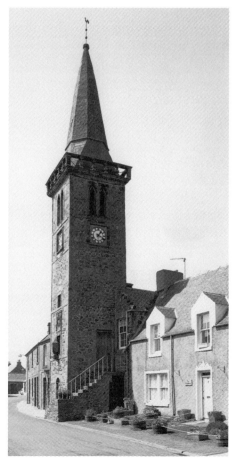

A. ***Strathmiglo Town-house*** *(No.82) from SE*   *(B 39424)*

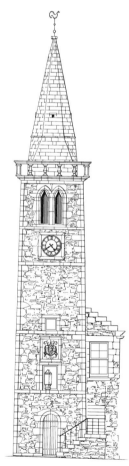

B. armorial panel and sundial   *(B 39429)*

clock stage

second floor

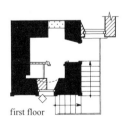

first floor

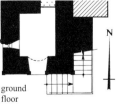

ground floor

C. S elevation and plans

m |_____5

	1734
	19th century
	20th century

83 STRICHEN TOWN-HOUSE
Aberdeenshire

NJ 9466 5516

The town-house, which is built in a castellated style and dates from 1816, stands in the NW angle of High Street and Bridge Street. Its architectural prominence is enhanced by its position at the centre of the village, which was laid out on a grid-plan in 1764.[1]

The gabled two-storeyed main block is rectangular on plan, measuring 12.6m from E to W by 7.5m, and an ornate steeple measuring 5.2m by 5.7m projects from its E end. The building is constructed of finely-wrought grey-brown granite ashlar, except for the inserted masonry surrounding the round-headed ground-floor windows of the S front, which is of light-brown granite. These windows have been inserted into an original four-bay open arcade, shown in a mid-19th-century painting of the building,[2] which presumably gave access to a market-area. At first-floor level there are three square-headed windows with heavy label-moulds, below a crenellated parapet. The N front is much plainer in character, and all three windows at first-floor level are blind.

The steeple has segmental-headed and broad-chamfered embrasures to S and E at ground-floor level, the former being the main access-doorway and the latter a blind window. At first-floor level the S and E fronts have paired lancets with traceried heads surmounted by hood-moulds. At the next level there are pairs of small round-headed blind windows, above which are circular clock-faces set within stepped label-moulds. The crenellated parapet is supported by tripartite corbels and has corbelled angle-turrets decorated with blind dumb-bell loops. The octagonal belfry stage, which is set within the parapet-walk, has pointed windows in each face, alternately louvred and blind, which are surmounted by a bold moulding and a diminutive crenellated parapet. Within this there is set the stepped base of the octagonal spire, whose faces are decorated with a horizontal moulding near the base, quatrefoils in alternate faces and a crenellated band towards the middle.

Internally the main block possesses few early features, and modern partitions have been inserted towards the E end of both floors, those at first-floor level cutting across a circular plaster centrepiece and cornice. The ceiling of the main first-floor room has been lowered. Fireplaces in the W wall on both floors have been removed and blocked. The steeple has a spiral stair which gives access to the first floor, and above this level a smaller spiral stair in the NW angle rises to the spire. The belfry houses a bell, 0.8m in diameter, which was cast by Thomas Mears of London in 1818.

HISTORY
The village of Strichen, which never achieved burgh status, was founded by Alexander Fraser, Lord Strichen, in 1764. The town-house was built at a cost of about £2,000 for his grandson's widow, Mrs Emilia Fraser, in 1816, during the minority of her son who later became the 12th Lord Lovat.[3] It was designed by the Aberdeen-based architect John Smith, known locally as 'Tudor Johnny' due to his preference for late Gothic forms, who subsequently designed the classical Strichen House for the same clients.[4] Shortly before 1875 the ground floor was fitted up for use as a female school, and the upper floor served as the town hall.[5]

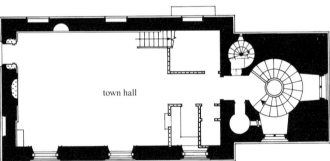

first floor

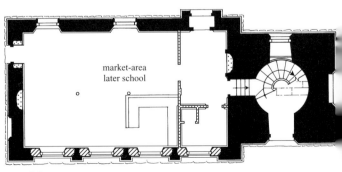

ground floor

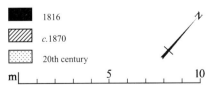

■	1816
▨	c.1870
▦	20th century

Strichen Town-house (No.83), S elevation and plans

A. **Strichen Town-house** (No.83), conjectural reconstruction

B. view from SE

(B 39697)

C. 19th-century view from SW (C 2587)

84 TAIN TOLBOOTH
Highland
NH 7800 8212

The castellated steeple of Tain Tolbooth forms a conspicuous landmark in the angle formed by the W end of High Street and the E end of Tower Street. The four-storeyed steeple is substantially the work of local mason Alexander Stronach in the first quarter of the 18th century. The two-storeyed sheriff-court abutting it to the SE, which replaced an earlier council-house, was built in 1848-9 to a baronial design by Thomas Brown, and extended in 1873.

The steeple measures about 7.9m square over 1.3m walls, and is built of sandstone ashlar quarried at Hill of Tain, which is used even for its roofs.[1] The round-arched entrance-doorway in the SW wall and the ground-floor window of similar form in the NW wall were recast in 1848-9, as were the two prominent string-courses, while the panel bearing a lion rampant above the doorway is dated 1848.[2] The rectangular broad-chamfered windows in the upper storeys of the tower, however, may preserve their original form.

The upper part of the steeple has a central spire framed by smaller corbelled angle-turrets which project only slightly beyond the main wall-line, and all are surmounted by ball-finials. The turrets and spire have small rectangular windows, and similar openings in the roofs have miniature triangular gablets cut into their lintels. Set between the angle-turrets there are circular clock-faces in square-headed surrounds which were added in 1877.[3] Below each of these there are four small water-spouts which drain the parapet-walks.

The stone-flagged ground storey contains a 19th-century stair to the first floor, and a doorway to the adjacent building which in its present form is of similar date. Access above first-floor level is by a spiral stair in the S angle, which is lit by three small windows in the SW front. This may originally have descended to ground-floor level, but any evidence for this is obscured by later masonry. Each floor contains a single chamber, originally used as prison-accommodation. That at second-floor level is barrel-vaulted and retains a plain original fireplace, now blocked, and a floor of flagstones supported on joists, which was installed in 1825-6 for reasons of safety and security.[4] The stair continues to the S angle-turret, which opens to the parapet-walk.

Two stones from an earlier tolbooth are built into the NE face of the spire. They are inscribed: THIS NEV WARK / BIGIT 1631 IHON / MACKULLOCHE BEING PROVEST / [...] BAILZIES. The lower stage of the spire contains a clock-mechanism of 1877 by Ritchies of Edinburgh which replaced a clock, with one dial only, of about 1750.[5] The bell, which is set above the clock, measures 0.64m in diameter and is inscribed, below a frieze of foliated scrolls: SOLI DEO GLORIA. MICHAEL BURGERHUYS ME FECIT ANNO 1630 ('Glory to God alone, Michael Burgerhuys made me, 1630').[6]

The collections of Tain Museum include several objects associated with the tolbooth, including manacles, a set of weights and measures, and a drawing and an early model of the steeple and the sheriff court-house of 1848-9.[7]

HISTORY
The new tolbooth referred to in the re-used inscription, which was at least partly thatched with heather, was built in 1631 on a site now occupied by part of the parish churchyard.[8] Extensive repairs were required during the 1660s, and in 1666 a burgess was convicted of 'down casting of three bartisanes stones from the top of the stible', implying that the masonry was in a poor state of repair.[9] A report in 1691 stated that the 'councill and prison house of this burgh are so ruinous and demolished that they ... cannot be made up in the same integrity it was formerlie without payment'.[10] After further damage by a storm in 1703, the building was demolished.[11]

IC

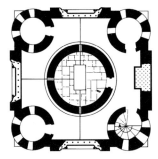

clock stage

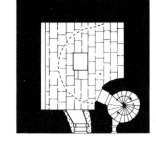

second floor

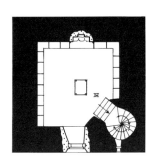

first floor

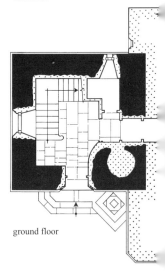

ground floor

■ 1706-8

▨ 1848-9 and later

m |_____|_____|_____|_____|_____| 5

Tain Tolbooth (No.84), SW elevation and plans

*A. **Tain Tolbooth** (No.84) from W* (C 45944)

B. steeple and court-house from SW, c.1850 (C 48791)

The present building was begun in 1706, having been funded in part by voluntary contributions collected in churches throughout Scotland and a grant of 500 merks from the Convention of Royal Burghs.[12] In 1708, a report to the convention stated that 'the said tolbuith and steeple with the pricket therof consisting of six storry high, together with the counsell house of tuo houses hight adjoyned thereto, are finished to the securing of the plateforme and bartisone head of the said steeple'.[13] The 'master meassone', Alexander Stronach, had already exceeded his contract price, and work appears to have stopped until 1712. Work halted again in 1720, when Stronach was engaged in work on Dornoch Castle, and he finally completed the 'bartizan', presumably the central spire, only in 1733.[14] Meanwhile, in 1715 a smith was ordered to 'make up ane ravell (balustrade) to the Counsell house stair efter the forme of the ravell of Inverness'.[15]

In 1778-80 the council-house received a new roof, and other repairs and improvements were carried out, at a cost of £59 6s 8d.[16] As early as 1818 the jail and court-house were described as 'insufficient and uncomfortable'.[17] A year later the walls of the steeple were described as 'easily gone through with a common chisel'. Its principal floors were described thus: 'the highest is appropriated to ordinary criminals, the centre one to civil debtors, and the lowest, which was considered the most secure, is generally appropriated to criminals of the deepest dye'.[18] In a letter of 1824 from the provost to the Lord Advocate, the steeple was described as 'perhaps the only building in the burgh which can lay claim to ancient grandeur', and this may have ensured its preservation when the main block was demolished.[19] In 1825 the foundation-stone was laid for 'the long contemplated and much required new Gaol and Court house of the burgh', which was completed in the following year to designs by Alexander Gordon. The cost of £1,130 was borne mainly by the burgh, with a contribution from the county, and the first floor was devoted to the court-room, with the council-chamber and burgh and county record-rooms below and three prison-rooms in the attic storey.[20]

The new building was destroyed in 1833, with the loss of three lives, in a fire which began in the top-floor cells, and the steeple once again became the only prison until a new one was opened in 1846.[21] Thomas Brown's court-house of 1848-9, which made use of the ground floor of the steeple as a vestibule, was enlarged to the SE in matching style by Andrew Maitland in 1873.[22]

C. inscribed stone in steeple (B 14594)

197

85 WEST WEMYSS TOLBOOTH
Fife

NT 3260 9466

This tolbooth is situated on the S side of the main street, abutted to E and W by later houses which encase both angles of its rear wall. The W part of the ground storey is occupied by a wide pend which gave access to the shore. While the main part of the building may be ascribed to the early 18th century, there appears to be a masonry-break at first-floor level and part of an earlier building may have been incorporated. The burgesses were granted the right to have a tolbooth when the burgh of barony was erected in 1525, and the building was mentioned in 1586, although its exact site is not known. [1]

The building is two-storeyed and rectangular on plan, measuring 11.4m across its main (N) front by 8.9m. At the centre of the main front there is a steeple, 18m high and only 3.1m square, which is abutted to the E by a simple forestair. The masonry is of harled rubble, with dressed margins to the main windows. The gabled roof of the main block is pantiled, while the steeple was formerly slated, [2] but is now covered with copper. A panel set into the S wall of the steeple, now badly weathered, preserves the outline of a coronet and remains of an inscription which has been recorded [3] as reading:

THIS FABRIC WAS BUILT BY EARL DAVID
WEMYSS & TOWN
FOR THE CRIBBING OF VICE AND SERVICE TO
CROWN.

A lower panel bears the arms of the Wemyss family, with the initials E / DW for 'Earl David Wemyss'. These probably refer to David, 3rd Earl of Wemyss from 1705 to 1720, rather than to the 2nd Earl who died in 1679.

Parallel to the street at ground-floor level there are two vaulted cells which were entered from the pend but whose doors are now blocked, along with the window of the S cell. The first floor now forms one large room, but this was formerly partitioned and the W portion retains a decorated plaster ceiling of late 18th-century type. The existence of two fireplaces in the E wall suggests that the E half was further divided. The roof-structure, which has been rebuilt, incorporated a number of ships' timbers. [4]

A bell for the tolbooth was 'brought home' in 1678 by a local mariner, probably from the Netherlands. The present bell and clock were installed in 1901 by James Ritchie and Son. [5]

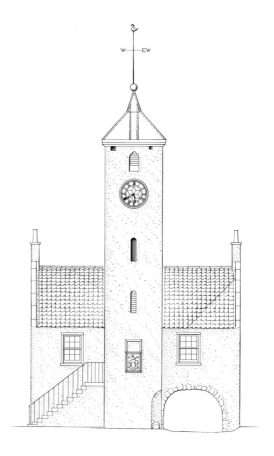

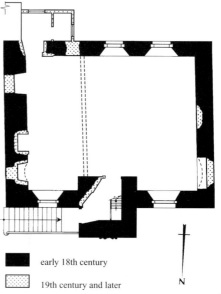

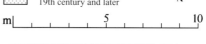

■ early 18th century

⬚ 19th century and later

N

m 5 10

B. N elevation and first-floor plan

*A. **West Wemyss Tolbooth** (No.85) from N* (B 39440)

*C. armorial panel
(B 39441)*

198

86 WHITHORN OLD TOWN HALL
Dumfries and Galloway

NX 4452 4020

Situated near the middle of the W side of George Street, the former town hall is of irregular T-shaped plan, having a two-storeyed main block to the street and a square steeple and two-storeyed wing to the rear. The gabled main block, which is of three bays and is inscribed '1814' on the blocking-course, presents a somewhat domestic appearance. The steeple is of traditional character, and it has been suggested that it is of early 18th-century date.[1] While the carefully-wrought ashlar of its conical spire may have been re-used, however, the building as a whole appears to be of early 19th-century date.

200   It measures 12.8m across the main (E) front by 7.2m, and the steeple and rear wing extend a further 9.9m to the W. The masonry is of rubble with dressed margins, the street frontage being harled. The main block has stepped quoins, and a channelled surround to the segmental-headed central doorway. To the N of this there is an inserted square-headed doorway, probably of late 19th-century date, which opens into the N ground-floor room. The shop-front in the S part of this frontage was inserted in the early 20th century, and the ground-floor rooms in the main block were probably entered originally from the central corridor.

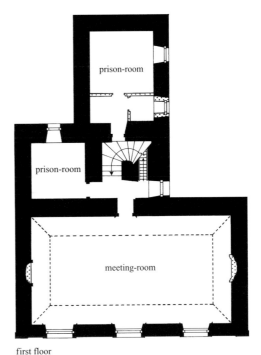

first floor

Whithorn Old Town Hall (No.86), E elevation and plans

ground floor

◼ *c.*1814

▨ late 19th century and later

m ___ 5 ___ 10

The steeple, which is of four stages, is set at the centre of the rear wall of the main block. It has narrow raised margins to the quoins and the three round-headed openings of the belfry stage. The top stage, which is slightly intaken above an ashlar band, contains circular clock-faces. Its cornice carries a balustraded parapet within which there is an ashlar-built conical spire, having a ship as weather-vane.

Internally, the building retains few early features, but the main meeting-room on the first floor of the main block has an original chimneypiece in the S wall and a coombed ceiling. There are two vaulted cells in the rear wing at ground-floor level, and the room above these, as well as the rooms at both levels in the SW re-entrant of the steeple and main block, were also used for prison-accommodation. [2]

In the steeple there hangs a bell, 0.51m in diameter and inscribed, between two bands of fleurs-de-lis: PETER VANDER GHEIN HEEFT MY GHEGOTEN INT IAER / 1708 ('Peter van den Ghein cast me in the year 1708'). [3]

HISTORY

Historical evidence is limited, but it is known that a tolbooth was in existence at Whithorn from at least the middle of the 17th century. A contract for its repair was made with a local landowner in 1664, and it was rebuilt in 1708-9. [4] A re-used stone inscribed '1709' is built into the rear wall of the present building. The local minister in 1795 stated that: 'About the centre of the town, there is a good hall for public meetings, adorned with a spire and turrets, and provided with a set of bells'. [5] It evidently stood on an island site, for in 1839 it was reported that 'the town-house and gaol were removed about twenty years ago from the middle of the street, where they formerly stood, and are now erected upon the west side of the street, about the centre of the town, and ornamented with a steeple'. [6] A new town hall was built in 1885, [7] but the upper floor of the old building remained in use by the local authority.

Whithorn Old Town Hall (No.86) *from E*   (B 47691)

87 WICK TOWN HALL
Highland
ND 3629 5090

The town hall is situated on the SE side of Bridge Street, 50m NE of the Bridge of Wick. It comprises a two-storeyed block about 13.5m square, with a square steeple advanced some 4.6m at the centre of the main (NW) front. When built in 1826-8 a courtyard to the rear contained two prison blocks, for criminals and debtors, but these have been demolished and part of the area is covered by later extensions. A new sheriff court-house to a Renaissance design by David Rhind was built in 1862-6 immediately to the NE, on the site of an earlier court-house.[1]

Flanking the steeple there are single-storeyed bays surmounted by balustraded parapets and with round-headed arches in both faces. These are linked by impost-bands to the steeple, and the side-bays form with it a continuous groin-vaulted open arcade. The central archway opens through the arcade to an entrance-doorway surmounted by a fanlight. The windows in the main block are disposed symmetrically, those in the first floor of the steeple and NW front having bracketed cornices. The building is constructed of rock-faced coursed masonry with dressed margins.

The third stage of the steeple is defined by a moulded cornice linked to that of the main wall-head and has horizontal recessed panels in all faces. The octagonal lower stage of the spire has four clock-faces surmounted by anthemions, set between recessed oblique faces. The cylindrical belfry-stage has a close-set arcade of round-headed and round-based openings, and its entablature carries a ribbed dome.

The ground storey originally contained four offices divided by a central hall, and two cells flanking the main stair at the rear.[2] The first floor contained further offices and the court-room, and the latter remains largely unaltered, housing a collection of portraits of local notables. The rest of the interior has undergone extensive later alteration. The original scale-and-platt staircase with flagstone treads was rebuilt in timber in 1932, when a rear extension was added.[3]

HISTORY
A jail was built on the N side of High Street following a parliamentary order of 1672. It was replaced in 1750 by a tolbooth a short distance to the E, in the NE angle of High Street and Tolbooth Lane (ND 3638 5101). By 1820 this building was 'extremely ruinous', the roof being 'almost entirely gone', and the town council suffered severe financial penalties at this period for the escape of prisoners.[4] Following consultations with the county authorities, locally-made plans for a new court-house and jail were rejected as inadequate. However a suitable site near the bridge was identified in 1821, and two years later designs were obtained from Robert Reid, 'his Majesty's Architect for Scotland'.[5]

Reid's first scheme, for a County Hall flanked by two prison wings and having a separate debtors' prison at the rear, was rejected on grounds of cost. A reduced design comprising two slightly larger prison blocks was accepted in 1826.[6] The Caithness county authorities paid £1,500 of the estimated cost of £3,270, the burgh being responsible for the remainder, and the contract was awarded to William Davidson, a local 'architect'. Work was completed in 1828, in which year the sheriff court was transferred from Thurso to Wick. Following legal and medical inspections the jail was declared a legal jail, which with the adjacent court-house and public offices was 'to be called the Tolbooth of Wick in all time coming'.[7] The two identical prison-blocks stood to the rear of the court-house, each containing 'two rather large rooms and four small rooms or cells'.[8]

*A. **Wick Town Hall** (No.87) from W*　　　　　　*(C 4343)*

B. portraits on staircase　　　　　　*(C 4349)*

APPENDIX
Demolished and much-altered buildings
(for abbreviations see p.xi)

ROYAL BURGHS

1 Annan (P 55)
A grant was made for repairs to the tolbooth in 1610 (*RCRBS (1597-1614)*, 301). In 1740 it was decided to add a steeple with a clock and bell to the town-house (Steel, A, *Records of Annan 1678-1833* (1933), 82). A 'Clock and Bell House' was built in 1795 and removed in 1841. In 1837 the old burgh prison contained five rooms, one used as a meal-house (*Prison Inspectors' Third Report*, 25-6). The building was demolished in 1875, and a town hall built to a Baronial design by R Smith of Glasgow.
(Steel, A, *The Church of Annan* (2nd ed., 1989), 52-4).

2 Anstruther Easter (P 60)
The old tolbooth, repaired in 1806 and demolished in 1872, was of three storeys, with a pend above which was the jail, and a first-floor school-room. The bell was taken when the tolbooth was 'plunderit by the Engleis' (Cromwellian soldiers), and a new one was 'brocht hame frae Holland' in 1668. The tolbooth was used both by the Jacobites and the militia in 1715.
(Conolly, *Fifiana*, 190; Gourlay, G, *Anstruther* (1888), 24-6).

3 Berwick-upon-Tweed (P 1)
The town hall occupies the island site of the 13th-century *tolbotha* (*supra*, p.1), bequeathed by a wealthy burgess. The 'berfrey' (bell-tower) was used as a jail in the 14th century, and Speed's map of 1564 shows a large crenellated tower (Harding, D W (ed.), *Archaeology in the North* (1976), 149, 163). A later tolbooth, which included shops, a prison, and a 'met' or weigh-house, collapsed in 1749 and was replaced in 1750-7 by the town hall (S and J Worrall, architects). This has a 46m steeple (with a peal of eight bells, 1754) above an end-wall portico, ground-floor arcades enclosing shops, and a jail on the second floor.
(Scott, J, *Berwick-upon-Tweed* (1888), 226-8, 249, 253, 256, 264-6, 307, 436).

4 Burntisland (P 57)
The building described in 1635 as 'a pretty towbeoth' (Lowther, *Journall*, 24) may have been the 'old tolbooth' shown on the peninsula E of the harbour-mouth on John Elphinstone's plan of 1746 (British Library, King's Maps XLIX 85-1). A building with a roof-top spire, shown in a drawing attributed to Slezer (National Gallery of Scotland), may have been its successor. This occupied an island site near the harbour, at the W end of High Street (King's Maps, loc.cit.; plan by J Wood, 1824). The town bell of 1595/1677 (*Inventory of Fife*, No.76) is preserved in the existing town hall, a Gothic design of 1843 by John Henderson.

5 Dornoch (P 73)
A *curia* (court-house) was mentioned in 1512 and a 'tolboothe', near the E end of the cathedral, in 1603. It was ruinous in 1730, when the council decided to build 'ane sufficient Town House consisting of ane Grand Council House, a Gentleman prison, and Clerks Room, with four shops in the lower storey, and ane stairs ascending in the outer'. A contract was made in 1735 with Donald Junior, mason in Tain, for a building 12.8m x 4.9m within walls, vaulted throughout and having a steeple 4.9m square with a turnpike; it was incomplete in 1750, and the cathedral chapter-house was used as the prison. Replacement of the tolbooth was proposed in 1811, and the material was sold by roup in 1813 when the 16th-century Bishop's Castle *(Cast. and Dom. Arch.,* **2**, 336-7),

A. ***Dornoch***   *(C 96618)*
Bishop's Castle and County Buildings from N

recently repaired by the Sutherland estate, was offered for use as a court-house and prison. The adjacent County Buildings and Jail, by Thomas Brown, were built in 1842.
(SRO, SC 9/84/6, 19, 20, 34 and 36; B 15/6/3; Bentinck, C D, *Dornoch Cathedral and Parish* (1926), 164, 270-80, 335, 342-8, 356-64; *Prison Inspectors' Second Report*, 56-7; *Ninth Report*, 39-40; Name Book, Sutherland No.9, pp.11-12; Groome, *Ordnance Gazetteer*, 362).

6 Dundee (P 29)
In 1325 Robert I granted a plot, 24.4m by 12.2m, probably in Seagate, to build a tolbooth and prison, and in 1363 David II added a strip 24.4m by 1.8m (*supra*, p.2). A later tolbooth on the NW side of High Street was used until the 16th century, possibly surviving until the late 18th century. A new tolbooth in St Clement's churchyard was completed in 1562, using material from Greyfriars, and the old church became a weigh-house. The tolbooth had a forestair to the council-house and prisons on the upper floors, with shops below; an octagonal belfry was added in 1590. It was ruinous and condemned in 1730 by William Adam, whose classical town-house (*Vitruvius Scoticus*, pl.104) was built in 1732-4 at a cost of £4,000. This had a seven-bay rusticated front 29.6m in length, with a three-bay advanced centre having paired Ionic pilasters at the upper level and carrying a pediment with armorial; the 42.7m steeple rose from the centre of the roof. The arcaded ground storey, enclosing shops, gave the local name, 'the Pillars'. The council- and guildry chambers were on the first floor, and the jail above. The town-house was repaired after a fire in 1771, extended to the rear in 1872, and demolished in 1932.
(TCM in Dundee City Record Office; Hay, W (ed.), *Charters ... of the royal burgh of Dundee* (1880); Stevenson, S J and Torrie, E P D, *Historic Dundee* (Scottish Burgh Survey, 1988); Kidd, W, *The Dundee Market Crosses and Tolbooths* (1901); Maxwell, A, *The History of Old Dundee* (1884); Steele, V, 'William Adam's Dundee Town House' (St Andrews University Dissertation, 1988, copy in NMRS); Millar, A H (ed.), *The First History of Dundee, 1776* (1923), 142, 162-5; Mackie, C, *Historical Description of the Town of Dundee* (1836), 138-9; Thomson, *Dundee*, 136, 174-7, 351).

xiiE

7 Dunfermline (P 3)
The gild court was held in the *tolbuth* in 1433 and the gild contributed to repairs in 1448-9 (Torrie, E P D, *The Gild Court Book of Dunfermline, 1433-1597* (SRS, 1986), **1**, 166-7). In 1607 it was proposed to repair the tolbooth and remove the council-house to a new site (Shearer, A, *Extracts from the Burgh Records of Dunfermline* (1951), 36), and it was probably rebuilt after a destructive fire in 1624. The tolbooth

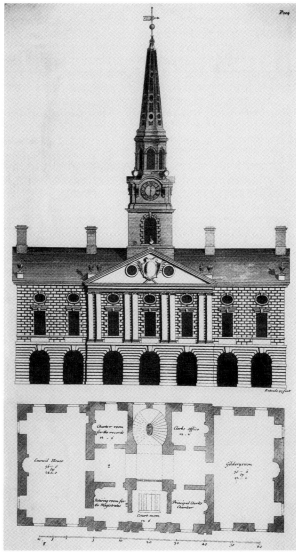

A. **Dundee Town-house**   (AND/159/1)
   first-floor plan and N elevation by Adam (scale, 1:400)

B. **Dunfermline Town-house** *from N, c.1810 (scale, 1:400)*   (C65823)

faced the E end of High Street and its long central forestair
spanned the Tolbooth Port, linking Kirkgate and Collier Row
(Bruce Street). It had a ground-floor meal-market, 'laich
prison', and pend; a first-floor council-room and clerk's
chamber; and a debtors' prison in the timber-built second floor,
with a small belfry on the wall-head (*NSA*, **9**, 319-20;
Chalmers, P, *Historical and Statistical Account of Dunfermline*,
2 (1859), pl. opp. p. 4). It was demolished in 1772 after an
adjacent town-house was built in 1769-71. Two storeys were
added to this in 1792, to form a three-storeyed five-bay
rectangle, with a slender end-wall steeple having an octagonal
belfry and slated spire (Fernie, pl. opp. p. 18). It contained a
ground-floor council/sheriff-court room, a first-floor town hall
and reading-room, and second-floor jail with debtors' room
and four cells (*Prison Inspectors' Second Report*, 95-8). Six
carved panels from the old mercat cross were built into the
exterior. It was demolished in 1876, and the City Chambers
built on an adjacent site, to a Baronial design by J C Walker, in
1875-9. These contain the Town Bell, cast by Henrick ter
Horst at Deventer (Netherlands) in 1654 (*Inventory of Fife*,
No.211). The Guildhall with its 41m spire, designed by
Archibald Elliot and built for the Guildry and subscribers in

1807-11, was intended for use as County Rooms but became
the Spire Inn from 1820 and the Sheriff Court from 1849/50
(SRO, RHP 45758, 45762, proposed alterations by Clarke and
Bell, 1849).
(Fernie, J, *A History of the Town and Parish of Dunfermline*
(1815), 18-20; Chalmers, P, *Historical and Statistical Account
of Dunfermline*, **1** (1844), 319-20; Henderson, E, *The Annals of
Dunfermline* (1879), 174, 296, 328-9, 457, 487-8, 492-3, 559,
564, 576-8).

C. **Dunfermline Tolbooth** *from SE, 1768*   (Chalmers)

8 Elgin (P 13)

The tolbooth is mentioned in 1541, although use was made in the 1570s of the parish church and Greyfriars for courts and of vaults in the latter for a prison. In 1602 a contract was made for a tolbooth, 18.3m by 6.1m, on the site of the old one. It was burnt down by a 'furious' prisoner in 1700 and rebuilt in 1709. The tolbooth, on an island site W of the parish church, was demolished in 1843. Early views (Mackintosh, opp.

*A. **Elgin Tolbooth** from SW, after Rhind*   *(MacGibbon and Ross)*

p.196; *Cast. and Dom. Arch.*, **5**, 98-9) show a massive early 17th-century tower, used as the prison, with a corbelled-out tapering stair-turret at the SW angle. A plain parapet enclosed the roof, which was used as an exercise-area for debtors, and a stone spire. The two-storeyed main block had a crow-stepped W gable, a Venetian window to the S, and two forestairs. Two carved stones, the bell of 1593 (recast by A Gely in 1713), and the clock-mechanism are in Elgin Museum.
(Mackintosh, H B, *Elgin Past and Present* (1914), 193-8).

*B. **Forres Tolbooth** from NW, c.1830*   *(Douglas)*

9 Forres (P 8)

In 1586 a proclamation was made from the 'bois windock' (bay-window) of the tolbooth, which was repaired in 1588 with 'bent' (grass). In 1620 a wardhouse was to be built upon the stairs. Repairs were made in 1670-7, but in 1698 a contract was made with James Anderson, mason in Forres, for rebuilding the tolbooth to the same dimensions, and with a forestair 'that three men may goe up collatrall'. In 1710 he was paid for building the 'piramede', but in 1717 it was decided that the 'prirket' (spire) should be of timber for lightness. Early views show a three-storeyed main block, with crow-stepped gables and a forestair rising to a pedimented doorway. The massive end tower had a crenellated parapet enclosing an inner tower, with conical angle-turrets, which carried the tall octagonal (?timber-built) belfry. By 1793 the court-room was in disrepair, having been used as a prison and a guard-house, and it was repaired by John Smith, mason in Forres. By 1835 a new court-house and jail were required, and the former was rebuilt in 1838-9 to a design by William Robertson which followed the style of the tolbooth. A former cholera hospital was used as a temporary jail, and a new one completed in 1849.
(Douglas, R, *Annals of the Royal Burgh of Forres* (1934), 275-84, pl. opp. p.280; *Cast. and Dom. Arch.*, **5**, 101-2).

10 Hamilton (P 58)

The 'old jail', which bore a date-stone of 1642 (Name Book, Lanarkshire No.38, p.21), stood in the old town at the edge of the Hamilton Palace policies. It had a low ground storey, pedimented openings to the two upper storeys, a wrought-iron

*C. **Hamilton Old Jail** from NE, c.1936*   *(LA/500)*

balcony of 1707-13 at the first-floor doorway, and a sundial. The centre-gable steeple, which contained a clock and bell, was remodelled in the 19th century and demolished in 1954. (*Cast. and Dom. Arch.*, **5**, 124; photos in NMRS; Burns, D, Reid, A and Walker, I, *Hamilton District: a History* (1995), fig. on p.24). The jail was used until the completion of a new prison and court-house about 1834, and a separate town hall stood nearby (*NSA*, **6**, 274-5, 292). It was repaired by the Hamilton estate in 1861 (Groome, *Ordnance Gazetteer*, 803), and demolished in 1951. A lock and key are preserved in Hamilton Museum. New Burgh Buildings were erected to a Baronial design by Clarke and Bell in 1863.

11 Inverurie (P 30)

Meetings were held in the *praetorium* 'a little after 1600', and a house was purchased for use as a tolbooth in 1642. The tolbooth built 1660-2 had a ground-floor prison (*Prison Inspectors' Second Report*, 35-6), and a council-room approached by a forestair with stone balustrade. It was demolished in 1868, and a new town-house was built on a different site in 1863.

(Davidson, J, *Inverurie and the Earldom of the Garioch* (1878), 349-50).

12 Irvine (P 45)

Robert II in 1386 granted a plot in the market street, 12.2m by 9.1m, to build 'a fitting and honourable house' for council-meetings. The tolbooth, which stood on an island site, was repaired in 1677 and 1710-11, and again in 1745 when the prison was rebuilt and the roof-level made uniform. The spire was altered from slate to stone in 1808. Early views show a two-storeyed main block (24m by 8m) of 18th-century character, having a tall steeple with double forestair at the centre of the S gable. In the 19th century the council-room and town clerk's office were on the ground floor, entered by a pedimented doorway. The guard-room, court-house or 'Great council room' (also used as a debtors' day-room) and cells were above, and the 'black hole' on an upper floor of the steeple. The lower rooms were vaulted, and those in the S end were said to be of older character (Pont, 218). The building was demolished in 1861 and an Italianate town-house built nearby in 1859-61. It contains two 17th-century armorial

2B

A. *Irvine Tolbooth* from NW, 1860   (*C 47324*)

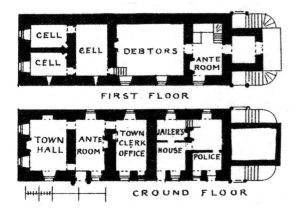

B. *Irvine Tolbooth,* plans (scale, 1:400)   (*MacGibbon and Ross*)

stones, and the inscribed 'tolbuith bell' of 1637 (Clouston, 'Ayrshire Bells', 228).

(Pont, *Cuninghame*, 215-18 and pl. opp. p.216; Dobie, J S (ed.), *Muniments of the Royal Burgh of Irvine* (1890-1), *passim* (with photographs of carved stones); Robertson, G, *Cunninghame* (1820), 417; *Prison Inspectors' Third Report*, 51 (two cells and two debtors' rooms); McJannet, A F, *The Royal Burgh of Irvine* (1938), 115-20; plans in *Cast. and Dom. Arch.*, **5**, 125-6; photograph *c*.1860 in Whatley, C (ed.), *John Galt 1779-1979* (1979), opp.p.161).

13 Kilrenny (P 66)

A tolbooth was built in the coastal settlement of Cellardyke in 1624, and replaced by a Gothic town hall of 1882-3. Early photographs show a two-storeyed building of late 18th-century domestic character with a gable bellcot and pantiled roof.

(Watson, H D, *Kilrenny and Cellardyke* (1986), 35, 130, 147, figs. on pp.128, 148).

14 Kirkcaldy (P 78)

The early tolbooth, whose vault was used as a jail in 1566, may have stood opposite Kirk Wynd. Its successor, at the junction of High Street and (the later) Tolbooth Street, was rebuilt in 1678, and in 1793 it contained a ground-floor guard-house, meal-market and weigh-house; a hall for courts and council-meetings; and a second-floor prison. The tower, with spire, contained the town clock and bell, and a record-room. In 1826 it was replaced by a town-house and jail in Romanesque style, to designs by William Burn, itself demolished in the 20th century.

(Torrie, E P D and Coleman, R, *Historic Kirkcaldy* (Scottish Burgh Survey, 1995), 30; *Stat. Acct.*, **18**, 3-4; drawings by Burn, 1825, in NMRS). *See also* Linktown (p.211).

15 Kirkwall (P 52)

James III granted the right to have a tolbooth in 1486, and a house at the foot of Strynd was acquired for this use in the mid-17th century. A timber guard-house was built in St Magnus's churchyard in 1703, and a new tolbooth proposed. A new tolbooth replaced the guard-house in 1742. The 13th Earl of Morton gave £200 and the use of stone from the royal castle, for the right to hold sheriff courts (formerly held in the cathedral) in the hall; it was roofed with slates from the Earl's Palace (TCM in Kirkwall Library; Tudor, J R, *The Orkneys and Shetlands* (1883), 232-3). The ground floor was a jail and lock-up, the first floor was used for courts and assemblies, and the second floor as a masonic lodge. The tolbooth was demolished in 1890, and a town hall was built nearby, to designs by T S Peace, in 1884-7.

(Hossack, B H, *Kirkwall in the Orkneys* (1900); pre-demolition drawing by T S Peace in Kirkwall Library).

16 Perth (P 5)

The tolbooth stood on the bank of the Tay at the E end of High Street, adjoining the harbour and the bridge that was swept away in 1621 by a flood which 'tuike down the gavill of the tolbuithe' (*The Chronicle of Perth* (Maitland Club, 1831), 22). It was believed to incorporate the medieval chapel of St Mary, and was of L-plan. A thin octagonal S tower included a first-floor oriel lighting the court-room. Council meetings were often held in the session-house of St John's Church, but in 1695-6 a S wing containing a council-chamber and clerk's chamber (*supra*, p.18) was built by William Milne, wright in Dupplin. Its ground storey included a stair, a pack- or weigh-house, and a pend to the North Shore, and a pend built at the S end in 1696 gave access to a small harbour. In 1790 a W wing was built to a design by George Sandeman, wright (TCM 4 January 1790), to contain the burgh court-room and record-rooms, the sheriff court remaining in the tolbooth. From 1789 the erection of new Town and County buildings and jail was discussed, and Robert Reid prepared several designs between 1806 and 1814. The buildings erected in 1815-19 to Sir

206A

11B

*A. **Perth Tolbooth and Council-chamber** from SW, c.1800*   (Cowan)

Robert Smirke's Greek Doric design were for the county only, but the adjacent jail was a joint enterprise. This allowed the tolbooth to be refurbished for burgh use until it was replaced in 1877-9 by municipal offices to Andrew Heiton's design. The council-house had been demolished in 1839 to open up the river-front.
(TCM; survey-plans of tolbooth, 1764 and 1810 (George Alexander, architect), and other views, in Perth Museum and Art Gallery; *NSA*, **10**, 82-3; Morison, W, *Memorabilia of the City of Perth* (1806), 18-20; Cowan, S, *The Ancient Capital of Scotland* (1904), *passim* and **1**, pl. opp. p. 332; Marshall, T H, *The History of Perth* (1849), 477-8).

17 Renfrew (P 11)
A grant for repair of the tolbooth was made in 1594 (*RCRBS (1295-1597)*, 440). It was rebuilt in 1670, and a wing containing a town hall above a new council-chamber was added in 1826. Early views show a three-storeyed block with a forestair, and a projecting tower with balustrade enclosing a square stone belfry with ogee roof (photograph in NMRS; *Cast. and Dom. Arch*, **5**, 123). It was replaced in 1872.
(Dunn, J A, *History of Renfrew* (1971), 63).

18 Rosemarkie (P 64)
This burgh was united with Fortrose (No.32), and no tolbooth existed in 1661 (*APS*, **7** (1661-9), 225). In 1686 there was a tolbooth and council-house, and heather was to be provided for roof-repairs (SRO, B 28/7/2, 28 June 1686).

19 Rutherglen (P 12)
A grant for repairs was made in 1599 (*RCRBS (1597-1614)*, 49). The town-house was rebuilt in 1767-8 (TCM 26 June 1767, 11 March 1768) as a three-storeyed seven-bay block with pedimented centre, and a portico carrying a first-floor balcony. It was demolished in 1900. The town hall was built to a Baronial design by Charles Wilson in 1861-2.
(TCM in Mitchell Library, Glasgow City Archives; Ure, D, *The History of Rutherglen and East Kilbride* (1793), 80; Shearer, W R, *Rutherglen Lore* (1922), 285 and pl. opp. p.285).

20 St Andrews (P 72)
The *Domus Urbis* ('Town's House'), on its island site in Market Street, appears on a 16th-century view of the town (McRoberts, D (ed.), *The Medieval Church of St Andrews* (1976), frontispiece and pp.151-2). This already shows the two parts of the building, a main block, 16m by 10m, whose ground storey was originally arcaded on three sides, and a prison-wing to the W whose gable bore an armorial panel of 1565. Before 1767 the E wall received a Venetian window and oculus above, with a gable bellcot; there was a forestair at the S wall and jougs reached by steps at the SE angle (pen-

21B

*B. **Renfrew Tolbooth** from S, c.1870*   (RE/2302)

drawing by John Oliphant, 1767, in St Andrews University Library). In 1817 a third storey was added to the main block, and photographs show large tripartite windows in the upper stages of the E wall, with a bellcot to the W. The town-house was demolished in 1862, after the completion of the Town Hall to a Baronial design by J A Hamilton. This houses the panel of 1565 bearing the arms of the burgh and of Provost Patrick Learmonth of Dairsie, and other artefacts are in Kinburn House Museum. The town bell of 1617 was recast by John Meikle in 1697.

6A

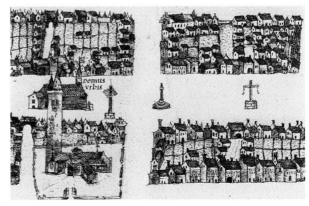

*C. **St Andrews** from S, c.1580,*   (National Library of Scotland)
showing tolbooth ('Domus Urbis'), pillory, mercat cross and tron

A. St Andrews Tolbooth from W, c.1860   (F/4543)

B. St Andrews Tolbooth, bell recast 1697   (C65088)

(Fleming, D H, *Handbook to St Andrews* (1927 ed.), 18-20, 127-9, 133-9; Cant, R G, in Proudfoot, E (ed.), *Three decades of historical notes* (1991), 77, 111-12; *Prison Inspectors' Second Report*, 84-5; *NSA*, **9** (Fife), 470-1; Roger, C, *History of St Andrews* (1849), 68, 165-6).

21 Wigtown (P 38)
Symson, writing in 1684-92, described the tolbooth, 'lately beautify'd with a Pyramis ... upon the top of the steeple, set round with pylasters' (*Geog.Coll*, **2**, 74). This building was demolished with gunpowder in 1747 and a town-house with a ground-floor piazza was built in 1747-9 by Bailie Samuel Kennan, mason, to a design by John Douglas (TCM 24 June 1747). By 1774 this was 'ruinous and decayed', and it was

rebuilt, with a tall spire, in 1776. The original design was heightened to allow a 'handsome ballroom', paid for by the masonic lodge, and it also included the parish school-room. There was a ground-floor vaulted cell (preserved in the later town hall) and further prison-accommodation on the upper floors. The town-house was replaced in 1862 by a town hall to a Gothic design by Wardrop and Reid.
(TCM in Stranraer Museum; Brewster, D, *Wigtown*, (n.d.)).

BURGHS OF BARONY AND REGALITY
(headings include dates of erection)

22 Airth (B, 1597; P 257)
In 1723, presumably in the old town near Airth Castle, 'there's building a tolbooth and fleshmarket' (*Geog. Coll.*, **1**, 327). A hollowed stone or salt-vat from a fireplace of the tolbooth is preserved locally (*Inventory of Stirlingshire*, **2**, No.415(ii)).

23 Alloa (Reg, 1620; P 173)
Payment was made in the 18th century for repairs to tolbooth doors, windows and stocks (SRO, GD 124/17/282/3). A new County Court-house was built in 1863-5, Municipal Buildings in 1872, and a town hall in 1888 (Groome, *Ordnance Gazetteer*, 42).

24 Bathgate (B, 1663; P 361)
18th-century drawings for a proposed town-house show a rectangle 8.5m by 6.1m, with a small clock-tower on the W gable above a pediment with a Hopetoun armorial. The ground storey was to have a 'vault for criminals', and two identical cells for men and women, each with window, fireplace and ?bed-recess. The first-floor court-room was to be reached by a projecting forestair at the E gable (Hopetoun Drawings, copy in NMRS, WL/402). The 'town jail' is shown as a plain hip-roofed building in a 19th-century photograph (Hendrie, W F, *Bathgate in old picture postcards* (1985), pl.3). Part was described in 1837 as very old, and part was rebuilt *c.*1830 (*Prison Inspectors' Third Report*, 57).

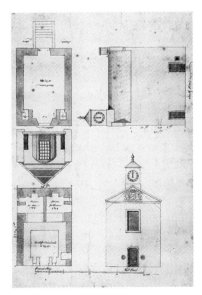

C. Bathgate, proposed town-house   (WL/402)
(scale, 1:400)

25 Biggar (B, 1451; P 138)
The tolbooth was 'a strong vaulted building', used as a courthouse and prison. It was probably ruinous by 1737, and thereafter courts were normally held in the bailie's house (Hunter, W, *Biggar and the house of Fleming* (2nd ed., 1867), 186). In 1837 there was a vaulted prison, 5.5m by 4m (*Prison Inspectors' Third Report*, 81).

26 Blairgowrie (B, 1634; P 331)
The town-house, which survives in much-altered form, was built about 1832 (*Prison Inspectors' Second Report*, 75). It is two-storeyed, with a seven-bay front, and a hall was added at the rear in 1860 to designs by John Carver.

27 Bo'ness (Reg, 1668; P 380)
Pennant in 1769 described a 'town-house ... in the form of a castle', a towered rectangle modelled on Inveraray Castle and intended to have a school on the second floor. A tower was added 1857, but the building collapsed (except for the tower) in 1882.
(Pennant, T, *A Tour in Scotland: MDCCLXIX* (3rd ed., 1774), 243; *Stat. Acct.*, **18**, 429; Lindsay and Cosh, *Inveraray*, 330).

28 Broughton, Edinburgh (non-burghal barony)
A two-storeyed rectangle, with a 1582 door-lintel, small dormers, crowsteps, and a central forestair. It became Heriot's Hospital property in 1636; was leased for storage, reserving a room for courts, *c*.1750; and was demolished in 1829.
(Wilson, *Memorials*, 2, 208-10; Steven, W, *History of George Heriot's Hospital* (1859), 59, 62, 96).

A. **Broughton Tolbooth** *from E, c.1850*   (*Wilson*)

29 Carnwath (B, 1451; P 139)
The tolbooth was a two-storeyed rectangle with crow-stepped gables and a date-stone of 1705 (information from Mr T Ward). It had two ground-floor cells in 1837 (*Prison Inspectors' Third Report*, 82). In 1874 there was a stair at the rear, a lock-up on the ground floor and domestic rooms above. After use as a garage, it was demolished in 1929.
(NMRS, plan dated 1874 (LAD/36/54), and early photographs, LA/1776).

30 Castle Douglas (B, 1791; P 469)
In 1832 there was 'a modern town-house', presumably the 'town hall with a clock-tower' that preceded the hall of 1862. In 1837 it had two prison-rooms on the first floor.
(Chambers, *Gazetteer*, 142; *Prison Inspectors' Third Report*, 30).

31 Colinsburgh (B, 1707; P 459)
A house of 1684 was used as the tolbooth in the 18th century, and had a bell on the W gable. The site is occupied by the 'Tolbooth shop'.
(Dick, R, *Annals of Colinsburgh* (1896), 17, 63-4).

32 Creetown (B, 1791; P 470)
In 1837 the prison was a 'quite new' building, with four prison rooms and two keeper's rooms on the ground floor, and a large upper room, 'intended to serve as the Town-hall,' (*Prison Inspectors' Third Report*, 34-5).

33 Crieff (B/Reg 1687; P 393)
A tolbooth was built in 1684-5 and demolished in 1842. It was a two-storeyed rectangle, with one gable crow-stepped and an octagonal tower, belfry and spire at the other gable (drawing in Perth Museum; Macara, D, *Crieff: its Traditions and Characters* (1881), vignette on title-page). The ground-floor jail contained an iron cage and iron stocks, which are

B. **Crieff Tolbooth** *from NW*   (*Macara*)

preserved (Sporne, *Stocks*, **2**, 70-1). In 1837 there was a lock-up under the former guard-house, probably the same building (*Prison Inspectors' Third Report*, 57). A bell of 1725 by Robert Maxwell, donated by Lord John Drummond, was re-cast in 1821 by Stephen Miller and now hangs in the town hall (*PSAS*, **122** (1992), 473).
(Porteous, A, *The History of Crieff* (1912); Macara, D, *Guide to Crieff, Comrie, St Fillans* (n.d.), 17-18; *NSA*, **10**, 498-9, 525; plan for proposed prison, 1764 (SRO, RHP 3413)).

34 Cromdale (B, 1609; P 284)
A building-contract for 'a tolbooth in the town of Cromdale' was made in 1738 between Ludovick Grant of Grant and Alexander Frazer, mason in Cromdale. It mentions the 'pitt',

C. **Carnwath Tolbooth** *from W, c.1925*   (*LA/1776*)

vaults, three shops, the front room and clerk's chamber. The floors were to be laid with flags, locks to be 'fitt for a prison', and the roof slated. The contract-price was £58 sterling. (SRO, GD 248/152/1)

35 Douglas (Reg, 1707; P 147)
The former 'Sun Inn', said to have been used as a barony court-house and prison, is a three-storeyed rectangle with crow-stepped gables, and a round-ended stair-tower at the rear. A door-lintel is dated 1621, and a skewputt is dated 1674. In 1837 there was a prison, 3.7m by 2.7m, on the ground floor of the town-house, 'an old building' (*Prison Inspectors' Third Report*, 83). An early 'town clock' is in the church tower.

A. **Douglas**, *former Sun Inn from SW*   (LA/689)

36 Dunblane ('city' but not burgh; P 96)
A tolbooth was built E of the churchyard gate in 1650 (Barty, A B, *The History of Dunblane* (1944), 83). The prison was 'ruinous' in 1773, and was repaired in 1775 to make 'four tenable prisons, an apartment for the jailer, and a good Court House' (SRO, E 727/41/3, nos.1-5). The prison in the town-house was 'very old, very small, and very insecure' in 1836, and a new jail was built in 1842 (*Prison Inspectors' Second Report*, 77-8; *Eighth Report*, 60). The town hall dates from 1887.

37 Duns (B, 1490; P 163)
Orders were given in 1629 to improve the tolbooth (p, 217, n.30). Money was collected in 1683 for building 'the croce and tolbuith' (decreet in Duns Library, folio 8, no.10). Drawings in the Duns Castle collection (copies in NMRS) include: (a) a rectangular 'Ould Town Hous' with forestair at angle; (b) a late 18th-century five-bay three-storeyed hip-roofed block, with projecting end-wall steeple; (c) estimates and drawings for a town hall with central steeple, almost identical with Selkirk (No.77) and naming Mr Lees as contractor, and a separate jail. Schemes (b) and (c) probably followed fire-damage to the town-house in 1795 (local guide), but it was not replaced until 1816. The new town hall, to a four-bay Perpendicular Gothic design by J G Graham, stood at the centre of the Market Square like its predecessor. Engravings show a spire modelled on that of Louth (Lincolnshire; cf. Montrose) above a centre-gable clock-tower, but the spire was removed before 1900, and the building was demolished in 1966.

38 Ellon (B, 1707; P 457)
The town-house presented a gable with a belfry to the square, and had a 'double outside stair' enclosing the entrance to the jail. A girnel and 'salmon house' were also on the ground floor. It was demolished in 1842, but an early 18th-century

dormer pediment with the arms of Bailie James Gordon is built into the wall of Number.7 the Square (NMRS photograph, AB/3561, and record-sheet).
(Mair, T, *Records of the parish of Ellon* (1876), 152-3; Godsman, J, *A history of the burgh and parish of Ellon* (1958), 51, 303-4).

39 Fordyce (B, 1499; P 175)
The W end of the medieval church was heightened to carry a double-bellcot dated 1661, and in 1671 money was collected 'for scletting and building off the stiple' (SRO, GD 16/46/33). In 1682 the kirk-session agreed to fit up the first floor of the steeple-house as a prison (Cramond, W, *The Church at Fordyce* (1912)). The three-storeyed gabled tower has a vaulted ground-floor porch, and a forestair against the S wall.

40 Fraserburgh (B, 1546; P 227)
A 'small and humble' court-house and jail, with a forestair on the gable facing the square, was replaced in 1856 by the Town Hall (Cranna, J, *Fraserburgh Past and Present* (1914), 36, 389).

B. **Duns Town Hall**, *engraving from S after Graham, c.1816*   (BWD/69/2)

41 Fyvie (B, 1671/3; P 131)
The burgh charter of 1673 allowed a tolbuith (*NSA*, 12, 330), and in 1723 there was 'an old village called Woodhead ... where is a stone Tolbooth and a stone cross' (*Geog.Coll.*, 1, 94). The tolbooth became a dwelling, and was replaced *c*.1840 by a farmhouse which contains re-used masonry.
(Name Book, Aberdeenshire No.35, p.127; Pratt, J B, *Buchan* (4th ed., 1901), 413).

42 Galashiels (B, 1599; P 264)
A tolbooth with thick 'clay built' walls was used for worship before the building of a church in 1617. The steeple, probably added, had a vane and clock-face dated 1669. In 1722 there was 'ane tolbooth with clock and bell & markit cross' (*Geog. Coll.*, 1, 362). It was ruinous for some years before its demolition in 1880, but the clock was transferred to the parish church, the jougs to Abbotsford, and the John Meikle bell of 1695 is at Old Gala House (*Inventory of Selkirkshire*, No.20). The town hall dates from 1867.
(Craig-Brown, T, *The History of Sekirkshire* (1886), 485-6; Hall, R, *The History of Galashiels* (1898), 26).

43 Glenluce (Reg, 1707; P 451)
In 1837 there was a vaulted lock-up in the former town-house, which was privately owned (*Prison Inspectors' Third Report*, 40).

44 Gorbals, Glasgow (non-burghal barony)
St Ninian's Chapel of 1494 was adapted as a court-house and prison. In 1720 the prison was moved to the upper storeys of the adjacent 'tower and fortalice', of early 17th-century date, which had square corbelled angle-turrets and a flat balustraded roof. The principal room in the tower was later used for courts and meetings, and the complex included a school-room. The

*A. **Gorbals**, chapel and tower, c.1827*   *(Swan)*

buildings were sold in 1827 to finance a new police-station, and they were demolished in 1869.
(Swan, J, *Select Views of Glasgow* (1828), pl. opp. p.84; *The Regality Club*, **4** (1912), 41, 44-6; *Glasgow Extracts (1823-33)*, p.xliv).

45 Grantown on Spey (Reg, 1694; P 432)
The planned town was established about 1766, and in 1793 it had 'an elegant town-house, covering a prison' (*Stat. Acct.*, **8**, 258). There was a prison at Grantown in 1841 (*NSA*, **14**, 443), and a court-house with police cells was built in the Square in 1868 (Name Book, Moray No.5, p.151).

46 Greenock (B, 1635; P 332)
Early council meetings were held in an inn. In 1765 a plan by James Ewing, mason, was 'improved' by Bailie James Watt (father of the engineer), and built by James Wallace, wright, and John Pye, mason, for £420. The town-house was a two-storeyed five-bay rectangle with rusticated quoins, having a central pend to a lane. The ground storey contained a prison and court-room, latterly shops, and the upper floor was used for assemblies and masonic meetings, and as a newsroom until 1814. Wings to house the council-room and town clerk's office were built at the rear in 1811 A castellated jail was built in 1810. The town clock and bell were housed in various improvised belfries and church steeples. The town-house was demolished in 1880, and new Municipal Buildings (H and D Barclay, architects) were erected in 1881-6.
(TCM (Watt Library, Greenock), 13 February, 3 April, 16 May, 19 June 1765; Weir, D, *History of the Town of Greenock* (1829), 26-7, 36; Williamson, G, *Old Greenock* (1st series, 1886), 119-20, 131-4, 174-5; Brown, A, *The Early Annals of Greenock* (1905), 127-30; McKelvie, J, *Views and Reminiscences of Old Greenock* (1891), pl.17 and text).

47 Hatton of Fintray (B, 1625; P 316)
Barony courts held in the tolbooth are recorded from 1719. It was demolished for building-materials in the 18th century, except for an arched section of a vault. (*Miscellany of the Third Spalding Club*, **1** (1935), 8, 15, 36, pl. opp. p.15).

48 Hawick (Reg, 1669; P 193)
The tolbuith, mentioned in 1682, was 'ruinous' in 1692 when Francis Gledstanes offered timber for rebuilding as an example to others (*Transactions of the Hawick Archaeological Society*, **6** (1867), 36). The tolbooth is said to have been 'at the back' of the later town-house, and was 'a low thatched

*B. **Hawick Town-house** from W, c.1880*   *(Robson)*

building' (Vernon, J J, *The Parish and Kirk of Hawick* (1900), 11, 199). It was demolished in 1781, and a 'neat council house' was erected with a £50 contribution from the 3rd Duke of Buccleuch (*Stat. Acct.*, **8**, 452). This had meal- and butter-markets on the ground storey, and photographs show infilled arcades in the three-bay gable-wall and part of the side wall, which also had a forestair (Robson, W S, *The Story of Hawick* (1937), 85, fig. on p.82). A 'spire like a may-pole' (Wilson, R, *History of Hawick* (2nd ed., 1841), 92) at the centre of the gable was a later addition, shown in a drawing of 1806 which refers to a contract with John Laing, mason in Hawick (drawing in Hawick Museum, copy in NMRS). The town-house was demolished in 1884 and replaced in 1885-7 by the Municipal Buildings, to a Baronial design by J C Walker.

49 Helensburgh (B, 1802; P 472)
As early as 1809 burgh courts were held in the 'New Theatre', which was converted to a town-house in the 1830s. It was replaced in 1878 by the Municipal Buildings, to a Baronial design by J Honeyman.
(Battrum, W, *Guide to Helensburgh and Neighbourhood* (1864), 10, 20; Maughan, W C, *Annals of Garelochside* (1897), 136).

50 Huntly (Reg, 1684; P 155)
The tolbooth was repaired in 1731 and 1736-8 (SRO, GD 44). Designs for a new court-house include a Gothic scheme which may be that prepared in 1826 by J B Papworth (SRO, RHP 31776-8, 31793; Colvin, *Architects* (2nd ed., 1978), 618). Archibald Simpson prepared unexecuted designs for a town hall in 1833, but the prison in 1835 was a former blacksmith's shop (*Prison Inspectors' First Report*, 63). A new hall was built in 1875 and repaired in 1887. The town bell was cast by J(ames) B(artlet), London, in 1656 (*PSAS*, **90** (1956-7), 156).

51 Kilmarnock (B, 1592; P 249)
The tolbooth was extended in 1711 to include a weigh-house (grant from 3rd Earl of Kilmarnock at Dean Castle). The council-house had a forestair facing the Cross and the prison was at the rear, with jougs fixed at the platform of its forestair. It was demolished and a town-house built in 1805, on the E side of the newly-formed King Street. This building, which was demolished about 1970, had a pedimented centrepiece, with a Venetian window, carrying a small octagonal belfry and spire. In 1837 there were three ground-floor police cells, later replaced by shops (*Prison Inspectors' Third Report*, 48). A bell by Robert Maxwell (Clouston, 'Ayrshire Bells', 231-2), which in 1711 was gifted by the 3rd Earl of Kilmarnock to the town 'for ther councillhouse', is displayed in the Dick Institute.
(Paterson, J, *History of the Counties of Ayr and Wigton* (1866), **3**, 374-9; M'Kay, A, *The History of Kilmarnock* (4th ed., 1880), 111-12).

52 Kilsyth (B, 1620; P 308)
In 1836 the prison occupied two vaults on the ground floor of the town-house, 'a very old building, standing on one side of a kind of square' (*Prison Inspectors' Second Report*, 103). The 'old barony court-house' was demolished in 1860 (plaque on site). An early 19th-century market-house was demolished in 1978 (NMRS, record-sheet).

53 Kincardine on Forth (B, 1663; P 360)
The early 19th-century Commercial Hotel is said to be a former town-house, erected by the local Shipmasters' Society (*PSAS*, **97** (1964-6), 301).

54 Kincardine O'Neil (B, 1511; P 201)
In 1725, 'there is a Tolbooth in the said town' (*Geog. Coll.*, **1**, 101).

55 Kingussie (B, 1464; P 148)
The 'Tolbooth of Baddenoch' was built in 1736-7 by Alexander Frazer, mason (SRO, GD44/52/254, p.43). In 1832 there was 'a small jail, with a court-room' (Chambers, *Gazetteer*, 650).

56 Kirriemuir (Reg, 1670; P 145)
The town-house, which stands on an island site in the market-place, was shown in 1860 as a plain two-storeyed hip-roofed rectangle, 11.4m by 7m (drawings by J Carver in possession of Lord Home of the Hirsel, copies in NMRS). The jail in the W half of the ground storey had walls up to 1.4m thick and may have survived from a supposed tower of 1604. An engraved view on the 18th-century town baton (Stirton, fig. on p.28)

Kirriemuir Town-house
N front engraved on town baton, c.1800
(Stirton)

showed a projecting and round-ended central forestair, whose footings were excavated in 1994 (report by Scottish Urban Archaeological Trust). In 1862 John Carver, a Meigle architect, altered the W end to a bow and added a second large bow and a clock-tower to the N (preliminary designs, 1860, loc.cit.). In 1896 the thick walls were thinned internally to make space for a post-office.
(Stirton, J, *Thrums and its Glens* (1896), 28-9; Reid, A, *The Regality of Kirriemuir* (1909), 186-7; *The Kirriemuir Observer*, 19 June 1896).

57 Largs (B, 1631; P 319)
In 1837 there was an insecure old prison in the market-place (*Prison Inspectors' Third Report*, 53).

58 Laurencekirk (B, 1779; P 467)
In 1846 there was a court-room in a building used also as a masonic lodge, and a lock-up was built about 1843 (Lewis, *Dictionary*, **2**, 157, *Prison Inspectors' Ninth Report*, 31).

59 Linktown, Kirkcaldy (B, 1663; P 363)
The town-house was 'a plain-looking old building', with a ground-floor jail (last used in 1822), and 'the upper story was the place of meeting for the Baron Bailie and other officers' until 1816. In 1855 it was the residence of the widow of the Baron Bailie, and 'the whole going to decay'.
(Name Book, Fife No.107, p.18; *NSA*, **9** (Fife), 159).

60 Logierait (Reg, 1671; P 387)
Freestone was supplied in 1707 for the regality court-house and prison. It was demolished in 1817-18, but the yett was removed to Ballechin House (Dixon, J H, *Pitlochry Past and Present* (1925), 34-5, pl.37).

61 Longforgan (B, 1672; P 392)
The church tower, which bears a 1690 date-stone, was used as a prison (information from Mr D B Taylor).

62 Macduff (B, 1783; P 468)
In 1832 there was a town-house (described in 1846 as a neat town hall) and jail (Chambers, *Gazetteer*, 752; Lewis, *Dictionary*, **2**, 225).

63 Mauchline (Reg, 1707; P 191)
A small prison was built *c*.1820 (*Prison Inspectors' Third Report*, 46).

64 Maxwelltown (B, 1810; P 473)
A plain court-house, above a jail with five cells, was built about 1811.
(Lewis, *Dictionary*, **2**, 239-40; *Prison Inspectors' Second Report*, 118-19).

65 Melrose (Reg, 1621; P 276)
In 1837 there was a vaulted lock-up on the ground floor of the 'town court-house', built about 1822. This had replaced 'a curious old one', from which a stone bearing the burgh arms was preserved.
(Chambers, *Gazetteer*, 764; *Prison Inspectors' Third Report*, 22).

66 New Tarbat (Reg, 1686; P 408)
In 1755 there was 'a court-house and a very good prison in Milntown (Milton) of Newtarbat' (Wills, V, *Reports on the Annexed Estates, 1755-1769* (1973), 37). In 1774 estimates were sought for re-roofing the court-house with heather or slate (SRO, E321/18, p.147).

67 Old Meldrum (B, 1671; P 385)
In 1724 the burgh had 'a convenient mercat place with a tolbooth (*Geog. Coll.*, **I**, 11). The town-house was a two-storeyed rectangle with (?later) tripartite first-floor windows; a forestair rose to the entrance in a projecting central steeple with ogee roof (photograph in NMRS). In 1836 there was a single vaulted ground-floor cell (*Prison Inspectors' Second Report*, 35). A panel of 1741 with the arms of the superior was removed from the steeple to the town hall that replaced the town-house in 1877, and which contains the bell of 1791 by Thomas Mears (*PSAS*, **91** (1957-8), 93).

68 Paisley (Reg, 1587; P 156)
A house in the high street was granted by the abbot for use as a tolbooth about 1490, and rebuilt in 1610. It was rebuilt in 1757, to a design by Bailie John White (Colvin, *Architects*, 1042), as a three-storeyed main block (rebuilt in 1821), with a tall steeple which was demolished in 1870. Castellated County and Town Buildings were built on the W bank of the River Cart in 1818-20 to designs by Archibald Elliot and

A. Paisley County and Town Buildings from S, c.1830   (*Mackie*)

William Reid (ibid., 340, 798; Mackie, C, *Historical Description of the Abbey and Town of Paisley* (1835), 148-51) and demolished in 1968. The George A Clark Town Hall (W H Lynn, Belfast, architect) was opened in 1882.
(Metcalfe, *Paisley*, 315-31; early views in NMRS; accounts for repairs, 1680, in Paisley Museum).

69 Portsburgh, Edinburgh (B, 1649; P 349)
In 1709 Edinburgh town council agreed to build a small

tolbooth or prison-house 'in the corner of the Toun wall at Bristo', later identified as 'the south-east turret' of the wall. It was to have ground-floor cells for men and women, a first-floor court-room with forestair, and second-floor rooms for male and female debtors. The estimated cost was £50.
(*Inventory of Edinburgh*, pp.lix-lx; *Edinburgh Extracts (1701-18)*, 168-9, 288).

70 Prestwick (B, 1600; P 267)
In 1723 there was 'a tolbooth and toun councell and twa Bailies' (*Geog. Coll.*, **1**, 410). In 1837 the prison-room opened off a school-room (*Prison Inspectors' Third Report*, 45). The Freemans' Hall of about 1837 (Groome, *Ordnance Gazetteer*, 1357) was later used as a school, a prison and, from 1906, as town chambers.

71 Rosehearty (B, 1681; P 414)
In 1721 it was reported that 'this town has a tolbooth' (*Geog. Coll.*, **1**, 41), and at the end of the 19th century it had 'a disused tolbooth' (Groome, *Ordnance Gazetteer*, 1383).

72 St Monance (B, 1596; P 255)
In 1836 both floors of the town-house were used as a prison, the ground floor being 'miserably bad' (*Prison Inspectors' Second Report*, 88; *NSA*, **9**, 354). In 1853 the town-house was 'the upper story of a dwelling house' (Name Book, Fife No.80, p.36).

B. Paisley Town-house from E, 1821   (*Metcalfe*)

73 Strathaven (B, 1450; P 137)
In 1837 there were two cells in the upper storey of the town-house, formerly ruinous but repaired by the Duke of Hamilton about two years earlier (*Prison Inspectors' Third Report*, 78).

74 Tarland (B, 1683; P 419)
About 1724 this was described as 'a Burrough of Regality, with a Tolbooth and Victuall house for the sale of meal and grain &c' (*Geog. Coll.*, **1**, 25).

75 Thornhill (Reg, 1664; P 366)
A tolbooth was in use in 1700 (Waugh, J L, *Thornhill and its Worthies* (2nd ed., 1913), 19-20). It was repaired in 1718 (Drumlanrig, Buccleuch Muniments, bundles 1533, 1549), and is shown on a plan of 1742 (SRO, RHP 37535).

76 Thurso (B, 1633; P 326)
The session-house at the E end of the church was used by sheriffs and magistrates as a court-house and prison. In 1726, 'above a dungeon ... there is a steeple and common clock' (*Geog. Coll.*, **1**, 170). In 1797 there was no prison, and a new town-house was proposed (*Stat. Acct.*, **20**, 529, 545). A Town and County Hall in Sinclair Street was built shortly before 1825 (Pigot, J, *New Commercial Directory of Scotland 1825-6*, 293), but the sheriff court was transferred in 1828 to Wick (No.87), and the hall was burnt down some years later. A Gothic town hall was built in 1870 (Groome, *Ordnance Gazetteer*, 1566).

77 Turriff (B, 1512; P 203)
In 1683 a contract was made for upholding the slate-work of the tolbooth (SRO, classified index to NRA). A market was mentioned, but no tolbooth, in 1723 (*Geog. Coll.*, **1**, 91-3).

78 Unidentified
An 18th-century drawing shows a three-storeyed rectangle, 11m x 7.8, with a central tower rising above a small wall-head pediment to a clock and ogee roof. The flanking bays have ground-floor arches, giving access to a newel-stair in the tower and to three cells (one for women) at the rear. There are granaries on the first floor, and on the next floor a Town Room, Sheriff Court Room and 'Smal Closet'. A note records that 'James Binning says to execute the above plan it will cost £330 besides the clock and bell'. (Hopetoun Drawings, no.3; copy in NMRS).

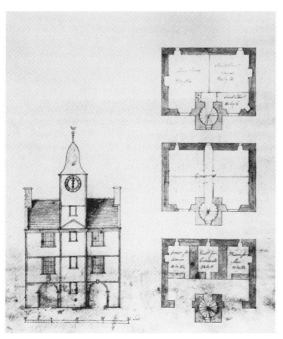

*A. **Unidentified town-house** (scale, 1:400)* (C 65822)

79 Unidentified
A design of 1820 by James Milne for a court-house and debtors' jail shows a two-storeyed five-bay classical building (Hamilton Drawings; copy in NMRS, UND/25/6).

NON-BURGHAL

80 Coldstream
Court House Lodge may be the jail shown on a plan of 1818 (Nat. Lib. of Scot.). In 1837 it was described as a good small prison, built about 1817, with two ground-floor cells below the jailer's rooms (*Prison Inspectors' Third Report*, 21-2). A town hall was built in 1862.

81 Drumlithie
'The Steeple', a circular ashlar pillar carrying a belfry, was erected in 1777 for the use of local weavers. It was repaired, and the bell recast, in 1868, and still stands at the centre of the village.
(Kinnear, G H, *The History of Glenbervie* (1910), 25-6).

82 Dufftown
The castellated clock-tower that stands in the central square was built by subscription 'at the time of the cholera' (about 1832), 'to frighten vagrants away', and contained two prison-cells (*Prison Inspectors' Second Report*, 41-2).

*B. **Dufftown Clock-tower** from E, c.1890* (BN/1356)

83 Ecclefechan
In 1723 this was described as the 'head Burgh of ... pairt of the Regality of New Dalgarnock ... having a Tolbooth in the middle of the town' (*Geog. Coll.*, **1**, 369).

84 Gifford
A clock from Edinburgh was housed in 1777 in a belfry on the roof of the town hall or tolbooth (Simpson, J H, *The Feuars of Gifford* (1986), 9). In 1837 there was a lock-up, 5.8m by 3m, the property of the Marquis of Tweeddale, and in 1853 the parish school-room was above it (*Prison Inspectors' Third Report*, 99; Name Book, East Lothian No.18, p.50). The school was rebuilt as the town hall in 1887 (Muir, J, *Gifford 1750-1850* (1913)).

85 Glass
In 1724 there was 'a litle village and tolbooth, which he [Sir George Gordon, d.1691] designed for a burgh of Baronie' (*Geog. Coll.*, **1**, 80). There was still a lock-up in the 19th century, on the site of a modern house, Braehead, at Haughs of Glass (Godsman, J, *Glass, Aberdeenshire* (1970), 162-3).

86 Gretna Green
An account of 1723 described 'the whole village with a tolbooth being lately built anew by [Col. James Johnston] after a new modell'. Another description referred to 'a Burgh of

Barrony in which there is a steeple and courthouse' (*Geog. Coll.*, **2**, 371, 382).

87 Keith
The tolbooth, demolished in 1841, had a vaulted jail, girnel and shambles below, and a double forestair led to a school-room and library above. The town bell was cast by John Mowat in 1763.
(Gordon, J F S, *The Book of the Chronicles of Keith* (1880), 64-5; *Prison Inspectors' Second Report*, 41).

88 Mid Calder
A detailed contract for building a two-storeyed 'prison house' was made in 1710 between Lord Torphichen and George Waddell, mason, 'conform to a draught drawn by Andrew Paterson of Kirktoun'. It was to measure 9.1m by 7.6m, with a ground-floor market-area and two vaulted cells and a first-floor 'councill house' reached by a forestair (SRO, RD 3/138, pp.102-6).

89 Portree
The court-house, with two vaulted prison-cells on the ground storey, was built in 1800-2 at a cost of £511, to a design by J G Graham, and is now used as a tourist office (Armadale, Clan Donald Centre, GD 221/15/1 and 28/2; *NSA*, **14**, 234).

90 Stewarton, Ayrshire
In 1837 there was an unsatisfactory cell, owned by the proprietor of the town, which was replaced in 1844 by a lock-up and court-room (*Prison Inspectors' Third Report*, 49; *Ninth Report*, 55). The former burgh offices appear to be of 19th-century domestic origin.

91 Ullapool
A 'tolbooth or court house' was proposed in 1756 by the surveyor Peter May (Adams, I H (ed.), *Papers on Peter May, Land Surveyor, 1749-1793* (SHS, 1979), 12, 267; SRO, RHP 3400).

OTHER LOCK-UPS IN 1837

(*Prison Inspectors' Third Report*).

92 Ayton (pp.20-1)
A two-room lock-up, built about 1817.

93 Catrine (p.47)
A lock-up under a spinning-mill aqueduct, lately replaced by two cells in 'part of an old corn-mill'.

94 Cockburnspath (p.21)
A hovel attached to the church.

95 Dunkeld (*Second Report*, p.74)
Three cells in the abutment of the Tay Bridge of 1809.

96 [East] Linton (pp.98-9)
A small cell in a wing attached to the turnpike-house.

97 Galston (p.48)
'Two very small cells made in the ruin of an old castle'.

98 Gatehouse (pp.33-4)
Two cells on the upper floor of the gate-keeper's house, built *c*.1825.

99 Kincardine, Perthshire (*Second Report*, p.77)
A lock-up with two cells, 'constructed a few years ago out of an old engine-house'.

100 Lasswade (pp.86-7)
Two cells, on the ground and first floors of the old church tower.

101 Lockerbie (p.26)
Two rooms, formed out of an old ruin *c*.1831.

102 Newcastleton (p.24)
A lock-up with two cells, built *c*.1820.

103 Old Cumnock (p.47)
A single cell, replaced by a prison and court-room *c*.1840.

104 Penicuik (pp.86-7)
The ground floor of the old church tower, adapted for use as a lock-up *c*.1830.

105 Portpatrick (pp.42-3)
A one-storeyed lock-up with two cells.

106 Tranent (p.97)
A small room in the constable's house, adapted about 1835.

ABBREVIATIONS USED IN THE REFERENCES

Aberdeen Extracts	Stuart, J (ed.), *Extracts from the Council Register of the Burgh of Aberdeen*, Spalding Club, 1844-8; SBRS, 1871-2.
APS	*The Acts of the Parliaments of Scotland, 1814-75.*
BOEC	*The Book of the Old Edinburgh Club.*
Brown, *Early Travellers*	Brown, P H, *Early Travellers in Scotland*, 1891.
Cameron, *Prisons*	Cameron, J, *Prisons and Punishment in Scotland*, 1983. .
Cast. and Dom. Arch.	MacGibbon, D and Ross, T, *The Castellated and Domestic Architecture of Scotland,* 1887-92.
Chambers, *Gazetteer*	Chambers, R and W, *The Gazetteer of Scotland,* 1832.
Chambers, *Reekiana*	Chambers, R, *Reekiana: Minor Antiquities of Edinburgh,* 1833.
Chapman, *Johnson and Boswell*	Chapman, R W (ed.), *Johnson's Journey to the Western Islands of Scotland and Boswell's Journal of a Tour to the Hebrides with Samuel Johnson, Ll.D.* (1934).
Clouston, 'Ayrshire Bells'	Clouston, R W M, 'The Church Bells of Ayrshire', *Ayrshire Archaeological and Natural History Society Collections,* second series, **1** (1947-9), pp.200-60. .
Colvin, *Architects*	Colvin, H, *A Biographical Dictionary of British Architects, 1600-1840,* third edition, 1995.
Conolly, *Fifiana*	Conolly, M F, *Fifiana: or, Memorials of the East of Fife,* 1869.
Dickinson, *Aberdeen*	Dickinson, W C (ed.), *Early Records of the Burgh of Aberdeen, 1317, 1398-1407,* SHS, 1957.
Edinburgh Extracts	*Extracts from the Records of the Burgh of Edinburgh,* 1869- .
Eccles. Arch.	MacGibbon, D and Ross, T, *The Ecclesiastical Architecture of Scotland,* 1896-7.
Elgin Records	Cramond, W (ed.), *The Records of Elgin,* New Spalding Club, 1903-8.
Geog. Coll.	Macfarlane, W, *Geographical Collections relating to Scotland,* SHS, 1906-8.
Gifford, *Fife*	Gifford, J, *Fife,* The Buildings of Scotland, 1988.
Glasgow Extracts	*Extracts from the Records of the Burgh of Glasgow,* 1876- .
Groome, *Ordnance Gazetteer*	Groome, F H, *Ordnance Gazetteer of Scotland,* new edition, 1901.
Gurney, *Prisons*	J J Gurney, *Notes on a visit made to some of the prisons in Scotland and Northern England,* 1819.
Historic Buildings at Work	Scottish Civic Trust, *Historic Buildings at Work: a Guide to the Historic Buildings of Scotland used* by Central Government, 1983.
Inventory of [County]	Royal Commission on the Ancient and Historical Monuments of Scotland, *Inventory of the Ancient Monuments in [the county stated],* 1908-92. .
Lanark Extracts	Renwick, R (ed.), *Extracts from the Records of the Royal Burgh of Lanark,* 1893.
Leighton, *Fife*	Leighton, J M, *History of the County of Fife,* 1840.
Lewis, *Dictionary*	Lewis, S, *A Topographical Dictionary of Scotland,* 1846.
Lindsay and Cosh, *Inveraray*	Lindsay, I G and Cosh, M, *Inveraray and the Dukes of Argyll,* 1973.
Lowther, *Journall*	Lowther, C, *Our Journall into Scotland,* 1894.
Mackenzie, *Burghs*	Mackenzie, W M, *The Scottish Burghs,* 1949.
Maitland, *Edinburgh*	Maitland, W, *The History of Edinburgh,* 1753.
Metcalfe, *Paisley*	Metcalfe, W M, *A History of Paisley, 600-1908,* 1909.
Mylne, *Master Masons*	Mylne, R S, *The Master Masons to the Crown of Scotland,* 1893. .
Name Book	Original Name-books of the Ordnance Survey (microfilms in NMRS and SRO).
Nat. Lib. of Scot.	National Library of Scotland.
Neild, *Prisons*	Neild, J, *State of the Prisons in England, Scotland and Wales,* 1812. .
NMRS	National Monuments Record of Scotland.
NSA	*The New Statistical Account of Scotland,* 1845.
OS	Ordnance Survey.
Pont, *Cuninghame*	Dobie, J S (ed.), *Cuninghame, Topographized by Timothy Pont, A.M., 1604-1608,* 1876. .
Prison Directors' First Report	*First Report of the General Board of Directors of Prisons in Scotland,* 1840.
Prison Inspectors' [ ] Report	*[ ] Report of the Inspectors appointed ... to visit the different Prisons of Great Britain, IV (Scotland),* 1836-50.
Pryde, *Burghs*	Pryde, G S, *The Burghs of Scotland, a critical list,* 1965.
Pryde, *Kirkintilloch*	Pryde, G S (ed.), *The Court Book of the Burgh of Kirkintilloch,1658-1694,* SHS, 1963.
PSAS	*Proceedings of the Society of Antiquaries of Scotland.*
RCRBS	*Records of the Convention of Royal Burghs of Scotland,* 1870-1915.
RMS	*Registrum Magni Sigilli Regum Scotorum,* 1882-1914.
RPC	*The Register of the Privy Council of Scotland,* 1887- .
SBRS	Scottish Burgh Records Society. .
SBRS Misc.	Marwick, J D (ed.), *Miscellany of the Scottish Burgh Records Society,* SBRS, 1881. .
Shepherd, *Modern Athens*	Shepherd, T H, *Modern Athens ... or Edinburgh in the Nineteenth Century,* 1829.
SHR	*The Scottish Historical Review.*
SHS	Scottish History Society.
Sporne, *Stocks*	Sporne, K R, *An Illustrated Catalogue of Stocks in Great Britain,* 1986-8.
SRO	Scottish Record Office.
SRS	Scottish Record Society.
Stat. Acct.	*The Statistical Account of Scotland,* 1791-9.
Storer, *Views*	Storer, J and H S, *Views in Edinburgh and its Vicinity,* 1820.
TCM	Town Council Minutes (for location see *infra*, p.216).
TDGNHAS	*Transactions of the Dumfriesshire and Galloway Natural History and Antiquarian Society.*
Thomson, *Dundee*	Thomson, J, *The History of Dundee,* new edition by J Maclaren, 1874.
Wilson, *Memorials*	Wilson, D, *Memorials of Edinburgh in the Olden Time,* second edition, 1891.
Wood's plan	Town plan in Wood, J, *Town Atlas of Scotland,* 1828.

LOCATION OF TOWN COUNCIL MINUTES

Aberdeen	Aberdeen City Archives.
Airdrie	Airdrie Public Library.
Anstruther Wester	St Andrews University Library (B 3/5).
Arbroath	Montrose Library, Angus Council Cultural Services Archive Unit.
Auchtermuchty	St Andrews University Library (B 5/5).
Ayr	Ayr, Carnegie Library.
Banff	Old Aberdeen, Aberdeen City Archives, former Grampian Regional Archives.
Brechin	Montrose Library, Angus Council Cultural Services Archive Unit.
Campbeltown	Lochgilphead, Argyll and Bute Archives.
Crail	St Andrews University Library (B 10/10).
Cupar	St Andrews University Library (B 13/14).
Dingwall	Dingwall Museum.
Dumbarton	Dumbarton Public Library.
Dumfries	Dumfries Archive Centre.
Dunbar	SRO (B 18/13).
Dysart	Kirkcaldy Town-house, Fife Council.
Earlsferry	St Andrews University Library (B 24/4).
Edinburgh	Edinburgh City Archives.
Falkland	St Andrews University Library (B 25/5).
Forfar	Montrose Library, Angus Council Cultural Services Archive Unit.
Fortrose	SRO (B 28/8).
Girvan	Ayr, Carnegie Library.
Haddington	SRO (B 30/13).
Inverkeithing	SRO (B 34/10).
Inverness	Inverness Library, Highland Council Archive.
Jedburgh	Hawick, Scottish Borders Council.
Kirkcudbright	Kirkcudbright, Stewartry Museum.
Kirkintilloch	Kirkintilloch Public Library.
Lanark	Lanark, Lindsay Institute.
Lauder	Newtown St Boswells, Scottish Borders Council.
Linlithgow	SRO (B 48/9).
Lochmaben	Lochmaben Town-house.
Montrose	Montrose Library, Angus Council Cultural Services Archive Unit.
Musselburgh	SRO (B 52/3).
Nairn	Inverness Library, Highland Council Archive.
New Galloway	Kirkcudbright, Stewartry Museum.
Newton on Ayr	Ayr, Carnegie Library.
Old Aberdeen	Aberdeen City Archives.
Peebles	SRO (B 58/13).
Perth	Perth, Sandeman Library.
Pittenweem	St Andrews University Library (B 60/6).
Port Glasgow	Greenock, Watt Library.
Rothesay	Rothesay, Argyll and Bute Archives.
Selkirk	Newtown St Boswells, Scottish Borders Council.
Stirling	SRO (B 66/21).
Stonehaven	Stonehaven, Aberdeenshire Council, South Division.
Stranraer	Stranraer Museum.
Tain	SRO (B 70/6).
Wick	Wick, North Highland Archive.

NOTES

Introduction

1   The intended sale of a property in Berwick to Bishop Archibald of Moray (1253-98) was proclaimed *in tolbotha* ('in the tolbooth') at three successive head courts by the vendor (*Registrum Episcopatus Moraviensis* (Bannatyne Club, 1837), 143).

2   *RMS*, **5** (1580-93), no.2356.

3   For the development of the word, see s.v. 'Tolbuith' in *A Dictionary of the Older Scottish Tongue* (forthcoming) and *The Scottish National Dictionary*. A similar range of meanings was used in England, but the related terms 'tolsel' (still current in Ireland, e.g. Kilkenny) or 'tolsey' were more common (*New English Dictionary*, s.vv.'Tolbooth', 'Tolsey'). For Loch Kinord see Name Book, Aberdeenshire No.19, p.145; Michie, J S, *Loch Kinnord* (new ed., 1910), 93-6 and pl.vi.

4   A late 16th-century map of St Andrews (*supra*, fig.206C; McRoberts, D (ed.), *The Medieval Church of St Andrews* (1976), frontispiece), names the *Domus urbis* ('house of the town'). At Wick (No.87) it was declared in 1828 that the new court-house and jail were 'to be called the Tolbooth of Wick in all time coming'.

5   In the 18th century the 'Town Hall' was commonly a single room intended for civic functions, such as the 'Great Room' of Aberdeen Town-house (No.1) and the hall in the Palladian extension added in 1740 to Glasgow Tolbooth (No.34).

6   General works include: Mackenzie, *Burghs*; Duncan, A A M, Nicholson, R G, Donaldson, G and Ferguson, W, *The Edinburgh History of Scotland* (1965-75); Lynch, M, *Scotland, a New History* (1991); Ewan, E, *Townlife in Fourteenth-century Scotland* (1990); Lynch, M, 'Towns and townspeople in 15th century Scotland', in Thomson, J A F (ed.), *Towns and Townspeople in the Fifteenth Century* (1988); Lynch, M *et al.*, *The Scottish Medieval Town* (1988); Lynch, M (ed.), *The Early Modern Town in Scotland* (1987); Pryde, G S (ed.), *Ayr Burgh Accounts, 1534-1624* (SHS, 1937); Pryde, *Kirkintilloch*; Smout, T C, *A History of the Scottish People, 1560-1830* (1969); Saunders, L J, *Scottish Democracy, 1815-1840* (1950). For individual towns see works cited *infra*, and the reports by the Scottish Burgh Survey (1978-). For tolbooths, see *Cast. and Dom. Arch.*, **5**, 98-129; Howard, D, *Scottish Architecture, Reformation to Restoration 1560-1660* (1995); MacGregor, C A, 'Buildings of Administration', in Fenton, A (ed.), *Compendium of Scottish Ethnology* (forthcoming); Stell, G, 'The earliest tolbooths: a preliminary account', in *PSAS*, **111** (1981), 445-53.

7   Commission on Municipal Corporations in Scotland, *General Report (Parliamentary Papers*, 1835, vol.29); *Local Reports on Royal Burghs* (ibid., and 1836, vol.23); *Local Reports on Burghs of Regality and Barony* (1836, vol.23).

8   This body, drawn from the landowners ('heritors') of the county, was responsible for imposing county taxes and maintaining public works (Whetstone, A, *Scottish County Government in the Eighteenth and Nineteenth Centuries* (1981), *passim*).

9   See Stevenson, D and W B, *Scottish Texts and Calendars* (SHS, 1987), 83-9 and index, s.v. 'Burghs'. Many of these volumes were edited, with valuable introductions, by distinguished scholars including Sir James D Marwick, town clerk successively of Edinburgh and Glasgow, and Marguerite Wood and Helen Armet, city archivists of Edinburgh.

10   Cameron, *Prisons*, 44-66; Neild, *Prisons*; Gurney, *Prisons*.

11   E.g., Laurie, J, 'Reminiscences of a town clerk', in *BOEC*, **14** (1925), 147-81; Conolly, *Fifiana*; Mitchell, J, *Reminiscences of my Life in the Highlands* (1883) (for Inverness).

12   Moir, D G (ed.), *The Early Maps of Scotland*, **2** (1983), 244-83.

13   Duncan, A A M (ed.), *The Acts of Robert I* (Regesta Regum Scottorum, 1988), no.282; Webster, B (ed.), *The Acts of David II* (Regesta Regum Scottorum, 1982), no.292.

14   For examples at Ayr and Banff see Dickinson, *Aberdeen Records*, p.cxxiv.

15   For a list and discussion of surviving pre-1707 tolbooths see Stell, op.cit.

16   'The first year of burgh reform' was celebrated by the inscription on a bell of 1834 at Dunbar (No.24).

17   *Prison Inspectors' Reports, passim*; Cameron, *Prisons*, 92-123.

18   For municipal buildings of this period in Britain, with a list including Scottish examples, see Cunningham, C, *Victorian and Edwardian Town Halls* (1981).

19   See Postan, M *et al.* (eds.), *The Cambridge Economic History of Europe, 3* (1963), *passim*. For English towns see Platt, C, *The English Medieval Town* (1976); Reynolds, S, *An Introduction to the History of English Medieval Towns* (1977); Tittler, R, *Architecture and Power* (1991).

20   Mackenzie, *Burghs*, 78-84; Pryde, *Burghs, passim*; Pryde, *Kirkintilloch,* introduction.

21   Sixty-seven burghs were listed as members of the Convention of Royal Burghs in 1753 by Maitland (*Edinburgh*, 381-2). Auchtermuchty, Earlsferry, Falkland and Newburgh were exempted from attendance at parliament and the convention (Pryde, *Burghs*, nos. 51, 54, 62, 75).

22   'Setts of the Royal Burghs [1708]', in *SBRS Misc.*

23   Hannay, R K, *The Parliaments of Scotland* (1924), 275-8.

24   *Prison Directors' First Report*, 3.

25   Webster, H A, in Groome, *Ordnance Gazetteer*, 1745-8.

26   Cf. the Dundee 'pirlie pig', now in the McManus Art Gallery and

27   Museum, which was acquired for this purpose in 1602 (Beatts, J M, *The Municipal History of the Royal Burgh of Dundee* (1873), 56-7). The town council of Edinburgh met twice-weekly in the late 16th century, and fines for lateness or non-attendance ranged from 18d to 5s (*Edinburgh Extracts (1573-89)*, 371, 457).

27   For the Edinburgh mace of 1616-17 and other civic insignia, see *Edinburgh 1329-1929*, 64-75. Four officers with halberds attended the magistrates at courts held in Leith Tolbooth in the 16th century (ibid., 106). Halberds used for this purpose are displayed in Selkirk Court-house (No.77).

28   See Galt, J, *The Provost* (1822 and later eds.), chs.8 and 10. Several burgh punch-bowls are preserved, including a set of three Chinese porcelain bowls presented to Cupar town council in 1784 (fig. 4B).

29   Whetstone, op.cit.

30   Mackenzie, W M (ed.), *The Poems of William Dunbar* (revised ed., 1970), 81-3. In 1629 the sheriff of Berwickshire and bailies of Duns were ordered 'to mak the tolbuith of Dunse patent for ressaveing of prisounaris, otherwayes the shireff courtis to be removed to Grenelaw' (*RPC*, 2nd series, **3** (1629-30), 145). In the 1820s there was prolonged contention between Thurso and Wick (No.87) over the location of the sheriff courts of Caithness.

31   *BOEC*, **13** (1924), 8, 18, 26.

32   *APS*, **1** (1124-1423), 92*.

33   For the elaborate ceremonies when Montrose's head was 'very honorablie and with all dew respectis takin doun', including the erection of a wall-head platform for trumpeters, see *BOEC*, **1** (1908), 31-46. For Argyll, see ibid., **5** (1912), 116; Willcock, J, *The Great Marquess* (1903), 331.

34   Metcalfe, *Paisley*, 318.

35   Edinburgh held the Scottish standard ell, Lanark the stone weight, and Linlithgow and Stirling the firlot and pint for dry and liquid measure. In Aberdeen and Edinburgh purpose-built weigh-houses were erected in the 17th century. The Commissioners are indebted to Dr A D C Simpson, Royal Museum of Scotland, for information on weights and measures.

36   A 15th-century ell-wand with chain attached is preserved in Huntly House Museum. Payment was made at Edinburgh in 1566 to a mason 'to hing (hang) the yrne elwand in the nether Tolobuith' (Adam, R (ed.), *Edinburgh Burgh Accounts* (1899), **2**, 236). In 1663 it was ordained that all burghs should have a standard foot-measure for the use of building-craftsmen, 'hung at their tolbuith doors or upon their mercat croces' (*APS*, **7** (1661-9), 488).

37   Robert Adam prepared designs for a separate Town and County Record Office in Aberdeen in 1772 (drawings in Soane Museum, copies in NMRS). It was built at the E end of Castle Street, to a different design, in 1779, but has since been demolished.

38   Treasurer's accounts, quoted in *Transactions of the Hawick Archaeological Society*, **6** (1867), 33.

39   The arcaded ground storey of the medieval town hall in Amsterdam (burnt down in 1652) was recorded in Pieter Saenredam's painting based on his drawings of 1641 (Nash, J M, *The Age of Rembrandt and Vermeer* (1972), pl.16).

40   Ellon Tolbooth, which was demolished about 1830, included a salmon-store (Mair, T, *Records of the Parish of Ellon* (1876), 153).

41   Thomson, *Dundee*, 175, 351.

42   All prices are here quoted in sterling.

43   Mackenzie, *Burghs*, 160-85.

44   Robertson, J, *The Book of Bon-Accord* (1839), 173-5.

45   Direct labour services, or money in lieu, were required at Aberdeen in 1407 (Dickinson, *Aberdeen Records*, 238). Carriage of stone from the quarry by all inhabitants who owned horses was required at Linlithgow (No.55) in 1668 and at Elgin in 1713 (*Elgin Records*, **1**, 388).

46   Hannay, R K and Watson, G P H, 'The Building of the Parliament House', in *BOEC*, **13** (1924), 1-78.

47   Dundee TCM (Dundee City Archive and Record centre), 15 January 1732.

48   'The Old City Debt', in Robertson, D and Wood, M, *Castle and Town* (1928), 221-56.

49   Mactaggart, C, *Life In Campbeltown In The Eighteenth century* (1923), 16.

50   Subscription-paper of 1741-2 in Haddington burgh records (SRO, B 30/21/105).

51   Taylor, L B, *Aberdeen Council Letters*, **1** (1552-1633), 141.

52   Act 59 George III, c.61.

53   Cameron, *Prisons, passim*; *Prison Directors' First Report*, 2-19.

54   Dickinson, *Aberdeen Records*, pp.cxxxix, 22.

55   *APS*, **4** (1593-1625), 141.

56   Glasgow Bridewell, as enlarged in 1823-4, was praised for its exceptional management (*Prison Inspectors' First Report*, 53-4, and *passim*). For a bridewell of 1789, see Jedburgh (No.41).

57   *APS*, **10** (1696-1701), 66.

58   Wick TCM, 17 April 1820. Cf. Dingwall (No.21, n.12).

59   *Geog. Coll.*, **3**, 199-200.

60   *Edinburgh Extracts (1557-71)*, 259. See Lynch, M, *Edinburgh and the Reformation* (1981), 192 and *passim*.

61   Cameron, *Prisons*, 34-7.

62   Lord Fountainhall, quoted in *BOEC*, **16** (1928), 135.

63   McDowall, W, *History of the Burgh of Dumfries* (1867), 485-6.

64 *Dictionary of National Biography*, s.v. 'Barclay, Robert', 'Jaffray, Alexander'.

65 John Swinton, 'ane fanatik persone and ane quaker', was warded in Edinburgh Tolbooth in 1660 until his trial for high treason (as one of the Cromwellian Commissioners for Justice), when he was sentenced to forfeiture and imprisonment in Edinburgh Castle (*BOEC*, **16** (1928), 58).

66 *The Heart of Midlothian*, note 1, quoting a petition from Scott's relatives, who asked for him to be transferred to Jedburgh where he could be kept away from other Quakers (Acts of Privy Council, 20 June 1665, 5 July 1666).

67 Cameron, *Prisons*, 24-6. At Edinburgh Tolbooth in the 1660s several men were detained for illegal pricking, or bringing false accusations of witchcraft (e.g. *BOEC*, **5** (1912), 97, 99).

68 E.g. Bessie Brabboner, hanged at Edinburgh in 1663 (ibid., 107). Helen Walker and her younger sister Isabella, of Irongray near Dumfries, were the models for Jeannie and Effie Deans (*The Heart of Midlothian*, introduction).

69 Chambers, *Reekiana*, 154-72.

70 In 1667 William Douglas almost escaped from Edinburgh Tolbooth, 'having cutt the stenchers (bars) of the windows with aqua fortis' (*BOEC*, **5** (1912), 135).

71 Dickinson, W C (ed.), *John Knox's History of the Reformation in Scotland* (1949), **1**, 357-8; *A Diurnal of Remarkable Occurrents* (Bannatyne Club, 1833), 283-5; Lynch, op.cit., 94-5.

72 Thomson, *Dundee*, 176-7.

73 *The Heart of Midlothian*, note 3.

74 Chambers, *Reekiana*, 158-9.

75 Dickinson, *Aberdeen Records*, p.cxxxix; Metcalfe, *Paisley*, 329.

76 The gad from Edinburgh Tolbooth is preserved in the Royal Museum of Scotland, as are the stocks which served a similar purpose at Canongate Tolbooth.

77 *Guy Mannering*, chapter 28.

78 Neild, *Prisons*, 474; Cameron, *Prisons*, 64.

79 For a concise survey of major examples, see Pevsner, N, *A History of Building Types* (1976), 27-62.

80 Letter from Lord Auchinleck to James Boswell, 8 October 1763, quoting a contract with the burgomasters of Amsterdam which was in his own possession (Pottle, F A (ed.), *Boswell in Holland, 1763-1764* (1952), 51-3). But the use of Scottish stone has been questioned (Fremantle, K, *The Baroque Town Hall of Amsterdam* (1959), 37-8).

81 Zeegers, G and Visser, I, *Kijk op Stadhuizen* (1981), 114.

82 Cf. the *Stadthuis* at Montfoort, Utrecht province (ibid., 117).

83 Guildry buildings were erected at Arbroath (No.4) in 1780, and at Dunfermline (appendix, no.7), to a design by Archibald Elliot, in 1807-11.

84 For this arrangement see the 16th-century plan of St Andrews (*supra*, fig.206C). The tron at Irvine appears in pre-demolition views of the town-house. An Edinburgh tron-beam of 1642 is preserved in Huntly House Museum, and other 17th-century examples survive from Alloa (Smith Institute, Stirling) and Jedburgh (Jedburgh Castle Museum). For surviving weights see A D C Simpson in *Northern Studies*, **29** (1992), 62-81.

85 The early-14th-century locations of the tolbooths at Aberdeen (No.1) and Dundee (appendix, no.6) were close to the harbours.

86 Brown, *Early Travellers*, 214.

87 Cameron, *Prisons*, 66.

88 Ruined church towers were also adapted for lock-ups, as at Lasswade and Penicuik (appendix, no.100, 104).

89 Cf. the difficulties experienced at Inveraray Castle in the 1750s (Lindsay and Cosh, *Inveraray*, 106-19).

90 For individual architects see Colvin, *Architects*, *passim*. The principal exceptions are James Gibbs, Robert Mylne (who unified the show-front of Inveraray with arcades, but did not alter the town-house itself) and W H Playfair.

91 Ibid., 35-45 .

92 Early engravings show a spire based on that of Louth Parish Church (Lincolnshire), which Graham was to use in 1832 as the model for Montrose Steeple.

93 See Walker, F, 'National Romanticism and the Architecture of the City', in Gordon, G (ed.), *Perspectives of the Scottish City* (1985), 125-59.

94 No legislation on this subject has been identified.

95 E.g. Delft, where de Keyser's town hall of 1620 encases a medieval tower (Zeegers and Visser, op.cit., 74).

96 Hay, G, *The Architecture of Scottish Post-Reformation Churches, 1560-1843* (1957), 170-7.

97 Ibid., 172.

98 *Cast. and Dom. Arch.*, **4**, 509.

99 Hay, op.cit., 174-7.

100 Adam visited St Martin's in the year of its completion, and subscribed to the first (1728) edition of Gibbs's *Book of Architecture* (Fleming, J, *Robert Adam and his Circle* (1962), 23; Friedman, T, *James Gibbs* (1984), 262).

101 Hay, op.cit., 167-70.

102 Loc. cit., *supra* n.31.

103 Dickinson, W C, *The Sheriff Court Book of Fife, 1515-1562* (SHS, 1928), pp.xx, 37, 56; Paterson, W, *History of the Counties of Ayr and Wigton*, **3** (1866), 375.

104 *Vitruvius Scoticus*, pl.104.

105 *BOEC*, **11** (1922), 117; Hannay, R K, *The College of Justice* (1933), 39-41; *Edinburgh Extracts, passim*.

106 In some burghs the assembly-rooms were separate from the town-house. For the various premises occupied in Edinburgh between 1710 and the opening of the present Assembly-rooms in George Street in 1787, see *BOEC*, **19** (1933), 31-91.

107 McCarter, W, *Ayrshire* (1832), 146-7.

108 Perth TCM, 14 September 1696.

109 Ibid., 21 December 1696.

110 Ibid., 11 October 1697.

111 Aberdeen TCM, 20 September, 15 November 1750.

112 Ibid., 3 October 1751.

113 Ibid., 3 October 1751, 26 May 1755; Guildry Accounts 1757-8.

114 Dr Johnson was made a freeman of Aberdeen in this room in 1773. Boswell commented 'It was striking to hear them all drinking 'Dr Johnson! Dr Johnson!' in the town-hall of Aberdeen' (Chapman, *Johnson and Boswell*, 16, 216).

115 TCM 1 September 1756; Guildry Accounts 1757-8. The painting is reproduced in Holloway, J, *Patrons and Painters: Art in Scotland 1650-1760* (1989), fig.73.

116 TCM 17 November 1755.

117 *Lanark Extracts*, 17. For the use of rushes and herbs over stone-flagged floors, see Thornton, P, *Seventeenth-century Interior Decoration in England, France and Holland* (1979), 143.

118 *Edinburgh Extracts (1701-18)*, 79.

119 *Glasgow Extracts (1760-80)*, 270.

120 E.g. *Edinburgh Extracts (1573-89)*, 117, 122; *Prison Inspectors' Reports, passim*.

120 *Glasgow Extracts (1739-59)*, 121.

121 Godsman, J, *Glass, Aberdeenshire, the story of a parish* (1970), 83.

122 *Elgin Records*, **1**, 428-9. Knappell wood was split oak, of a size smaller than wainscot.

123 Montrose TCM, 17 April 1765.

124 Ibid., 4 March 1767.

125 Allen, C, *Old Stirling Clockmakers* (1990), 28.

126 *Supra*, n.27; *Edinburgh Extracts (1589-1603)*, 210-11.

127 Ibid. *(1665-80)*, 314.

128 The town council of Edinburgh paid for the equestrian statue of Charles II that was erected in Parliament Square in 1685 (*BOEC*, **17** (1930), 82-90). The mounted bronze figure of William III, formerly placed in front of the town hall of Glasgow and now in Cathedral Square, was presented to the burgh in 1734 by James McRae, a former governor of Madras (Eyre-Todd, G, *History of Glasgow*, **3** (1934), 161-3).

129 Gilbert, C, *English Vernacular Furniture, 1750-90* (1991), figs.297, 303.

130 This panel is now displayed in the town hall (*Inventory of Fife, etc.*, No.480).

131 *Inventory of Edinburgh*, No.168.

132 *BOEC*, **14** (1925), 161. The inscription was 'in large gilt letters on a black-board', and disappeared some years before 1857.

133 View by James Gordon of Rothiemay (*BOEC*, **13** (1924), frontispiece); *PSAS*, **53** (1918-19), 30-3.

134 *Edinburgh Extracts (1665-80)*, 234.

135 This lintel is now displayed in Perth Museum.

136 An almost identical inscription is painted above the magistrates' bench at Much Wenlock, Shropshire (Tittler, R, *Architecture and Power* (1991), pl.12).

137 *BOEC*, **1** (1908), 32-3.

138 See the series of articles by F C Eeles and R W M Clouston in *PSAS*, vols. **82-124**, and Clouston, 'Ayrshire Bells'.

139 Particularly after the Disruption of 1843, the exclusive right of the established church to have its services marked by town bells was challenged. The case at Peebles (No.69) in 1873-5 went to the House of Lords.

140 For a detailed study of bells and bell-founding in the Netherlands, see Lehr, A, *Van Paardebel Tot Speelklok*, (1971).

141 Four of these bells are displayed in Huntly House Museum.

142 The Irvine bell, probably by Albert Daniel Gely, was recast and again broke when being rung for Queen Victoria's Diamond Jubilee in 1897 (Clouston, 'Ayrshire Bells', 227).

143 Extracts from the council minutes of several burghs are included in Smith, J, *Old Scottish Clockmakers* (2nd ed., 1921).

1 Aberdeen

1 Gordon, J, *A Description of Both Touns of Aberdeen* (Spalding Club, 1842), 45; Anderson, P J (ed.), *Charters ... of the Royal Burgh of Aberdeen, MCLXXI-MDCCCIV* (1890), no.15. A contemporary note on the seal-tag of the original charter in Aberdeen City Archives gives the dimensions as 26.5m by 12.8m.

2 View by James Gordon of Rothiemay, 1661, reproduced in Gordon, op.cit (*supra*, fig.25).

3 Building-contract registered in TCM 6 March 1616 (*Aberdeen Extracts (1570-1625)*, 338-44).

4 Part of the N wall is also visible from the atrium of the adjacent Sheriff Court.

5 *Extracts (1570-1625)*, 338-40.

6 Ibid., 339. A special allowance of aquavitae and ale was made to the

workmen who cleaned out the 'sink' (cess-pit) in 1704 (Dean of Guild Accounts).

7 See plans by John Smith, 1820 (originals in Aberdeen Art Gallery, copies in NMRS); OS 1:500 plan, 1852 (Aberdeenshire sheet 75.11.14).

8 Views of Castle Street by Robert Seaton (1806) and Hugh Irvine (1812). In 1705 payment was made to the masons 'for sorteing the old hewen work' (Dean of Guild Accounts). A similar retention of early features is seen in the continuation of the string-course along the N part of the E wall, but as with the parapet it was not repeated on the new N wall.

9 On the repairs required see a report by John Smith in TCM, 10 May 1839. Blaikie's name and the date 1841 appear on the lead roof of the adjacent Clydesdale (formerly North of Scotland) Bank.

10 *Extracts (1570-1625)*, 357.

11 Payment was made in 1704 for 56 steps to the stair (Dean of Guild Accounts).

12 Work on the tolbooth door and stair was recorded in 1559-60 (Treasurer's Accounts), and new doors, including that of the prison, were made in 1596-7 (Dean of Guild Accounts).

13 *Extracts (1570-1625)*, 339.

14 The nature of the access 'to gang doun to the lauch vault' is obscure, and there may be an omission in the contract as recorded in TCM, 6 March 1616. (The published text (ibid.) is an accurate transcript. In the following section, however, the published 'crann' is an error for 'croun').

15 Ibid., 338-9. Similar work survives behind wall-facings to the W, where two of the arches were preserved until 1871 as recesses in the court-room. Fragments from the arcade were then incorporated in a summer-house in Duthie Park (record-sheet in NMRS). The central arch was preserved until 1820 as an entrance to the court-room, and the outer arches were infilled in rubble whose plaster covering bears the incised date '1764'. A painted colour-scheme of yellow and white, separated by a black band, was applied at this period to the vestibule and the infill of the outer arches.

16 Douglas, F, *Description of the East Coast of Scotland* (1782), 77; Kennedy, W, *Annals of Aberdeen* (1818), **1**, 404-5. In 1698 the jailer's house was on the S side of Castle Street (Kennedy, W, manuscript Index of Council Register, s.v. 'prison').

17 Kennedy, *Annals*, **1**, 404-5; Douglas, loc.cit.

18 *PSAS*, **94** (1960-1), 284-5. An earlier recasting was carried out in London in 1732-3 (Dean of Guild Accounts).

19 *Extracts (1398-1570)*, 149-50; *(1570-1625), 341*.

20 TCM 25 January 1597/8; *Extracts (1570-1625)*, 158; Dean of Guild Accounts, 1733-4; *Cast. and Dom. Arch.*, **5**, fig.1481 on p.366.

21 Dickinson, *Aberdeen Records*, pp.cxxiv, 13, 15, 17. Gordon stated in 1661 that 'the ruins of the old tolbooth is to be seen at the posterne gate of the Laird of Pittfoddells hous opening towards the shore' (op.cit., 9).

22 *Exchequer Rolls*, **1** (1264-1359), 547. This account covered the period 1348-58.

23 Dickinson, *Aberdeen Records*, pp.cxxiii-v, 22, 238.

24 *Extracts (1398-1570)*, 77, 281, 366-7; Treasurer's Accounts.

25 *Extracts (1570-1625)*, 153, 157; Treasurer's Accounts. The lean-to roof of this structure appears to be shown in Gordon's view.

26 *Extracts (1570-1625)*, 306, 321, 334-5, 338-44.

27 Taylor, L B (ed.), *Aberdeen Council Letters*, **1** (1552-1633), 141-2. The council claimed that 'for the use of our awin inhabitantis, the tolbuith itselff wes alreddie a sufficient wardhous'.

28 *Extracts (1570-1625)*, 342, 358-9, 376, 379; *(1625-43)*, 24-6; Mylne, *Master Masons*, 113.

29 Treasurer's Accounts, 1627-8.

30 Taylor, op.cit., **5** (1670-5), 220-6. For subsequent repairs see *Extracts (1643-1747)*, 285, and *Geog.Coll.*, **3**, 90.

31 Kennedy, *Annals*, **1**, 404; Dean of Guild Accounts, 1704-6. Two letters were subsequently received from Smith.

32 Dean of Guild Accounts, 1704-6 (the amount stated by Kennedy, loc.cit., is the *income* for the first year). The amount paid was about two-thirds of the contract-price of Dumfries Mid steeple (No.23).

33 TCM 5 and 7 November, 26 December 1729, 11 April, 13 and 20 June, 14 September 1730; Dean of Guild Accounts, 1729-33. A 'section of the principal room in the new worke' by William Crystall, who was paid in 1731-2 'for boxing the new room' (drawing in Aberdeen City Archives), shows that the room was panelled throughout, with a segmental-headed overmantel. Adam's plan was for an extension of 9.1m (TCM 5 November 1729), but the OS plan of 1852 shows the W block as 6.1m wide, and a little deeper than the main block.

34 TCM 7 March 1750 and 1750-5, *passim*; Kennedy, *Annals*, **1**, 406; watercolour by A D Longmuir, 1871, in Aberdeen City Archives.

35 TCM 27 February 1756; views by Irvine and Seaton, and on Aberdeen Assurance Co. certificate dated 1805 (Aberdeen City Archives, 17/A/4).

36 TCM 30 January 1734; Dean of Guild Accounts, 1734-5. From 1694 this area had been used by the sheriff-clerk (information from Miss J Cripps).

37 Smith drawings in Aberdeen Art Gallery (copies in NMRS); engraving of Castle Street, c.1850, by J Allen; elevations in drawings by Archibald Simpson, c.1839, and Peddie and Kinnear, 1865-7 (copies in NMRS, ABD/162/7 and 448/1-3).

38 TCM 3 June 1819, 29 September 1824, 7 July 1825, 5 July 1831; *Prison Inspectors' First Report*, 22-5.

39 Simpson drawings in possession of Clydesdale Bank (copies in NMRS, ABD/162); TCM 10 May 1839.

40 Drawings of preliminary schemes in possession of Dick, Peddie and Mackay, Edinburgh (copies in NMRS, ABD/448); Cunningham, C, *Victorian and Edwardian Town Halls* (1981*)*, fig.44 on p.113; Aberdeen City Archives, minutes of Aberdeen County and Municipal Buildings Commissioners, 1866-73, *passim*; papers on County and Municipal Buildings, especially nos.65-74, 83.

2 Airdrie

1 OS 1:500 plan, Lanarkshire sheet 8.10.1 (1858-61); 'Its inhabitants', *The Book of Airdrie* (n.d.), 59.

2 Knox, J, *Airdrie, a historical sketch* (1921), 65; *Prison Inspectors' Third Report* , 72-3. The town-house was used for burgh courts until the erection of a new court-house in 1887 (Knox, loc.cit.; Russell, J D, *The Airdrie Court House* (1915), 7).

3 TCM 28 June 1821, 9 April 1822.

4 TCM 27 May 1824 to 8 March 1825, *passim*; MacArthur, J, *New Monkland Parish* (1890), 223-4.

5 TCM 15 and 22 March, 6 April, 3 and 23 June 1825, 14 March, 15 August, 12 December 1826; MacArthur, op.cit., 224.

6 TCM 22 March 1825, 4 December 1827, 28 January 1828; *The Book of Airdrie*, 61-3.

3 Anstruther Wester

1 *Inventory of Fife, etc.*, No.38. The town hall is believed to occupy the site of the parsonage-house (Gourlay, G, *Anstruther* (1888), 8).

2 This and other minor work was carried out by the St Andrews architect Charles Anderson (TCM 23 May and 26 June 1911).

3 The church was formerly dedicated to St Nicholas. In the 1970s it was converted for use as the Hew Scott Hall of St Adrian's Church.

4 TCM 24 March 1742, 12 January, 12 February, 21 June 1827.

5 *Stat.Acct.*, **3**, 86.

6 TCM 14 October 1741, 17 September 1794; Stevenson, S, *Anstruther* (1989), 72.

7 TCM 19 July 1798, 15 September 1812; Stevenson, op.cit., 73.

8 Name Book, Fife No.82, p.63; Stevenson, loc.cit.

4 Arbroath

1 Hay, G, *History of Arbroath* (1876), 91, 163.

2 Ibid., 306, 342-3, and frontispiece; Carragher, P C, *The Town House of the Royal Burgh of Arbroath* (1907), 4-5.

3 TCM 2 July 1807, 28 April 1808; Hay, op.cit., 365-6; Carragher, op.cit., 5-6, 11-12. The mason-contractor was John Croal (TCM 20 July 1809).

4 *Prison Inspectors' First Report*, 26-7; *Eighth Report*, 37.

5 TCM 8 March, 16 May, 25 July 1844; Hay, op.cit., 365-6; Carragher, op.cit., 13, 18.

6 TCM 12 and 22 June 1820; Carragher, op.cit., 12, 21; Hay, op.cit., 366. Wood's plan (1822) shows the bridge at the W end of the N wall.

7 TCM 8 March 1844; Carragher, op.cit., 18-19, 23.

8 TCM 28 June 1814, 18 March 1819; Carragher, op.cit., 12, 27, 30.

9 Carragher, op.cit., 21.

5 Auchtermuchty

1 *RMS*, **3** (1513-46), no.168.

2 TCM 3 November 1727, 12 May, 27 September 1728, 19 September 1729.

3 TCM 23 March 1733 (reference to 'houses near the old tolbooth').

4 Leighton, *Fife*, 213.

5 Shown on a plan dated 1946 in NMRS (FID/45/1-2).

6 *Prison Inspectors' Second Report* (1837), 81; Leighton, loc.cit.

7 TCM 3 November 1727, 12 May 1728. The earlier repair was by George Scott of Canongate, Edinburgh, and that of 1841 by Robert Clark, Newburgh.

8 TCM 12 May 1728, 4 June 1740.

6 Ayr

1 Strawhorn, J, *The History of Ayr* (1989), 26, 39-40; Pagan, J H, *Annals of Ayr in the Olden Time* (1897), 52-5; Pryde, G S (ed.), *Ayr Burgh Accounts, 1534-1624* (SHS, 1937), 138-42, 261-4, and *passim*. Payment of 12s. was made in 1574-5 for a coat-of-arms on a glass window, and of £5 to James Scott in 1577-8 for painting a coat-of-arms (ibid., 138, 142).

2 Paterson, J, *History of the Counties of Ayr and Wigton* (1863), **1**, 59-60. See Carrick, J C, *The Tower of S. John the Baptist at Ayr* (1913), 104-5, for the re-use of this masonry in Racecourse Road after 1825.

3 Paterson, op.cit., 61-4; Strawhorn, op.cit., 87-8; TCM 1830-2, *passim*; architect's drawings in Carnegie Library, Ayr (copies in NMRS).

4 McCarter, W, *Ayrshire* (1832); Bryden, R, *Etchings of Auld Ayr*; Morris, J A, *The Brig of Ayr* (1912), frontispiece; plans, 1754, in Carnegie Library, Ayr; drawings of steeple by Robert Adam, 1785, ibid. and in Soane Museum (copies in NMRS); report on Ayr Jail by James Paterson, 1812, in SRO, GD 142/47 (printed in Anon., *Reminiscences of Auld Ayr* (1907), 418-26).

5 TCM 2 March 1814, 26 April, 18 October 1815.

6 Ibid., 2 March 1814, 26 April 1815; Ayr, County Buildings, CO3/7/1, 5 December 1814, 24 April 1815. Hamilton received £65 12s for his rejected designs, which survive (ibid., 12 May 1815; copies of drawings in NMRS). Advice was also sought, without success, from Thomas Harrison of Chester (ibid., 5 December 1814, quoting letter with full specification of rooms required; 24 April 1815).

7 SRO, GD 142/78/10 (intimation for laying foundation-stone, 23 April 1818); CO3/7/6, 23 October 1817 (estimate of £20,814 by J McCall, mason); CO3/7, *passim*; McCarter, op.cit., 136-44; *NSA*, **5** (Ayrshire), 22-3.

8 CO3/7/1, 25 August 1812; TCM, 5 December 1814, 26 April 1815, 16 September 1818; Shaw, [Shaw,] J E, *Ayrshire 1745-1950* (1953) 93-4. The tolbooth was not demolished soon enough for this offer to become effective.

9 CO3/7/14, agreement to build wings, 1820.

10 CO3/7/6, 23 October 1817, 25 July 1818; CO3/7/8, 28 October 1820.

11 In 1820 Wallace supplied a model of a slightly cheaper design for the staircase, with a 'direct approach', but the original spiral design was retained (CO3/7/8, 30 June, 7 July, 5 September 1820).

12 TCM and Hall Committee Minutes, 1878-81, 1901-3, *passim*; plans in Carnegie Library (copies in NMRS); schedule of measurements, 1901 (NMRS, MS 237).

13 Correspondence in Burgh Letter-book, 1827-8. Hamilton had examined specimens from three quarries and 'gave decided preference to Cullaloe both for its beauty and for its durability for the great weight of the building' (TCM 30 January 1828).

14 TCM 9 May 1827. On 18 November 1829 the town council approved Hamilton's amended design for the steeple, 'giving an additional elevation ... which he stated would add greatly to the beauty and grandeur of the structure'.

15 Hamilton's working-drawings of July 1827 and his perspective-drawing of the same year (Carnegie Library, Ayr; copies in NMRS) show the lions replaced eagles, and that the corbelled cornice was also a late alteration. For the possible derivation of the lions and foliage-ornament from etchings of 1803 by C H Tatham, see Rock, J, *Thomas Hamilton, Architect, 1784-1858* (1984), 28, 32, and pl.14.

16 TCM 3 February, 9 June, 1 December 1836; Burgh Letter-book, 28 and 30 January 1836.

17 TCM, *passim*; McCarter, W, *Ayrshire*, 145-7; *NSA*, **5** (Ayrshire), 23-4.

18 Clouston, 'Ayrshire Bells', 210-11. Thomas Mears was paid £149 for the large bell, whose mountings were the subject of much discussion (Burgh Accounts, 1830-1; TCM 1831, *passim*).

19 TCM 22 May 1824, 19 January, 2 February, 2 and 9 March 1825. For Hamilton's local connection, through his design of the Burns Monument at Alloway, see Fisher, I, 'Thomas Hamilton of Edinburgh, 1784-1858' (Oxford University BA thesis, 1965; copy in NMRS).

20 TCM 21 February, 14 and 28 March, 1 December 1827, 23, 24 and 30 January, 20 February, 14 and 26 March 1828, 17 November 1830; Burgh Accounts 1827-8, 1831-2.

7 Banff

1 *NSA*, **13**, 34-5.

2 TCM 11 August 1797.

3 TCM 13 February 1767. Forty guineas were paid for this clock, and it was specified that the W face should have a copper dial, but that the S and E faces should have wooden dials and hour-hands only (ibid.). The diameter of the bell corresponds exactly to the 30 inches specified in 'Mr Adam's' plan of the steeple (ibid.).

4 The bailies were commanded 'til big thare tolbuth incontinent, and that thai spend thair commone gude apone the samyn' (*Acts of the Lords of Council*, **3** (1501-3), 85). For later references see Cramond, W, *The Annals of Banff* (1891-3), **1**, 18, 379.

5 *RCRBS 1(677-1711)*, 355.

6 TCM 15 March, 13 July, 6 December 1762, 20 December 1763, 13 February 1767.

7 TCM 13 February, 2 March 1767 (including payment to John Marr, 4 August 1763, 'for drawing plans'); Cramond, op.cit., **1**, 311n. For Marr's work under John Adam's direction at Cullen House, and his later career at Inveraray, see Lindsay and Cosh, *Inveraray*, 390 n.13, 425.

8 Cramond, loc.cit.

9 TCM 29 September 1794, 29 August 1795, 19 January, 27 February, 3 and 8 March 1796, 16 March 1797 (*sic* for ?1796), 2

July, 11 and 22 August 1797, 30 January, 28 February 1798, 9 January 1799. For the mason contractors, John Rhind and James Robertson, see also Barclay, W, *The Schools and Schoolmasters of Banffshire* (1925), 16-17.

8 Beith

1 *NSA*, **5** (Ayrshire), 601-2; *Prison Inspectors' Third Report*, 50.

2 Anon., *The Book of Beith* (1933), 43-4.

3 Clouston, 'Ayrshire Bells', 216.

4 *NSA*, **5** (Ayrshire), 601.

9 Brechin

1 TCM 13 December 1854, 14 February, 11 April, 28 June 1855, 9 January, 13 February 1856.

2 Thoms, D B, *The Council of Brechin* (1977), 10-11, 30-1, 44-5, 97, 140, 143-4; Black, D D, *The History of Brechin to 1864* (2nd ed., 1867), 45, 112; *SBRS Misc.*, 101; TCM 7 April 1788, 28 January 1789.

3 Thoms, op.cit., 144; TCM 30 March, 25 May 1789, 20 January 1790.

4 Thoms, loc.cit.; Black, op.cit., 164-5; TCM 28 January, 9 and 23 February, 25 May 1789, 20 January, 9 September 1790.

5 TCM 20 November 1789; Gurney, *Prisons*, 34-5; *Prison Inspectors' First Report*, 35-7; *Second Report*, 26-7; *Third Report*, 95; *Ninth Report*, 31; *NSA*, **11**, 133; Black, op.cit., 281.

10 Campbeltown

1 *Inventory of Argyll*, **1**, No.323.

2 TCM 23 June 1778; Lindsay and Cosh, *Inveraray*, 408.

3 TCM 28 June 1865. For Douglas, see *Inventory of Argyll*, **7**, pp.194, 548.

4 An elevation-drawing dated 25 June 1788 (perhaps in error for 1778) shows a tall steeple whose lower section is identical with the existing one, but whose upper stages are more elongated and with a two-stage spire. This may be a preliminary design by Brown (copy in NMRS, AGD/76/2).

5 Quarterly, 1st, a castle triple-towered; 2nd, gyronny of eight; 3rd, a galley, sail furled; 4th, a fret. The motto is: IGNAVIS PRECIBUS FORTUNA REPUGNAT ('Fortune opposes idle prayers').

6 OS town plan. In 1843 the building contained 'besides the town-council chambers, a large hall, in which the courts are held' (*NSA*, **7** (Argyll), 465).

7 TCM 4 August 1779.

8 MacTaggart, C, *Life in Campbeltown in the 18th Century* (n.d., c.1923), 15.

9 Ibid.

10 TCM 4 November 1757, 10 January 1759.

11 Argyll and Bute District Council Archives, Commissioners of Supply Minutes, 18 May 1758.

12 TCM 13 July 1767. The application concluded 'as you're all masons and have no objection to any innocent amusements, its hoped you'll comply with the above request'.

13 TCM 23 June 1778, 4 August 1779.

14 Municipal Corporations Report, quoted in Teignmouth, Lord, *Sketches of the Coasts and Islands of Scotland, and of the Isle of Man* (1836), **2**, 377-8; *Prison Inspectors' Third Report* (1838), 64.

15 *Prison Inspectors' Ninth Report* (1844), 22-3; Name Book, Argyll No.78, p.111.

16 TCM 28 June 1865; Burgh Accounts. The Glasgow firm of Galbraith and Winton supplied a chimneypiece of Kintyre marble for Inveraray Castle in 1871 (Lindsay and Cosh, *Inveraray*, 415).

11 Canongate

1 *Inventory of Edinburgh*, No.105.

2 View of Edinburgh by James Gordon of Rothiemay. Possibly as a result of this demolition, repairs to the tolbooth were required in 1690, 'the gavill (gable) thereof being lately fallen' (*Edinburgh Extracts (1689-1701)*, 48).

3 *Extracts (1665-80)*, 318.

4 Plans dated 1875 and 1908 in NMRS; *Edinburgh Evening News*, 18 and 24 September 1953, 8 July 1954.

5 *Supra*, n.2.

6 A pre-1871 photograph in NMRS (ED/7045) shows this lintel above a doorway (subsequently contracted to a window) at the E end of the ground floor of the main block. Morham replaced this opening by a wider archway.

7 Photographs in NMRS.

8 An old clock from the 'High Steeple' was installed in the Canongate Steeple in 1726, and was repaired in 1762 (Edinburgh TCM, 20 June 1726, 8 July 1765). Early photographs show the painted dates 1855 and 1871. Storers' *Views* (1820) shows straight timber supports for the platform, but Shepherd's *Modern Athens* (1829) shows curved metal ones of the existing type.

9 Smith, J A, 'Notice of the shingled roof of the tower of the Canongate Tolbooth, Edinburgh', in *PSAS*, **9** (1870-2), 162-7. One of the shingles is displayed in Huntly House Museum.

10 The gable is shown, without the cap-house, in Gordon of Rothiemay's view of 1647.

11 Excavation report by N Holmes in 'Medieval Archaeology Research Group Newsletter, November 1988'.

12 *Extracts (1689-1701)*, 232.

13 Cowan, I B and Easson, D E, *Medieval Religious Houses Scotland* (2nd ed., 1976), 90; Pryde, *Burghs*, nos.84, 239.

14 *RMS*, **2** (1424-1513), no.1329; Wood, M (ed.), *Book of Records of the Ancient Privileges of the Canongate* (SRS, 1955), 332-7.

15 Smith, op.cit., 165; *RPC*, 1st series, **4** (1585-92), 550.

16 *RMS*, **9** (1634-51), no.929; *Edinburgh 1329-1929*, 222-4; *Inventory of Edinburgh*, pp.liii-iv.

17 *Extracts (1665-80)*, 294, 318, 347; ibid. *(1681-9)*, 20, 118; ibid. *(1689-1701)*, 10, 44, 48, 162, 232.

18 Ibid. *(1689-1701)*, 232.

19 *Prison Inspectors' Second Report*, 126-7; *Eighth Report*, 77-8; *NSA*, **1**, 720.

12 Ceres

1 *RMS*, **7** (1609-20), no.2111.

13 Clackmannan

1 *Inventory of Fife, etc.*, No.587.

2 *APS*, **3** (1567-92), 583. The building was to be paid for by an assessment of £284 on the whole sheriffdom of Clackmannan (ibid.).

3 Gordon, T C, *The History of Clackmannan* (1936), 82, 192. The bell has been removed, and the present clock has an electric mechanism.

4 *Stat. Acct.*, **14**, 608; Gordon, op.cit., 170.

5 *PSAS*, **23** (1888-9), 160; *Inventory of Fife, etc.*, No.612; Watson, W J, *The Celtic Place-names of Scotland* (1926), 103.

14 Coupar Angus

1 *Stat. Acct.*, **17**, 5; *RMS*, **6** (1593-1608), no.2002. The date 1767 is given in *NSA*, **10**, 1149, which states that the steeple was built by local subscription.

2 *Prison Inspectors' Second Report*, 75-6; *NSA*, **10**, 1149; Name Book, Perthshire No.18, p.37. J M Wilson (*The Imperial Gazetteer of Scotland* (n.d.), **1**, 344), refers to 'a town-house and prison with a steeple' where courts were held. No other early sources refer to a separate court-house.

3 *Prison Inspector's Second Report*, 75-6.

4 *PSAS*, **122** (1992), 470-1.

15 Crail

1 TCM 31 October, 20 November 1598, quoted in Beveridge, E, *The Churchyard Memorials of Crail* (1893), 269-70. The specified internal dimensions of 15.2m by 5.5m correspond closely with those of the present building, but it was claimed in 1814 that the town council was 'enlarging the site' of the tolbooth (TCM 16 June 1814). The suggested date of 1517 (Rogers, C (ed.), *Register of the Collegiate Church of Crail* (Grampian Club, 1877), 26) is based on the record of a meeting held in the tolbooth in that year, but a tolbooth already existed in 1506 (Conolly, *Fifiana*, 124).

2 *RCRBS (1597-1614)*, 239.

3 This carving, in relief within a moulded surround, shows the device of the burgh as on the burgh seal: a galley with a pennon on the masthead and a crescent moon with six stars. Four figures are shown aboard the vessel. The date, now much abraded, is at the top, and at the bottom there is the name CRAIL.

4 TCM 8 and 10 April 1776.

5 TCM 15 February, 21 July 1811, 31 December 1813, 11 March, 16 June 1814, 27 September 1815.

6 TCM 23 May, 6 and 16 June, 28 September, 7 November 1814. The agreement of 7 November stipulated that doors and windows in 'the back gavel' should be blocked.

7 Letter from J Hale, architect in St Andrews, to the town council, 2 March 1866 (St Andrews University Library, MS B10/14/630/1); TCM 20 December 1865, 18 March 1866.

8 TCM 4 February 1886; *Prison Inspectors' Second Report* (1837), 85-6.

9 Beveridge, op.cit., 59-60. For the 1614 bell by Peter van den Ghein, which is 0.46m in diameter and bears the burgh arms and the name CRAIL, see ibid.; *Inventory of Fife, etc.*, No.121.

10 This medallion is identical with one on the rather smaller bell of 1526 at Dunning, Perthshire, which is attributed to Willem van den Ghein (*PSAS*, **122** (1992), 479-80).

11 TCM 16 June 1814, 3 March, 25 April 1815.

16 Cromarty

1 The Commissioners are indebted to Mr David Alston, Cromarty, for generously making available the results of his research on this building.

2 *NSA*, **14**, 14.

3 SRO, SC 24/21/7, un-numbered Sheriff Court papers.

4 *Prison Inspectors' Second Report*, 61-2.

5 Miller, H, *Scenes and Legends of the North of Scotland* (1857), 451-7.

6 According to Mackenzie, W M, *The Royal Burgh of Cromarty* (1924), 8, 13, the surviving cross dates from 1578, replacing a 14th-century cross.

7 Pryde, *Burghs*, nos. 36, 423.

8 SRO, E 721/18 (Minutes of Forfeited Estates Commissioners, 1768-84), pp. 18, 92.

9 Ibid., pp. 11, 113, 132; E 727/41/1-2.

10 *Inverness Courier*, 19 April 1843, 19 June 1844.

17 Cullen

1 Early photographs also show consoles on the first-floor windows of the NW front (e.g. GWW 6207; copy in NMRS).

2 Wood, D, *Cullen - A Pictorial History* (n.d.), 13.

3 Contract with James Smith, wright in Forres, and other tradesmen (SRO, Seafield Papers, GD 248/784/5/55).

4 Ibid.

5 Ibid.

6 Cramond, W, *The Annals of Cullen 961-1904* (1904), 26, 30-4. 'Upputing and edifeing the tolbuith' was also carried out in 1642 (ibid., 38).

7 Ibid., 66-7.

8 Ibid., 88.

9 Soane Museum, Adam Drawings, vol.1, no.210 (copy in NMRS).

10 Soane Museum, Playfair Drawings no.4/6 (copy in NMRS); SRO, RHP 2545/1.

11 SRO, GD 248/800/4.

12 Plans in SRO (Seafield Drawings A20-1); copies in NMRS.

13 SRO, GD 248/784/5/55. The contract was made by Col. F Grant of Grant, as curator-in-law for the 5th Earl of Seafield.

14 *NSA*, **13** (Banffshire), 328.

15 Ibid., 328, 353; building-contract, loc.cit.; *Prison Inspectors' First Report*, 37.

18 Culross

1 *Inventory of Fife, etc.*, No.158 (7).

2 Ibid.; Beveridge, D, *Culross and Tulliallan* (1885), **2**, 304.

3 Drawings in NMRS, W373.

4 Beveridge, op. cit., **1**, 124. 'The ground of the auld tolbuith' is mentioned in 1594 (*APS*, quoted ibid., **2**, 305).

5 *Prison Inspectors' Second Report*, 76-7. In 1859 the building still contained a lock-up, and residences for a policeman and a town officer (Name Book, Perthshire No.20, p.108).

6 Ibid., 76; Beveridge, D, *Between the Ochils and Forth* (1888), 191.

7 Apted, M R, 'Painting in Scotland from the 14th to the 17th centuries' (Edinburgh University PhD thesis, 1964; copy in NMRS), **2**, 278.

8 Beveridge, loc.cit.

9 The shield bears: within a bordure a saltire, on a chief three mullets, with a lion's head as crest and two wild men as supporters; a label bears the motto FUIMUS ('We have been') and the date 1628. The panel closely resembles the armorial at the apex of Sir George Bruce's monument in Culross Abbey Church (*Inventory of Fife, etc.*, fig.166).

10 For council minutes recording this donation of 2,000 merks, and the decision to erect a 'lasting memorial', see Beveridge, D, *Culross and Tulliallan*, **2**, 92-4.

11 Cf. the seal illustrated in Bute, John, [3rd] Marquis of, *The Arms of the Royal and Parliamentary Burghs of Scotland* (1897), 69-73.

12 Saint Ninian's Row was in the Calton area of Edinburgh. The small bell bearing the initials T.L., which was in the garret in 1928 (*Inventory of Fife, etc.*, loc.cit.), is no longer in the building.

19 Cupar

1 TCM 29 March 1816.

2 TCM 28 September 1816.

3 TCM 22 April 1818.

4 TCM 6 May 1818; Name Book, Fife No.113, p.33

5 *Liber Sancte Marie de Melros* (Bannatyne Club, 1837), 564-5. See also Dickinson, W C (ed.), *The Sheriff Court Book of Fife, 1515-22* (SHS, 1928).

6 Anon., *Historical Notes and Reminiscences of Cupar* (1884), 16-17.

7 *Stat. Acct.*, **17**, 141-3; Anon., op.cit., 20.

8 TCM 13 October 1810.

9 TCM 1 June and 30 November 1809, 30 October 1810; minutes of Jail Commissioners, 1809-15, including plan signed by J Gillespie [Graham] and Maurice Finlay, builder, 19 September 1811 (St Andrews University Library, B 13/21/2); SRO, GD 12/32/1. For the

building, which ceased to be used as a jail in 1844, see record-sheet and photographs, 1991, in NMRS; Gifford, *Fife*, 164-5; *Prison Inspectors' Second Report*, 82-4.

10   Gifford, *Fife*, 164-5.
11   TCM 26 April 1815; Anon., op.cit., 17-18.
12   TCM 27 July 1815.
13   TCM 9 December 1818.
14   TCM 27 July, 2 November and 15 December 1815, 28 September 1816.
15   TCM 18 August 1819.

20 Dalkeith

1   *Inventory of Midlothian, etc.*, No.77.
2   Survey-drawing by Sir Frank Mears and Partners, 1958 (NMRS, MLD/26/1); photographs in NMRS.
3   *NSA*, **1**, 531.
4   Ibid.
5   Ibid.
6   *RPC*, 1st series, **10** (1613-16), 616; **12** (1619-22), 269.
7   SRO, Buccleuch Muniments, GD 224/390/6/1 and 3. A court was held *in pretorio burgi* in 1633 (GD 224/390/1/1).
8   SRO, GD 224/390/6/1.
9   *NSA*, **1**, 532.
10   *The Dalkeith Advertiser*, 23 February 1984.
11   *Scotland's Magazine* (December 1966), 42.

21 Dingwall

1   TCM 24 February 1902; *The Inverness Courier*, 23 September 1902; *Cast. and Dom. Arch.*, **5**, fig.1223 on p.103.
2   TCM 21 June 1732.
3   Ibid.
4   Macrae, N, *The Romance of a Royal Burgh* (1923), 251.
5   TCM 21 June 1732.
6   See *PSAS*, **22** (1887-8), 308-9. This is presumably the 'grated iron door' of an opening in the former straight forestair, which gave access to a cell in the steeple (*Cast. and Dom. Arch.*, **5**, 102-3). Early photographs show that after the alteration of the forestair the yett was fixed to the S wall of the town-house.
7   *RCRBS (1677-1711)*, 660.
8   TCM 16 December 1729.
9   TCM 21 June 1732, 4 April 1734.
10   TCM 10 October 1735, 27 September 1745.
11   Macrae, op.cit., 231; TCM 2 February, 31 March, 5 May 1773. The clock was made by Thaites of London, and is now displayed in Dingwall Museum.
12   Macrae, op.cit., 251-2; *Prison Inspectors' Second Report*, 70-2. The inspector was told that formerly 'prisoners were sometimes allowed to go to supper parties! and this with the key of the prison in their pockets!' One of the debtors for whose debt the burgh was made liable had no intention of absconding, but had attended a public meeting, 'which was held in the court-room adjoining his cell'.
13   Ibid., *Ninth Report*, 39.

22 Dumbarton

1   Record-sheet (DBR/2/1) and photographs in NMRS.
2   OS 1:500 plan; TCM *passim*.
3   TCM 31 May 1861; MacLeod, D, *Dumbarton Ancient and Modern* (1893), pl.24 and text.
4   Building-accounts, and payments for repairs to its predecessor, in Roberts, F and MacPhail, I M M (eds), *Dumbarton Common Good Accounts 1614-1660* (1972), *passim*; MacLeod, op.cit., pls 5 and 11.
5   TCM 20 September 1794.
6   TCM 2 August 1819, 26 April, 23 November 1821, 3 and 18 April 1822, 13 November 1823, 28 January, 30 April 1824, 21 November 1825; account of laying of foundation-stone in *The Glasgow Herald*, 23 July 1824.
7   TCM 8 February, 8 March, 19 April, 31 May 1861, 4 July 1862.

23 Dumfries

1   Edgar, R, *An Introduction to the History of Dumfries* (ed. by R C Reid, 1915), 44-5; Shirley, G W, in *TDGNHAS*, 2nd series, **23** (1910-11), 201-14.
2   TCM 7 March 1709. Sibbald drew two designs, and the council chose the more expensive one.
3   Pencil drawing of High Street and Midsteeple by G H Johnson, 1828, in Dumfries Museum; early drawings and photographs in Dumfries Museum and NMRS. A redrawn sketch which shows a pediment (*PSAS*, **20** (1885-6), pl.5 opp.p.186), is said to be 'of 1780', but it shows the yard-measure in the S wall and is probably later. The portico of 1830 was re-erected in 1910 at Rotchell House, 29 Rotchell Road, Dumfries.

4   Pre-1909 views indicate that the first-floor window of the S front originally had a plain surround like those above. The cornice of the S window on the E front has been removed since 1912 (*Inventory of Dumfries-shire*, Fig.43).
5   Ibid., 48.
6   Ibid. The Commissioners are indebted to Charles J Burnett, Ross Herald of Arms, for his comments on these carvings.
7   Shirley, op.cit., 206-7.
8   *Inventory of Dumfries-shire*, fig.44 on p.49. It has been stated that these were the ancient arms of the burgh (*Stat.Acct.*, **5**, 122-3). J Barbour identifies them as the arms of the Brown family, and assumes that a figure of St Michael has been broken off (*TDGNHAS*, 2nd series, **12** (1895-6), 96-9, with photographs of both stones on p.98 and ibid., **17** (1900-5), 198).
9   *PSAS*, **20** (1885-6), pl.5 opp.pp.186. The Commissioners are indebted to Dr A D C Simpson, Royal Museum of Scotland, for discussion of this measure. Although normally referred to as an 'ell', it is a 'plaiding yard' of 38 inches (0.97m) for measuring unfinished cloth, with two inches allowed for further shrinkage.
10   Steeple Minutes, 11 August, 30 October, 16 December 1707, 4 and 6 October 1708.
11   Ibid., 25 September 1708.
12   Ibid., 16 December 1707, 10 and 16 November 1708.
13   Edgar, op.cit., 43-4, 147-8; A E Truckell in 1986 reprint of McDowall, W, *History of the Burgh of Dumfries* (1867); *RPC*, 1st series, **2** (1569-78), 24; **4** (1585-92), 129; *Stat.Acct.*, **5**, 122-3; *NSA*, **4**, 14.
14   Edgar, op.cit., 45-7; Anon., *Notes on the established churches of Dumfries, to which is appended the story of the building of the Dumfries Mid-steeple* (1865), 39-40; McDowall, op.cit., 537-8.
15   Original minute-book, 1703-9, in Dumfries Archive Centre (copy in NMRS); detailed summary in Anon., op.cit., 39-52; McDowall, op.cit., 538-42; *PSAS*, **20** (1885-6), 187-9.
16   The younger James Smith (d.1705) was a cousin and former apprentice of his celebrated namesake (Colvin, *Architects*, 894).
17   Steeple Minutes, *passim*. It has been suggested, on the basis of similarities in the fenestration of the steeples, that Moffat also designed St Peter's Church, Liverpool, of 1700-4 (*Transactions of the Historical Society of Lancashire and Cheshire*, **130** (1981), 1-14).
18   TCM 30 April 1703; Anon., op.cit., 40.
19   Edgar, op.cit., 43-4, 147-8; *Stat.Acct.*, **5**, 123-4.
20   Edgar, op.cit., 45; *Stat.Acct.*, **5**, 123, 127; Anon., op.cit., 52; McDowall, op.cit., 884; *PSAS*, **20** (1885-6), 186-7; *NSA*, **4**, 14; Name Book, Dumfries-shire No.26, p.133.

24 Dunbar

1   *Inventory of East Lothian*, No.37.
2   *The Haddington Advertiser*, 28 April 1911, records that 'all the old lime has been scraped off the building and the stones washed with the fire hose'.
3   Plans by George Simpson, architect (SRO, RHP 32708-10). The building was constructed of cast concrete imitating stone.
4   *The Haddington Advertiser*, 10 January 1913; *Cast. and Dom. Arch.*, **5**, fig.1231 on p.113; early photographs in NMRS.
5   For a similar open gnomon, cf. a dial at Inveresk (*Cast. and Dom. Arch.*, **5**, fig.1475 on p.363). In 1686 the town council decided 'to agrie with the painter for culloring the orlage of the steeple' as well as for painting the royal arms (TCM 12 February 1686).
6   'The toun's steeple' needed 'to be helped' in 1707, when its wright-work was repaired (TCM 17 February 1707). In 1816 an estimate was accepted for 'the top part to be taken down as far as where it is at present slated, a new roof put on, slated again, the bell also to be removed and hung lower down' (TCM 23 February 1816).
7   Neild, *Prisons*, 175.
8   TCM 21 March 1818. Some years earlier Neild (loc.cit) found that the debtors' room on the first floor was used for this purpose.
9   *Prison Inspectors' Third Report*, 99.
10   TCM 12 February, 19 March, 19 April and 3 May 1686; Mackay, H, 'The Armorial Panels of Dunbar Town House', in *Transactions of the East Lothian Antiquarian and Field Naturalists' Society*, **11** (1968), 12-16. Mackbyth was also commissioned to paint a second panel with the burgh arms and the inscription 'justice seat for the Magistrats and Councill', to adjoin the royal arms 'at the bak of the councill-hous seat' (TCM 3 May 1686).
11   Lost council records quoted in *The Haddington Advertiser*, 11 October 1912. Cf. *RCRBS (1295-1597)*, 440 (three-year exemption from attendance at convention, 1594).
12   TCM 23 May, 19 October, 5 November 1705, 17 February 1707; Act of Parliament quoted in *The Haddington Advertiser*, 10 October 1902.
13   TCM 4 October 1723.
14   TCM 23 February 1816, 9 December 1818.

25 Dysart

1   *Inventory of Fife, etc.*, No.225.
2   Muir, W, *Notices From The Local Records of Dysart* (Maitland Club, 1853), 25.
3   View of Dysart Tolbooth *c.*1920, by J B White, Dundee.
4   This tree resembles a palm, but is probably intended to represent a thorn-tree, the arms of the burgh.
5   TCM 11 February, 20 September 1825, 20 June 1876. Plates attached to the mechanism bear the names of the makers and of the burgh magistrates and officials for 1876. The Commissioners are indebted to Mr J Swan, Dysart Preservation Trust, for information about the clock and bells.
6   TCM 8 July 1808.
7   The final word is damaged and illegible, but presumably meant 'announces' or 'bestows'. The reference is possibly to John the Baptist
8   Muir, op.cit., 24-5, 38. Previously the council had met in the steeple of St Serf's Church (ibid., 27, 38).
9   *NSA*, **9**, 135.
10 TCM 14 June and 15 July 1707, 26 May 1719; Dysart Accounts, 13 June 1719.
11 TCM 9 May 1743. The council had previously obtained plans for rebuilding the tolbooth from John Thompson (TCM 23 January 1743). For Douglas's work at Dysart House in 1748, see SRO, GD 164/5/38.
12 TCM 14 April and 9 May 1743, 21 September 1744; Dysart Accounts, 1744-5.
13 *NSA*, **9**, 134-5; TCM 25 March 1811, 27 February 1815.
14 TCM 7 May 1765.
15 Late 19th-century views (Muir, op.cit., frontispiece; *Cast. and Dom. Arch.*, **5**, 118) show a two-storeyed range extending S from the steeple and abutted by a house which conceals most of its W wall.
16 Photograph by I G Lindsay in NMRS (1934), showing large window. The 1576 date-stone was reset above the new window.

26 Earlsferry

1   OS 6-inch map, Fife sheet 26 (1853/5). The position of the tower, NW of the central axis of the hall, suggests that it was widened. In 1872 the town council acquired a house to the NE, and a strip of ground behind the old hall, to enlarge the site (TCM 17 January 1872).
2   *RMS*, **5** (1580-93), no.1652.
3   Leighton, *Fife*, **3**, 119; *Prison Inspectors' Second Report*, 89.
4   TCM 12 October 1849.
5   TCM 26 January, 19 February, 25 April, 13 May, 5 June, 2 September 1872, 12 and 31 March 1873.

27 Edinburgh

1   The extensive literature includes: *Inventory of Edinburgh*, No.80; *Edinburgh Extracts, passim*; Edinburgh TCM (extracts in Edinburgh Public Library, Boog Watson notebooks); Chambers, *Reekiana*, 122-72; Wilson, *Memorials*, **1**, 238-54; Miller, R, *The Municipal Buildings of Edinburgh* (1895), 1-38; Miller, P, 'The origin and early history of the Old Tolbooth of Edinburgh', in *PSAS*, **20** (1885-6), 360-76; Fairley, J, 'The Old Tolbooth: with extracts from the original records', in *BOEC*, vols.**4-13** (1911-24), *passim*; Kerr, H F, 'The Old Tolbooth of Edinburgh', ibid., **14** (1925), 7-23. Floor-plans are given in Chambers, *Reekiana*, opp.pp.126, 130, and elevations by J Sime in *PSAS*, **20**, pls.vi, and Illustrations include pre-demolition views by D Somerville (*BOEC*, **4**, 74, 77) and A Archer (drawings in Royal Museum of Scotland library and NMRS), and later views by Storer (*Views*), Nasmyth (Cooksey, J C B, *Alexander Nasmyth, H.R.S.A., 1758-1840* (1991), cat. F29-30, K2, O9), and Wilson (*Memorials*, **1**, pl. opp. p.92).
2   Webster, B (ed.), *The Acts of David II* (Regesta Regum Scottorum, 1982), no.350; Marwick, J D (ed.), *Charters and other documents relating to the City of Edinburgh, A.D.1143-1540*, no.7 and pl.
3   Marwick, op.cit., no.13 and pl. The building was described by Robert Reid in 1808 as measuring 18.9m by 10.05m (Miller, R, op.cit., 18).
4   *Infra*, n.6.
5   *Extracts (1403-1528)*, 89-90.
6   *Extracts (1557-73)*, 130-1, 133. In 1575 the treasurer was ordered 'to tak doun the west gavill of the towre of the auld tolbuith quhilk is rottin and rewynus ... and to reedifie and big vp the samyn agane in substantious manner' (ibid. (*1573-89*), 38).
7   *Extracts (1604-26)*, 52, 55, 61, 67. The total cost was £7,330 10s 4d Scots, almost £611 Sterling (Miller, R, op.cit., 22).
8   For a visit by Scott and Alexander Nasmyth when the 'cage' was being demolished, see Smiles, S (ed.), *James Nasmyth, Engineer; an Autobiography* (1897), 83-4 and pl. opp. p.82.
9   Symsoun agreed in November 1610 'to big ane other hous (storey) heicht in proportioun lyke to the nixt hous under the samyn' (*Extracts (1604-26)*, 67).
10 Two of the niches are preserved at Abbotsford, along with the timber door and other carved fragments. The 'gad' or iron bar to which condemned prisoners were manacled, and other items from the tolbooth, are in the Royal Museum of Scotland (Grant, J, *Old and New*

Edinburgh (n.d.), **1**, fig. on p.129).
11 This may be the ashlar-built tower on which work was in progress in 1501.
12 Kerr, op.cit., 15-17.
13 In 1714 the town council ordered 'that the great windows on the east syde (of the tolbooth) be built up with strong stone and lime at least the half of the height of the said windows' (*Extracts (1701-18)*, 278). A similar alteration in the N window is visible in Sime's elevation.
14 Chambers, *Reekiana*, 126-7; drawing of hall by Archer. The pulpit does not appear in other views of the hall (Cooksey, op.cit., cat.K2; Miller, R, op.cit., pl. opp. p.29). For the order to obtain a portable pulpit in 1568, see *supra*, p. 9.
15 *Extracts, passim*; Miller, R, op.cit., 54. A detailed description and plan of the courts in the church in 1629 are given in Lowther, *Journall*, 26-30, 34, 49-56.
16 *Extracts (1557-71)*, 154; Miller, R, op.cit., 54, 57 and 41-69, *passim*.
17 See plan in Wilson, *Memorials*, **2**, opp.p.296.
18 *Inventory of Edinburgh*, No.23; Miller, R, op.cit., 111-33, 137-43; Gray, W F, 'The Royal Exchange and Other City Improvements', in *BOEC*, **23** (1938), 1-27; Youngson, A J, *The Making of Classical Edinburgh* (1966), 52-9.
19 For the plan as executed and a late 19th-century view of Writers' Court, see Miller, R, op. cit., pl. vi and opp.p.114. See also the left-hand side of the view in Shepherd, *Modern Athens*, opp.p.46.
20 A description of the screen with the shops is contained in Name Book, Edinburgh No.105, pp.94, 151. At that date (1852) the E side of the court was occupied by the Clydesdale Bank, and Paxton's Royal Exchange Coffee House and Tavern kept 'good refreshments'.
21 For the history of this statue, discovered in a chest in St Giles's Church in 1810, see *Inventory of Edinburgh*, p.89n and references cited. An 18th-century French origin is suggested in Pearson, F (ed.), *Virtue and Vision: Sculpture and Scotland 1540-1990* (1991), 14.
22 For details, see Gifford, J, McWilliam, C, Walker, D, *Edinburgh* (Buildings of Scotland, 1984), 177-8.
23 Morris, M, 'Mary King's Close, An Architectural Survey' (Heriot-Watt University dissertation, 1986); Name Book, Edinburgh No.105, p.146.
24 Miller, R, op. cit., 116-17; engraved frontispiece by J Fergus to 'Contract of Agreement for Building an Exchange' (copy in NMRS).
25 For accounts of the funding of the scheme and the disposal of the rooms, see Laing, D, 'Note respecting the Royal Exchange, Edinburgh, and the Original List of Subscribers, in 1752', in *PSAS*, **4** (1860-2), 593-7; Miller, R, loc. cit.; Gray, loc. cit.; *Inventory of Edinburgh*, 88 and refs cited.
26 City Architect's Department, Edinburgh (copies in NMRS): plans by David Cousin dated 1855-62; plans dated 1870-1; plans by Robert Morham 1875-9; *The Builder*, 16 December 1899, 22 December 1900, and 22 June 1901.

28 Falkirk

1   *Inventory of Stirlingshire*, **2**, No.253.
2   Elevation-drawing signed by Hamilton and the stentmasters, 1812 (Falkirk Museum, A58.342); Falkirk Stentmasters' Minutes (Central Region Archives, FA1/7/1), 11 February, 3 March, 16 October 1812; Reid, J, 'The Stentmasters of Falkirk', in *Calatria*, **5** (1993), 25-44. Hamilton received twelve guineas for the plan and specifications (Minutes, 22 May 1812).
3   Hamilton's elevation-drawing, and a copy (in Falkirk Museum), signed by Robert Smith and also dated 1812, show the four-storeyed block attached to the rear (E) of the steeple.
4   St Enoch's Church (now demolished), was built in 1780-2 to a design by James Paterson (*Transactions of the Scottish Ecclesiological Society*, **8** (1924-7), 160).
5   Love, J, *Local Antiquarian Notes and Queries*, **3** (1925), fig. on p.264. The stentmasters had discussed the possible re-use of the weather-cock from the old steeple (Minutes, 29 April 1814; Reid, op.cit., 38).
6   Minutes, 6 September 1814 ('the shop or under flat of the steeple'); *Prison Inspectors' Third Report*, 61; *Ninth Report*, 9; *Thirteenth Report*, 5.
7   The original clock of 1815 was made by the celebrated local clockmaker John Russell, 'watchmaker for Scotland to his Royal Highness the Prince Regent' (inscription on clock-mechanism; Love, op.cit., **2** (1910), 18-22; **3** (1925), 268-72). The mechanism and two of the illuminated dials, which were installed by subscription in 1846, are now in the Royal Museum of Scotland.
8   *PSAS*, **84** (1949-50), 76-7; Love, op.cit., **2**, 113-15; *The Steeple of Falkirk* (Falkirk Rotary Club, n.d.); Reid, op.cit., 38-9.
9   *PSAS*, **84** (1949-50), 77.
10 Love, op.cit., **3**, 265; Lawson, L, *A History of Falkirk* (1975), 53-4.
11 Love, op.cit., 265-8; Lawson, op.cit., 53-4; Reid, op.cit., 33-5.
12 Reid, op.cit., 35-6; *The Glasgow Courier*, 11 September 1811 (typescript copy in Falkirk Museum).
13 Stentmasters' Minutes, 14 December 1812, 26 February 1813. The final price, including the bell and clock, was about £2,000 (Reid, op.cit., 37-9, 41).
14 *The Falkirk Herald*, 21 September 1927; Lawson, op.cit., 111-12; Scott, M and Astbury, T, *Falkirk's Yesterdays* (1983), figs. on p.17. For previous repairs see Love, op.cit., **2**, 293-5.

29 Falkland

1   *Prison Inspectors' Second Report*, 81-2; information re door from Mr C Bayne, Falkland.

2   TCM 28 June 1799 (proposal to build school at 'the Gowk's Tree'), 20 October, 28 November 1800, 9 February, 4 and 29 April 1801.

3   Leighton, *Fife*, **2**, 226.

30 Fochabers

1   The Commissioners are grateful to Smiths Gore, Fochabers, for copies of two sheets of drawings which, although unsigned, are clearly in Baxter's hand.

2   The slater was James Marquis and some 7,600 slates were supplied (account in SRO, GD44/51/388).

3   A staircase with similar balusters is preserved in the manse.

4   The plasterer was Philip Paterson, whose account for 1791-2 included 'ceiling of the large room with cove — 65 yards' (ibid.). He also supplied 31 1/3 yards (28.7m) of cornice, which matches the dimensions indicated on Baxter's plan. This shows the court-room extending the full depth of the building, and its existing SW wall (which although 0.45m thick has no support in the ground storey) is presumably an insertion.

5   SRO, Gordon Muniments, GD 44/51/379 and GD 44/52/254, p.40 (accounts, 1735-42, amounting to £73 6s 2d); plan by A R[oumieu] (SRO, RHP 2374); Name Book, Banffshire No.4, p.78; NMRS record card NJ 35 NW 2. Stone for the tolbooth was freighted from Covesea to Speymouth.

6   SRO, RHP 2370.

7   Simpson, A and J, 'John Baxter, Architect, and the Patronage of the Fourth Duke of Gordon', 53, in *Bulletin of the Scottish Georgian Society*, **2** (1972), 47-57.

8   Ibid., 55-6; SRO, GD 44/51/388.

9   Drawings in possession of Smiths Gore, Fochabers. A one-room lock-up, 'formerly used as a guard-room', was in use in 1835, but it is not stated whether it was in the town-house (*Prison Inspectors' First Report*, 47).

10 Name Book, Banffshire No.4, p.65. A contract for a clock for the old tolbooth, at a price of £18, had been made in 1735 with John Mowat, smith in Old Aberdeen (SRO, GD 44/51/379).

31 Forfar

1   Reid, A, *The Royal Burgh of Forfar* (1902), pl. on p.81.

2   Ibid.; OS 6-inch map, Angus sheet 38 (1st ed., 1861/5).

3   A thin birdcage bellcot was erected on the S pediment, possibly in 1804, and was removed in 1879 (Reid, op.cit., 81, 260; McCulloch, W M S, *A history of the Town and County Hall, Forfar* (n.d.), 12, 17).

4   *Stat. Acct.*, **6**, 523.

5   McCulloch, op.cit., 14-15; Reid, op.cit., 260.

6   Letter from Playfair, 27 January 1787 (copy in NMRS). In 1790 an inserted stair in the council-room was to be lit by a window in the W gable (TCM 23 March 1790).

7   Anon., 'The Royal Burgh of Forfar: a review of the administration of the town's affairs, 1660-1965' (typescript, 1965), 14.

8   McCulloch, op.cit., 21-7. Raeburn's portrait of Henry Dundas was donated by William Maule of Panmure to replace a Romney portrait which Maule, a political opponent of Dundas, had damaged by fire in 1807 (ibid., 22).

9   *RPC*, 1st series, **4** (1585-92), 538.

10 *Geog. Coll.*, **1**, 271-2; McCulloch, op.cit., 1.

11 Summary of contract, 16 December 1785 (copy in NMRS). Playfair himself prepared two schemes, to cost £1,100 or £1,300 (letter dated September 1785, to R Graham of Fintry, SRO GD 151/11/32). Three undated schemes, by Thomas Gibson, Alexander Thompson and an unknown designer, are also preserved (copies in NMRS).

12 Copies in NMRS. Both schemes showed a five-bay main elevation with a rusticated ground storey, having advanced end-bays which at first-floor level were framed by (i) single and (ii) paired pilasters. The first floor was to have a large County Hall to the W and a Sheriff Court E of the 'great stairs'.

13 Playfair letters, 19 June 1786, 27 January 1787, 22 January 1786; TCM 24 January 1787; McCulloch, op.cit., 11-12.

14 Drawings dated 1821 in NMRS, RIAS collection. The building is rectangular but with an apsidal N end. Its five-bay W front has a tetrastyle centrepiece of giant engaged Ionic columns, which are repeated on the N bow.

15 McCulloch, op.cit., 14-16; Anon., op.cit., p.15.

32 Fortrose

1   MacDowall, C G, *The Chanonry of Ross* (n.d., c.1960), 134.

2   *Eccles. Arch.*, **2**, 401-2; Fawcett, R, *Beauly Priory and Fortrose Cathedral* (1987), 16-19.

3   *Prison Inspectors' Second Report*, 62.

4   *APS*, **7** (1661-9), 225.

5   TCM 3 May 1698, 16 March 1700, 30 September 1706 and *passim*;

6   *RCRBS (1677-1711)*, 241, 265; MacDowall, op.cit., 134-5.

6   TCM 30 September 1700, 21 July 1721, 31 December 1723.

7   TCM 30 July 1716; MacDowall, op.cit., 88-9.

8   For Sir Hector Munro's distinguished career in India see *Dictionary of National Biography*, s.v. 'Munro'. For repairs at this period, see *Stat. Acct.*, **11**, 342-3.

9   *Prison Inspectors' Second Report*, 62-4; Name Book, Ross and Cromarty No.28, p.14. In 1851 the undercroft was being used as a coal-cellar, and it was recommended that a cross-wall which had formed a 'black hole' in the W end should be demolished (report to Office of Works by R Matheson, SRO, MW 1/525).

10 Fawcett, op.cit., 29; SRO, MW 1/525-34.

33 Girvan

1   TCM 14 January 1825; Valentine, W B S, 'Girvan Town Council — The Early Days', 54-5, 57, in Cunningham, J H *et al.*, *Girvan 1668-1968* (1968), 44-64; *The Carrick Herald*, 18 August 1911, pp.2-3.

2   *The Carrick Herald*, loc.cit.; *The Ayr Advertiser*, 23 March 1939, p.7.

3   The existing weather-vane in the form of a sailing-ship is not shown in early photographs, and evidently dates from after the fire of 1939.

4   *Prison Inspectors' Third Report*, 44.

5   TCM 8 July 1825; Valentine, op.cit., 58.

6   Ibid., 63; Clouston, 'Ayrshire Bells', 226.

7   Valentine, op.cit., 50-1.

8   Early views and maps show the town hall as a plain two-storeyed gabled building, about 19m from N to S by 6.6m (McMeikan, M, *Girvan Memories* (1993), pls.49, 50; OS 1:500 town plan).

9   TCM 23 February 1825, 15 January 1827; Valentine, op.cit., 58, 63.

10 *Prison Inspectors' Third Report*, 44.

34 Glasgow

1   Sir William Brereton (1634) and Richard Franck (1658), in Brown, *Early Travellers*, 150-1, 191.

2   Anon., *Description of Ceremonial on the occasion of Laying the Foundation Stone of the Municipal Buildings in George Square, Glasgow* (1885), 131ff.; Gomme, A and Walker, D, *Architecture of Glasgow* (1968), 104-5, 198 (no.451), fig.77.

3   Young, W, *The Municipal Buildings, Glasgow* (1890); Gomme and Walker, op.cit., 191-4.

4   The Great Bell of 1554 is now in the Peoples' Palace Museum. It measures 0.81m in diameter and below an arabesque frieze it is inscribed: KATHELINA BEN IC GHEGOTEN VAN JACOB WAGHEVENS INT JAER ONS HEEREN MCCCCLIIII ('Catherine am I, cast by Jacob Waghevens in the year of Our Lord 1554'). Four plaques bear figures of St Catherine, a mitred bishop, a robed man holding a long-shafted cross, and griffins supporting a shield which bears a griffin rampant (*PSAS*, **82** (1947-8), pl.36; *The Regality Club*, **2** (1893), 38-41).
A bell measuring 0.69m in diameter, which was cast by Gerard Koster at Amsterdam in 1663 and bears the city arms, is also displayed in the Peoples' Palace Museum, having been used from 1792 to 1881 in the Calton church. This is evidently one of the 'paill [peal] of belles', having 'the tounes armes fixit on them' which the town council ordered from Holland in 1663 (ibid., 40, 42-4).
In addition to the 'Great Bell', the following bells were found in the steeple when it was cleared out for new chimes in 1881 (ibid., 41-2): (a), twelve bells dated 1735, presumably from the set of music bells ordered from London in the following year; (b), six bells dated 1738, and eight others, similar but undated; one was inscribed 'Ormiston & Cunningham Edinburgh Fecit for Glasgow 1738', another 'These 29 tuned by John Fyfe for Glasgow 1738', and a third bore the motto 'Let Glasgow Flourish'; (c), three bells by Mears and Stainbank dated 1843, and two dated 1845.

5   *Liber Collegii Nostre Domine* (Maitland Club, 1846), 176.

6   *Glasgow Extracts (1573-1642)*, 8, 22, 451-2, 456, 460.

7   Ibid., 346, 349, 351-3, 361-3, 366, 374, 480-2; Neil, G, 'A few brief notices of the old Tolbooth at the Cross of Glasgow', in *Transactions of the Glasgow Archaeological Society*, **1** (1868), 8-28); MacGregor, G, *The History of Glasgow* (1881), 180-2; Anon., *Ceremonial*, 103-10.

8   Descriptions in McUre, J, *A view of the City of Glasgow* (1736), 255-6; Denholm, J, *An historical account and topographical description of the City of Glasgow* (1797), 110-11; view by R Paul, *c*.1760 (Stuart, R, *Views and Notices of Glasgow in Former Times* (1847), pl. opp. p.81).

9   Franck, in Brown, op.cit., 191.

10 A royal armorial, said to be from the tolbooth, is illustrated in Renwick, R and Lindsay, J, *History of Glasgow*, **1** (1921), pl. opp. p.288. The inscription, which occurred in translation at Perth (p.22), was recorded by McUre (loc.cit.) as:
HAEC DOMUS ODIT, AMAT, PUNIT, CONSERVAT, HONORAT, NEQUITIAM, PACEM, CRIMINA, JURA, PROBOS.
('This House doth hate all wickedness, Loves peace, but faults corrects, Observes all laws of righteousness, And good men it erects').

11 Loc.cit.

12 *The Regality Club*, **2** (1893), 40. For the murder of town clerk Robert

Park by Major Menzies see Eyre-Todd, G, *The History of Glasgow*, **3** (1934), 25-7.

13 These portraits were transferred in 1740 to the new town hall (Stuart, op.cit., 96-7). With later additions to the collection, including Allan Ramsay's portrait of the 3rd Duke of Argyll (*Extracts (1739-59)*, 319 (payment of £42 to 'Andrew' Ramsay, limner, 1750); MacMillan, D, *Painting in Scotland, the Golden Age* (1986), col.pl.3) and Flaxman's statue of William Pitt the Younger, they are now in Glasgow Art Gallery and Museum, Kelvingrove.

14 *Extracts (1718-38)*, 351.

15 Ibid., 511, 515; *(1739-59)*, 44, 70, 97, 121. Lustres for the hall were obtained from London in 1744 at a cost of £68 5s (ibid., 149, 185).

16 Ibid., 490, 514, 525-6, 547, 549. A fine wooden model of the building in its extended form, attributed to Dreghorn's workshop, was acquired by the Royal Museum of Scotland in 1990. The Commissioners are indebted for information about this model to Mr H Cheape.

17 Denholm, J, *An historical account and topographical description of the City of Glasgow* (1797), 107-10.

18 *Extracts (1781-95)*, 509, 534, 556, 560, 606. This extension, which had a Venetian window to the E, is described in Denholm, op.cit., 111-12.

19 *Extracts (1809-22)*, pp.xxvii-ix, 176-7, 209, 211, 213, 232-5, 237-9. The rebuilt tolbooth dominates John Knox's painting of the Trongate *c*.1826, in Glasgow Art Gallery and Museum (MacMillan, op.cit., fig.68 on p.147; *supra*, fig.xiiB).

20 Eyre-Todd, op.cit., 165, n.8.

21 *Extracts (1796-1808)*, pp.xlii, 673-4.

22 *Extracts (1809-22)*, pp.xxiii-vii, 2, 43-4, 64-5 (decision to have only one row of pillars in the portico), 72 (laying of foundation-stone, 18 September 1810), 200 (certificate of completion, 2 November 1813); Anon., *Ceremonial*, 119-26. The competition plans are preserved in the Mitchell Library, Glasgow.

23 *Prison Inspectors' First Report*, 49-53; Anon., *Ceremonial*, 130-1; Williamson, E *et al.*, *Glasgow* (Buildings of Scotland, 1990), 194; *Historic Buildings at Work*, 185.

35 Greenlaw

1 Vignette in Armstrong's Map of Berwickshire, 1771 (*Inventory of Berwickshire*, fig.89 on p.93).

2 Chambers, R, *Picture of Scotland*, quoted in Gibson, R, *An Old Berwickshire Town* (1905), 156.

3 Undated survey-drawings in NMRS, BWD/34/2.

4 *Eccles. Arch.*, **3**, 574-5, suggests a 15th-century date. The Commissioners are indebted to Dr C Brooke (University of Nottingham) for the information that ultra-violet photography suggests that the lower two storeys are of a different build from those above, and the first-floor openings are distinguished by relieving-arches. However, so far as can be seen through the thick harl-pointing of the tower, there is no significant difference in masonry between it and the church. The contract for building the latter in 1675 specifies that 'ane bell house' should be put on 'the wester gable', and there is no mention of an existing tower (Gibson, op.cit., 43-4).

5 Gibson, op.cit., 153-4.

6 Information from the clock-winder, Mr D Smith.

7 Gibson, op.cit., 156.

8 In 1730 it was reported that the stair-tower on the E face of the steeple 'will hinder the putting of a dial plate and hand to go on that side' (letter to 2nd Earl of Marchmont, SRO, GD 158/1340, p.99).

9 Thomas Broumfield bequeathed 400 merks in 1667 'for to buy ane good bell for the paroche church of Grinlaw' (Gibson, op.cit., 124).

10 Ibid., 145-9.

11 Ibid., 155-6. The earl's benefaction was recorded on a plaque, now set above the E doorway of the walled garden at Marchmont House. Now much-weathered, it is said to have borne the date 1712 (ibid.) and is inscribed: D(OMINUS) [PATRICIUS H]UME COMES DE MARCHMONT &c / [HOC] BURGI PRETORIUM SUIS SU[MPTIB]US AEDIFICARI FECIT ('Patrick Hume, Earl of Marchmont, etc., had this burgh court-house built at his own expense'). A further four-line inscription, largely illegible, begins: EXURGE DOMINE ('Arise, O Lord').

12 Ibid., 43-4.

13 Photographs in NMRS; *Prison Inspectors' Third Report*, 18-20; *NSA*, **2** (Berwickshire), 48. The style of the building suggests that it may have been designed by J Gillespie Graham.

14 Colvin, *Architects* (2nd ed., 1978), 247; plans in SRO, RHP 49497 (copies in NMRS, BWD 34/4-8); Gibson, op.cit., 171-4; *NSA*, **2**, 43-4; correspondence, 1831, in SRO, GD 158/774/1 and 4.

15 Gibson, op.cit., 175-6; Small, J W, *Scottish Market Crosses* (1899), pls.86-7.

36 Haddington

1 The contract stipulated that the town-house was to measure 18.3m by 11m (TCM 10 June 1742). The SE block was extended by 0.9m to the E in 1824-5 (TCM 19 June 1824). The N end of Adam's building, which was hip-roofed, had tall round-headed first-floor windows

2 (*supra*, fig.103A; engraving in *Illustrated London News*, 27 August 1853; copy in NMRS).

2 Martine, J, *Reminiscences of the Royal Burgh of Haddington* (1883), 105-6; TCM, *infra*.

3 TCM 3 December 1788.

4 Gray, W F, *A short history of Haddington* (1944), 140.

5 Survey plans, 1941, in NMRS (ELD/71/1-15).

6 *Edinburgh Evening News*, 5 March 1956.

7 Ibid.; drawing of window-head, 1941, in NMRS.

8 TCM 10 June 1742, 24 February 1750, 3 May 1783; Gray, op.cit., 140.

9 It is possible that this was obtained following the council order 'to buy ane yrne kyst in Flanders' (TCM 29 January 1533/4).

10 Notes on bells and clock by J Robb, 1879, in Local Studies Centre, Haddington Library.

11 TCM 19 March 1700. The original inscription (Robb, op.cit.) read: IOANNES MEIKLE EDINBURGI ME FECIT FOR THE TOWNE OF HADINGTOWNE 1700.

12 TCM 23 October 1669.

13 TCM 20 February 1425/6.

14 Gray, op.cit., 142.

15 TCM 21 March 1571/2, 12 July 1658, 20 January 1683; Gray, op.cit., 142.

16 *SBRS Misc.*, 80. The upper part of the steeple appears in Slezer's view of Haddington.

17 TCM 3 August 1732, 2 and 8 December 1740.

18 TCM 2 March, 9 November 1741; obligation by subscribers, 1741-2 (SRO, B 30/21/105); contract with Robert Reid, mason and George Pirie, wright, 7 June 1742 (entered in TCM 10 June 1742).

19 TCM 24 February, 7 November 1743, 19 June, 10 November 1744, 10 June 1745.

20 TCM 19 June 1744 (extra £10 to be paid); Martine, op.cit., 23, 105-6.

21 TCM 24 February 1750, 29 March 1775, 3 May 1783.

22 TCM 14 December 1774, 1 November 1788; Gray, op.cit., 140.

23 TCM 1 November, 3 December 1788.

24 See D Walker in *Country Life*, 10 August 1972, 319-20.

25 TCM 26 June 1823, 20 March, 5 and 17 April, 19 June 1824. The Treasurer's Accounts (SRO, B 30/19/4) include payments of about £480 to Alexander Wilson and Peter Dickson, and of £18 15s 6d to William Burn.

26 TCM 26 March 1830.

27 TCM 13 April, 2 July 1830; record placed in foundation-stone, 15 June 1830, printed in *The East Lothian Literary and Statistical Journal, 1831* (reprinted in *The Haddington Courier*, 20 August 1921). For James McWatt, builder, see Martine, op.cit., 23. The Treasurer's Accounts for 1830-3 (SRO, B 30/19/4) record payments of £1,150 to McWatt and £61 5s 6d to Graham for his design.

28 *Prison Inspectors' Second Report*, 129-31; *Thirteenth Report*, 10; TCM 1 December 1848; Name Book, East Lothian No.22, p.32.

29 TCM 7 February, 21 March, 20 October 1854, 16 February, 22 March, 24 May 1855.

37 Inveraray

1 *Inventory of Argyll*, **7**, No.209. For the old and new towns of Inveraray, see ibid., Nos.199-210; Lindsay and Cosh, *Inveraray*, *passim*.

2 Lindsay and Cosh, *Inveraray*, fig.56 on p.159.

3 Argyll and Bute Archives, Commissioners of Supply Minutes, 19 October 1773.

4 Ibid., 2 May 1759; Lindsay and Cosh, *Inveraray*, 163-4.

5 Lindsay and Cosh, *Inveraray*, 19-23, fig.7 on p.27; *Inventory of Argyll*, **7**, pp.428-9.

6 *Inventory of Argyll*, **7**, No.209; Lindsay and Cosh, *Inveraray*, 157-65.

7 Lindsay and Cosh, *Inveraray*, 272, 315-16.

8 Ibid., 315-19; *Inventory of Argyll*, **7**, No.205; Fraser, A, *The Royal Burgh of Inveraray* (1977), 48-9.

9 Information from former provost A MacIntyre.

38 Inverbervie

1 Gove, R, *Inverbervie: "the story of the royal burgh"* (1992).

2 *NSA*, **11** (Kincardineshire), 8.

3 Ibid. A larger room on the ground floor was also in use as a lock-up cell in 1836 (*Prison Inspectors' Second Report*, 27).

4 Gove, op.cit.

39 Inverkeithing

1 The medieval mercat cross was moved from the High Street to a position in front of the town-house in 1799 (Stephen, W, *History of Inverkeithing and Rosyth* (1921), 24). It has recently been returned to its original site.

2 Ibid., 25.

3 Ibid., 26, where it is suggested that the lower stages of the steeple preserve earlier masonry; TCM 26 March 1755.

4 TCM 12 and 18 December 1769, 15 March 1770, 9 April 1771;

Stephen, loc.cit.

5   TCM 17 January, 31 March 1777.

40 Inverness

1   Maclean, L (ed.), *The Hub of the Highlands* (1975), 175.
2   John Hossack was provost of Inverness in the middle of the 18th century. There is no record of a bell-foundry at Leicester in 1759 (information from Leicestershire Record Office), but a bell was sent to London for recasting in 1758 (Pollitt, A G, *Historic Inverness* (1981), 84), as had been done in 1674 and 1724 (Mackay, W and Boyd, H C, *Records of Inverness* (New Spalding Club, 1911-24), **2**, 259; SRO, GD 23/4/74/13 and 64).
3   Fraser-Mackintosh, C, *Invernessiana* (1875), 108-9.
4   Pollitt, op.cit., 83.
5   Mackay and Boyd, op.cit., **2**, 216, 353, 355-6.
6   TCM 14 March 1692.
7   *Prison Inspectors' Second Report*, 64; Fraser-Mackintosh, C, *Antiquarian Notes*, **1** (1865), 16; Neild, *Prisons*, 291-2. For the bridge, see Mackay and Boyd, op.cit., **2**, 284, 285-6, 295, 306, 309, 317, 319, 331, 335, 347-8. It was swept away in the floods of 1849.
8   Mackay and Boyd, op.cit., **2**, 262, 272, 274, 353; *Transactions of the Inverness Scientific Society*, **8** (1912-18), 291.
9   TCM 23 September 1707 (council-meeting 'within the new session house'); Name Book, Inverness-shire No.33, p.125; Pollitt, op.cit., pl.4; view by P Delavault in Barron, E, *Old Inverness* (1967). The site is said to have been occupied by the Forbes of Culloden mansion (Fraser-Mackintosh, *Antiquarian Notes*, 230), or that of the Frasers of Lovat (Maclean, op.cit., 179). The building was used in 1746 as the headquarters of the Duke of Cumberland after the Battle of Culloden (Pollitt, op.cit., 48).
10   Lawson, A, *A Guide to Inverness Town House* (n.d.); Pollitt, op.cit., 38-40, 42-9. The royal and burgh armorials were carved for the gateway at the E end of the bridge by James Smith (ibid., 40; Mackay and Boyd, op.cit., **2**, 335, 348).
11   SRO, GD 23/4/74 (Inverness Treasurer's Accounts); Barron, op.cit., s.v. 'the steeple'.
12   TCM 1 May, 31 July 1786, 27 March 1787, 28 July 1788; memorial dated 1786 in Fraser-Mackintosh, op.cit., 17-18.
13   TCM 25 June 1787, 27 April 1789, 16 and 30 May 1791.
14   TCM 28 June 1818 (replies to queries by House of Commons committee).
15   TCM 29 April, 25 May, 27 July 1789, 20 September 1790; Pollitt, op.cit., 84-5.
16   Laing is described as architect by Barron (op.cit., s.v. 'the steeple'). TCM 7 February 1791 states that Charles and James Smith, masons, had carried out the work as agreed 'to a certain height', but another undertaker was being employed, through their agent in Edinburgh, for completing it. Sir William Forbes described 'a very handsome spire, built by Stevens, who erected that of St Andrew's Church at Edinburgh' (letter to Lady Forbes, 1 July 1794; Nat. Lib. of Scot., MS Acc. 4796/46/5). The statement in *Stat. Acct.*, **9**, 623, that 'the spire was built by the architect of St Andrew's Church in Edinburgh' presumably refers to Stevens, who also built the steeple of St Cuthbert's Church, Edinburgh. It has been assumed to be a reference to William Sibbald, who himself spent some time in Inverness (Maclean, op.cit., 175; Colvin, *Architects*, 592, 867, 924).
17   TCM 21 September 1789, 20 September 1790, 7 February, 26 September 1791, 9 January, 18 June, 3 December 1792.
18   Miller, H, *My Schools and Schoolmasters* (1852 and many editions), ch.19. Miller described 'the neat, well-proportioned, very uninteresting jail-spire of the burgh' as 'a fifth-rate piece of ornamental masonry'.
19   TCM 28 June 1818; *Prison Inspectors' Second Report*, 64-8; *NSA*, **14** (Inverness), 16, 34.
20   Pollitt, op.cit., 86 (quoting *The Inverness Courier*, 26 May 1853), 92.

41 Jedburgh

1   *Inventory of Roxburgh*, **1**, No.426.
2   Ibid., fig.39; photographs in NMRS.
3   Jeffrey, A, *The History and Antiquities of Roxburghshire* (1859), **2**, 112, 154. The burgh seal (ibid., pl. opp. p.153) shows a Jeddart staff rather than a spear.
4   Ibid.
5   The first-floor room was in use as a jury-room for the adjacent circuit court in 1859 (OS 1:500 plan, 21.5.9).
6   *Inventory*, **1**, 214.
7   TCM 29 May, 16 December 1779, 10 March, 5, 6 and 19 July 1780, 2 April, 29 June 1781.
8   Jeffrey, op.cit., **2**, 99; TCM 25 August 1809 ('extensive and commodious' building proposed, site and old materials valued at £1000), 28 March, 12 May 1810. Jeffrey describes the building as the 'Town Hall', but it is named as the 'County Hall' in 1859 (Name Book, Roxburgh No.20, p.48), and both descriptions are used in TCM, 1810-1861, *passsim*.
9   OS 1:500 plan.
10   TCM 18, 24 and 28 January, 6 and 11 February 1861. Rhind estimated the cost of the proposed work as £3,200.

11   Nicholson, R, *Scotland, the Later Middle Ages* (1974), 568. But the source quoted (Lesley, J, *The History of Scotland* (Bannatyne Club, 1830), 81) does not mention the tolbooth.
12   Watson, R, *Jedburgh Records* (n.d.), 55.
13   TCM 16 December 1779.
14   TCM 29 July 1756.
15   TCM 26 November 1755, 17 May, 2 and 29 July 1756; Jeffrey, op.cit., **2**, 99-100. Application was made to the heritors in 1756 to re-use the masonry of the old Latin school for the steeple. James Winter, who was later described as 'architeck' (TCM 15 October 1772), may have been the mason-architect of that name who worked at Blair Castle in 1743-4 and 1747-58 (Colvin, *Architects*, 1070). Sir Hew Dalrymple represented the Haddington group of burghs, which included Jedburgh, from 1761-8.
16   TCM 16 December 1783 (council-house); 8 and 29 April 1815, 10 September 1818 (need for new jail, discussion of burgh contribution); MacIvor, I, *Jedburgh Castle, a Georgian Prison* (1972), 2-3 and *passim*; *Prison Inspectors' Second Report*, 132-4. The burgh offered a site for the Bridewell anywhere on Castlehill, but it was built SE of Abbey Bridge, and demolished in 1972 (TCM 17 September 1785; MacIvor, op.cit., 2; Wood's plan (1823); photograph in NMRS (RX/2598).

42 Kelso

1   Jeffrey, op.cit., **3**, 11.
2   Ibid.; *Stat. Acct.*, **10**, 598; painting in private possession (photograph in NMRS).
3   *The Builder*, **89** (1904), 396.
4   Engraving in Haig, J, *A Topographical and Historical Account of the Town of Kelso* (1825), opp. p. 98; photograph, *c.*1880, in NMRS (RX/1644).

43 Kilbarchan

1   MacKenzie, R D, *Kilbarchan, a parish history* (1902), 156-7, 238; Anon., *Kilbarchan Steeple* (appeal leaflet, *c.*1955).
2   MacKenzie, op.cit., 281-2. The upper part of the original painted timber statue, by Archibald Robertson, a Greenock figure-head carver, is preserved in the 'Ladies' Room'.
3   A clock-face on the NW is said to have been provided in 1755, and the others were added in 1782 *(Kilbarchan Steeple Leaflet)*. The clock-mechanism, which is undated, may date from the same period.
4   MacKenzie, op.cit., 156.
5   Ibid., 157.
6   *Kilbarchan Steeple Leaflet.*

44 Kilmaurs

1   OS 6-inch map, Ayrshire sheet 18 (1st ed.,1854-6); copy of drawing dated 1895, and photographs of 1950s-60s, in NMRS.
2   Pont, *Cuninghame*, 274 ('a Town-house, with steeple and clock bearing the date 1709'); Gibson, M, 'Transcription of Minute Book of Kilmaurs Town Council 1719-99' (typescript at Dean Castle, Kilmarnock), p.34.
3   Gibson, op.cit., (1800-52), p.9.
4   Ibid., pp.9, 10.
5   Clouston, 'Ayrshire Bells', 233.
6   McNaught, D, *Kilmaurs, Parish and Burgh* (1912), 266-7; Gibson, loc.cit.
7   A demolished single-storeyed building known as the 'old tolbooth', formerly situated at the NW angle of Main Street and Irvine Road, may also have included a prison (McNaught, op.cit., 276 and pl. opp. p.276).
8   Close, R, *Ayrshire and Arran, an illustrated architectural guide* (1992), 118; Sporne, *Stocks*, **2**, 210-11.

45 Kinghorn

1   *Cast. and Dom. Arch.*, **5**, 116-17.
2   Contract with James [?]Walls, mason in Dunfermline, 17 March 1829 (Kinghorn Burgh Register of Deeds (1810-34), fols. 104-9). The contract price was £1,707, but it has been stated that the final price was £2,500 (Reid, A, *Kinghorn* (1906), 19).
3   *Prison Inspectors' Second Report*, 93.

46 Kinross

1   Lowther, *Journall*, 40; SRO, GD 29/25. Bruce had been granted a burgh of regality at Kinross in 1685 (Pryde, *Burghs*, no.218), and the jailer was to serve as officer for the sheriff and regality courts.
2   *NSA*, **9** (Kinross), 19; transcript of lost Steeple Committee minutes, in Sandeman Library, Perth.
3   *NSA*, **9** (Kinross), 14; letter from Thomas Brown to William Adam,

August 1824, enclosing plan and specification (Blair Adam papers, section 4/995). For the Duke of Hamilton's approval of the design, see p.177.

4 Steeple Committee minutes, 29 March 1831; *NSA*, **9** (Kinross), 14; Name Book, Fife and Kinross No.89, p.24; date-panel above E door of Town Hall.

5 Some branches of the Bruce family used the lion rampant as crest, but the version holding the shield has not been identified.

6 Steeple Committee minutes, 23 April 1751, 27 June 1755.

7 Ibid., 16 January 1778.

8 The original intention was to build a turnpike stair, but in 1751 timber was obtained from 'Sir John (Bruce)'s Parks' to make trapdoors 'to lead from one floor of the steeple to another' (ibid., 12 May 1742, 29 April 1751). A S doorway leading into the church was blocked after its demolition (ibid., 5 March 1833).

9 Ibid., 7 June 1751, 27 June 1755, 4 December 1758, 5 February 1759 (contract with R Millar), 28 August 1760, 10 January, 9 April 1761.

10 Ibid., 19 January 1816, and notes by D Marshall.

11 Ibid., 8 and 31 March, 3 and 12 May 1742, 23 and 29 April, 3 May, 7 and 13 June 1751, 27 June 1755, 25 August 1758; SRO, Kinross Kirk-Session minutes (CH 2/487/3), 12 June 1742.

12 The building was described as the County House in 1771 (*infra*), as the Tolbooth in 1797 (Steeple minutes, 20 January 1797), and as 'Town House and Tollbooth' in Wood's plan of 1823.

13 Gurney, *Prisons*, 40-1.

14 For a description of the interior in 1946, see Eland, G (ed.), *Shardeloes Papers of the 17th and 18th centuries* (1947), 137-8.

15 Blair Adam papers, letter from John to William Adam, 10 November 1772, quoted by A Rowan in *Journal of the Royal Society of Arts*, **122** (1974), 660-1; letter from William Drake, 26 June 1779 (Eland, op.cit., 137). Robert Adam was Member of Parliament for Kinross-shire from 1768 to 1774.

16 Note in Steeple Committee minutes; information from Mr S Connolly, Sandeman Library, Perth, quoting Commissioners of Supply minutes.

47 Kintore

1 *PSAS*, **91** (1957-8), 87.

2 Ibid., 87-8.

48 Kirkcudbright

1 *Inventory of Kirkcudbright*, p.115; TCM 14 June 1760.

2 There is a rough vertical joint at the junction of the two phases, and the original length is uncertain. The turnpike that was altered in 1732 (*infra*) appears to have been some distance from the W gable, and a cellar at the W end was acquired in 1754 to allow the building of the prison.

3 A similar pend is preserved in one of the houses E of the tolbooth.

4 TCM 27 May 1732, 7 December 1751('the Tolbooth yeat'), 6 July 1752 ('the present entry of the Tolbooth').

5 *Cast. and Dom. Arch.*, **5**, 114-15; *Inventory of Kirkcudbright*, p.114.

6 Sporne, *Stocks*, **2**, 214-16.

7 The blocked window, and the slit-window W of the doorway, are wrought with half-rolls within two quirks, as is the fourth-stage window which appears to belong to the repairs of 1724.

8 The W belfry-opening is displaced to the N to accommodate a chimney-flue, presumably part of the work of 1724.

9 *Kirkcudbright Records (1606-58)*, 774; *Inventory of Kirkcudbright*, p.115.

10 *Records*, 380, 394.

11 *Inventory of Kirkcudbright*, fig.79.

12 Ibid. A collection of early locks at the tolbooth includes a padlock dated 1754, presumably made for this extension.

13 *Inventory of Kirkcudbright*, p.115.

14 *PSAS*, **99** (1966-7), 202-3; *Records*, 774.

15 *PSAS*, loc.cit.; TCM 23 November 1723 ('the litle bell hath sustained a great damadge'), 28 August 1725 (account for £6 1s 6d sterling to Thomas Maxwell, shipmaster).

16 *TDGNHAS*, 2nd series, **13** (1896-7), 113-15.

17 Robison, J, *Kirkcudbright* (1926), 164-5; *Records*, 51-3, 102, 114-15.

18 *Records*, 106, 216, 289, 382, 341; *RPC*, 1st series, **13** (1622-5), 728.

19 *RPC*, loc.cit.; *Records*, 323-4, 341-3, 380, 393-4. A small-scale excavation inside the E end of the main block in 1991 found no evidence of earlier occupation (report by Scottish Urban Archaeological Trust). Two rigs of land belonging to the tolbooth were sold in 1628 (*Records*, 280).

20 TCM 4 January 1642, quoted in *TDGNHAS*, 2nd series, **13** (1896-7), 114; *Records*, 662, 723, 734; Robison, op.cit., 11.

21 TCM 14 November, 7 December 1723, 29 November 1725.

22 TCM 27 May 1732, 8 January, 2 April 1733.

23 TCM 10 October 1744, 7 December 1747, 7 December 1751, 6 July 1752, 30 January 1754. A cellar W of the tolbooth entry was purchased before work began, and was presumably demolished.

24 14 June 1760, 5 and 23 March (subscription begun), 21 July (£140 raised), 26 October 1763, 11 July 1764.

25 TCM 6 November 1725, 19 September 1764, 22 February 1774. In 1774 the records were moved to the council-house from the 'under

shop' of the tolbooth, which was considered too damp, and more suitable as a house for the bellman.

26 TCM 25 July 1774, 19 and 20 June 1787, 5 April, 16 June 1788. The hall was to be at least 9.1m square, and with an 'alcove roof' (?coved ceiling) 5.5m high. It was agreed to omit an intended 'pyramid' (?pediment). The OS 1:1056 plan of 1850/4 shows a three-bay court-house about 9m square over all.

27 Scott, Sir W, *Guy Mannering* (1815 and many editions), ch.28.

28 Neild, *Prisons*, 318.

29 Contract and specification, 1815, in Stewartry Museum; *Prison Inspectors' Third Report*, 30-3; *NSA*, **4** (Kirkcudbright), 24-5.

49 Kirkintilloch

1 Martin, D, *The Story of Kirkintilloch* (1987), 25. In 1808 the Council resolved to negotiate with a Mr Lang whose house at the Cross was considered 'an eligible situation' for a town-house and schoolhouse (TCM 26 March 1808).

2 TCM 17 October 1815 (council-room), 31 May 1823 (court-room). Horne, J (ed.), *Kirkintilloch* (1910), 48, describes the school-room. For the jail see TCM 13 December 1816 (application to have it declared a legal burgh jail); *Prison Inspectors' Second Report*, 104; *NSA*, **8**, 201-2.

3 A previous clock was installed in 1822 (TCM 16 February 1822).

4 TCM 18 April and 17 October 1829, 11 June 1835, 12 March and 21 May 1836, 26 April 1849. For description see *PSAS*, **82** (1947-8), 189.

5 Pryde, *Kirkintilloch,* 4.

6 Agreements of 1749 quoted in TCM 5 May 1808 (transcripts in Horne, op.cit., 45-8).

7 TCM 9 March, 13 April 1813, 20 December 1814. The building-committee's accounts (TCM 26 February 1820), are confusing, and different totals have been quoted (NSA, **8**, 202; Horne, op.cit., 48; Johnston, T, *Old Kirkintilloch* (1937), 171).

8 TCM 17 October 1815, 31 May 1823; Treasurer's Accounts, 1815.

9 TCM 30 October 1860; Horne, op.cit., 73-6.

50 Lanark

1 Set in a recess in the E wall of the town-house there is a carving with a unicorn and a double-headed eagle, part of the burgh arms, which is believed to be a remnant of the mercat cross (information from Mr P Archibald, Lindsay Institute, Lanark).

2 Robertson, A D, *Lanark: the Burgh and its Councils 1469-1880* (1974), 44-6; Name Book, Lanarkshire No. 42, p.34.

3 Information from Mr P Archibald.

4 TCM 28 November 1777, 13 May 1779. The dimensions originally agreed for the hall were 13.7m by 7m.

5 Robertson, op.cit., 63-4, pl. between pp.48 and 49. The recasting of 1740 was by the Edinburgh founder William Ormiston (ibid., 63).

6 *Lanark Extracts*, 1-2.

7 Ibid., pp.xxii, 49-50, 62, 64-5, 67, 69-70.

8 Ibid., 158-9, 284, 287.

9 TCM 28 November 1777.

10 TCM 28 November, 4 December 1777, 15 January, 23 June, 9 July 1778, 13 May 1779.

11 *NSA*, **6**, 29.

12 *Prison Inspectors' Third Report*, 79-81; Fullarton, A, *Gazetteer of Scotland* (1843), **2**, 209; Robertson, op.cit., 44-6.

51 Langholm

1 Glen, D, *Hugh MacDiarmid, out of Langholm and into the World* (1992), 12.

2 OS 6-inch map, Dumfries-shire sheet 45 (1857/62).

3 *Prison Inspectors' Third Report*, 25.

4 *Geog. Coll.*, **1**, 389.

5 Telford, T, *Life of Thomas Telford, Civil Engineer, written by himself* (1838), 5.

6 SRO, Buccleuch Muniments, GD 224/657/13/1/34. For Elliot's work at Drumlanrig in 1813, see *Country Life*, 8 September 1960, p.489.

7 Library Committee Minutes in Langholm Library.

52 Lauder

1 Drawing by General William Hutton (d.1827) in Nat. Lib. of Scot., Adv. MS 30.5.22, fol.34; photographs in NMRS.

2 Romanes, R, *Papers on Lauder* (1903), 144.

3 Ibid., 67.

4 Thomson, A, *Lauder and Lauderdale* (n.d.), 33.

5 Ibid., 34; *Calendar of State Papers relating to Scotland, 1547-1603*, **13**, part 1 (1969), 207. In 1606 the Earl of Home and others received a royal pardon for the slaughter in 1598 of Bailie William Lauder, known as 'William at the West-Point', within the *pretorium* (Pitcairn, R, *Ancient Criminal Trials in Scotland* (Bannatyne and Maitland Clubs, 1833), **3**, part 1, 116).

6   TCM [-] March 1729, 13 November 1734; Thomson, op. cit., 36-8. This one-handed clock, made by John Kirkwood (cf. No.35), was moved to Mellerstain stables when the present clock by R and R Murray, Lauder, was installed in 1859 (ibid.).

7   Thomson, op.cit., 34; TCM 21 April, 3 May 1773.

8   Thomson, op.cit., 35-6; Romanes, op.cit., 143-5.

53 Leith

1   *RMS*, **3** (1513-46), no.3088. It has been suggested (*Inventory of Edinburgh*, pp.lxi, 267) that the earlier tolbooth stood at Restalrig, but the charter of 1545 states that the inhabitants of Leith were deprived of their court-house 'through the burning of the said town by the English'.

2   *Edinburgh Extracts (1557-71)*, 169, 180-1 (quoting Mary's letter of 5 March 1563/4. The armorial panel, now displayed in the porch of South Leith parish church, is illustrated in Robertson, D H, *The Sculptured Stones of Leith* (1851), pl.2; Irons, J C, *Leith and its Antiquities* (1901), **1**, 295.

3   *Extracts (1557-71)*, 207-8; Irons, op.cit., **1**, 352-6; *Inventory of Edinburgh*, pp.lv-lix.

4   Irons, op.cit., **2**, 148-9.

5   Letters from Sharpe to Scott, suggesting the retention of the original façade (Partington, W (ed.), *The Private Letter-books of Sir Walter Scott* (1930), 309-10; Allardyce, A (ed.), *Letters from and to Charles Kirkpatrick Sharpe, Esq.* (1888), **2**, 288-9); Wilson, *Memorials*, **2**, 196. For illustrations see: ibid., **1**, pl. opp. p.104; Storer, *Views*; watercolour by J Skene in Edinburgh Public Library (Butchart, R, *Prints and Drawings of Edinburgh* (1955), pl.56; *BOEC*, **27** (1949), pl. opp. p.121); Robertson, op.cit., pl.3.

6   Edinburgh TCM 8 June 1569.

7   Ibid., 9 June 1726; Maitland, *Edinburgh*, 495.

8   Robertson, D, *The Bailies of Leith* (1915), 198-200 and 185-204 *passim*.

9   Robertson, D, *South Leith Records*, **1** (1911), 121; *Extracts (1665-80)*, 344 (ordering the city treasurer to 'caus theik the top of the steeple with lead').

10   Robertson, *Sculptured Stones*, pl.3.

11   Robertson, *Bailies*, 201-4; *Prison Inspectors' Third Report*, 84; signed drawings in NMRS (DC 6699-6708). Sharpe's description of 'the new barbarity, designed by Mr Gillespie' (Partington, op.cit., 309) presumably refers not to Gillespie Graham (as assumed in Colvin, *Architects*, 421), but to the contractor George Gillespie, builder, who signed the contract-drawings on 12 August 1824, and subsequently went bankrupt (SRO, CS 96/362).

12   *BOEC*, **20** (1935), 64.

13   *The Builder*, **26** (1868), 406; **61** (1891), 374.

14   Plans dated from Simpson's office (19 Charlotte Street, Leith), 26 December 1878, in possession of City of Edinburgh Council Property Services. A single-storeyed three-bay classical building in this position is shown in an undated illustration (Marshall, J S, *The Life and Times of Leith* (1986), 174) and, as part of the Town Hall, in Moffat, W, *Geometrical and Geological Landscape from Leith to Edinburgh* (1837), no.12.

15   *The Builder*, **84** (1903), 146; *Edinburgh Evening News*, 1 October 1983.

16   *BOEC*, **20** (1935), 64.

17   These consoles are probably a late 19th-century addition, replacing an original lintel at springing-level (cf. engraving in Shepherd, *Modern Athens*).

18   *The Builder*, **61** (1891), 374; *Journal of Decorative Art*, **12** (1892), 72. The Corinthian doorcase leading from the stair to the council-chamber bears the burgh arms and the date 1904-5.

19   Robertson, D, 'The Magistrates and Masters of Leith', in *BOEC*, **20** (1935), 61-77; Robertson, *Bailies*, 186, 204, 235-7.

20   *Edinburgh Evening News*, 1 October 1983.

54 Lerwick

1   Shetland Archives, Commissioners of Supply Minutes (CSM), 29 January 1767 (order to send to Scotland for corner-stones); 1 November 1770 (£60 paid 'for free stone brought from Leith and Orkney'). The Commissioners are indebted to Mrs M Robertson, Lerwick, for providing references to these documents and for making available a copy of her typescript notes on 'The Lerwick Tolbooth' (1992).

2   A widened platform at the entrance-doorway, and the existing raised band at first-floor level, are shown in *Cast. and Dom. Arch.*, **5**, fig. 1248 on p.129, but not in earlier views (*infra*, n.4).

3   CSM 22 February 1790; Manson, T, *Lerwick during the last half century* (1923), 201.

4   Watercolour by Sir Henry Dryden, 1855 (NMRS, SHD/73/1); *Cast. and Dom. Arch.*, **5**, fig.1248 on p.129; photographs in NMRS; Scott-Moncrieff, G (ed.), *The Stones of Scotland* (1938), pl.119 opp. p.80.

5   CSM 4 November 1772, 13 July 1780; Robertson, op.cit., pp.6-8. The spire may originally have been lead-covered (ibid., p.7).

6   Strong, T, 'Lerwick Past and Present', in *The Shetland Times*, 1887; undated plan of basement in Shetland Archives, sheriff-court deed

4439; *Prison Inspectors' Second Report*, 45; Robertson, op.cit., pp.6-8.

7   William Aberdeen's perspective view of Lerwick (1766) shows a substantial gabled building on what is probably the same site (Irvine, J W, *Lerwick — the birth and growth of an island town* (1985), 36).

8   CSM 17 July 1755. Scalloway Castle, which had previously been used as a prison, was in disrepair (ibid.).

9   CSM 4 December 1762, 20 June 1766, 29 January 1767; Sandisson, W, *A Shetland Merchant's Day-Book in 1762* (1934), 4, 38-9.

10   CSM 29 and 31 January, 25 August 1767, 29 November 1772, and 1759-67, *passim*; Robertson, op.cit., pp.1-3.

11   CSM 29 January 1767, 1 November 1770 (detailed account of expenditure); Robertson, op.cit., pp.2-5; *The Shetland News*, 1 August 1908 (laying of foundation-stone 'with masonic honours').

12   Low, G, *A Tour through the Islands of Orkney and Schetland ... in 1774* (1879), 66; Robertson, op.cit., p.6.

13   Robertson, op.cit., pp.6-8.

14   Ibid., pp.7-8; *Prison Inspectors' Second Report*, 45-7; Irvine, op.cit., 144.

15   Name Book, Shetland No.1, p.141; Robertson, op.cit., p.8; Nicolson, J R, *Lerwick Harbour* (1977), 78.

16   *Handbook to Lerwick Town Hall* (1984), 43-4.

55 Linlithgow

1   TCM 6 and 21 July 1847. The council accepted Thomas Brown's proposal for 'taking down the front wall of the whole of the upper storey, facing anew with hewn stone the whole of the front of the middle storey, and rebuilding the upper storey over it all in the same style and exactly in the form of the present building' (TCM 7 January 1848).

2   The original access was by a double forestair, rising from the E and W ends of the S front, which is shown in a plan attributed to John Smith (*infra*) and in one of Slezer's views of Linlithgow. This was replaced in 1810 by a cast-iron verandah (*infra*).

3   TCM 7 April 1848. A Hill-Adamson calotype (Bruce, D, *Sun Pictures* (1973), 136-7) shows the building before the fire of 1847.

4   Cf. Smith's contract dated 4 February and 18 March 1668 (SRO, B 48/18/116); report by T Brown (TCM 7 January 1848).

5   Wood's plan of 1820 shows in the NW re-entrant a building which was presumably the two-storeyed grain-market (subsequently used as a house for the burgh officer) to which a storey was added for use as a debtors' prison (*Stat. Acct.*, **14**, 568; TCM 12 December 1829, 1 November 1847).

6   The E and W clock-faces are later additions, occupying blocked window-recesses.

7   Memorial for town council (TCM 1 November 1847), confirmed by Smith's contract (*supra*, n.4) and numerous entries in TCM.

8   A stair is shown in this position in Smith's plan (*infra*, n.18), but his contract mentions the possibility of a vault there; the plan also shows two rooms in the W end.

9   TCM 23 October 1824, 19 May 1827, 12 December 1829, 1 November 1847.

10   TCM 7 January 1848. The previous arrangement of this storey is uncertain. In 1848 the floor was raised by 0.3m to heighten the court-room below, thus concealing the lower parts of the fireplaces, and a new coved ceiling extended into the former garret-space.

11   SRO, GD 215/1822; B 48/17/1; Fergusson, J, *Ecclesia Antiqua* (1905), 290.

12   SRO, GD 76/1/2/5.

13   SRO, B 38/18/60, and TCM 12 April 1656 (both quoted in Mylne, *Master Masons*, 241). As well as providing building-materials for the Cromwellian forces, the demolition of the tolbooth may have removed a military hazard overlooking the palace.

14   SRO, B 48/18/114 and 115.

15   TCM 23 January 1668; contract dated 4 February and 18 March 1668 (SRO, B 48/18/116).

16   SRO, B 48/18/109 and 117; contract of 4 April 1670 between the burgh and James Young, 'Quarreour at Kingcavill Quarrell' (Mylne, *Master Masons*, pl. opp. p.241).

17   TCM 24 May, 7 June 1673.

18   Mylne, *Master Masons*, pls. between pp. 240 and 241. These may be the 'plans of Town Hall, 1667' included in an inventory of burgh records in 1884 (TCM 1 July 1884).

19   The discrepancies, including the newel-stair extending to the ground floor and the division of an original single W room, are explained by Smith's contract (SRO, B 48/18/116), which shows that the council was undecided on these details. The dimensions specified in the contract are those of this plan, and of the existing building.

20   TCM 18 March 1710, 3 February 1722, 14 October 1752, 20 January, 21 May 1753, 18 May 1754, 11 November 1786, 1 November 1847.

21   TCM 22 and 29 May, 31 July, 4 September 1790.

22   TCM 3 November 1810, 12 June 1813.

23   An extension in this position appears to be shown in Wood's plan of 1820.

24   *Supra*, n.9. For the prison in its final state, see report in TCM 12 December 1829, and *Prison Inspectors' Third Report*, 58-9.

25   TCM 6 July 1847 - 3 November 1848, *passim*.

26   TCM 22 December 1847; cf. *supra*, n.1.

27   TCM 23 April 1857; Waldie, G, *A History of the Town and Palace of Linlithgow* (1858), 17. The clock has been replaced, but the bell remains in a low bellcot on the roof of the tower. A hand-bell cast from the bell that was destroyed in 1847 is in Linlithgow Museum.

28   Plans and descriptive note by J R Walker (SRO, RHP 42374-88; B 48/18/200); plans by W Scott, 1905, in possession of Dick Peddie and Mackay, Leith.

29   Copy plans in NMRS.

30   TCM 24 July, 14 August 1819, 7 May 1825. The date 1821 is incised on a window-lintel (Name Book, Linlithgowshire No.38, pp.39-40).

56 Lochmaben

1   OS 6-inch map, Dumfries-shire sheet 42 (1857-61); views by Aitken (Dumfries Museum, copy in NMRS) and in *Lochmaben Almanac, 1867* (Wilson, J, *The Royal Burgh of Lochmaben* (n.d.), cover).

2   See early views; TCM 26 December 1840 and *passim*.

3   *TDGNHAS*, 3rd series, **29** (1950-1), 89.

4   Precept signed 'James R', 31 January 1625 (SRO, GD 124/10/297; Fraser, Sir W, *The Annandale Family Book* (1894), **2**, 332).

5   TCM 20 July 1627.

6   *RCRBS (1677-1711)*, 375.

7   TCM 1720-2, *passim*; Wilson, op.cit., 25; Wilson in *TDGNHAS*, **52** (1976-7), 152-3. But note the reference to a forthcoming meeting with 'Deacone Meen and the measones' (TCM 9 November 1730).

8   TCM 17 August 1741.

9   Drawing in NMRS. The tolbooth is shown as a hip-roofed block with one first-floor window to each side of the steeple, as at Lochmaben, but with an arcaded ground floor.

10   TCM 30 November 1765, 23 February 1844, 15 April 1847; *NSA*, **4** (Dumfries-shire), 392; *Prison Inspectors' Third Report*, 26-7.

11   TCM 7 February 1825, 8 May 1826, 10 and 14 January 1839, 9 March, 14 December 1869, 17 January 1870.

12   TCM 15 February, 26 December 1877; Schedule of measurement for mason-work, D and J Bryce, 11 November 1876 (MS in NMRS).

57 Maybole

1   'A Description of Carrict' by Rev W Abercrummie (*Geog. Coll.*, **2**, 17; *Cast. and Dom. Arch.*, **3**, 498). This was presumably written before Abercrummie (d.1723) was deposed as minister of Maybole in 1690.

2   For views from NE see: Billings, R W, *Baronial and Ecclesiastical Antiquities of Scotland* (1852), **4**, pl.4; Maybole burgh seal (Lawson, R, *The Capital of Carrick* (1897), 15; Gray, J T, *Maybole, Carrick's Capital* (1973), fig. on dust-wrapper; carving in gable of 1887 Town Hall); engraving in Lawson, op.cit., 26. A distant view from S appears in a pre-1887 photograph by G W Wilson (GWW 2514; copy in NMRS).

3   A small square opening, visible in Wilson's photograph, survives, blocked, in the present SW gable.

4   The bold treatment of the mouldings bears general comparison with other late 16th-century work in SW Scotland, including fragments preserved at Blairquhan itself (photographs in NMRS). The cusped motif is found on a fireplace at Hoddam Castle, Dumfries-shire (ibid.), but the closest parallels are in Cumbria, at the Two Lions Inn of 1585 in Penrith and at Barwise Hall, Hoff, of about 1579 (RCHME, *Inventory of Westmorland*, pl.31). One 19th-century engraving (Lawson, loc.cit.) shows a larger opening of similar form in the NE end-wall, but the burgh seal and Billings both show only a small window in this position. The wall is now concealed by the town hall.

5   Loc.cit.

6   Clouston, 'Ayrshire Bells', 238-9

7   SRO, GD 25/9/44/bundle 5.

8   SRO, GD 25/8/633. A contemporary endorsement states 'of the house in Mayboill, to be ane tolbuith'.

9   Letter of thanks from the burgh, 13 October 1798, in SRO, GD 25/9/44/5.

10   Gray, op.cit., 55, 127.

11   *Prison Inspectors' Third Report*, 44.

12   Lawson, op.cit., 27.

58 Moffat

1   Groome, *Ordnance Gazetteer*, 1166; contract plan of 'the School house, Court house and Prison in Moffat', signed by Stevens, 18 June 1770 (SRO, RHP 85766). For Stevens, who was celebrated as a designer of bridges, see Colvin, *Architects*, 923-4.

2   Drawings by William K[?em]p (copies in NMRS); 18th-century view of Moffat showing old steeple, at Moffat House Hotel.

3   Plan by A Stevens (*supra*, n.1); Groome, loc.cit.; Forman, S, *Moffat ... A Backward Glance* (2nd ed., 1987), 20.

4   Stevens's plan (*supra*) shows a stair rising parallel to the line of the present one, but to the W side of this wall.

5   Groome, loc.cit.; account dated 1665 in Annandale Papers, bundle 606.

59 Montrose

1   The sandstone used originally was quarried at Lauriston in the Mearns (Low, J G, *Highways and Byeways of an Old Scottish Burgh* (1938), 99).

2   The W pediment bore the date 1819 and the names of the Edinburgh sculptors, D Ness and Co., Leith Walk, and of the stonecarver R Dow (ibid., 100).

3   TCM 12 May 1762 ('anent altering the entry to the churchyard'); Low, op.cit., 98-9.

4   This vault contains several graveslabs, table-tombs and mural tablets, including the table-tomb erected in 1761 by the town clerk, William Speid (d.1774), which bears an ink-pot and quill-pens in a Rococco cartouche. Later monuments name relatives of another town clerk, Thomas Stewart, and an undated tablet commemorates Robert Dunbar, who 'was one of the proprietors of this vault'.

5   TCM *passim*; plans by William Smith, 12 April 1819, in Montrose Art Museum (copies in NMRS); Name Book, Angus No.72, p.53.

6   Mitchell, D, *History of Montrose* (1866), 80.

7   TCM 17 April, 13 November 1765, 4 March 1767.

8   Information from the former bellringer, Mr C Campbell, and Mrs R Benvie, Montrose Museum. See also Low, J G, *Memorials of the Church of St. John the Evangelist ... the Parish Church of Montrose* (1891), 125-33, 142-5; Morrison, D and Mouat, A, *Montrose Old Church, a history* (1991), 25-30; photograph of curfew bell in Fraser, D, *East Coast Oil Town before 1700* (1974), 105.

9   Original charter dated 15 December 1375 in Montrose Museum, WC/2. The commissioners are indebted to Mrs F Scharlau for a transcript of this charter. See also Low, *Highways*, 29.

10   Low, *Highways*, 29-30. The 'jail' is shown on John Wood's plan of Montrose (1822), and in paintings by Milne (1826) and Madoland (1832-7) (*infra*).

11   Low, op.cit, 29-31; *Stat. Acct.*, **5**, 32; *Prison Inspectors' First Report*, 67-8.

12   Another version of Madoland's painting, with figures added, is preserved at Sunnyside Hospital, Montrose, and is illustrated in Presly, A S, *A Sunnyside Chronicle 1781-1981* (1981), 1.

13   TCM 15 August 1759, 11 April, 20 and 27 May 1761.

14   TCM 12 May 1762, 16 November 1763. The land-surveyor John Hutcheson claimed payment in 1763 for 'a plan of the intended new Town Hall', which 'had been produced before the Court of Session' (petition dated 31 August 1763, Montrose Museum, Burgh correspondence 5/54). It is probable that this plan was made during the prolonged litigation about the site (TCM 1761-3 *passim*; Low, op.cit., 98-9), and was not an architectural design.

15   TCM 18 December 1765, 5 February 1766.

16   Chapman, *Johnson and Boswell*, 11, 205.

17   TCM 2 and 9 December 1818, 21 April, 5 May 1819; Johns, T, 'The Guildhall 1763-1848' (typescript notes, copy in NMRS). The use of the town-house for balls is commemorated in the local name, 'the ba' hoose' (information from Mr N Atkinson).

18   Johns, loc.cit.

60 Musselburgh

1   TCM 18 February 1828, 15 September 1885.

2   TCM 21 July 1758; Paterson, J, *History of the Regality of Musselburgh* (1858), 85.

3   TCM 14 July 1744 (order to repair steeple, 'in great danger of falling down'); Paterson, op.cit., 85.

4   TCM 16 June 1773; Paterson, op.cit., 83.

5   TCM 20 January 1811, 3 April 1899, 13 November 1900, 21 June, 9 July 1901; Groome, *Ordnance Gazetteer*, 1214.

6   A brass plate bearing this information was stolen 'a good many years' before 1839 (*NSA*, **1**, 273-4).

7   TCM 14 November 1901.

8   TCM 29 October 1821, 27 September 1822.

9   *Inventory of Midlothian*, No.114.

10   *RPC*, 1st series, **2** (1569-78), 232-3.

11   *Stat.Acct.*, **16**, 5-6.

12   TCM 25 March 1700, 14 July 1744, 1 and 21 July 1758; Paterson, op.cit., 84-5.

13   TCM 16 January 1716; Paterson, op.cit., 85.

14   TCM 25 January 1731, 4 August, 22 September 1733. Crighton may have designed the building; he was allowed an extra £7 sterling 'for his pains and attendance' when his account was settled (ibid.).

15   TCM 26 January 1811.

16   TCM 25 May 1885, 9 November 1897, 3 April 1899, 13 November 1900, 19 March, 21 June, 9 July 1901.

61 Nairn

1   Photograph, *c*.1860, in Ellen, D M, *Nairn in old picture postcards* (1987), pl.2.

2   TCM 15 February 1843; Bain, G, *History of Nairnshire* (1893), 313.

3   *Prison Inspectors' Second Report*, 43.

4   Ibid., *Eighth Report*, 68; *Ninth Report*, 37; plans by T Brown in SRO, RHP 21567-971. OS 1:500 plan, Nairn (surveyed 1868), shows a

spiral stair in the area linking the main block to the cell-range, which
has been much altered.

5   Bain, op.cit., 312-16.
6   Copy of engraving in Nairn Highland Council Office, Technical
Services Department, Bain, op.cit., 383-4.
7   TCM 28 September 1816, 27 September 1817, 25 September 1819, 11
December 1822 (final accounts).
8   *The Inverness Advertiser*, 4 February, 14 July 1868; Groome,
Ordnance Gazetteer, 1220.

62 Newburgh

1   TCM 5 September 1815. The 1869 bell, which was recast by
subscription, measures 1.22m in diameter. An uninscribed bell
displayed in the building is believed to have come from a local church.
2   Anderson, J (ed.), *The Protocol Book of Sir Alexander Gaw, 1540-
1558* (SRS, 1910), 16.
3   TCM 1 June 1796.
4   TCM 19 August 1800, 1 February, 12 May 1808. Bailie John
Adamson lent £700 to the building-committee in 1808 (TCM 22
August 1820).
5   TCM 7 August 1806, 14 December 1807, 1 and 8 February 1808.
6   TCM 24 May 1808.
7   TCM 20 June, 18 September 1810, 3 January, 1 February 1815.
8   TCM 30 March 1824; *Prison Inspectors' Second Report*, 80;
Leighton, *Fife*, **2**, 160.
9   A H Millar (*Fife: Pictorial & Historical* (1895), **2**, 362) records that
work was carried out by the Dundee architects C and L Ower. He
suggests that the town-house was extended, but in fact a Jubilee Hall,
now demolished, was built on a separate site to the W.

63 New Galloway

1   Inscription on plaque below W wall-head. The architect was Francis
Armstrong, Dalbeattie (TCM 4, 8 and 22 September 1874).
2   TCM 4 and 15 January 1874.
3   TCM 3 March 1875.
4   TCM 12 June, 12 October 1895.
5   The shield is charged: gules, on a cross azure a boar's head sable, a
coronet or in chief. The supporters are: dexter, a wild man holding a
club; sinister, a ram. Above the helm there is a boar's head as crest,
and a coronet. Cf. Groome, *Ordnance Gazetteer*, 682.
6   TCM 30 January, 1 March, 21 May 1872.
7   Distant view of New Galloway and Kenmure Castle by J C Nattes.
8   TCM 26 April, 18 May 1878.
9   The OS 6-inch map of 1849/53 (Kirkcudbrightshire sheet 24) appears
to show the tower extending N of the main block.
10   *Third Prison Inspectors' Report*, 29.
11   TCM 13 December 1871.
12   *Scots Peerage*, **3**, 351; **5**, 126-9, 135. The larger bell, which was
cracked, is said to have been recast at the Dumfries foundry of 'Mr
McKinnel' at the expense of Mrs Louisa Bellamy Gordon of Kenmure
(TCM, summary of expenditure, 1871-2). However, it closely
resembles the work of John C Wilson, Glasgow (*PSAS*, **99** (1966-7),
206). The older inscriptions are: (1) FOR WILLEAM VISCONT OF
KENMUR. R.M. FECIT. EDIN: 1711. (2) EX DONO MAGISTRI
GULIELMI COCHRAN. KILMARNOCK. R.M. FECIT. EDR.
1711.

65 Newton on Ayr

1   TCM 23 March 1776.
2   Photographs in NMRS; OS 1:1056 town plan.
3   OS town plan; Name Book, Ayrshire No.5, p.11.
4   Clouston, 'Ayrshire Bells', 207.
5   *RMS*, **6** (1593-1608), nos.359, 1048; Murray, D, *Early Burgh
Organization in Scotland* (1932), **2**, 257; TCM 11 October 1649 x
3 January 1650.
6   TCM 14 December 1791; Community Book 15 December 1791, 4
January 1792.
7   TCM 31 May, 30 August 1793, 8 March 1794, 1 October 1795;
Community Book 14 March, 6 May, 7 October 1795.
8   Community Book 14 March, 5 August, 7 October 1795; TCM 7 and
11 September 1795.

66 Newton Stewart

1   One of the local names for the building in 1846 was 'the Market
House' (Name Book, Wigtownshire No. 30, p.24).
2   *Prison Inspectors' Third Report*, 35; *NSA*, **4**, 179, 193.
3   *Stat. Acct.*, **3**, 341.
4   Name Book, loc. cit.

67 North Berwick

1   Visible at wallhead of N front in NMRS photograph EL/1865, dated
1970.
2   Swan, D B, 'The Records of the Burgh of North Berwick' (typescript
in SRO, B 56/15/5), 1801-83.
3   Ibid. (1727-1800), p.8; *Prison Inspectors' Third Report*, 97. The
abutments for substantial cross-walls are visible about 3.2m from the
W gable at both levels.
4   Ibid., p.8; account, 1735 (SRO, B 56/16/98).
5   Ibid., p.8. In 1725 Maxwell sued Hugh Dalrymple, advocate, for
payment for a bell weighing 175 stones, and the latter was reimbursed
by the burgh (SRO, B 56/16/nos.68 and 71).
6   Ibid., '16th-century records', quoting protocol-book of Sir Robert
Lauder, 1540-62.
7   Ibid. (1727-1800), p.7. The masons were Archibald and John Broun
in North Berwick, and Patrick Forgan in Hauch. A bond for 1,000
merks, in connection with the erection of the tolbooth, was discharged
by Sir James Dalrymple in 1729 (SRO, B 56/16/nos.76, 78-9).
8   Ibid., p.20. The coping of the staircase is probably original.
9   Ibid., p.8; account, 1782 (SRO, B 56/16/128).
10   In 1774, because of 'hurt to the furniture of the Councill Roome', an
advance payment of 5s. per night was imposed on these companies
(Swan, op.cit. (1727-1800), p.7).

68 Old Aberdeen

1   TCM 14 July 1789.
2   Munro, A M (ed.), *Records of Old Aberdeen*, **1** (New Spalding Club,
1899), 188; Kennedy, W, *Annals of Aberdeen* (1818), **2**, 311.
3   TCM 23 February, 1 March 1712 (Munro, op.cit., 177-8); Orem, W, *A
Description of the Chanonry, Cathedral and King's College of
Aberdeen in the Years 1724-5* (1830), 191-2.
4   *PSAS*, **94** (1960-1), 284, 294-5. Mowat used the motto AD SACRA
ET IURA ('legal affairs') VOCAMUS.
5   TCM 12 May 1726 (Munro, op.cit., 184); Orem, op.cit., 192.
6   Orem, op.cit., 189-90.
7   Ibid., 190-2; TCM 31 January 1702 (Munro, op.cit., 168).
8   TCM 31 May 1769 (Munro, op.cit., 198), 9 October 1787.
9   TCM 29 March 1779 (ibid., 198), recording the decision to build a
new town-house, to be paid for by public subscription; 9 October
1787, 5 February 1788 (ibid., 202).
10   TCM 5 February 1788 (ibid., 202).
11   TCM 29 March 1779 (ibid., 198).
12   TCM 5 April 1788.
13   TCM 28 October 1822; Treasurer's Accounts, 1809-10.

69 Peebles

1   *Inventory of Peebles-shire*, **2**, No.543.
2   TCM 12 March 1752.
3   Buchan, J W (ed.), *A History of Peeblesshire* (1925), **2**, 153.
4   'Peebles Bridgegate excavations 1985-7' (interim report by Dr P
Dixon, Border Burghs Archaeology Project, 1987); Buchan, op.cit., **2**,
16, 187; Chambers, W, *Charters and Documents Relating to the
Burgh of Peebles 1165-1710* (1872), 128 (works at tolbooth, 1458),
214 (use as school).
5   Buchan, op.cit., **2**, 16, 187, 207-8; Chambers, op.cit., *passim*.
6   TCM Michaelmas 1722; Buchan, op.cit., **2**, 97-8, 105, 283. The
'tolbooth' shown in M J Armstrong's 1775 plan *(Inventory of Peebles-
shire*, **2**, pl.53) on the N side of High Street, opposite the town-house,
was a vault acquired in that year to replace the jail in the old steeple,
and it was used for that purpose until 1798 (Buchan, op.cit., **2**, 105-6).
7   Buchan, op.cit., **2**, 90; TCM 19 July 1749.
8   TCM 12 March 1752, 25 June 1756.
9   Buchan, op.cit., **2**, 97-8, 283-8. The church was rebuilt in 1885, when
the burgh's ownership of the steeple was acknowledged. The existing
bell bears the arms of the burgh and an inscription recording that it
was recast in 1886 'from two bells formerly in the tower of the Old
Cross Church' (ibid., 157-8). From the prolonged litigation in 1873-5
over the town council's authority to have the bells rung for the time of
service at dissenting churches, see Gunn, Dr [C B], *The Parish
Church of Peebles, A.D. 1784-1885* (1917), 126-31.

70 Peterhead

1   An original straight forestair had been replaced in 1859 by a double
forestair and balcony (Neish, R, *Old Peterhead* (1950), 71-3 and
fig.18 on p.70).
2   Arbuthnot, J, *An historical Account of Peterhead* (1815), 21. For the
many subsequent changes of use, see Neish, op.cit., 71-3; Findlay, J
T, *A History of Peterhead* (revised ed., 1933), 274-6.
3   *Prison Inspectors' Second Report*, 37.
4   *PSAS*, **91** (1957-8), 91, 99; Neish, op.cit., 72.
5   Findlay, op.cit., 60-1; Neish, op.cit., 65-6.
6   Neish, op.cit., 67-9. Findlay (op.cit., 62) states that the tolbooth was
demolished in 1788.

7 Arbuthnot, op.cit., 21.
8 Ibid., 22; Findlay, op.cit., 274.
9 Neish, op.cit., 71.
10 Ibid., 72.
11 Ibid., 71-3. Findlay (op.cit., 274-5) refers to 'Mr Stuart, architect'.

71 Pittenweem

1 *Inventory of Fife, etc.*, No.444.
2 Wood, W, *The East Neuk of Fife* (2nd ed., 1887), 301-4; Conolly, *Fifiana*, 214-15; Cook, D, *Annals of Pittenweem, 1526-1793* (1867), 13-15; *APS*, **3** (1567-92), 552-3; *RMS*, **5** (1580-93), no.2356. For the church see record-sheet FIR/61/1, in NMRS.
3 Cook, op.cit., 84.
4 Ibid., 104. An undated (?late 17th-century) account states that the tolbooth and grammar-school were situated S of the church, and that the court of the regality of Pittenweem was held in the tolbooth (*Geog.Coll.*, **3**, 219-20).
5 *Inventory of Fife, etc.*, No.445.
6 An apparent straight joint visible in early photographs suggests that the gable is a later addition to the tower, although it formerly incorporated a roll-moulded window-surround.
7 A square block, set above the lower corbel-course in the centre of the SW front, may have been intended to carry a sundial or an inscription.
8 Martin, P, *What to see in Pittenweem* (1990), 8.
9 Ibid., 9.
10 *Inventory of Fife, etc.*, p.224.
11 *Stat. Acct.*, **4**, 376. The steeple may have been garrisoned, along with other places in the town, at the outbreak of the 'Bishops' Wars' in 1639 (Conolly, *Fifiana*, 215).
12 Conolly, *Fifiana*, 218-19.
13 Drawing of Priory from NE, 1784 (Nat. Lib. of Scot., Hutton Collection, Adv.MS 30.5.23, fol.23a).
14 A simpler porch is shown in early photographs.
15 *Inventory of Fife, etc.*, p.223.
16 *Prison Inspectors' Second Report*, 88; Martin, op.cit., 8.
17 Name Book, Fife No.82, p.43.
18 TCM 16 July 1821.
19 TCM 18 June, 7 and 16 July 1821,

72 Pollokshaws

1 McCallum, A, *Pollokshaws, Village and Burgh, 1600-1912* (1925), 45-6, 50; *The Evening Citizen*, 14 December 1935.
2 Early photographs in Mitchell Library and NMRS; McCallum, op. cit., pl. opp. p.170; *The Evening Times*, 6 April 1909; *The Evening Citizen*, 26 October 1934. The N frontage was further extended by one-storied cottage-like wings with pedimented SE and NW gables.
3 McCallum, op. cit., 45-54.
4 Ibid., 106-7, 134-5, 157; *The Evening Times*, 6 April 1909.

73 Port Glasgow

1 TCM 18 April 1815.
2 TCM 11 February 1814.
3 *Prison Inspectors' Third Report*, 54-5.
4 *APS*, **7** (1661-9), 649.
5 Groome, *Ordnance Gazetteer*, 1342-3.
6 TCM 14 December 1803.
7 TCM 23 April, 9 November 1813.
8 TCM 11 February, 10 March 1814.
9 TCM 18 April 1815, 14 November 1816.
10 Groome, loc.cit.; TCM 15 May 1813, 15 and 17 May 1815, 20 April 1816.
11 TCM 9 August 1860, 5 February 1861, 20 January, 4 February, 4 March, 29 April, 6 May 1862.
12 TCM 24 December 1883, 4 February 1884.
13 TCM 1 July 1889, 6 March, 13 October 1890, 12 and 19 January, 4 February, 16 March 1891.

74 Rothesay

1 Groome, *Ordnance Gazetteer*, 1403; drawings dated 1888 for alterations to W half of site, and earlier undated ground-plan, in possession of Argyll and Bute Council.
2 Anon., *Random Records of Rothesay* (1842), 15; *Prison Inspectors' Third Report*, 68.
3 Groome, loc.cit.
4 Reid, J E, *History of the County of Bute* (1864), 123.
5 *NSA*, **5** (Bute), 104; Wood's plan (1825).
6 TCM 17 March 1688, 28 September 1689; Hewison, J K, *The Isle of Bute in the Olden Time* (1895), **2**, fig.opp.p.188.
7 TCM *passim*; Hewison, op. cit., 203. Blain, writing about 1820, described the town-house as small, comprising a court-room above two prison vaults, and a 'modern' part containing 'very genteel apartments occupied as an office for the town and sheriff clerk, and

two prison rooms for debtors' (Ross, W (ed.), *Blain's History of Bute* (1880), 305-6).
8 Act 1 and 2 William IV, cap.34; Reid, op.cit., 122.
9 Letter from R Brown, Hamilton Palace, 9 April 1831 (Argyll and Bute Archives, BR 21/3).
10 Miscellaneous Court House Papers (ibid., BR 22); TCM 3 July 1833 (contract with Andrew Napier, mason, and others); *NSA*, **5** (Bute), 105. Reid (op.cit., 122) says that the foundation-stone was laid on 20 June 1832, but the local masons' lodge petitioned on 7 June 1833 for a procession to the ceremony (BR 22/2).

75 Saltcoats

1 Carragher, P C, *Saltcoats Old and New* (1909), 91. The trustees of the Eglinton estate gave free access to the quarry.
2 Early drawings and photographs in North Ayrshire Museum, Saltcoats.
3 *The Ayr Advertiser*, 22 September 1825.
4 *NSA*, **5** (Ayrshire), 198.
5 *Third Prison Inspectors' Report*, 52.
6 Clouston, 'Ayrshire Bells', 243. Information about present location of clock and bell from Mrs J McColl, Ardrossan Library.
7 Pryde, *Burghs*, no.212; Carragher, op.cit., 14-15.
8 'Articles of the Saltcoats Town-House Society, 1823' (copy in North Ayrshire Museum, Saltcoats); statement deposited in foundation-stone (*Ardrossan and Saltcoats Herald*, 28 August 1891); Carragher, op.cit., 91. The mason was Alexander McGibb and the joiner John Service, 'both in this place'.
9 *Ardrossan and Saltcoats Herald*, 28 August 1891; Groome, *Ordnance Gazetteer*, 1445-6.

76 Sanquhar

1 Simpson, R, *History of Sanquhar* (new ed., 1865), 63.
2 Wilson, T and McMillan, W, *Annals of Sanquhar* (1931), 167.
3 Brown, J, *The History of Sanquhar* (1891), 245-6. In 1837 only one ground-floor cell and one on an upper floor were in use (*Prison Inspectors' Third Report*, 27).
4 Brown, op.cit., 246.
5 *Inventory of Dumfries-shire*, No.563.
6 Wilson and McMillan, op.cit., 181-3, 190.
7 Sporne, *Stocks*, **2**, 220-1.
8 Brown, op.cit., 244; Wilson and McMillan, op. cit., 90, 116, 161, 166. For a remarkable skirmish in 1653 between two parties of Cromwellian soldiers, started by a Royalist prisoner in the tolbooth, see *Geog. Coll.*, **3**, 199-200.
9 Buccleuch Muniments, Drumlanrig Castle, bundle 1638 (copies in NMRS). The Commissioners are indebted to the Duke of Buccleuch for access to this material, which includes detailed accounts for quarrying and masonwork, and the supply and carriage of timber, lime and other materials.
10 Ibid., letter dated 1 September 1735 from James Erskine; account dated 20 June 1738.
11 Ibid., passim; Wilson and McMillan, op.cit., 167; Simpson, op.cit., 65.
12 Account for 'throwing down stones from the old Castle of Sanquhar for building the townhouse', 1737 (Buccleuch Muniments, bundle 1638); *TDGNHAS*, **21** (1936-8), 4; Simpson, op.cit., 63-4. The lead on the cupola may also have been re-used from the castle (Brown, op.cit., 167; Wilson and McMillan, op.cit., 167).
13 Brown, op.cit., 232-3, 246, 249; Wilson and McMillan, op.cit., 275.
14 Brown, op.cit., 246.

77 Selkirk

1 *Inventory of Selkirkshire*, No.23.
2 Craig-Brown, T, *The History of Selkirkshire* (1886), **2**, plan opp. p.130. Its position is now marked by cobbles, and the monument to Sir Walter Scott stands on the site of the court-room.
3 Wood's plan (1823).
4 Painting in Selkirk Museum; stereo photographs, c.1870 (copies in NMRS, SE/680).
5 For early views of the court-room, see Craig-Brown, op.cit., fig. opp. p.140; photograph in NMRS (SE/656).
6 Craig-Brown, op.cit., 30, 39-40.
7 *Geog. Coll.*, **1**, 355.
8 Craig-Brown, op.cit., 109.
9 Ibid., 113, 117.
10 Ibid., plan opp. p.130.
11 Ibid., 130; TCM 4 September 1801, 16 September 1803 (old town-house being taken down).
12 TCM 4 September 1801, 17 March, 31 May 1802, 2 February 1803. In 1805 it was reported that a balance of £556 was due for the building, and the town council agreed to give a further £100 (TCM 12 June 1805).
13 TCM 17 March, 22 November 1802, 17 January, 18 February, 1 March 1803.
14 TCM 1 March 1803; appendix, no. 37 (p.209).

15 Southey, 'Commonplace book', quoted in Craig-Brown, op.cit., 132.
16 Wood's plan (1823); *Prison Inspectors' Third Report*, 12-13 (prison with nine cells, 'better than most'); Craig-Brown, op.cit., fig. on p.111.
17 Information from Mr I Brown, Selkirk Museum.

78 South Queensferry

1 TCM 1 and 25 November 1641; Mason, J, 'History of South Queensferry' (typescript, 1963; copy in NMRS), pp.99, 352.
2 *Cast. and Dom. Arch.*, **5**, fig.1230 on p.112; TCM 1 December 1812, 1 March 1813.
3 Parted per pale: dexter, a cross between five martlets (for St Margaret of Scotland); sinister, a standing figure in a ship.
4 TCM 23 July, 4 September 1807, 25 April 1808; Mason, op.cit., pp.423-5.
5 TCM 31 January 1832; Mason, op.cit., pp.351-2.
6 TCM 6 February, 3 and 10 November 1817; Mason, op.cit., pp.306-7.
7 *Inventory of Midlothian, etc.*, No.375; TCM 9 January 1750.
8 Mason, op.cit., p.90; *RCRBS (1615-76)*, 343.
9 TCM 21 June 1703. For the 'Black Hole' see also TCM 31 January, 20 March 1832.
10 TCM 29 February 1720, 18 November 1732. The building-committee for Kinross Steeple (No.46) ordered a clock 'upon the same plan with the steeple clock of South Queensferry which (as is reported) was made by Mr Dunlop, Watchmaker at London' (Kinross Steeple Committee minutes, 5 February 1759).
11 TCM 29 February 1720, 5 March 1740.
12 TCM 30 April, 23 July 1770, 16 August, 2 September 1784.
13 Mason, op.cit., 432-5; *The Builder*, 8 December 1894. An undated set of drawings for a related scheme (SRO, RHP 3672) bears the address of the Edinburgh architect J M Henry.

79 Stirling

1 *Inventory of Stirlingshire*, **2**, No.232.
2 Dunbar, J G, *Sir William Bruce, 1630-1710* (1970), 19.
3 Renwick, R (ed.), *Extracts from the Records of the Royal Burgh of Stirling (1667-1752)*, 97, 99.
4 The 'sufficiencie or insufficiencie' of the gable of an adjoining property to the E was examined in 1702 (ibid., 97).
5 Ibid., 112.
6 Porteous, A, *The Town Council Seals of Scotland* (1906), 274.
7 The existence of the earlier doorway indicates that the E block was integrated with the 1703 building from the first. The N doorway is not indicated on plans of 1805 and 1862 (SRO, RHP 1884/8 and 21699).
8 Repairs to the roof were recorded in 1729, 1739 and 1749 (*Extracts (1667-1752)*, 204, 245, 288).
9 Sketch elevation by Brown and Wardrop, 1862 (SRO, RHP 21706). The stone balustrade of the forestair described in *Inventory of Stirlingshire* was replaced by an iron railing in the 1960s.
10 *Prison Inspectors' Second Report*, 101.
11 Name Book, Stirlingshire No.24, p.60.
12 For all of the bells see *PSAS*, **84** (1949-50), 93-5; Allan, C, *Old Stirling Clockmakers* (1990), 48-54.
13 *Extracts (1667-1752)*, 3, 6.
14 Ibid., 205. The founder of these bells was probably John Waylett (*PSAS*, **84** (1949-50), 95).
15 Renwick, R (ed.), *Charters and other documents relating to the royal burgh of Stirling. A.D.1124-1705* (1884), 39-42, 184-5; SRO, B 66/25/35-40.
16 Ibid., 212; *Extracts (1519-1666)*, 86, 143, 146-7, 204; *(1667-1752)*, 377, 379-80.
17 Ibid. *(1667-1752)*, 87-8, 97-8, 347.
18 Ibid., 98, 347; TCM, 9 January, 25 December 1703, 29 January, 8 April 1704.
19 *Extracts (1667-1752)*, 104, 112.
20 Ibid., 122.
21 Ibid., 181.
22 TCM 5 April 1785.
23 TCM 28 October 1806, 8 October 1808; plans initialled 'RC' in SRO, RHP 1884; *Inventory of Stirlingshire*, **2**, 293.
24 *Prison Inspectors' Second Report*, 101.
25 Name Book, Stirlingshire No.24 (1860), pp.43 (new prison), 60-1 ('Town and County Buildings').
26 SRO, RHP 21696-707 (town-house, 1862), 21689-96 (court-house, 1862), 21708-46 (court-house, 1871-6).

80 Stonehaven

1 *NSA*, **11** (Kincardine), 223; Watt, A, *Highways and Byways round Stonehaven* (n.d.), 19; record-sheet and photographs of 19th-century cell-block, 1983 (NMRS, KCR/8/1). A plan of *c*.1821 by John Smith (copy in NMRS, UND/4) shows a four-bay rectangle to which he proposed to add recessed wings, and Wood's plan (1823) shows the 'County Hall, Jail &c' in this form. In 1836 there were five cells, opening into a central lobby, on the ground floor of the court-house

(*Prison Inspectors' Second Report*, 27-9). The additions of 1863-5 were designed by J C Walker.
2 A contract for building 'Stonehaven Town House' in 1784 is said to be in private ownership (information from Mrs B Cluer), but no details are available.
3 Watt, op.cit., 57-61; Name Book, Kincardine No. 20, p.20, which describes the spire as the 'Town Steeple'.
4 Napier, J, *Stonehaven and its Historical Associations* (n.d., *c*.1870), 3.
5 The S jamb of this opening, which appears to be early, projects a little N of the line of the straight joint between the upper floors of the main and N blocks. It may perpetuate an early single-storeyed wing in this position.
6 Anderson, J, *The Black Book of Kincardineshire* (1879), 37-8.
7 *APS*, **4** (1593-1625), 246. It was stated that at Kincardine, the former head burgh, 'thair is nather ane tolbuith nor any hous to pairties to ludge Into for thair Intertenement'. The status of Stonehaven as seat of the head courts was confirmed in 1607 (ibid., 374-5).
8 Spalding, J, *Memorialls of the trubles in Scotland and in England. A.D. 1624 - A.D. 1645* (Spalding Club, 1850-1), **2**, 459
9 *Geog.Coll.*, **3**, 235.
10 Watt, op.cit., 42; Napier, op.cit., 1-2.
11 Anderson, op.cit., 25-35; Napier, op.cit., 4-5; Watt, A, *The Tolbooth* (n.d. [1963]). The Rev John Troup is said to have entertained the congregation after week-day services by playing the bagpipes or, according to another source, the violin (ibid.).
12 TCM 3 June 1788, 13 May 1789.
13 Watt (*Highways*, 29) states that the 1793 bell was cast by Moon.
14 TCM 3 June 1788, 10 March, 4 and 23 May 1789, 3 May 1790, 12 May 1792, 3 August 1793.

81 Stranraer

1 TCM 17 June 1886. This panel is set in an earlier round-headed feature, now concealed except for its projecting sill-course (photograph dated May 1962, in NMRS).
2 The present bell was cast in 1935 by John Taylor, Loughborough.
3 In 1776 the town council threatened boys caught playing ball and marbles in 'the Peaches (piazzas) or sheds of new Tolbooth executed lately' with imprisonment in the 'laigh Tolbooth' (TCM 11 May 1776). The short impost-bands at the outer ends of the N front may relate to such arcades.
4 TCM 6 and 16 October 1779, 22 November 1819.
5 OS 1:1056 town plan (1847); Name Book, Wigtownshire No.35, p.47.
6 Photograph displayed in Stranraer Museum.
7 In 1772 a prisoner petitioned to be removed to the upper tolbooth, 'where he may have the benefit of a fire' (TCM 14 January 1772). For references to the tolbooth in 1596 and later, see Torrie, E P D and Coleman, R, *Historic Stranraer* (Scottish Burgh Survey, 1995), 46-7.
8 TCM 1 and 24 April 1775, 1 June 1776.
9 TCM 1802, *passim*; 16 April 1846 (plans by Mr Boyd, architect, submitted), 22 September 1853, 18 May 1854, 14 June 1855. The site of the corn-exchange encroached on the adjacent churchyard, and two burials were identified inside the building in 1989 (*Discovery and Excavation Scotland, 1989*, 14).
10 Information from Miss A Reid, former curator of Stranraer Museum.
11 *Inventory of Wigtownshire*, No.461; *TDGNHAS*, 3rd series, **57** (1982), 76.
12 TCM 28 November 1815, 11 May 1820, 22 September 1821, 20 September 1823; Boyd, J S, *The Royal and Ancient Burgh of Stranraer, 1617-1967* (1967), 39.
13 Name Book, Wigtownshire No.35, p.49; castle guidebook.
14 The central of the three two-light windows in the S wall at third-floor level is a dummy, and may reflect the original intention to have three rather than two debtors' rooms (TCM 11 May 1820).
15 In 1837 it was stated that there was no exercise-area except for the corridor outside the debtors' rooms (*Prison Inspectors' Third Report*, 40-1).
16 Ibid.

82 Strathmiglo

1 Leighton, *Fife*, **2**, 183.
2 The Balfour family owned the nearby castle of Strathmiglo, stones from which are said to have been used in the construction of the town-house (ibid.).
3 Gifford, *Fife*, 414.
4 Leighton, loc.cit.
5 Ibid.

83 Strichen

1 See development-plans by D G Lockhart in Parry, M L and Slater, T R (eds.), *The Making of the Scottish Countryside* (1980), 266.
2 Anonymous painting in Strichen Library.
3 *NSA*, **12**, 692; Smith, A, *A New History of Aberdeenshire* (1875), part 2, 1253; Pratt, J B, *Buchan* (4th ed., 1901), 196-7; *Scots Peerage*, **5**, 545-6.

4

Colvin, *Architects*, 898-900. 'Town House, Strechin' is no.130 in a list of drawings by John Smith (NMRS MS 2/8).

5

Smith, A, loc.cit.

7 TCM 15 March 1826, 4 and 11 March, 18 June, 25 November 1828.
8 *Prison Inspectors' Second Report*, 52. By 1847 the large rooms had been sub-divided (*Thirteenth Report*, 42).

84 Tain

1 MacGill, W, *Old Ross-shire and Scotland*, **2** (1911), 89.
2 This panel is signed by [G] Beauclerk, a London sculptor.
3 Munro, R and J, *Tain Through the Centuries* (1966), 74.
4 TCM 23 December 1826.
5 Munro, op.cit.,123.
6 A bell dated 1820, which is preserved in the sheriff court-house, is of unknown provenance.
7 The model does not include the armorial panel of 1848 above the steeple doorway, and it was presumably made to show Brown's original proposals.
8 MacGill, op.cit., **1** (1909), 122-3; **2**, 131.
9 Ibid., **2**, 73, 82, 131.
10 *RCRBS (1677-1711)*, 642; Munro, op. cit., 73.
11 MacGill, op. cit., **2**, 130; Taylor, W, *Researches into the History of Tain* (1882), 84-5.
12 *RCRBS (1677-1711)*, 355, 454.
13 Ibid., 468.
14 Ibid.; MacGill, op.cit., **2**, 89, 130-2; Munro, op.cit., 74.
15 MacGill, op.cit., **2**, 92-3.
16 Account due to Alexander Ross (SRO, SC 34/28/88/1); TCM 11 February 1779, 20 June 1780.
17 TCM June 1824.
18 *Inverness Journal and Northern Advertiser*, 6 August 1819.
19 TCM 21 October 1824.
20 TCM 30 November 1824, 9 June 1825, 8 and 23 December 1826.
21 *Prison Inspectors' Second Report*, 59-61; *Thirteenth Report*, 42; plans for Tain prison by Thomas Brown (SRO, RHP 21800-23).
22 *Historic Buildings at Work*, 77; plans dated 1848 and undated (?1873) in Highland Council Archive.

85 West Wemyss

1 Cameron, M and Johnstone, D, *West Wemyss: a Village Tale* (n. d., *c.* 1995), 2, 8; Fraser, W, *Memorials of the Family of Wemyss* (1888), **2**, 313.
2 *Inventory of Fife, etc.*, No.538.
3 Inscription 'taken from an old record', quoted in letter from S Tod to RCAHMS, 30 July 1928, and given with minor variations in *Inventory of Fife*, loc.cit. But G P H Watson in 1928 noted the following readings, perhaps due to recutting of the panel, which are still partially legible: 'Earl of Wemyss' for 'Earl David Wemyss', and 'crushing crime' for 'the cribbing of vice' (RCAHMS notebook in NMRS, MS 36/90).
4 Information from Mr C Tod, architect to Wemyss Estates.
5 Cameron and Johnstone, op.cit., 8, 66.

86 Whithorn

1 Radford, C A R, 'The Bells of Whithorn', in *TDGNHAS*, 3rd series, **28** (1949-50), 75.
2 *Prison Inspectors' Third Report*, 38.
3 Radford, op.cit., 75-6. The bell cast by Evert Burgerhuys in 1610, now in the Priory Museum (ibid., 77), was lying in the town hall in 1877 (McIlwraith, W, *The Visitors' Guide to Wigtownshire* (2nd ed., 1877), 58), but was evidently cast for the cathedral.
4 Contract between the burgh and Alexander Stewart of Physgill for repairs to the harbour and tolbooth of Whithorn, 24 October 1664 (*Miscellany of the Scottish History Society*, **11** (1990), 271, 285-9); grant of £5 sterling for rebuilding, 1708 (*RCRBS (1677-1711)*, 463).
5 *Stat. Acct.*, **16**, 276.
6 *NSA*, **4**, 54. The *Prison Inspectors' Third Report*, 38, stated in 1837 that the town-house 'was built about 22 years ago'.
7 Groome, *Ordnance Gazetteer*, 1613.

87 Wick

1 *Historic Buildings at Work*, 64.
2 OS 1:500 plan, Caithness sheet 25.5.4 (1872/4). At this period all four ground-floor offices were occupied by the town-clerk's department, but the use of rooms may have been different before the completion in 1866 of the adjacent sheriff-court building.
3 Information from Mr A Begg and Mr W Mowat, Wick.
4 *APS*, **8** (1670-86), 90; Name Book, Caithness No.14, p.9; Horne, J, *Ye towne of Wick in ye oldene tymes* (1895), 10-20; TCM 17 April 1820, 15 March 1826. The former tolbooth of 1750 was converted to shops after 1828, and survived until the end of the 19th century (Horne, loc.cit.).
5 TCM 17 April, 2 September 1820, 10 May 1821, 8 May 1823.
6 TCM 8 May, 27 November 1823, 7 July 1825, 15 March 1826, 25 November 1828.

233

GLOSSARY

This glossary covers terms not included, or defined in a different sense, in the 7th edition of *The Concise Oxford Dictionary* (1982).

Acroteria: simplified pedestals, often carved with palmettes, set at the angles of a pediment.

Aedicule: a niche with moulded surround; a portico framed by two columns, entablature and pediment.

Baron-bailie: the principal administrative officer of a barony (*Scots*).

Bell-cast: in architecture, of a roof having a bell-shaped profile..

Blocking-course: a plain course of stones crowning a wall.

Cap-house: a small chamber at the top of a spiral stair.

Caulked ashlar: a type of masonry with small stones inserted into the mortar between blocks of ashlar.

Column in antis: a recessed column.

Coomb: a sloping or curved element between a wall and a ceiling.

Dado: a decorative lining applied to the lower part of the walls of a room and representing a continuous pedestal.

Dentillated: in classical architecture, of a cornice having small square blocks or projections in the lowest moulding.

Dog-leg stair: a stair without a central well in which the flights are parallel.

Drip-course: a projecting course of stones which prevents water from running down a wall.

Forestair: an external access-stair.

Gablet: a small gable, usually formed on a crow-step or dormer-window.

Garderobe: a medieval latrine, often served by a mural soil-shaft.

Gibbs-surround: the surround of an opening with projecting blocks of stone punctuating the jambs and arch-head.

Girnel: a granary (*Scots*).

Guildry: a guild or incorporation of the merchants (and sometimes craftsmen) in a burgh (*Scots*).

Guttae: small triangular projections under the triglyphs of an entablature, or supporting the ends of a panel.

Jougs: an iron neck-collar for the restraint or public humiliation of miscreants.

King-post: a roof truss containing a central vertical member which joins the tie-beam to the ridge.

Lucarne: a dormer-window, or a small window in a spire.

Lugged: having an 'ear' or projecting piece (*Scots*).

Oculus: in architecture, a circular window.

Off-set: of the margin of an opening, or quoin-stones, slightly advanced from the wall-surface.

Pend: a covered passage (*Scots*).

Pretorium: a council-house or court-house (*Latin*).

Scabbled: of stone, roughly faced.

Scale-and-platt: of a stair having straight flights of steps with landings.

Segmental arch: an arch whose arc is less than a semi-circle.

Skews: the copings of a gable.

Skewputt: the lowest stone in the coping of a gable.

Thermal window: a tripartite window having a semicircular or segmental head springing directly from the sill.

Tuskers: stones projecting from the surface of a wall to allow the bonding in of another wall.

Wardhouse: a place of confinement (*Scots*).

Yett: a grated iron door with interlacing bars (*Scots*).

INDEX

Abbotsford (Roxburghshire), 210, 223.
Abercrummie, Rev William, 142, 229.
Aberdeen (Aberdeenshire): 120, 190, 194; bridewell, 31; early tolbooth, 30, 218, 219; county and municipal buildings, 3, 15, 18, 24, 31, 219, fig.3A; 'great room'/town hall, 18, 19, 31, 217, fig.17B; market-place, 2, 11, 12, 24, figs.25, 31A,B; prisons, 8, 30, 31; record office, 217; tolbooth/town-house/wardhouse, 1, 2, 3, 6, 7, 8, 9, 12, 15, 16, 18, 19, 20, 21, 23, **24-31**, 217, 218-19, figs.2A, 20A, 25-31C; weigh-house, 217. *See also* Old Aberdeen.
Abernethy Forest (Inverness-shire), 13.
Actors, 7, 142, 161.
Adam, James, architect, 100.
Adam, John, architect, 8, 12, 13, 15, 23, 44, 82, 87, 106, 220, 230.
Adam, Robert, architect, 8, 38, 64, 118, 119, 217, 218, 220, 227.
Adam, William, architect, 3, 7, 8, 13, 16, 17, 18, 31, 103, 105, 180, 181, 202, 219, 225.
Adamson, Bailie John, 8, 228, 230.
Airdrie (Lanarkshire), town-house, 7, 13, **32**, 219, fig.32A.
Airth (Stirlingshire), tolbooth, 207.
Ale tax, 8, 77, 136, 219.
Alexander, Cosmo, artist, 18.
Alexander, George, architect, 206.
Alexander, James, artist, 19.
Alexander, John, artist, fig.4A.
Alloa (Clackmannanshire): 13, 74, 118; old parish church, 55; tolbooth, 207; tron-beam, 218.
Alloway (Ayrshire), Burns Monument, 13, 220.
Amsterdam (Netherlands), 11, 188, 217, 218, 224.
Anderson, Charles, architect, 219.
Anderson, Herbert, mason, 126.
Anderson, James, mason, 204.
Annan (Dumfries-shire), tolbooth/town-house, 202.
Annandale, George Johnstone, 3rd Marquis of, 8, 140.
Annandale, Johnstone family of, 143.
Annandale, steward of, 140.
Anne, Queen, 18.
Anstruther Easter (Fife), tolbooth, 202.
Anstruther Wester (Fife): church, 12, 20, 33, 219; tolbooth, 11; town hall, 6, 14, 20, 21, **33**, 219, figs.32B-33B.
Arbroath (Angus): abbey, 13; guildry building, 34, 218; market-area, 11; tolbooth, 34; town buildings/sheriff court, 18, **34-5**, 219, figs.34-35B.
Arcades, 16, 27, 82, 87, 92, 93, 99, 106, 112, 144, 148, 150, 165, 191, 194, 201, 207, 219.
Archer, Alexander, artist, 223, figs.5A,B, 84B.
Archibald, Bishop of Moray, 217.
Architects, 13 and *passim*.
Ardrossan (Ayrshire), sandstone-quarry, 178, 231.
Argyll, Archibald Campbell, Marquis of, 5.
Argyll, Archibald Campbell, 9th Earl of, 49.
Argyll, Archibald Campbell, 3rd Duke of, 12, 49, 225.
Armorial paintings and panels, 18, 20-22 and *passim*, figs.1A, 17A, 20B,C,D, 21A,B, 33B, 63B, 67A-C, 73B,C, 77A,B, 90B,C, 111, 131B, 140B, 157A, 163C,D, 168B, 174A,C, 184B, 185C, 190B, 193B, 198C.
Armour, 6, 8.
Armour, Robert, plumber, 50.
Armstrong, Francis, architect, 230.
Arnold, Dent and Co., clockmakers, 176.
Arran, 39, 177, 226.
Assembly-rooms, 3, 6, 7, 17-18 and *passim*.
Auchtermuchty (Fife): burgh, 36, 217; town-house, 15, 20, 23, **36-7**, 219, figs.36-37D.
Ayton (Berwickshire), lock-up, 214.
Ayr (Ayrshire): 217; assembly rooms, steeple and town-house, 3, 7, 12, 13, 14, 15, 16, 18, 19, 23, **38**, **40-2**, 220, figs.3C, 14B, 38B, 40A-42C; county buildings/sheriff court, 3, 7, 8, 11, 17, 19, 20, **38-40**, 42, 220, figs.39A,B; fort, 13, 38; high tolbooth/'dungeon clock', 8, 12, **38-9**, 42, 219-20, figs.38A,C-E; new bridge, 38, figs.14B, 38A; old bridge, fig.38B; old tolbooth, 38; St John's Church, 38; Wallace Tower, 38.

Bachup, Tobias, master-mason, 7, 13, 74.
Badenoch, *see* Kingussie.
Baird, Alexander, 32.
Balfour, Margaret, of Burleigh, 21, 193, 232.
Ballachulish (Argyll), slate-quarry, 13.
Ballantine, Bailie Duncan, 48.
Balmerino, Lords, 56.
Bancroft, John, clockmaker, 73.
Banff (Banffshire): tolbooth, 18, 44, 220; town-house, 13, 15, 16, 18, 23, **43-5**, 217, 220, figs.43A-45C.
Barbour, James, architect, 74, 222.
Barclay, David, of Urie, 9.
Barclay, George, bell-founder, 22, 73.
Barclay, Hugh and David, architects, 210.
Barclay, Hugh and David, masons, 115.

Barclay, Provost, 106.
Barclay, Robert, of Urie, 9.
Barclay, Thomas, mason, 91.
Barron, Patrick, wright, 31.
Bartlet, James, bell-founder, 211.
Bass Rock (East Lothian), prison, 9.
Bathgate (West Lothian), town-house, 207, fig.207C.
Baxter, John, architect, 12, 64, 92, 165, 167, 224.
Beauclerk, G, sculptor, 233.
Beith (Ayrshire), town-house, 4, 7, **46**, 220, fig.46.
Bellcots, 14, 16, 46, 47, 107, 140, 158, 177, 205, 206, 209, 224, 229.
Bellenden, Sir Lewis, 51.
Bellie Parish Church, *see* Fochabers.
Bells, 2, 5, 8, 13, 21, 22-3 and *passim*, figs.22B, 42C, 43B, 53A, 58B,C, 61A, 80, 91B, 101A, 125A-D, 142B,C, 207B. *See also* bell-foundries *under* Edinburgh, Glasgow, London *and* Old Aberdeen.
Bennet, Captain James, 108.
Berwick-upon-Tweed (Northumberland): tolbooth, 1, 2, 5, **202**; town hall, 202.
Biggar (Lanarkshire), tolbooth/prison, 208.
Binning, James, ?mason, 213.
Black holes, 9, 19, 20, 47, 69, 80, 110, 130, 135, 165, 205, 224. *See also* Thieves' holes.
Blaikie, John, plumber, 26, 219.
Blairgowrie (Perthshire), town-house, 208.
Blairquhan House (Ayrshire), 229.
Blairquhan, Kennedy family of, 12, 141, 142, 229.
Bo'ness (West Lothian), town-house, 208.
Bonnar, Thomas, decorative painter, 133.
Boog, John, architect, 70, 223.
Boswell, James, 7, 148, 218.
Boyd, John, master of works, 13, 100.
Boyd, Mr, architect, 182, 232.
Brabboner, Bessie, child-murderess, 218.
Brechin (Angus), town-house, 7, 12, **47**, 220, figs.47A-C.
Brereton, Sir William, traveller, 100, 224.
Bressay (Shetland), quarry, 134.
Bridewells, 9, 31, 111, 217, 226.
Bridger, James H, clockmaker, 110.
Bristo (Edinburgh), 212.
Bristol (Gloucestershire), 48.
Brodie, Deacon William, 13.
Broughton (Edinburgh): barony, 53, 208; tolbooth, 208, fig.208A.
Broumfield (Brovnfield), Thomas, 102.
Broun, Archibald, mason, 230.
Broun, John, mason, 230.
Brown and Wardrop, architects, 188, 207, 232.
Brown family, 222.
Brown, David, mason, 169.
Brown, John, mason, 48.
Brown, Peter, surveyor, 64.
Brown, Thomas (of Uphall), architect, 118, 138.
Brown, Thomas, architect, 61, 110, 131, 138, 152, 188, 196, 197, 202, 228, 233.
Bruce family, 227.
Bruce, Sir George, of Carnock, 21, 67, 221.
Bruce, Sir Henry, 55.
Bruce, Sir John, of Kinross, 118.
Bruce, Sir William, of Kinross, architect, 13, 118, 186, 188, 232.
Brussels (Belgium), 11.
Bryce, David and John, architects, 139, 229.
Bryson, Robert and Sons, clockmakers, 102.
Buccleuch, Francis Scott, 2nd Earl of, 69.
Buccleuch, Henry Scott, 3rd Duke of, 129, 211.
Building-materials, 12-13 and *passim*.
Buncle, Deacon James, wright, 137.
Burgerhuys, Evert, bell-founder, 233.
Burgerhuys, Jan, bell-founder, 53, 104.
Burgerhuys, John, bell-founder, 108.
Burgerhuys, Michael, bell-founder, 22, 91, 125, 196.
Burges, David, bell-founder, 127.
Burn, James, architect, 105.
Burn, William, architect, 103, 105, 110, 135, 138, 172, 205, 225.
Burntisland (Fife), tolbooth, 202.
Bute, John Crichton-Stuart, 2nd Marquis of, 176.

Campbell, Provost Alexander, 48.
Campbell, Archibald, of Danna, 106.
Campbell, Archibald, of Stonefield, 106.
Campbell, Robert, mason, 71.
Campbell, Sir William Hume, of Marchmont, 102.
Campbell Douglas and Sellars, architects, 41, 78, 80.
Campbeltown (Argyll), town-house, 7, 8, 15, **48-50**, 220, figs.48-50C.
Canongate (Edinburgh): 219; Huntly House, 21, 51; tolbooth, 2, 4, 5, 9, 12, 13, 15, 16, 18, 21, **51-3**, 218, 220-1, figs.17A, 51-53C.

Printed in Scotland for The Stationery Office by (3808)
Dd 29335 C10 10/96

**Published by The Stationery Office
and available from:**

The Stationery Office Bookshops
71 Lothian Road Edinburgh EH3 9AZ
(counter service only)
South Gyle Crescent Edinburgh EH12 9EB
(mail, fax and telephone orders only)
0131-479 3141 Fax 0131-479 3142
49 High Holborn London WC1V 6HB
(counter service and fax orders only)
Fax 0171-831 1326
68-69 Bull Street Birmingham B4 6AD
0121-236 9696 Fax 0121-236 9699
33 Wine Street Bristol BS1 2BQ
0117-926 4306 Fax 0117-929 4515
9-21 Princess Street Manchester M60 8AS
0161-834 7201 Fax 0161-833 0634
16 Arthur Street Belfast BT1 4GD
01232 238451 Fax 01232 235401
The Stationery Office Oriel Bookshop
The Friary Cardiff CF1 4AA
01222 395548 Fax 01222 384347

**The Stationery Office publications
are also available from:**
The Publications Centre
(mail, telephone and fax orders only)
PO Box 276 London SW8 5DT
General enquiries 0171-873 0011
Telephone orders 0171-873 9090
Fax orders 0171-873 8200
Accredited Agents
(see Yellow Pages)
and through good booksellers